Software Product Management

Hans-Bernd Kittlaus

Software Product Management

The ISPMA®-Compliant Study Guide and Handbook

Second Edition

 Springer

Hans-Bernd Kittlaus
InnoTivum (www.innotivum.com)
Rheinbreitbach, Germany

ISBN 978-3-662-65118-6   ISBN 978-3-662-65116-2   (eBook)
https://doi.org/10.1007/978-3-662-65116-2

This Springer imprint is published by the registered company Springer-Verlag GmbH, DE part of Springer Nature.
The registered company address is: Heidelberger Platz 3, 14197 Berlin, Germany

Preface

The author is very grateful to all contributors without whom I would not have been able to write a book as comprehensive as this. Here is some information on author and contributors:

Author

Hans-Bernd Kittlaus is the founder and CEO of InnoTivum Consulting (www. innotivum.com) and works as a consultant and trainer for software organizations, in particular in the areas of software product management and organizational aspects of software organizations. Before he was a Director of SIZ GmbH, Bonn, Germany (German Savings Banks Organization) and a Head of Software Product Management and Development units of IBM. He has published numerous articles and books, in particular *"Software Product Management—The ISPMA-Compliant Handbook and Study Guide,"* Springer, 2017 (with Samuel Fricker) and *"Software Product Management and Pricing—Key Success Factors for All Software Organizations,"* Springer, 2009 (with Peter Clough). He is a Diplom-Informatiker, ISPMA Certified Software Product Manager, Certified Scrum Product Owner (CSPO), Certified PRINCE2 Practitioner, and a member of ACM and GI. Hans-Bernd lives near Bonn, Germany. He is a founding board member and current chairman of ISPMA. Contact email: hbk@innotivum. de, Blog: www.innotivum.com/en/publications/spm-blog/

Contributors

Peter Clough was a Senior Vice President and management consultant with InnoTivum Consulting specializing on software pricing. Previously, he was an Enterprise Software Sales Executive and Manager of Software Offerings in IBM's Software Group and influenced, participated in or managed every major IBM software terms development between 1983 and 2008, after holding previous positions in IBM's hardware and software marketing and sales. Peter lives in

New York, USA. He served as a reviewer of the complete book. Contact email: pnclough@gmail.com

Samuel Fricker is a Professor at the University of Applied Sciences and Arts Northwestern Switzerland (FHNW) and a Head a.i. of the FHNW Institute for Interactive Technologies. He received his Ph.D. degree in 2009 from the University of Zurich. Samuel spent his career in both industry and academia. Important industry stays were with Ericsson, ABB, and Zuehlke. In academia, he had a position as an Assistant Professor at the Blekinge Institute of Technology (BTH). His applied research focuses on requirements engineering, socio-technological alignment, and validation of innovative digital products and platforms. Samuel is the coordinator of the Horizon2020 project GEIGER, participated in FP7 and Horizon2020 projects in various roles, and assists the European Commission as an expert reviewer and rapporteur. Samuel lives near Zurich, Switzerland. He is a founding member and former chairman of ISPMA. Samuel was a co-author of the first edition of this book. Contact email: samuel.fricker@fhnw.ch

Gerald Heller works as a consultant and trainer on the topics of software product management and requirements management. Gerald has 30 years of experience in the IT field. During his career, he has covered various aspects of the product development life cycle. He holds a degree in computer science and is a member of the German informatics society (GI). Gerald lives near Stuttgart, Germany. He is a founding member and current board member of ISPMA. Gerald served as a reviewer of parts of this book. Contact email: gerald.heller@pd7.group

Barbara Hoisl is an independent consultant and trainer. She specializes in Exponential Strategy—helping businesses thrive in a world driven by exponential change. Barbara draws on more than 30 years of experience in the software industry, including 14 years with the software business unit at Hewlett-Packard (HP). She holds a master's degree in Computer Science with a minor in Business Administration from the Technical University of Kaiserslautern. Barbara lives in Stuttgart, Germany, and is a fellow member of ISPMA. She contributed text to Chap. 5 and served as a reviewer of parts of this book. Contact email: info@barbarahoisl.com

Andrey Maglyas, D.Sc (Tech) is a managing director at Maglyas Consulting. His consulting work for product companies includes coordination and execution of projects based on business goals and key performance indicators in accordance with the client's strategy. Before that he was responsible for a scientific project called Need4Speed (N4S). During that time he was a postdoctoral researcher and project manager in the Department of Software Engineering at LUT University (http://lut.com), Finland. His research interests included empirical investigation of software product management practices, methods, and tools. In addition, he is an active member of product management community in Finland and Russia, and a co-founder of ProductCamp Helsinki. Andrey lives in St. Petersburg, Russia. He is a fellow member of ISPMA. He contributed text to Chap. 7 and served as a reviewer of parts of this book. Contact email: maglyas@gmail.com

Andrey Saltan is a postdoctoral researcher and lecturer at LUT University in Finland and HSE University in Russia. His areas of research and teaching expertise include product management and pricing of software services, data and business analytics, business strategies for digital services and platforms. Andrey is an Extended Board Member of ISPMA, where he focuses on marketing operations. He contributed text to Sect. 3.10 and served as a reviewer of parts of this book. Contact email: andrey.saltan@lut.fi

I would like to thank ISPMA e.V. as an organization for allowing me to make use of ISPMA's published material. In addition to the colleagues listed above, I also thank all the other ISPMA members who contributed to ISPMA's syllabi: Jonas Als, Magnus Billgren, Erik Bjernulf, Prof. Dr. Sjaak Brinkkemper, Prof. Dr. Christof Ebert, Prof. Dr. Tony Gorschek, Rainer Grau, Prof. Dr. Georg Herzwurm, Dr. Marc Hilber, Robert Huber, Prof. Dr. Slinger Jansen, Dr. Mahvish Khurum, Daniel Lucas-Hirtz, Haragopal Mangipudi, Lars Olsson, Dr. Katharina Peine, Dr. Karl Michael Popp, Greg Prickril, Niklas Rosvall, Prof. Dr. Guenther Ruhe, Dr. Peter Stadlinger, Dr. Kevin Vlaanderen, Dr. Inge van de Weerd, and Prof. Dr. Krzysztof Wnuk.

Though I acknowledge the contributions of all these colleagues, the contents of this book including any mistakes, omissions, and judgments are the sole responsibility of the author.

I would also like to recognize Samuel Fricker, Peter Clough, Christoph Rau (†), and Juergen Schulz, my co-authors of my previous books on software product management [KittFric17, KittClou09, KiRaSch04], for all the work that they put into them and that helped with this publication. I thank Petra Steinmüller and Sophia Leonhard from Springer-Verlag for the good cooperation. I thank Sjaak Brinkkemper, Utrecht University, Netherlands, Inge van de Weerd, Free University of Amsterdam, Netherlands, and Gartner, Inc. for giving me some graphical images for publication. Thanks also to Strategic Pricing Group, Thomas Nagle, and John Hogan for allowing me to reproduce their Strategic Pricing Pyramid. Last but not least, special thanks go to my better half for her moral support.

Rheinbreitbach, Germany
May 2022

Hans-Bernd Kittlaus

Software Product Management

What readers of "*Software Product Management: The ISPMA-Compliant Study Guide and Handbook*," first edition, said:

"Software-intensive products are at the heart of many businesses, so product management is a paramount business activity. But how can businesses be perfect at it? This book is the answer. It is your vade mecum for all product management topics and aspects."

Dr. Karl Michael Popp, Chief Product Expert and Director Corporate Development, SAP SE, Walldorf, Germany.

"A book that goes beyond platitudes and offers concrete methods and frameworks to product managers working with software intensive product development. The authors have a sound footing in both practice, but also state-of-the-art research, and manage to combine the two."

Prof. Dr. Tony Gorschek, Blekinge Institute of Technology, Karlskrona, Sweden.

"By reading and applying the lessons from the new book "*Software Product Management: The ISPMA-Compliant Study Guide and Handbook*," you will gain strategic advice, practical techniques, and great insights into how to accelerate software product management (SPM) success. These practices and methods will be useful to executives and practitioners in this demanding area—and those who aspire to a level of software excellence—in both their current jobs and future careers, as they work to help organizations deliver superior value and effective software solutions to a world of increasingly demanding customers."

Michael Eckhardt, Managing Director, CHASM Institute, Palo Alto, California, USA.

"Call her/him a linchpin, a rudder or even a conscience keeper, the role of Software Product Manager (SPM) is extremely critical for the viability as well as sustainability of any software product business. This book is a "must read" as well as "must have," not just for every SPM but for all the key stakeholders and decision makers connected with a software product business. And for all the business leaders in the software services industry aspiring to extend their success into software product business, here's your definitive reference."

Haragopal Mangipudi, Adjunct Professor, Indian Institute of Management, Bangalore, India; CEO, guNaka, Bangalore, India (formerly Infosys SVP and Global Head of Finacle).

"Software has been turning into the dominating value driver in most traditional industries like automotive and banking. I recommend this book not only to software professionals, but also to managers in these other industries. It provides comprehensive structural and operational help how to set up and run product management of software-intensive products. Particularly fascinating are the authors' highly topical ideas to extend the discipline of SPM into the management of industrial ecosystems to tackle the increasing complexity with an integrated consistent approach."

Wilhelm Gans, CTO, DSV Group (German Savings Banks Organization), Stuttgart, Germany (banking industry).

"This book provides a comprehensive and enlightening knowledge foundation for both practitioners and researchers in the increasingly important domain of software product management."

Prof. Dr. Bjorn Regnell, Lund University, Sweden.

"This compendium based on industry best practices provides a toolbox for software product managers and executives to ensure sustainable success of software products along their life cycles. The authors have vividly described the multi-faceted role of a software product manager—the mini CEO—and his embedding into the corporate organization. Special emphasis is put on areas relevant for SPM such as pricing models, legal aspects, ecosystem management and orchestration that are not covered too well in the available literature. A must-read for everyone interested in the software business aspects in all industries."

Michael Conrad, Director Portfolio Management, AVL List GmbH, Graz, Austria (automotive industry).

Praise for "*Software Product Management and Pricing*," Hans-Bernd Kittlaus' previous book (with Peter Clough) which continues to be the only extensive publication on software pricing:

"These two seasoned practitioners have masterfully distilled the essence of the software business and the art and craft of the increasingly important and challenging field of software product management. Worthwhile to any who want an appreciation of the evolving world of product management, seasoned veteran and new entrant alike."

Richard Campione, Senior Vice President, Business Suite Solution Management and CRM On Demand, SAP, Germany/USA.

"Mr. Kittlaus and Mr. Clough have used their considerable knowledge and experience to succinctly lay out the value chain that is essential to the development of a financially healthy software company. If you want to understand how to turn software technology into a long-term profitable company this is the book to read."

Paul Kaplan, Vice President, Worldwide Enterprise Software Sales, Software Group, IBM, USA.

"This book on Software Product Management and Pricing is the first book that treats the business of software in a systematic way. Although software products were already shipped in the seventies of the last century, there are hardly any books providing an overview of all issues a company faces when playing a role in this industry. Product management and pricing are key processes, and this book informs the reader of the essentials. It is a must-read for anyone involved in software products, be it in business or in research."

Prof. Dr. Sjaak Brinkkemper, Information and Computing Sciences, Utrecht University, Netherlands.

Contents

Introduction

1

Why write yet another book on software product management (SPM)? What is special about software product management compared to other products?

Product management is a discipline which many industries have utilized for decades, above all the consumer goods industry. The invention of product management as an explicit management concept is attributed to Procter and Gamble. In 1931, the company assigned one product manager to each of two competing soap products (see [Gorche11]). Since then, this basic idea has become widespread. In fact, it makes sense for any company to explicitly manage the products that generate its revenue and that, as assets, represent the company's sustainable value. But what does product management mean? Unfortunately, only parts of this question have a general answer. The activities of the product manager depend largely on the type of product involved, the culture, history, and company organization, and the target and reward systems. Product management means planning and coordinating all relevant areas of a product inside and outside the company with the aim of sustainably optimizing product success.

The focus of this book is to describe the tasks of a software product manager, and how to perform those well. We follow a best-practice approach and make use of any techniques that help product managers, from whichever methodology they come, be it lean, agile, kanban etc. In our experience, while methodologies come and go over time, the same tasks remain. Therefore, we do not use temporarily marketable terms like "Agile Product Management" or "Lean Product Management". The prime objective of a product manager is not to follow any particular fashionable methodology, but to take care of his tasks in the best possible way, and thereby make his product successful over its life cycle.

Software has become highly pervasive. There is hardly any industry that is not increasingly dependent on software, be it as part of their products or as the backbone of their business operations. A good example of that phenomenon is the automobile industry. The software contents of cars have increased significantly over the last 10 years. In more and more industries software is turning into the number one value driver.

© Springer-Verlag GmbH Germany, part of Springer Nature 2022
H.-B. Kittlaus, *Software Product Management*,
https://doi.org/10.1007/978-3-662-65116-2_1

Another example is corporate IT organizations. For many of them, it has become apparent that they need to manage their software applications explicitly as crucial assets with a life cycle perspective, i.e. as software products. The realization that companies from non-IT industries are suddenly becoming "standard software suppliers" by providing apps to their customers may also have contributed to this development.

Software has become important also in our private spheres. Many use software to manage their private lives and to communicate with others. Software has also started to be critical for addressing the big challenges of our societies. For example, in the healthcare area, internet-based apps empower patients and their caregivers to make decisions for themselves. This empowerment allows expert healthcare staff to serve more patients for less cost per patient.

Software product management—as we define it—applies to all these organizations:

- Vendors of software products and software-intensive technical services, be they licensed products, or Platform-as-a-Service (PaaS), or Software-as-a-Service (SaaS), or apps running on all kinds of smart devices (software industry),
- Vendors of software-intensive products (all industries), e.g. cars or smartphones,
- Vendors of professional human services (all industries) in which software is used to increase productivity, and
- Corporate IT organizations (all industries).

In several decades of experience in the software industry, the authors have come to realize that knowledge and experience acquired in other business areas and with other types of products are only partially transferable to software. We believe that software is the most complex product of human invention that we know of (see Chap. 2). That complexity implies that the management of software products is special and puts unique demands on the persons responsible for this task (see also Sect. 2.6).

A software product manager's job is special because software is special, i.e. the characteristics of software are different from most other products and have a strong influence on what a software product manager does. The most conspicuous differences are:

- High frequency of change over the life cycle of the software with the resulting great importance of requirements management,
- High complexity,
- Ability to interact with customers through the product,
- Flexibility of re-configuring the product and adapting it to new purposes and usage contexts,
- Culture of searching for lightweight, agile approaches to building and evolving software,
- No or little need for physical manufacturing and distribution.
- Increasing returns through network effects,

- Special financial picture due to high initial development costs followed by low marginal cost.

When Hans-Bernd Kittlaus published his first book on Software Product Management [KiRaSch04] and his second book on "Software Product Management and Pricing" [KittClou09], there were not too many publications on this subject available. Since then, the situation has changed significantly. The number of SPM-related publications has increased, there is more focused research in academia, and there is an increasing number of commercial SPM training offerings available.

These changes are to some degree due to the establishment of International Software Product Management Association (ISPMA e.V., www.ispma.org). "ISPMA" is a registered trademark of ISPMA e.V. First convened in 2009, ISPMA is a non-profit organization whose fellow members are SPM experts from the industry and academia. Various types of membership are open to interested companies and individuals. ISPMA's goal is to foster software product management excellence across industries (for more information see Sect. 7.4). ISPMA's fellow members have developed a curriculum and a Certifiable Body of Knowledge (SPMBoK) that have become the basis for a high number of commercial training offerings and university courses. Hans-Bernd Kittlaus is one of the founders of ISPMA, and its current chairman.

1.1 About this Book

This book provides an integrated view of software product management for all the organizations and scenarios listed above. We consider the similarities between the scenarios that are induced by the specifics of software as more significant than differences in organizational views. Nevertheless, there are some differences that require different priorities regarding the individual tasks (see Sect. 7.3).

The target group of this book is everyone involved or interested in software product management, be it on the academic side or in organizations in the scenarios listed above.

With this book, the author intends to provide a state-of-the-art update of [KittFric17] that is compliant with ISPMA's Body of Knowledge (as of May 2022) documented in these syllabi:

- ISPMA SPM - The Foundation V.2.1
- ISPMA SPM - Excellence in Product Strategy V.2.1
- ISPMA SPM - Excellence in Product Planning V.2.0
- ISPMA SPM - Excellence in Strategic Management V.2.0
- ISPMA SPM - Excellence in Orchestration V.2.0.

ISPMA has just released a new syllabus on "SPM for Startups", that is focused on SPM for new product development in a startup mode which can take place in startups as well as in more mature companies. This subject is covered in [KittMang22].

The reader can use this book in a supporting role to prepare for the ISPMA certification exam. However, the primary source for preparation is always the current release of the corresponding syllabus and the corresponding training.

We introduce the ISPMA software product management (SPM) framework in Chap. 2. The remaining chapters will follow that structure. Software pricing will be addressed in this book (see Sect. 3.10), but not as extensively as in [KittClou09].

The wealth of publications related to SPM over the last couple of years make it impractical to provide an exhaustively comprehensive bibliography. Our bibliography focuses instead on publications most often cited and which we find particularly useful. By reading this book, the reader will learn about the most influential results of research aimed at SPM topics.

Effective discussion across the breadth of software product management requires establishing some clear boundaries. Despite important interfaces between development and software product management, we will discuss neither the topics of software development management nor project management. We have also omitted consulting issues, nor do we cover bookkeeping, administration, and payment for the software licenses acquired and used in a company. Likewise, we exclude software product line management, i.e. the management of development variants based on the same product platform.

The book structure is as follows. Chapter 2 looks at software as a business and how we suggest managing it in terms of business models and organizational. We define relevant terms and introduce the ISPMA SPM Framework. Chapter 3 describes the tasks and activities related to product strategy. Chapter 4 focuses on product planning. Chapter 5 covers strategic management. Chapter 6 describes the orchestration of the organization's functional areas. Chapter 7 looks at SPM's state-of-practice, the application of SPM in different business scenarios, as well as the future of SPM.

At the end of the book, we provide a glossary, i.e. a list of definitions of all relevant terms used, aligned with ISPMA's glossary as of January 2022.

1.2   Conventions

Before we begin our in-depth discussion of SPM, we need to clarify several conventions used throughout this book. Terms such as "manager" or "director" are meant to be gender-neutral, that is they refer equally to female and male persons. While women increasingly participate in IT management, we have chosen a convention of referring to such positions using the male pronoun. This is not intended to be in any way discriminatory and was chosen simply for the purposes of easier readability. We use terms like development or marketing with small characters when we mean the activity, with capital characters when we mean the organizational unit.

We use the term "software vendor" to mean companies whose primary business is the development and provision of software for commercial purposes for a relatively large number of consumer and business customers. Examples are Microsoft, SAP, Oracle, IBM, Google, Samsung and Huawei. We use the term "corporate IT organization" for organizational units that are part of companies in all industries and whose primary mission is to provide software or IT support for the parent company or corporation, which we call "corporate customer". In that sense, software vendors are corporate customers of their internal IT.

The term "service" has many different meanings (see Webster's Dictionary). The following three meanings are relevant to this book:

- Useful labor that does not produce a tangible commodity (as in "professional services").
- A provision for maintenance and repair (as in "software maintenance service").
- The technical provision of a function through a software component that can be accessed by another software component. Such access often occurs over a network and executed on a remote server (as in "web services", "Software-as-a-Service", or "Service-Oriented Architecture").

Whenever we use the term "service" in this book, we try to make it clear which meaning we intend. When we use the term "controlling" we mean "performing the functions of a (business or financial) controller".

And now, we can jump right into the secrets of software product management.

Management of Software as a Business

2

Product management has become an established discipline in many industries since Procter and Gamble introduced it in 1931. During recent decades, most software product companies—like Microsoft, IBM, and Google—implemented Software Product Management (SPM). So did some corporate information technology organizations across essentially all industries, as well as some companies that produce software embedded in software-intensive products and services. The role of software product manager has emerged during this time as being of strategic value since it is crucial to the economic success of a product.

This chapter puts software product management into the context of software as a business. It outlines the historical context, defines relevant terms and characteristics, looks at software from a business perspective, introduces ISPMA's SPM Framework, and discusses the role of SPM and its positioning in a software organization. The business context, definitions, and scenarios will help the reader to understand how to implement the many practices that a software product manager has available to him to ensure the success of his product.

2.1   A Little History

To understand the business aspects of software, a short detour into the history of this young industry is helpful before we analyze the current business drivers in more detail.

The term "software" was first coined in a 1958 article by Tukey from AT&T's Bell Labs [Tukey58]. The term has become an integral element of the English language and has been taken up in many other languages. At the beginning of the computer era, the computer was considered a mere machine. Just as we tell an automobile motor to run faster by pressing the gas pedal, the computer was told what to do one instruction at a time. Manufacturers sold the computer as a physical machine and added the operating system and rudimentary software at no additional cost. Not before the early 1960s was software considered independent and separate,

© Springer-Verlag GmbH Germany, part of Springer Nature 2022
H.-B. Kittlaus, *Software Product Management*,
https://doi.org/10.1007/978-3-662-65116-2_2

and at the same time entrepreneurs started to see an opportunity for a software products business [Cusuma04, p. 90].

Several technical developments triggered this decoupling of software programs from the machine. In the beginning, the instruction sets were computer-specific, i.e. each processor had its individual assembler language. That is why programs were tied to the respective processor and could not be ported to any other processor. From the late 1950s on, the first higher-level programming languages like FORTRAN and ALGOL were created that enabled programming on a more abstract logical level. Compilers that transformed high-level source code into different assembler languages were offered for these languages. High-level languages enabled the programmer to develop programs for different processors. Porting a program from one processor to another came into reach, even though Java's slogan "Write Once, Run Everywhere" was still considered a vision when it was introduced in the mid-1990s. IBM released the/360 processor series in 1964 that contained processors at a broad spectrum of performance points that could be programmed with the same assembler language. This development allowed the decoupling of software from the machine, the understanding of software as something independent, separate. Under pressure from the U.S. Department of Justice and facing antitrust lawsuits, IBM announced on June 23, 1969, that it would unbundle hardware and software in the future. This announcement can be seen as the birth date of the software industry as we know it today. Within a few decades, it has developed into an enterprise software market with a volume that Gartner estimates at 517 billion US$ in 2021, with an annual growth rate (CAGR) in the range of 10.8% [Gartner21a].

In spite of the overwhelming success of software as an industry, there is an immense risk in the software business. Compared to more traditional industries, the software industry is characterized by high speed, a rapid succession of technological changes and much irrational hype. In some aspects, it is still quite immature. When the term "software engineering" was coined at a NATO conference in Germany in 1968, the intention was to bring the reliability and scientific approach of other engineering disciplines to software development. However, even today the failure rate of software development projects is still considerably higher than in those other engineering disciplines. Nevertheless, software has pervaded most other industries to an amazing—and sometimes frightening—degree.

Over the last 50 years, the world of business both in developed and in emerging economies has gone through change at a pace and extent of impact mankind has never experienced before. Over the last 25 years, the pace has accelerated. Most of this change is enabled if not driven by information technology. The fundamental drivers behind that are Moore's Law and the Internet.

2.1.1 Moore's Law

In 1965, Gordon Moore observed that the number of transistors that could be placed on an integrated circuit was doubling every 2 years. Since the mid-70s, it has been doubling every 1.5–2 years, currently slowing down a bit. Recently this increased density no longer translated into speed increases in single CPUs, which is the reason we see multi-core architectures emerging which continue to provide significant performance and availability improvements when compared at the same price level. For storage, the price per storage unit has been going down by a factor of 2 per year. These exponential improvements have led to today's situation that people have much more processing power and storage capacity in their smartphones than a mainframe computer in a water-cooled computing center had 40 years ago. Processors and storage, as well as software, are embedded in all kinds of products like cars, cameras, or mobile phones. Some industries have been totally transformed by this shift from analog to digital, accompanied by an increasing dependency on chip manufacturers. Though Moore's Law no longer holds on the chip level, there continues to be good reason to expect further exponential growth in computing for the foreseeable future [DenLew17]. The impact of new technologies like quantum computing is not yet predictable.

2.1.2 The Internet

With its origins in the military communications network ARPAnet in the US in the late 1960s, the internet has turned into the world's premier communications infrastructure. Hundreds of millions of people use it all over the world. It enables them to communicate via email, instant messaging and other paths. Since the introduction of HTML and the web browser in the mid-90s, people have been able to access information with unprecedented ease and speed. The internet has given rise to entirely new applications and business models many of which were not previously possible. Examples are search engines like Google Search, social networks like Facebook, internet banking, brokerage, and retail platforms like Amazon and eBay.

All industries make extensive use of IT today. IT may be an integral part of products, a major factor of development and manufacturing systems, or the backbone of business systems. Banking, financial services and music are just some examples of industries that have already been fundamentally influenced and radically changed due to IT and in particular software:

- The worldwide financial markets are fully dependent on IT, in terms of numbers of transactions and speed of execution. Prices and returns on many innovative financial products can only be calculated with the help of IT. This dependency on IT led to the fact that some players in the industry consider themselves more as IT companies than banks.
- When the music industry switched from LP to CD, i.e. from analog to digital, in the early 80s, they did not foresee the consequences. In the digital domain, a copy is identical to the original whereas in the analog domain it is not. With the proliferation of PCs and the internet, making digital copies and distributing them has become as easy as a mouse click. The music industry has been helplessly watching its revenues decline. The pinnacle of humiliation was the success of Apple, an IT company, with iTunes, the music download platform that

demonstrated how to be successful with music in the digital domain. Today streaming dominates the video and audio entertainment industries.

Before we look further at the current drivers of software as a business, we need to define our vocabulary.

2.2 Product Management for Software: Terms and Characteristics

Software is an intangible economic good, with no physical form. Only the functionality is perceptible, e.g. via a user interface, or visible in the results of transactions controlled via software, e.g. as account movements. As with many highly technical products, many people do not understand how software products work. Software is therefore in the truest sense of the word "intangible." Software thus contrasts greatly with other business investments or acquisitions of consumer goods. In particular, the customer does not acquire the product when buying software but specific, precisely defined rights of use as specified in a license or a Software-as-a-Service (SaaS) contract. However, investments in software today represent a larger proportion of spending for IT infrastructure than investments in hardware. Software contracts with large companies often amount to multiple millions of dollars.

Software belongs not to the three classic economic factors of capital, land, and labor, but to the new fourth category of "knowledge." Software is the manifestation of human know-how in bits and bytes. This form possesses the invaluable advantage that software can be easily copied and quickly circulated over any distance—which can also be a disadvantage as the example of the music industry above demonstrates. The right software, used appropriately, can represent a more important strategic competitive advantage in today's economic life than all the other factors. Software can be crucial for competitiveness in production processes, functionality, the availability of service products, and thus for a company's success or failure on the market. But what is a software product and what is it not—or not yet? What role does the price play? How should we classify services offered on the basis of software?

We find it reasonable not to limit the term "software product" to the world of software vendors, but also to use it in the world of corporate IT organizations. Is, for example, an online account with a direct bank, a mobile phone in combination with a special mobile phone tariff or the membership in a chat community a software product? In this chapter, we attempt to define the term "software product" and to discuss certain features of software and their relevance to products and product management.

Marketing defines the term "product" as follows: "a product is anything that can be offered to a market for attention, acquisition, or consumption that might satisfy a want or need." (see [KotArm15, p. 256]).

While products typically address bigger markets, if not "mass markets", we want to include internal customer-supplier relationships as well. Therefore, we consider the relationship between two parties as the core of our definition.

Product = A combination of material or intangible goods and services, which one party (called vendor) combines and evolves in support of their commercial interests, with the intention to transfer defined rights to one or more second parties (called customers).

Software product = Product whose primary component is software.

The phrase "in support of their commercial interests" should make clear that it refers to business but does not necessarily lead to payment. There is also a commercial interest behind Open Source. Even a product free of charge (e.g. Adobe's Acrobat Reader) has a commercial goal—to increase market penetration of another product from the same software vendor that is subject to a fee. The phrase "defined rights" expresses that there is some room for variation here, e.g. right of use (possibly with restrictions), property right, and right of resale. Details are typically defined in the software vendor's licensing terms or an individual contract between the parties concerned.

This product definition should also be construed as meaning that an item may already be a product before it has actually been purchased by a single customer. Software does not become "product" through the process of being purchased but through the intention to make it available as a useful entity to third parties, either inside or outside one's corporation, for monetary consideration or not.

In establishing the boundaries of what a software product is and is not, we have knowingly chosen a "flexible" phrase: the word "primary" should make it clear that there is room for discretion.

Still, a mobile phone is not a software product according to our definition (rather a telecommunication product), even if software is an important part and may have absorbed a large proportion of the development costs. In this case, we would be talking about embedded software. Here, embedded software "serves" most of the functionality and is, therefore, an underlying part of the whole product. The embedded software cannot be bought separately. We define:

Embedded software = Software parts of software-intensive systems that are not marketed, made available, and priced as separate entities.

Embedded software does not manage and operate only a computer or a processor, but rather is included in a technical system that consists of other components. All components together allow the whole thing to become a product. Embedded software can be the software for programming and managing a machine, diagnosis software for finding errors in an automobile, or software for servicing a dialysis machine in medicine. These programs serve highly specialized interfaces, which are typically very closely integrated with hardware.

The requirements and the product management for embedded software are driven by the functionality of the complete system that we call a "software-intensive system." Software-intensive systems can be products from many industries like cars, airplanes, and smartphones. Software-intensive services, often delivered as cloud or internet services, can also be products from any industries like financial, insurance, gaming, social software, or personal services based on software support. To facilitate the reading of this book, we will use the term "software products" to include software-intensive products.

Another important term in this context is "OEM product". OEM stands for Original Equipment Manufacturer. We define:

OEM software product = software product of software vendor A that is used by company B as a component under the covers of one of B's products.

The term "OEM" was originally coined in the hardware business and later transferred into the software world. It means that one manufacturer sells one of his products to another manufacturer who uses it as a component in one of his products without showing its origin openly. We differentiate "OEM" companies from integrator companies, the former offering products to customers, the latter a system development service to a specific customer.

Notice that B's product can be, but does not have to be, a software product. A vendor is usually willing to sell his products as OEM products at a significantly reduced price to increase his volume while protecting retail price by not revealing overtly the presence of his product or its OEM price.

Let's look at some more examples. A games console is also not a software product (rather a games product). The same arguments are valid here as for the mobile phone. A game for this console—purchased separately, separately packaged with its price and own terms of licensing—is by our definition a software product, however.

An online bank account is not a software product in our terminology. Rather, the account is a banking product implemented with the help of software products. The bank's customer receives online access to his account from his bank, which allows him to carry out bank transactions (bank balance enquiries, transfers, establishment of standing orders, etc.) at home or wherever he happens to be. The software is only useful and usable in connection with the account. So the account is the primary component.

A search offering like Google qualifies as a software product even though that may be contrary to some people's intuitive understanding. It does fulfill all the criteria of our definition: there is a commercial interest, the customer gets the right to use it, and its primary component is software. This approach builds on the "Software as a Service" model (SaaS).

The term "solution" is quite popular from a marketing perspective since it implies that a customer's problems are addressed and solved. It is used by both product vendors and professional service organizations.

Solution =

(a) A product that is a combination of other products, human services, and possibly some glue code and customization.
(b) A combination of products and customer-specific code that is developed and implemented for a specific customer.

An example for (a) are SAP's solutions for different industries or lines of business. An example for (b) is the result of a customization project in which a professional service provider customizes an SAP system for a specific customer.

2.2.1   Platform, Family, and Line

In the software product space there are a number of terms that need clarification. One of them is "product platform". McGrath defines [McGrat01]: "A product platform ... is a collection of the common elements, especially the underlying defining technology, implemented across a range of products. A product platform is primarily a definition for planning, decision making, and strategic thinking. The choice of a defining technology in platform strategy is perhaps the most critical strategic decision that a high-technology company makes." So we define:

Product Platform = the technological foundation on which several software products are based.

A product platform is not necessarily an independent product, but rather a combination of technological elements used in various products. Such a product platform often constitutes a valuable asset and serves as a market differentiation factor known as defining technology. Therefore, the product platform requires cautious management, since errors will immediately have serious consequences for all products based on the platform and thus for the company as a whole. When such a product platform is not offered as a product of its own, it is embedded in products that are based on it.

The term "product platform" is different from "platform in an ecosystem" which is a technical product that the platform owner as well as third parties use as a foundation for conducting their own respective businesses. This may include technological collaboration and integration, as well as commercial interaction and financial transactions. There are two non-disjoint types of platforms [CusGaYof19]:

- **Innovation Platform** = Technological foundation upon which the owner and other firms develop complementary innovations.
- **Transaction Platform** = Intermediary or online marketplace that makes it possible for people and organizations to share information or to buy, sell, or access a variety of goods and services.

An innovation platform is always based on a product platform that is turned into a product and thereby made available to third parties. An example of an innovation platform is the SAP core system that serves as the basis for all SAP components. With software, there can be platforms that are not under the control of the software vendor, but which nevertheless may have a key influence on the success of his product. For example, for any smartphone software the question of the operating system platforms needs to be answered. I.e. a vendor must define whether the software shall run on Apple's iOS, Google's Android, and/or some other platform.

An interesting example is Amazon. They have a highly successful e-commerce platform, which is both a transaction platform and an innovation platform. With Amazon Web Services (AWS), they have a pure innovation platform.

A third type of platform called coordination platform is not yet as well defined. It serves the organization of players in a system, e.g. a supply chain. While existing transaction platforms are highly successful in B2C, coordination platforms have a high potential of value creation in B2B.

Notice that there are authors like Choudary [Choudary21] who see the terms "product" and "platform" as opposites. For them, products have a "pipeline" business model with a linear flow of value from vendor to customer, whereas platforms have an ecosystem-based business model. In our view, innovation platforms are primarily governed by a pipeline business model, and we consider them as software products. A product manager who manages an innovation platform faces special challenges, in particular in ecosystem management and with the tailorability strategy.

For transaction and coordination platforms which have an ecosystem-based business model, the platform management is usually separate from the product management of the underlying software. Platform management, in particular for multi-sided platforms, is highly domain-specific and complex, e.g. the business model requires ongoing balancing so that all stakeholders get sufficient benefits from using the platform. Ecosystem management requires significantly more attention compared to non-platform products since achieving win-win-situations with a high number of stakeholders is a key success factor for a platform. Platform management is not fully covered by ISPMA's SPM Body of Knowledge nor by this book. We refer to [CusGaYof19, ParAlsCho16]. Product management of the underlying software is fully covered by ISPMA's SPM Body of Knowledge and this book. The way product management is done in this scenario is very similar to software product management in corporate IT organizations (see Sect. 7.3.5).

The establishment of a product family in the market is purely for marketing reasons. We define:

Product Family = A group of software products that are marketed as belonging together under a common family name.

A software vendor can group various products together under a "family name". That family name allows marketing the products more efficiently than with a single-product marketing approach. This product family approach suggests that the products belong together, implying that they are either technologically similar or that together they provide a solution for specific problems. The technological similarity can be a common product platform, e.g. SAP products. Microsoft Office is an example of a product family comprising a group of products that address specific problems, in this case, office tasks, even if the components of Office have not always had a seamless relationship.

The above examples illustrate that the terms "product platform" and "product family" sometimes coincide. Products based on a common product platform can be—but do not have to be—marketed as a product family. Conversely, products marketed as a family can have—but do not have to have—a common product platform. Whether or not it is advisable to establish a family concept is primarily a marketing decision. That decision has an impact on the requirements for the products. Customers expect products belonging to a product family to exhibit more common features in terms of integration of product combinations or interface similarities in the case of technologically similar products. If the products do not adequately meet customer integration expectations, the family concept can have a negative market impact. An examination of Microsoft Office will reveal a high percentage of queries and complaints related to differences between GUIs and transferability between applications even though generally this is considered the gold standard office suite of products.

The term "product line" has gained a lot of attention, primarily in, but not restricted to the area of embedded software. We define:

Product Line = A set of products based on a common product platform with defined (static or dynamic) variability tailored to different markets and users.

The Amazon e-commerce platform can serve as an example. Amazon has one code base as a product platform for all its international websites which is adapted to local requirements. Product lines are established for both business and technology management considerations.

All these concepts, platform, product platform, product family, and product line, increase the complexity of software product management. However, when used appropriately, they can accelerate development and marketing and increase return-on-investment.

2.2.2 Cloud Computing

One innovative area that has changed the IT landscape significantly is "cloud computing". The term came into use around 2007, but the underlying concept is older. Since then, the concept has been extended into the mobile space. For this book, we will use the following definition:

Cloud Computing = Service and delivery model for the provisioning of IT components through the internet based on an architecture that enables a high level of scalability and reliability.

Cloud computing can be offered for

- IaaS: Infrastructure as a Service, e.g. processor capacity or storage,
- PaaS: Platform as a Service, i.e. infrastructure plus pre-installed enabling products, e.g. a database,
- SaaS: Software as a Service, i.e. infrastructure plus middleware plus application software, e.g. a customer relationship management (CRM) software.

Examples for IaaS are Amazon's Simple Storage Service (S3) and Elastic Compute Cloud (EC2) in the public cloud. Companies like IBM or HP help corporate IT organizations of larger enterprise customers to build private clouds that use internet technologies, but are strictly separate from the public internet.

IaaS providers have started to extend their IaaS offering into a PaaS offering that allows third-party developers to develop and offer their software products rapidly. Governments have also invested in PaaS platforms. For example, the European Commission developed FIWARE, a platform which was adopted by a large number of startup companies even in its early years.

A well-known SaaS provider is Salesforce with its CRM application. Many interpret search engines like Google also as SaaS. This model means that the vendor does not sell a license to the customer, but a software-enabled service. The vendor will host, i.e. install and run the software on his own or a subcontracted computing center and take care of the installation of any updates. The customer gets the right to access the software via the internet and use it according to its contractual terms which may have the character of a Service Level Agreement (SLA). The customer stores his data on the vendor's system. SaaS promises unprecedented levels of scalability for customers without any significant investments in their infrastructure or operations. A lot of implementations follow a hybrid model where one software component runs on the user's device and communicates directly with the cloud component. The hybrid model is very popular with mobile app providers.

The SaaS delivery model may seem financially attractive. However, compared to a customer's on-premise total cost of ownership, SaaS providers' real cost savings are confined to the savings gained from centralized management and infrastructure. These are higher if the software supports multi-tenancy which means the ability to run multiple clients in parallel on the same runtime instance of the software. Those savings are what the providers can share with their customers. Additional business benefits for a provider, especially in the consumer business, can come from opportunities based on the data that customers provide. The Google business model of offering targeted advertisements based on the customers' search profiles is a good example of this.

From a customer perspective, SaaS has several advantages:

- The customer does not have to deal with the operations aspects of installation, maintenance, data storage, and backup.
- The software is automatically on the latest release level (which is hopefully compatible with the previous release level).
- The customer usually perceives the new pricing models as advantageous compared to the traditional license model.
- In most jurisdictions, customers have a financial advantage since periodic payments for SaaS are handled as operating expenses whereas investments in infrastructure and software licenses are considered as capital expenses.

The disadvantages are:

- The data is stored under the control of the vendor. The customer needs to have sufficient trust in the vendor, the reliability and long term availability of his service, and the vendor needs to ensure an appropriate level of security.
- The availability of the service is dependent on the availability of the internet that is typically neither controlled by the vendor nor the customer. The delivery of software services at the location of the customer is a business opportunity for telecom companies that they pursue under the name "mobile edge computing".

SaaS was preceded in the 1990s by the Application Service Provider (ASP) model. ASPs leased telecommunication lines instead of using the internet. Most ASP applications were customer-specific whereas SaaS offers standard software in a multi-user mode that the individual customer can only customize to a limited extent. The lease-based single-tenant approach never gained significant momentum in the market. The trend towards SaaS was predicted by [RusKan03] as early as 2003 when the authors still called it e-service. According to the market intelligence firm Gartner, the Corona crisis has accelerated the trend [Gartner21b]. Gartner predicts worldwide public cloud services end-user spending to increase from 270 billion US$ in 2020 to 397 billion US$ in 2022.

2.3   Software as a Business

Consideration of software as a business implies consideration of the what and why of the software: the definition of the product and the markets, the delivery and sourcing of the product, and the competitive positioning. A software product manager who wants to define such a product strategy needs to have an excellent understanding of the software industry, its trends and drivers, and the relevant markets for the product.

What we have seen in the banking or music industries has only been the beginning. Software penetrates the core of more and more industries, be it software-based diagnosis and personalized care systems in the healthcare industry, software-controlled engines and brakes in the automotive industry, and even cars which no longer even need a driver. This importance of software is quite new to these industries. It requires not only technical but also cultural changes that can be facilitated by introducing software product management in these organizations.

At the same time, more and more IT components become commodity products, like storage, processors, or inexpensive or free software apps. For a company from any industry, the challenge is finding the right combination of low-cost commodity IT and differentiating non-commodity elements that improve the company's competitiveness. Enablers of competitiveness are the attractiveness of the company's products, the effectiveness and efficiency of the business processes of the company, the abilities of the employees, and the design of the customer interface. It is a basic element of our economic system that these factors have been, are, and will be enabling differentiation in the market. Investments in IT that support these factors will be highly relevant for competitiveness in the future. Well known current examples of companies that are differentiating themselves in the market in exactly this way are Amazon, Apple, and Samsung. Their success is primarily based on innovative processes and customer interfaces that could only be implemented with IT. Commodity products can be part of those solutions, but they alone will not result in competitive advantage. Of course, when commoditization leads to lower prices for both hardware and software and thereby higher performance per $, then innovative offerings become financially feasible that were not feasible before.

2.3.1   Low Capital Investment

For software products, almost the entire product cost is incurred during development. As a consequence, a certain minimum revenue or minimum number of licenses must be achieved to reach the break-even point. In other words, software is one of very few products for which any additional revenue beyond the break-even point is almost pure profit. This characteristic of software products means that there is a high incentive—or necessity—for software companies to offer their products internationally to achieve the largest possible sales volumes. Internationalization usually requires translation of usage interfaces and documentation into the respective languages and addressing the specific requirements of each targeted country. The software market, in general, is international though there are some successful vendors for regional software solutions. This international orientation is an important element of the job of a product manager in software companies.

Compared to traditional industries that develop and produce physical goods, a software company needs relatively little capital and investments initially and in the course of its development. In principle, for software development "only" good know-how, a development environment, and a few PCs are required. Creation of software product deliverables is cheap because it can be done by duplication of media and printing of brochures and handbooks. Such production activities may not even be needed in case of internet distribution. In reality, even in the software industry it can be a bit more complicated, but the famous garage start-ups are not just myths. Anyone can start a software company—but not necessarily make it succeed. As is true for all startups, the secret of success is good know-how and professional management, with the difficult transition of company leaders from start-up entrepreneurs to businessmen. Eric Ries claims that "entrepreneurship is management" [Ries11, p. 8]. This sentence works both ways. Entrepreneurship means building an institution that automatically involves management [Ries11, p. 15]. On the other hand, a manager in an established company can benefit a lot from acting like an entrepreneur and applying ideas of Ries' "Lean Startup".

The low capital investment means low market entry barriers. Somewhere in this world, new software companies are founded daily—and die daily. The most significant asset of software companies—human know-how—is in the brains of the employees, i.e. highly mobile. The fluidity of such know-how leads to very high innovation in the software industry. Technological innovations spread quickly and get introduced into new product versions. Many software products have ideas at the core of their value which may not be patentable, copyrightable, or intellectual property protected via "trade secret." This high speed of innovation and adoption lowers the technical entry barriers, i.e. the software market is characterized by low market entry barriers and extremely high competition and fluctuation compared to other industries.

In the IT industry, the hardware manufacturers are in constant competition. A manufacturer of goods fears nothing so much as commoditization, i.e. the ability of his customers to easily replace his products with those of his competitors. The end user faces no big functional or economic barriers if he wants to change for example, the brand of car he buys. Therefore, manufacturers of products which are commoditized invest heavily in brand and image marketing. Also, they invest in bells and whistles that attempt to differentiate the product or make it to some degree proprietary (though the latter may backfire).

With software, competition is different. There is significant effort and risk involved in switching from an installed software product to a competitive product, more than for any other element of the IT infrastructure. This statement is valid for enterprise software, but also to some degree for consumer software. The main reason is that software is rarely used in an isolated way, but instead as an integral part of the complete software landscape, in an enterprise environment usually including self-developed applications. Unless there is a major quantifiable and visible-to-end-user improvement in a replacement product, the IT professional will correctly reject any decision to replace a working product. He will receive zero credit if he succeeds (no visible benefit), and the wrath of all his end users if the product fails. Another aspect is the high level of company-specific customization. The degree of interdependence of a product with the other components of the software landscape is extremely high and very often not properly documented. That is why software once installed, integrated and used is very difficult to replace. It also means that ongoing product development, maintenance of older releases, and compatibility of new to old releases and versions have high importance and are a key success factor for software product management.

2.3.2 Law of Increasing Returns

As pointed out in [HoRoPL00], the software industry is governed by the law of increasing returns that was first described by the economist Brian Arthur [Arthur96]. This law says that a software product with a high market share will experience a further improvement of its market position just because of this high market share whereas a low market share leads to a further decrease. In other words, trends in market share intensify themselves. There are three main reasons for this phenomenon: the network effect, the increasing cost of switching, and the trust in the market leader.

The network effect was described by Katz and Shapiro in [KatSha85]: "The utility that a user derives from the good depends on the number of other users who are on the same network." There are direct effects like standardization of interfaces that allow users of the same software product to exchange data and user experience more easily—they speak the same language. With users in different companies, this leads to a trend towards standardization of software products across companies. Indirect effects come from complementary products and services whose number increases when more customers use the base product (see [BuDiHe12, p. 21]).

The increasing cost of switching characterizes how software "sticks" in a customer environment. The longer a user or company has a certain software product in use (e.g. text processing software), the larger the effort of switching to a different product. The data created with one program cannot necessarily be interpreted by the other program. Imagine the difficulties in a company that has changed from text processor "A" to "B." If, a year or two later, it is necessary to refer to or change a document created under "A" there must be a way to do that. So in some way the older program must either be kept or conversion provided for, which is a significant inhibitor to change. Also, the switch usually means significant education effort.

The trust in the market leader describes some of the behavior of customers when they make buying decisions. Consumers, as well as big companies, tend to rely on established brands and leading products. An established brand gives the investment the security that the chosen product will not disappear from the market the next day. Customers interpret the market leading position as a quality seal since many have already decided for the product. The standardization of interfaces and data is also relevant in this context.

The importance of market share for a software product is different depending on the level of maturity of the market in which competition takes place. In an early technology phase, there are typically a large number of young products with similar functionality and the customers are in an orientation phase. The first products are tested; some early adopters make product decisions and invest in installations. In this phase, there is no market leader, but trends and camps emerge. The power and prestige of the respective camps will usually determine the market leader of the future. During the growth phase of a product market, two or at most three dominating products and vendors can be identified very quickly, i.e. within 12–18 months. In the maturity phase, one can observe all three of the effects described above. The combined effect is a consolidation and disappearance of the smaller vendors, and often a concentration on two or only one dominating product.

The law of increasing return makes market leadership more important for software products than for most other products. Of course, market leadership is an important competitive advantage for most products, be it for cost efficiency through economies of scale, be it as a marketing argument. But nowhere is market leadership so important for the future of a company in a market as with software products, and even more so with platforms. That is why in the short term the goal of market leadership in a chosen market segment has priority over other company goals like revenue or profitability.

One note of caution on the law of increasing returns and the network effect in particular: they alone do not guarantee sustained success when new technologies emerge. For example, Nokia dominated the phone market before Apple and Android-based smartphones took over. The disruption happened even though Nokia's market position seemed well established. A vendor must be vigilant, particularly as new technologies are introduced. The best strategy appears to be continuous evolution and improvement and never resting on your laurels. An example is Adobe's Photoshop. Although Adobe's high price strategy created a price umbrella for others to come in under and compete with compatible or similar products, the product continued to be successful for a long time. Nevertheless, Adobe made a radical switch to a SaaS model for most of their products.

New software technologies develop and drive new markets for software products. These markets show fast, often drastic growth, during which a high number of competitors boil down into a few winners and lots of losers. Software technologies and their markets can be compared to layers of an onion. New layers are created continuously, and the old ones dry out and die. The art of running a software company is to leave the drying outer layers in time and jump onto a juicy inner layer, a new market in which there is a new fight for market leadership.

2.3.3 The Financial Life Cycle of a Software Product

As just discussed, the start-up capital requirements for a software company are modest. If one has a good idea, and perhaps the beginnings of a demo or prototype, venture capital can be found which is sufficient to begin. Still, just as in almost any startup, there will be a great deal of expenditure before the first dollar of revenue is earned for a software product. Software is unique in that most of the capital outlay occurs during this pre-revenue period. As soon as revenue is earned, excepting major enhancements, the software product incurs small variable cost and high marginal profit. With SaaS, variable cost is a bit higher than a one-time electronic distribution of the software due to hosting.

To earn revenue with a software product, two common revenue models compete with each other: the one-time charge (OTC) model and the periodic charge model. Once sales begin, there will be pressure to show profits, certainly pressure to show dramatic yearly increases in revenues. In a periodic charge model with recurring charges, there is no acceleration of revenue through initial sales. Revenue is earned over time as the product is used. This revenue model contrasts with the up-front revenue model that is based on the sale of a one-time charge (OTC) perpetual license. Like someone who owns an apartment building and rents out the apartments, a software company with attractive products who licenses them using recurring charges may make a great deal of money in the long term. However, deferred recurring revenue is not the way to show the most dramatic financial growth as one might want to do in a start-up, particularly if one were contemplating an Initial Public Offering (IPO). This communication problem may influence a company to offer its licenses on an OTC basis, relying on maintenance charges to provide a recurring stream of revenue following the initial sale. With SaaS, periodic charge models have turned into the standard.

As the product becomes established, the objective shifts to wanting to maintain price and preserve revenue stream with less regard for quick growth. Achieving this shifted objective requires clarity of strategy, strength of will, and discipline in terms of discounting, periodic enhancements, continued marketing to increase share. As explained in the previous section, there is no fear as great as that of commoditization during this phase. Most software businesses will need the cash being generated by their successful products to finance the development of enhancements and new products, as well as potentially the acquisition of companies with interesting and innovative products. So the objective in the medium term is often to prolong product life as much as possible with modest expenditures to maximize profits, yet retain market leadership.

As companies grow, they often choose to grow by acquisition, particularly if they have cash. One can see this clearly with IBM, Oracle, SAP and others. They have been acquiring software companies at an increasing rate of more than one per month for several years. Reasons can be to buy innovation and shorten the time-to-market, to buy market share, or to get specific skills fast [Popp13].

Eventually most products move into a sunset phase where they reach their end of life, replaced by a new product in the vendor's portfolio (hopefully) or perhaps by a competitor. However, a product may be devilishly difficult to replace if it is tightly integrated into a company's infrastructure. Therefore, it behooves the vendor to provide an easy, effective, and financially attractive migration to his replacement product. If the migration to the vendor's follow-on product is difficult or expensive, the sunset will invite the customer to consider competitive alternatives. For customers who have a perpetual license, it is even harder to get them to migrate to a new product. Microsoft and their challenge to motivate customers to migrate to newer versions of Windows or Office is a good example. Microsoft tried to address this issue by offering Windows 7 and 8 users in the consumer market a free migration to Windows 10 for the first year following availability. And they are providing a path for Windows 10 users to migrate to Windows 11 at no charge (in terms of software).

2.4   Business Models

A business model describes the "rationale of how an organization creates, delivers and captures value by interacting with suppliers, customers and partners" [OstPign10, p. 14]. The business model reflects how a company intends to make money. The term "business model" has become popular with Internet businesses, as the Internet has opened up a wealth of new possibilities to earn money. The term can be applied to any business organization though it is often considered at the corporate or business unit level. A business model of a company or business unit describes which products and services are offered by a company, which value they offer to which market segments, and how cost and revenue streams relate to the different products and services. The business model concept can also be applied to an individual product.

A business model analysis can be helpful for a software product manager when analyzing potential partners. While relevant for an individual product, its consideration can also make sense for a solution that spans multiple products and services. We will come back to this in the chapter on Product Strategy.

2.4.1   Describing a Business Model

A Business Model is a conceptual model that describes the products and services considered and how revenue streams relate to these products and services. Teece provides some scientific foundations to the concept [Teece10]. Business models can

Business Model Matrix		Type of Products and Services			
		Financial	Physical	Intangible	Human
Archetypes	Creator	Entrepreneur	Manufacturer	Inventor, Developer, Author	./.
	Distributor	Financial Trader	Wholesaler, Retailer	IP Distributor	./.
	Lessor	Financial Lessor	Physical Lessor	IP Lessor	Contractor
	Broker	Financial Broker	Financial Lessor	IP Broker	HR Broker

Fig. 2.1 Business model matrix [PoppMey10]

be classified according to three dimensions: "the type of products or services provided, the business model archetype, and a revenue model" [PoppMey10]. A business model is constructed by choosing one or more combinations of the three elements of a business model (see Fig. 2.1).

According to [PoppMey10], types of products or services can be

- Financial products (cash and other assets),
- Physical products (real, physical products, durable and non-durable goods),
- Intangible products (software but also other intellectual property, knowledge and brand image), and
- Human services (people's time and effort).

Business Model Archetypes are basic patterns of doing business. Available archetypes are creator, distributor, lessor, and broker:

- A creator uses supplied goods and internal assets and transforms them to create a product sold to customers or used by other creators. It is important to know that the main work done by the creator is designing the product. An example is Apple. Apple designs the iPod in California. So Apple is a creator.
- A distributor buys a product and provides the same product to customers. Obvious examples are companies in the wholesale and retail industries, like Amazon, or Apple's online retail store for applications, the AppStore.
- A lessor provides the temporary right to use, but not own, a product or service to customers. Examples are landlords, lenders of money, consultants and software companies that license their software to customers. For human services, human resource lessors lend their employees' time to customers.

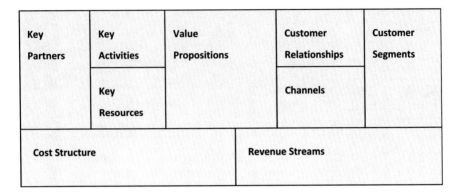

Fig. 2.2 Business Model Canvas [OstPign10]

- A broker facilitates the matching of potential buyers and sellers. A broker never takes ownership of the products and services. An example is a traditional stock broker. A software-based example is eBay, which provides a transaction platform that matches buyers and sellers.

Single products and services may be offered stand-alone, or they may be offered as a bundle, which is a combination of products and services. Software vendors are typically offering intangible products and act as a creator and lessor of software, but also offer human services like consulting, maintenance and support.

A revenue model describes how revenue is generated from the product offering. Details will be discussed under Pricing (Sect. 3.10).

One of the widespread tools for reviewing and evaluating existing business models is the Business Model Canvas. It is also used to systematically invent new ones that change the way a product competes. The Business Model Canvas consists of nine segments, see Fig. 2.2. On the right-hand side, we find the segments representing market- and customer-facing views (e.g. customer segments and revenue streams). On the left-hand-side, we find those representing company internal and supplier-facing views (e.g. key resources and cost structures). In the middle, the value proposition links the two sides or views.

Each of the dimensions of a business model leads to particular entries in the Business Model canvas. The entries are as follows:

- Products, services, or bundles are compensated by the customer. Compensation can be monetary (revenue streams) or non-monetary (exchange of products, services or information). For each product there always is compensation, which in many cases is a revenue stream.
- Products, services, or bundles have a corresponding value proposition.
- For each type of product, service, and bundle there is a specific cost structure.
- Business models are executed by activities, some of them being key activities. Activities are carried out by resources, some of them being key resources.

There is an example in the next section.

2.4.2   Business Models in the Software Industry: Software Product Company

The prototypical company in the software industry is the software product company, or software vendor, which develops, offers, and maintains software products. The customer buys a license, and installs and runs the software on-premise or as a cloud-based offering. To do the latter, the customer signs a contract for a cloud-based service where the vendor runs the software, and the customer accesses the service over the internet.

Figures 2.3 and 2.4 give a description of a software vendor's business model. We assume that the vendor has both on-premise and Cloud-based businesses (which requires hosting, shown in Fig. 2.3 as "Physical Lessor"). The vendor develops software, distributes it directly and/or indirectly, and sells licenses, i.e. act as a lessor. Also, the vendor offers product-related human services like maintenance, shown in Fig. 2.3 as "Contractor". Figure 2.3 demonstrates that the vendor covers five elements of the matrix. The business model canvas (Fig. 2.4) shows more details of the business model.

The business model of a software vendor assumes standard software products that are suitable for a large number of customers.

Business Model Matrix Software Vendor		Type of Products and Services			
		Financial	Physical	Intangible	Human
	Creator	Entrepreneur	Manufacturer	Inventor, Developer, Author	./.
	Distributor	Financial Trader	Wholesaler, Retailer	IP Distributor	./.
	Lessor	Financial Lessor	Physical Lessor	IP Lessor	Contractor
	Broker	Financial Broker	Financial Lessor	IP Broker	HR Broker

Fig. 2.3 Software Vendor's business model matrix

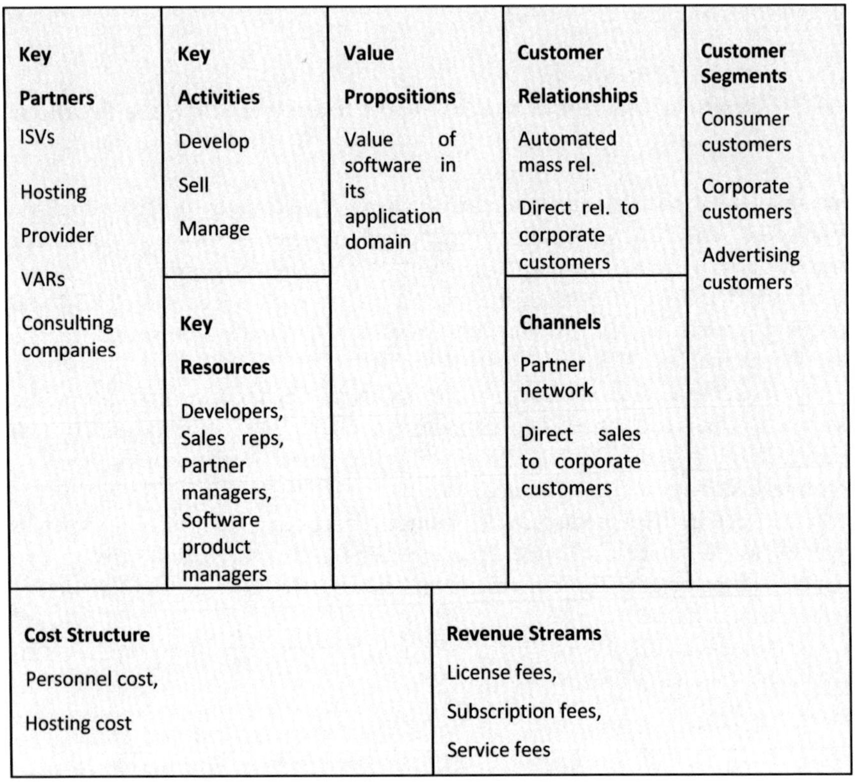

Key Partners	Key Activities	Value Propositions	Customer Relationships	Customer Segments
ISVs	Develop	Value of software in its application domain	Automated mass rel.	Consumer customers
Hosting Provider	Sell		Direct rel. to corporate customers	Corporate customers
VARs	Manage			Advertising customers
Consulting companies	**Key Resources** Developers, Sales reps, Partner managers, Software product managers		**Channels** Partner network Direct sales to corporate customers	

Cost Structure	Revenue Streams
Personnel cost, Hosting cost	License fees, Subscription fees, Service fees

Fig. 2.4 Software Vendor's Business Model Canvas (example)

The sales of a software product can be combined with product-related services that can be priced based on actual effort, or as a package with the software license, or as a subscription as is customary for product maintenance. According to Cusumano [Cusuma03]: "A general rule of thumb is that, over the lifetime of using a software product, enterprise customers pay between one and two dollars in service and maintenance fees per dollar of software license fees (the up-front product cost)." In particular, when the economy is bad and product sales are down, the importance of this income for the survival of a software vendor becomes obvious. That is why maintenance fees and even more so the pricing model of recurring charges are so attractive (see Sect. 3.10). There is no large up-front payment, but smaller monthly payments. This pricing model can be a pleasant pillar for vendors since it results in a more balanced, smoother revenue stream. The stock market deplores nothing as much as unpredictable earnings. With SaaS, the recurring pricing model has returned under the name 'subscription fee'.

2.4.3   Business Models in the Software Industry: Professional Service vs. Product

While both the software product and the professional services business models are attractive, there are significant differences that make them difficult to combine. In this context, it is important to differentiate between the different meanings of the term "service" that we introduced in Chap. 1. There is a continuum from services to products that can be confusing. It is illustrated in Fig. 2.5.

Of course, a company can follow the business model of a professional service company that develops customer-specific software. This business model means that the development of software is paid for, either based on effort expended or at a fixed price. The focus is not on a software product, but on projects and the employees who deliver the service. The goal is to implement an application, according to the requirements of the customer. It is typically not designed for a broad and flexible spectrum of usage scenarios.

The "service" in SaaS or PaaS is a technical service. For these offerings, it makes more sense to look at them as product offerings. Directly product-related services like maintenance or training ought to be managed as part of the whole software product offering. The term "whole product" was popularized by Geoffrey Moore [Moore14]. It means the combination of the base product and additional products and services by the same or different companies that together provide a convincing solution to customers in the target market.

In contrast, customer-specific human services like custom software development constitute a professional service business. This differentiation is required because service (or project) and product businesses have different business models as shown in Fig. 2.6.

In most cases, the financial characteristics of software products are opposed to those of professional services. Software requires high upfront investment and has

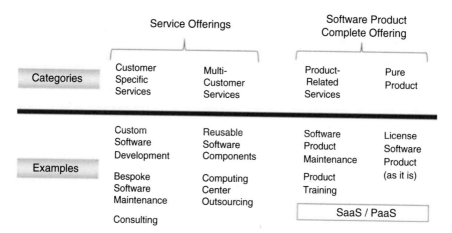

Fig. 2.5 Service-product continuum

	Service Business	Product Business
Focus	Customer, Project	Market, Product
Financial model	Small investment, Low risk, Continuous moderate profit	Significant upfront investment, Higher risk, Potentially high profit
Price calculation	Cost-based (cost + margin), Existing software usually included	Value-based, Software product usually priced separately from services
KPI	Utilization, Average daily rate	Market share, Profit
Market evaluation	Moderate	Much higher

Fig. 2.6 Differences between (professional) service and product business

low revenue-dependent variable cost. Once the original investment is recouped, additional sales result in very high profit margins. Professional services, in contrast, require low upfront investment and have high revenue-dependent variable cost. Of course, once a services team is hired the personnel costs can be considered as fixed. It would be difficult to lay off staff when there is no work to keep the employees busy and rehire the same skill pool when there is more work. Pricing is fundamentally different. For professional services the standard pricing approach is cost-based, whereas for software products it is value-based (see Sect. 3.10). Key performance indicators (KPIs) are different as well. For services, companies look at utilization rate, i.e. the percentage of work time of service employees that is paid for by customers. If that KPI is applied to a product business that business is killed because the required upfront investment would never be made. The reason why many service companies want to start a product business is the market valuation of the company. For a service business, it tends to be in the range of 2–3 times the annual revenue, for a product business often in the range of 10.

Software product management has been common practice for most software vendors. However, this does not mean that all software vendors manage their products explicitly. Often start-up companies are founded with the intention to go to market as software vendors, but lack the capital needed to develop the first release. If venture capital or bank credits are not available, an alternative is driving development through customer-specific projects that the customer pays for. Customers can often be found on the basis of sufficiently attractive prototypes.

An interested customer may be willing to pay for the way from a prototype to a commercially usable product that meets his specific requirements. However, he will be watchful that his money is not "misused" on the way to a more widely usable software product. That is why this approach frequently does not succeed and often leads to separate code bases for each customer and not to a more widely usable product. As long as further development and maintenance of these code bases is paid for by the respective customers according to effort, the model can work. But it is the business model of a service company, not of a software vendor. When company and customers switch to the software vendor model, the customers only pay standard maintenance fees that would be sufficient for maintaining a common product code base, but not separate customer-specific code bases. A mix of customer-specific development and standard maintenance frequently results in economic problems for the vendor.

Our experience suggests the following rules of thumb:

- The relation of the effort for a prototype versus a piece of software commercially usable in one customer environment is 1:3.
- The relation of effort for software commercially usable in one customer environment versus a software product that can be used by a higher number of customers is again 1:3.

What can we conclude from this? The executive management of a company must be clear in what the company is supposed to be, i.e. which business model it intends to follow. Michael Cusumano, professor at MIT Sloan School of Management, writes in [Cusuma03]: "Regardless of the balance of products and services they choose, managers of software companies must understand what their primary business is, and recognize how the two differ—for selling products requires very different organizational capabilities than selling (professional) services." The cultural differences between software and service companies often lead to failure whenever a service company tries to turn a piece of software that developed based on a service contract into a standard product. However, this cultural change is possible. An example is the CAD software CATIA developed by Dassault in France that became a very successful software product.

These are the reasons why all major IT companies that have both product and service business used to separate them strictly on the executive management level. A good example is IBM, who tried to establish a PaaS/SaaS business run out of IBM's service division that had a lot of outsourcing experience. It did not work too well. So in 2014, IBM relaunched its PaaS/SaaS business under the name Bluemix managed by IBM's product group. With their 2015 reorganization, IBM left that proven path of separating product and service business by establishing business units like Analytics or Commerce that combine software products, additional partner products, and product-related services. This experiment bore a lot of risk, but seems to work through a separation of product and service business in those units. In 2019, IBM bought Red Hat for the staggering amount of 34 billion US$ in order to make up for lost time in its cloud business.

The flexibility of software in combination with human services opens up a wide space for creative business model innovation, in particular in connection with the internet and mobile services. This ongoing innovation has increasingly led to companies using different business models for different products.

2.4.4   Business Models in the Software Industry: Open Source

Usually, ownership of software code rests with the company that develops it. In case of custom software development for an individual customer, it is a matter of contract negotiation whether ownership is with the customer, the professional service company or both. We cannot recommend strongly enough that this be crystal clear in the contractual wording in order to avoid later conflicts over intellectual property, royalties, right to market, etc.

With the emergence of open-source software like the Linux operating system, an alternative to the product ownership paradigm has proven its feasibility. A growing community of developers contributes in a self-managed and parallel way to the development of a complex system that has gone through the metamorphosis from a cult object to a de facto industry standard. Through the internet, the Linux code is available to everybody at no cost whereas the packages of Linux distributors that add installation and implementation tools and documentation to the code have a price tag.

Given the success of the open-source movement with software like Linux, Apache, the middleware JBOSS, or the MySQL database, there is some speculation that all software may be free of charge over time. We think this extrapolation is misleading. The history of open source shows that motivations can be observed that are clearly rooted in specific characteristics of the contributing programmer community. There is a strong anarchic element that favors the elegance and beauty of a technical solution versus any economical considerations. This element tends to rebel against restrictions that companies put on their employees or that the economic system puts on its market participants. A key factor of the open-source community has always been resistance against companies dominating the market, in former times IBM, then Microsoft. In the community, recognition by peers, i.e. other acknowledged specialists, is more important than economic success. However, many of these programmers use the recognition for getting well-paid jobs. The contradiction between the economic interest of the individual whose work as a programmer has to pay the bills and the anti-economic attitude of the community characterize the movement. Since this community consists exclusively of "techies", i.e. technically oriented programmers, it does not surprise that the primary focus has been on infrastructure software, i.e. operating systems and middleware. In recent years, there has been an increasing number of application-oriented open source projects, but none has reached market share comparable to the open source flagships like Linux or Apache. Applications can only be developed in cooperation with specialists from the application domain who typically do not share the anti-economic attitude of the open-source community. Over time, some companies have embraced the open source model for their own commercial reasons, e.g. Netscape [Hecker99]. Other companies work with hybrid models by combining proprietary and open source software [BoGiRo06]. Demil and Lecocq [DemLec06] look at open source ecosystems as controlled by "bazaar governance".

Today most commercial software includes open source code—primarily in order to improve productivity of the development teams. But vendors need to beware of legal implications and risks (see Sect. 3.13). Once a piece of open source software has gained a certain market share, it becomes interesting for commercial software companies. Based on the open source code, software products can be sold with packaging and product-related services justifying the price tag. Examples are companies like Red Hat (acquired by IBM) or Suse (acquired by Novell) in the Linux area. Established vendors have also embraced open source. Examples are Sun's acquisition of MySQL (now Oracle), or IBM that has jumped on the Linux bandwagon. What is the motivation behind this? The effort of a software company for the continuous development of complex software like an operating system is enormous. For this to make sense for the bottom-line, either the product price has to be high—an example is IBM's DB2 for z/OS—or the volume has to be high—as for Microsoft's Windows. A relevant open-source operating system, which is offered at almost no cost, may encourage a manufacturer to support that open source project, while making sure that his hardware will continue to be supported. Such cooperation may be financially more attractive than a self-developed software product.

Apps in app stores can usually not be considered as open source software even if their price is zero. They are usually developed by individual developers, not by a community, and their code is not made available to the public. Also, the developer will often try to generate revenue in other ways described below.

2.4.5 Business Models in the Software Industry: Free Commercial Products

Besides open source, there are a lot of commercial products that do not cost anything or very little. They can usually be downloaded or used on the internet. Low-cost pricing is typically driven by commercial interests and marketing strategies. The following variants are known: freeware, trial-ware, or upgrade-ware.

Freeware is the offering of a product at no charge. Examples are viewer or player products like Adobe's Acrobat Reader or Real Audio's player. Here, the software vendor intends to make the usage and exchange of files in its format easy and at the same time to create demand for its costly full-function product that is needed to create the files.

Trial-ware is the offering of a product either as a web download or sometimes media (CD or DVD) which offers a trial period after which it requires payment of a fee for continued use. Demo versions often have restrictions in functionality or capacity or become unusable after the trial period. This type of software does have the character of products, is part of a product family and is managed by the respective product management organization. A plan is needed that specifies the functions to be made available and for how long they should be available since this product behavior has to be implemented by Development.

Upgrade-ware (or Freemium) is the offering of a product with a base version at no charge and with enhancements that require payment. The user is encouraged to upgrade to obtain additional functions. Base versions may range from full-function products, where the upgrades offer additional bells and whistles, to limited (or no) function programs that simply tell you what they would do if they were fully functional. Especially with online games, this business model is also known as the freemium model where users can play a game for free, but as soon as they want extra features, they need to pay. A B2B example is the middleware company Talend that offers their base product as open source—with only their own developers working on it, additional functionality as commercial products. A variant of this is Adware where the software can be used for free, but contains advertisements. If the user wants to get rid of the ads he needs to pay a fee.

SaaS may be offered for free and be financed through advertising. Examples are search engines like Google or Yahoo and Google Apps, Google's office and collaboration suite. Google Apps can be seen as Google's attempt to transfer its extremely successful search business model that is based on advertising revenues to software market segments whose business models have traditionally been based on license fees. Social media platforms like Facebook are also trying to monetize their reach through advertisement. From a customer perspective, these offerings do not require monetary payment. However, there is a price to be paid in terms of being exposed to ads and revealing information about one's identity or interests. An increasing number of apps in the app stores of Apple or Google also fall into this category, i.e. the app developers try to generate revenue through ads.

Both open source and SaaS offerings providing revenue through the support of paid advertisements are examples of Wikinomics at work. The term "Wikinomics" was coined by Don Tapscott and described in his book of the same name [TapWil06]. It stands for the emergence of new business models that are based on the network effect enabled by the internet. We can expect to see more innovative business models over time in this context, in particular in connection with platforms like social and business communities on the net, some of which will impact software vendors.

In addition to these business models of software vendors and internet companies, there are other business models in software ecosystems. Examples are Value-Added Resellers (VARs), System Integrators, Hosting Providers, etc. [Kittlaus14]. We will come back to these ecosystem-oriented business models when we discuss software ecosystems in Sect. 3.12.

In software-intensive industries, the business models are governed by their respective products. These are not software business models. However, given the increasing importance of software in the products of almost all industries, software influences these business models. Software may even lead to disruptive business model revolutions, as in the music industry or the newspaper industry.

2.4.6 Business Considerations for Corporate IT Organizations

Corporate IT organizations have traditionally not had the view that they developed, marketed and sold software products. Typically, they saw themselves as the master and caretaker of an IT system that consisted of hardware and an applications landscape that was difficult to comprehend and manage because it was most often not thoroughly documented. Where and when a new function was implemented was often more a case of arbitrary organizational responsibilities and informal relationships than of a forward-looking planning of individual applications or the complete landscape. This randomness of decision-making was typically accompanied by severe communication problems between IT and the business units. The increasing dissatisfaction of the internal contract givers with the price and performance of IT—whether justified or not—has led to initiatives over the last 30 years aiming at making the IT organizations more manageable.

One area has been in providing more "customer" control, replacing the former dissatisfying fixed cost allocation with a more cause-oriented, sometimes transaction-based cost allocation. Also, there have been attempts to destroy the former monopoly of the IT organization by introducing competition. In some companies, the business units were allowed to order hardware and software without coordinating with the IT organization. This competition succeeded in weakening the IT organization, but unfortunately it also weakened the whole company because the inexperience of the business units sometimes led to poor decisions or was taken advantage of by the vendors. This situation resulted in an unmanageable collection of badly integrated islands with increasing data redundancy and risk of data loss. Over the last couple of years, we have been seeing a very similar trend with SaaS offerings. Since the pricing of SaaS allows business units to book the cost as operational expenses, they can easily work with SaaS without involving the IT departments unless governance rules forbid this.

The idea of introducing competition was also the main corporate motivator for outsourcing IT organizations into independent companies that were still fully owned by the parent corporation. The unfortunate executives of these companies were expected to achieve the square of the circle: strengthen customer orientation, lower cost, and develop new business as a service provider on the open market. It has hardly ever worked. Customer focus suffered because established communication paths were disrupted by the new organizational and often physical separation. The cost structures could only be improved long term. In fact, since many of these separated IT companies were expected to turn a profit and executive incentives were established to promote that, the companies added a profit margin to the fees they charged their largest customer, their parent, thereby increasing corporate costs for IT. This in turn provided additional incentive for business units to buy their own small computers or outsource their work to outside service organizations with more aggressive pricing. In Europe, the work councils made sure that at least in the short term no employee suffered due to the outsourcing. In the US, social pressures and potential loss of government incentives often had similar effects. And the new business did not materialize because selling on the open market was foreign to the company's culture and not realistic as any potential customer knew that he would always have second priority versus the parent corporation. Another issue was the lack of focus of the outsourcer on his client and in the welfare of the client's business.

Then there was a trend of external outsourcing to big IT service providers that imposed their outsourcing management and processes and often took over a large number of employees. Outsourcing a data center can lead to significant cost savings if the vendor passes on the cost savings realized by the consolidation. For software development, this is rare. Even if the service provider can develop more efficiently and at a lower cost, his profit orientation will jeopardize the benefits for the host company. Also, a formal requirements management process will limit the service provider's ability to cooperate flexibly. Only if additional customers for the application landscape can be won, significant cost advantages can be enjoyed. Successful examples are joint IT service providers of major German banking groups that provide services to a higher number of banking institutions, or service companies like First Data in the US that achieve significant economies of scale.

So far, attempts to make internal IT more manageable have led to mixed results. There is one positive outcome: The executives of the IT organizations—whether outsourced or not—have gained a much stronger entrepreneurial view of their organizations. Business units are today considered more as customers than as solicitors. The willingness to understand and manage the offerings as products and services has increased. This product and service orientation has made these IT organizations similar to software vendors, with the result that software product management has started to be accepted as a useful concept by the corporate IT organizations as well. The core elements of SPM are the same for software vendors and corporate IT organizations. The priorities may differ.

The increasing pervasiveness of IT and in particular software across most industries is leading to a changing view of high-ranking executives. This change is visible both in corporate IT organizations responsible for business infrastructure and in software development units that produce software embedded in the company's products and services. Meeting the increasing expectations in terms of value contribution, time-to-market, and innovativeness is very challenging for these organizations. Software product management can help a lot in these environments to improve communication and cooperation, and to focus more on business value.

2.5   The Software Product Management Framework

Given the broad spectrum of tasks and responsibilities of a software product manager, some structure is welcome. The first attempt to provide structure is the Reference Framework for Software Product Management developed by Inge van de Weerd, Willem Bekkers, Sjaak Brinkkemper, and colleagues at the University of Utrecht, Netherlands in 2006 [WBNVB06], see Fig. 2.7. It focuses on the core activities of a software product manager in the areas of product planning and includes recommendations for portfolio management, product roadmapping, release planning, and requirements management.

The framework's structure is based on the entity hierarchy portfolio, product, release, and requirement that are managed with a set of activities. These activities are performed by a product manager. The activities belong to the core activities in the ISPMA framework. When interpreted as a process, the Utrecht framework shows the

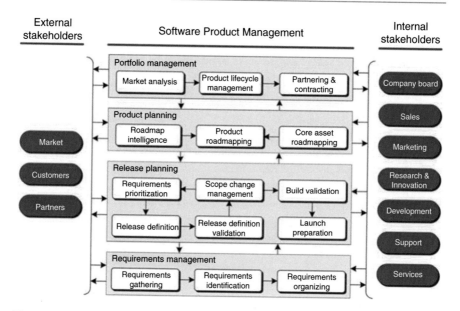

Fig. 2.7 Reference framework for software product management [WBNVB06]

core of what some software vendors call their product life cycle management (PLM) process which is an iterative process for software repeated for every release.

We consider this framework as very helpful and shall come back to it when we discuss the individual activities. However, it does not cover all tasks of a software product manager. For example, economic aspects such as the business case are only indirectly reflected in this framework. In our view, to create truly successful products, the business aspects must play a much more prominent role in a software product management framework.

Bekkers e.a. published a detailed specification of the framework in [BVSB10], which they had developed and evaluated by studying a large number of small and mid-size enterprises (SMEs). The focus is on ways to improve practices. In Fig. 2.8, "→" points to the practice of next-higher maturity, hence what the next practice is that should be adopted for increasing maturity.

Other frameworks consider such business aspects. One is the Pragmatic Framework® [PragInst19]. It mixes product management and product marketing aspects, however. Kittlaus and Clough [KittClou09] defined the roles of product manager and product marketing manager as separate and focused only on the software product manager in their SPM Framework. Also Ebert [Ebert07] focused on product management when he proposed how to manage a software product along the product's lifecycle phases of strategy definition, concept development, market entry and development, and evolution.

The ISPMA SPM Framework [ISPMA21] in Fig. 2.9 is an integration and consolidation of the three frameworks from Utrecht, Kittlaus, and Ebert. The International Software Product Management Association (ISPMA) facilitated a

Practices	Improvement Sequence
Portfolio management	**Market analysis**: trend identification → market planning → customer win/loss analysis → competitor analysis

Partnering & contracting: service level agreements → intellectual property management → distribution channels reviews → pricing model reviews

Product lifecycle management: product lifecycle analysis → portfolio innovation → portfolio scope analysis → business case reviews → product lines |
| Product roadmapping | **Roadmap intelligence**: product analysis → society, technology, and competition trend reviews → partner roadmaps

Core asset roadmapping: asset identification and registration → make or buy decisions → core asset roadmapping

Product roadmapping: short-term roadmap → internal consultation → theme identification → long -term roadmap → external roadmap |
| Release planning | **Requirements prioritization**: internal stakeholder involvement → structured prioritization → customer involvement → cost-revenue consideration → partner involvement

Release definition: capacity consideration → standardized release definitions → internal communication → optimized requirements selection

→ multi-release definition

Release validation: internal validation → formal approval → business case definition

Change management: change requests → milestone monitoring → impact analysis → scope re-planning

Build validation: internal validation → external validation → certification

Launch preparation: internal communication → formal approval → external communication → training → launch impact analysis → update external documentation |
| Requirements management | **Requirement elicitation**: passive basic registration → centralization → automation → proactive internal stakeholder involvement → proactive customer and partner involvement

Requirements definition: uniform documentation → requirements validation → grouping by similarity → automation

Requirements structuring: requirements typing → requirements lifecycle management → requirements dependency linking |

Fig. 2.8 Recommended improvements to product planning practices [BVSB10]

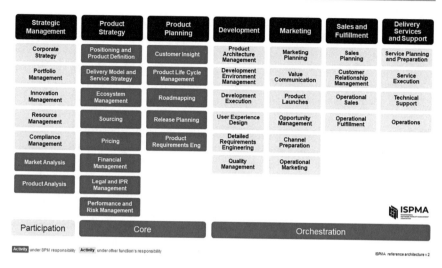

Fig. 2.9 ISPMA SPM framework V.2.0 [ISPMA21]

consensus between these academic and industrial opinion leaders [Fricker12]. In contrast to other reference models, the scope and contents of the ISPMA SPM Framework continues to evolve by being discussed and adjusted by the product management experts that are members of the ISPMA knowledge network. It hence adapts to the evolving understanding of the discipline.

The SPM framework provides a holistic view of the activities of software product management. It can be used as a model to establish and improve the discipline of software product management in an organization. It is structured in the following way:

- The horizontal structure (columns) is based on the functional areas of a software organization.
- Vertically, i.e. within the columns, the structure is based on a top-down approach, i.e. from strategic and long-term to operational and short-term. However, the interdependencies of the elements within each column (and also across columns) are more complex than can be fully expressed in a two-dimensional structure. There are a number of cases where the actual doing requires iterative processes that go back and forth between elements until everything is synchronized. A good example is the Product Strategy column where this kind of iterative approach is mandatory between most elements before a product manager gets to a consistent strategy. Also, there are elements like "Ecosystem Management" and "Customer Relationship Management" (CRM) that contain both longer-term and shorter-term aspects.
- There is an additional overlay structure with "Core SPM", "Participation" and "Orchestration". For Market Analysis and Product Analysis in the Strategic Management column, corporate functions are typically responsible in larger

companies with the product manager acting as a participant, whereas, in smaller companies, the product manager may be responsible. In any case, obtaining reliable information about the market and product on a frequent basis is part of the core SPM responsibilities. Activities under Orchestration are under the responsibility of the respective functions. However, the activity of Orchestration itself is a core responsibility of SPM.

Typically, software product managers have direct responsibility for the activities marked as "Core SPM", in particular, "Product Strategy" and "Product Planning" [MaNiSmFr17]. For the activities under "Strategic Management", software product managers participate by representing their products on the corporate level. For example, in portfolio management, product management provides input and makes use of the results. For the activities under "Development", "Marketing", "Sales and Fulfillment", and "Delivery Services and Support", the direct responsibility lies typically with other units in the company. A software product manager has to orchestrate these activities so that they are performed in line with product strategy and plan. Given the broad set of responsibilities, prioritization is needed on an ongoing basis and can be based on the estimated impact of prioritization decisions on short and long-term profitability.

2.5.1 The Four Software Product Scenarios

While we consider the role definition of software product manager described above as universal, its implementation and priorities depend on the type of product a software organization offers. But here we see a trend towards increasing heterogeneity. We look at four scenarios for software vendors.

Figure 2.10 shows a classification by using two types of runtime environments for software product instances and two software product life cycle phases.

Vendor-controlled means that the software vendor decides which changes are made when in the runtime environment. Vendor control is typical for rather unregulated environments like business-to-consumer (B2C) internet platforms and SaaS or B2C license products that offer automated maintenance over the internet. Customer-

Software Product Scenarios		Life Cycle Phase	
		New Product Development	Existing Product Evolution
Runtime Environment	Vendor-Controlled	Powerboat	Speedboat
	Customer-Controlled	Icebreaker	Cruise Ship

Fig. 2.10 Software product scenarios for software vendors [Kittlaus15]

controlled means that customers want to supervise the runtime environment, often because of quality, security, or regulatory concerns. Customer control is typical for business-to-business (B2B) software license products, but can also be found with B2B SaaS, in particular when tied to business process outsourcing.

The classifications also differentiate between the initial development of a product and the evolution of an existing product which already has customers. With new product development, there is a high level of uncertainty and risk, so the focus is on releasing a minimum function viable product as fast as possible. Once the product is rolled out, the focus shifts to extending the product scope and target market. At this point in the product life, compatibility and migration become relevant. We will take a more detailed look at the later phases of the product life cycle in Sect. 4.4.

In particular, release planning and product requirements engineering in the SPM Framework's Product Planning column work differently in the four resulting scenarios:

Powerboat

In the Powerboat scenario, we look at new product development for vendor-controlled runtime environments. For this type of product, SPM focuses on defining the minimum viable offering for the first customers. This goal requires a close link between product management and development, where the product manager often assumes the product owner role (in Scrum terminology), and extensive prototyping. In parallel SPM needs to work with potential customers on contents and business model, and with Marketing on positioning and pricing. Investments need to be justified based on a strategic perspective. The product vision (aggressive), the business model (one-page canvas), the product strategy (very high-level), the roadmap (high-level), and the business plan (aggressive) play an important role. Short-term experimentation drives release planning and requirements engineering lead to drastic changes of the product's direction, which is known as "pivoting". A product example is a new internet e-commerce platform before its initial launch. This scenario is described in much more detail in [KittMang22].

Speedboat

In the Speedboat scenario, we look at the evolution of an existing product for vendor-controlled runtime environments. SPM focuses here on extending the product scope and thereby increasing the target market. These goals require ongoing analysis of the actual usage of the product, of the market, and of competition. Depending on the organization's size, SPM and product owner roles may be separated, but remain closely linked. Product strategy and high-level roadmapping become important in combination with life cycle management. Release planning focuses on prioritization of individual requirements and scoping of development iterations. Requirements engineering is a mix of analysis and experimentation through customer discovery (see [Torres21]). If the organization does not implement governance functions like Architecture, things can become messy very quickly. Governance, compatibility, and migration tend to decelerate the velocity of the organization compared to the Powerboat phase. A product example is Google Docs.

Icebreaker

In the Icebreaker scenario, we look at new product development for customer-controlled runtime environments. SPM focuses here on defining the minimum viable product for the first customers. In the customer-controlled context, this goal requires extensive domain analysis with potential customers as a basis for requirements engineering and planning of the first release with a special emphasis on regulatory requirements. If a pilot customer is involved, a major SPM task is making sure that requirements are sufficiently generalized so that the first release does not become overly customer-specific. The interface between SPM and Development depends on the chosen development methodology. Product strategy and roadmap already need some focus to support internal investment decisions and to allow B2B customers to understand the longer-term perspective before they make their investment decisions. A product example is a new middleware software that is supposed to run on-premises, like Docker before its first release.

Cruise Ship

In the Cruise Ship scenario, we look at the evolution of an existing product for customer-controlled runtime environments. SPM focuses here on extending the product scope and thereby increasing the target market. Since customers do not want to test and install new releases in the customer-controlled environment often, the frequency of releases is low, often one or two per year. As a consequence, the new and changed contents of these releases is more significant and requires thorough release planning based on analytical requirements engineering. Product strategy and roadmap continue to be important as is life cycle management. A product example is the Oracle database.

These four scenarios may not fit each and every situation. However, from our experience they are quite representative. We will refer to the four scenarios in this book whenever this differentiation is needed.

When software organizations adopt agile approaches, they often use Scrum as a basis that they adapt to their specific needs. For a detailed description of Scrum, we refer to the Scrum Guide [SchwSuth20], books like [Rubin12], and articles like [Kittlaus12]. Scrum was originally developed and described as a methodological framework for software development, where it has proven to be valuable in many scenarios.

Scrum defines the role of a product owner as a member of the Scrum Team. The product owner feeds the team continuously with work that is specified with a prioritized list of user stories, called backlog. The user stories correspond to requirements. The product owner is the interface to the outside world and shields the rest of the team so that it can focus on development with optimal productivity. Implemented like this, the product owner is a rather operational full-time role whose tasks overlap with a software product manager's in the areas of requirements engineering and release planning.

Process and role definitions need to clarify the responsibilities within this overlap. Some Scrum consultants claim that the most productive solution is one person who

Software Product Scenarios		Life Cycle Phase	
		New Product Development	Existing Product Evolution
Runtime Environment	Non-Mission-Critical and Less Regulated	**Powerboat**	**Speedboat**
	Mission-Critical and/or Highly Regulated	**Icebreaker**	**Cruise Ship**

Fig. 2.11 Software product scenarios for corporate IT organizations

assumes both the product owner and product manager roles and all tasks attached to them—which they call product owner. Unfortunately, this is wishful thinking for most organizations! The approach may work in some environments with one Scrum Team, but it can hardly scale up. The poor person who gets this combined product owner and product manager role will always be pushed by the team to prioritize his operational tasks. Over time, the more strategic tasks are neglected—to the disadvantage of the product and the organization. Alternatively, operational tasks can be delegated to other Scrum Team members, but that boils down to an implicit split of the two roles again.

In most environments, it makes more sense to have the two roles of product owner and product manager separated. They should remain strongly linked for optimal communication. They should have clearly defined distinct tasks and responsibilities [Kittlaus12] that are comparable to those of the strategic and technical product managers. Product owners can either be part of the Development organization with a strong connection into SPM or be a part of the SPM organization that is delegated to the Scrum Teams [Leffing11]. For larger organizations that want to scale up Scrum, Leffingwell's Scaled Agile Framework (SAFe) is the most popular approach [KnasLeff20] which connects nicely with the SPM approach described in this book.

In the scenarios where the vendor controls the runtime environment, agile and lean approaches are dominant and increasingly extended into continuous delivery, based on continuous development, integration, and deployment [HumFar10]. While this approach can result in significantly improved time-to-market, it requires high investment in software architecture. Its success depends on fine-grained service-oriented architecture, on test automation, and on infrastructure such as the sophisticated configuration management and deployment system Apollo of Amazon [Vogels14].

For corporate IT organizations, the four software product scenarios also apply, but instead of using the control of the runtime environment as one criterion, it makes more sense to look at the criticality of the software product for the organization (see Fig. 2.11).

For mission-critical and/or highly regulated application areas, Development and Operations are usually strictly separated, with rigorous processes established to bring new and changed software code into the runtime environment with a rather formal handover and a lot of checks and balances. By doing it this way, these organizations have managed to reach ambitious quality and security objectives even with quite monolithic software applications, typically back-end legacy applications. For non-mission-critical and less regulated areas, the focus is usually on tighter integration of Development and Operations. This approach is also known as DevOps, which is a prerequisite for continuous delivery approaches described above [BasWebZh15]. Companies can apply this, for example, to most front-end applications and newly developed non-critical applications. A lot of corporate IT organizations use hybrid approaches by running older applications as cruise ships. They start new non-critical application development and deployment as powerboats and later run them as speedboats (see the highly entertaining novel [KimBeSp14]). Mc Kinsey calls this a two-speed approach [AveBePe15].

2.6   The Role and Organization of SPM

A software product manager handles the management of software with the objective of achieving sustained economic success over the life cycle of the software product, family, or line. Software product managers have business responsibility across different versions, variants, and associated services of a product. They have to manage a broad set of product-related activities as shown in the ISPMA SPM Framework (Fig. 2.9).

2.6.1   Objectives and Success Measurements

Sustainability—in an economic, not in an environmental sense—is a common corporate management objective for companies aiming at ensuring their long-term existence, even if investors have been demanding ever more short-term success. Sustainability should be included in the corporate vision statement and strategy (see Chap. 3) and become part of a lasting business model. For instance, an IT consulting firm cannot suddenly become a software vendor company and vice versa. Such a change, even if feasible, would take several years.

Successful products are not automatically sustainable. In the music business, for example, concert tickets are seasonal articles that lose any value when the concert is over. Companies who promote or arrange concerts can have a sustainable business model and a sustainable product family—as long as concerts are possible—, but their individual products are not sustainable. Furthermore, a music group can serve as a brand name, so to speak, and thus be sustainable.

The examples show that even if a company has an inherently sustainable business approach, its individual products will not necessarily be sustainable, but its product families and business model may be. Sustainability is found in a company's assets, i.e. in the company's true values, that need to be protected and developed. Together, the assets will determine the company's sustainability. The purpose of product management is to manage such product-related assets systematically on a long-term and sustainable basis, regardless of whether this involves single products, product families or product platforms.

In the case of software products, the single product itself is usually sustainable, at least for a time. An exception are low-priced consumer products, such as computer games. Here, the individual product may enjoy a burst of popularity and then fade away. The game product family or platform is the determinant for sustainability and should be managed accordingly. Software product management refers to the management of a software product (or product family or platform) over its entire life cycle in accordance with corporate level objectives.

Corporate management may press strongly for short-term success. It may routinely assign higher priority to exigencies than to essentials. Such pressure generates the need for caretakers whose job it is to pursue and attend to all urgent major and minor demands in the company. In our opinion, such caretaker tasks are best organized in a staff function like a "management assistant." Such an assistant can deal with them across the organization. Alternatively, corporate management may be geared more to a sustainability concept. In that case, it will need people with managerial skills to manage the corporate assets according to the strategies and objectives that are laid out. It is the software product manager's task to manage these assets insofar as software products (or product families or platforms) are involved.

In reality, of course, a company is never quite as black-and-white as these described models. The emphasis on sustainability does not imply that a company need not quickly and actively take care of urgent customer problems, for instance. Nevertheless, we find such an exaggerated comparison useful for defining software product management objectives and job descriptions. A software product manager cannot work strategically on software products as sustainable company assets, and at the same time be burdened with endless day-to-day tasks. This combination would only create another caretaker function with a new name. Such a function can be useful and important for the company, but it would not be software product management as defined in this book. Alternatively, the software product management function can be staffed with enough personnel so that employees can be assigned to individual tasks, with caretakers, branding, business analysts, and requirements management specialists all cooperating. In any case, software product managers, as defined here, and caretakers must work closely together.

In our view, the primary objective of software product management is to achieve sustainable success over the life cycle of the software product (or product family or platform). This objective refers to economic success, which is ultimately reflected by the profits that the product generates. Since profits lag behind investments, e.g. an investment phase involving losses may be followed by an extended highly profitable phase, customer satisfaction is often considered as a significant measure of software product management success. This significance is based on the hypothesis that there is a strong correlation between customer satisfaction and customer loyalty to the product and the producer. According to recent publications and based on our experience, this is only partly true [Reichh96]. Of course, an extremely dissatisfied customer is likely to switch to a different product and producer. Conversely, a high degree of customer satisfaction will not guarantee that a customer will not switch to a different product or producer. However, only if the functionality of a replacement product is much better (e.g. it is considered to be a "technology leapfrog") or one is very dissatisfied with the current product, is it worth the risk of changing. So there is value in customer satisfaction, and it is an important factor to be taken into consideration. However, the measurement of the concept is challenging as we will outline in Sect. 5.7.

In certain situations, and with some products, software product management does not focus primarily on profits attributable to a single product. For example, it could be in the interest of the company to achieve a maximum number of installations of a particular product platform as a prerequisite for selling other profitable products. One example of this has been the pre-installation of the Microsoft Windows operating system on new computers, for which the computer manufacturers pay Microsoft a relatively small license fee. By doing this, Microsoft ensures the continued dominance of its Windows operating system on desktop and laptop computers, which in turn serves as a platform for a large number of profitable software products sold by Microsoft and other vendors. In this case, market share is a better measure than profits. However, large market share with perpetual low or negative profit hardly makes for a profitable company.

Two thoughts emerge from this discussion: A conflict exists between software product management and executive management. Product management, by definition, has a long-term focus. Executive management has the desire to define objectives and variables that can be linked to business periods and thus evaluated annually. Development cycles or product success may not fit neatly into the business cycles that management will want to use for checking whether product management is on the right course and, if necessary, to make corrections. Also, there is the need to set individual objectives for each staff member and meet with them once a year to discuss performance and a salary increase. Unfortunately, this conflict is usually resolved in favor of more short-term objectives and measurements.

The sentence that a high-ranking American manager had hanging up as a poster in his office saying "Measurement Systems Do Work!" is true. If a company uses measurement systems to evaluate the performance of its employees and perhaps even makes bonuses and salary increases dependent on the results of such an evaluation, it must assume that the employees will try to optimize those measurements. This optimization means that, unless the measuring system uses measures that reflect what is intended exactly, the employees will be optimizing the wrong things. Since measurement systems are supposed to be simple so as to minimize the amount of time and effort necessary for evaluation, we often observe that the objectives become distorted and the wrong things are optimized. The inadequacies often have absurd consequences. Sometimes software licenses are unnecessarily given away to achieve certain target values with respect to the number of licenses installed. This debases the value of the product in the marketplace and the price it can command. Sometimes more effort is invested in the manipulation of figures to meet poorly conceived measurements than in actual business achievements.

We do not have any easy solution regarding the topics of "objectives and variable elements of compensation". In the end, the only possible solution is for software product managers and their superiors to talk about the problems we have described and reach an agreement together. This agreement should include important, period-linked objectives regarding actual individual employee tasks. Yet at the same time they should ensure that the product manager will still be able and willing to pursue the objective of sustainable product success. There are some available levers: milestone payments, employee rankings, longer term quotas and evaluations, career enhancement (many levels in a professional position). Richard Campione, SAP's former Senior Vice President of Suite Solution Management, confirms this: "The core concern is that the measurable key performance indicators (KPIs) tend to be significantly lagging indicators, and so while good for communicating intentions, and useful for long term, they frequently are inadequate for the short term. Here one needs to blend the solid, quantifiable KPIs with softer measurements and people's judgment." He uses criteria like product usage, deliverables, market responses to the product, and 360-degree evaluations involving responsible counterparts in the other units of the company like Sales, Marketing, Development, etc.

2.6.2 The Role of the Software Product Manager

Should corporate management choose to implement product management as a role in their company organization, they must clearly define the purpose and objective of this role and communicate it throughout the company. They must also ensure that all the stakeholders touched by the role find the job description acceptable. Regardless of how a company is organized, responsibilities will always be incompletely defined. Some issues and problems will always be neglected because no one feels responsible. Product management is therefore often misunderstood as being a universal caretaker responsible for all such issues and problems. Corporate management must deal with this problem by defining and delimiting the scope of all relevant tasks. It also must ensure that the software product management function is instituted with a genuine focus on sustainability.

The software product manager is supposed to be the person chiefly responsible for all relevant aspects concerning his product. Management skills are individual, personal qualities, but they can also be backed up organizationally. A management position tends to be easier to fulfill when it has managerial authority. Product managers frequently lack such authority, however, so often this is about leading without authority.

The following chapters detail the broad spectrum of issues and tasks for which a software product manager is responsible. Irrespective of the scope of his managerial authority, the software product manager has a cross-organizational role, requiring a high degree of communication and coordination between all functional, organizational units. Condon describes this challenging task in detail [Condon02] as does Sandy [Sandy20].

A job description should include the skills required for this position, i.e. the knowledge and experience needed to perform the tasks associated with the job. It should reflect the scope of responsibility of the software product manager's position as discussed in this chapter. This approach to the software product manager position is problematic because the scope of responsibility is so extensive that it will hardly be possible to find a candidate who can meet all the qualifications. Richard Campione, formerly SAP's Senior Vice President of Suite Solution Management, says: "If you try to find a person who fulfills the complete list of requirements you end up with the null set." This statement does not mean that a "software product manager" position should not be established and filled. Such a position should rather be created with the understanding that a candidate cannot be equally experienced and knowledgeable in all aspects of the job. So what is really important?

It is a management position for which it is more important to work in cooperation with specialists from all relevant organizational units, ask the right questions and be able to draw conclusions. Required are:

- Managerial skills, in particular leading without authority,
- Business acumen,
- Understanding of how software development works (this does not mean that the product manager needs to be able to develop software by himself),
- Domain knowledge (in particular for application software)

If the software product management function is staffed with enough personnel to allow a specialization by skill the individual product manager may not need to fulfill all these requirements.

Software organizations can have different foci for the role of SPM which translates into different priorities regarding these three areas:

- Business aspects.
- Product contents.
- Product Marketing.

We see three typical manifestations in the industry that are shown in Fig. 2.12. The size of each circle represents the priority of the area.

We consider Product Marketing Manager as a role separate from SPM. However, in some organizations both roles are assigned to the same person and may be called SPM or Product Marketing Manager. The strategic SPM is the business leader or "mini-CEO" [Ebert07]. The technical SPM is more focused on defining the contents of the product than the other two specializations.

Software Product Management's orchestration task—as shown in the SPM Framework (Fig. 2.9)—means to optimize the cooperation of all other units to achieve product-related goals. This task is conflict-laden in several dimensions. If

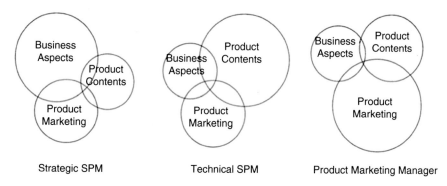

Strategic SPM   Technical SPM   Product Marketing Manager

Fig. 2.12 SPM manifestations

the company has more than one product or product family, there is competition, not in the market, but internally regarding the limited resources. In the competition that takes place in strategy discussions and planning processes, each product manager represents his own product. He is expected to take a strong position and to be biased. On the other hand, it may not help his career if he questions the executive management's strategy. These inherent conflicts are the reason why a product manager needs not only broad competence, but also a high degree of diplomatic dexterity when dealing with conflicts of goals and culture, human factors, and corporate politics. This aspect is well described with real world examples by Condon [Condon02]. Executive management can and must help here by clearly defining and separating tasks, responsibilities, and competencies [Gorche11] and by acting as referee in case of escalation. Corporations use various titles for the software product manager's position, such as product manager, program manager, solution manager, offering manager or brand manager. Terms like "application manager" or "(application) service manager" may appear in corporate IT organizations. These come from an ITIL role of the same name [Axelos16]. Essentially, most of these names refer to the software product manager described in this book, although some differences do exist.

2.6.3   Organizational Aspects of SPM

We have already indicated the broad spectrum of topics and tasks that a software product manager has to handle. Software product management is not primarily focused on a single development project or a single marketing action, such as a product launch. These are "merely" steps taken in the pursuit of long-term sustainable objectives. Software product management is the combination of all the tasks described in this book. It can therefore be conceived neither as a project which by definition would have a beginning and an end nor as a process which by definition would consist of a well-defined sequence of process steps. Only some tasks can be interpreted or organized in this manner. Requirements management, for instance, can be described as a process with respect to individual requirements (see Sect. 4.2), whereas the development of a new product release is often considered to be a project.

In conformance with the economic sustainability of the software product (or product family or platform), software product management viewed collectively as a combination of tasks is an ongoing activity. This f is a rather unpopular fact at a time when many people would like to believe that they can measure the efficiency of an organization by the share of its project or agile work. This idea stems from a vague feeling that unproductive colleagues might just comfortably while away their time performing ongoing tasks, whereas strictly organized project work—maybe based on agile methodology—would force everyone to be productive. In over 30 years of experience in the software business, we have not found any reason to support such views. We have experienced many unproductive projects and highly productive employees who perform ongoing jobs. Perhaps one way to explain this to organization members with a "project" orientation is to demonstrate to them that many tasks need to be recursive in order to provide true product and company sustainability. Furthermore, ignorance of ongoing critical tasks, such as market analysis or personnel development, tends to create enormous problems in the medium term for the company as a whole. Our observations show that good corporate management and a good working atmosphere help significantly to influence productivity. Software product management, in particular, is a good example of an ongoing task that is one of the most challenging jobs in a company. It requires a high degree of personal commitment and diligence for the product manager to be successful in the medium and long term.

A number of product management tasks, in particular in product strategy, are tied to the company's annual cycle for strategy and financial planning. For these tasks, an annual schedule may help product managers to prepare their inputs in time for the company's planning schedule. However, there are other tasks like dealing with legal aspects that are often triggered by outside events like a customer situation. And some tasks like performance management are really continuous tasks, i.e. require the product manager's attention at least once a month.

In big companies, product managers can be organized in a team that can exploit the different skills of the team members with an intelligent division of work. In a small company, such a division of work in a product management team is usually not possible. In addition, the success of a small company is so tightly connected to the success of the one or the few products that executive management handles the most important product management tasks themselves, particularly the financial ones. Still, the holistic product view is important for smaller companies as well. A single executive cannot cover the holistic approach for time and skill reasons and might neglect core elements like product planning and legal considerations.

The holistic entrepreneurial component in software product management suggests a company should be structured so that the SPM unit is close to executive management, i.e. as a staff function. The probability of success of this structure depends on the company's culture and the attitude of the people involved, in particular of executive management. The staff function has a lot of responsibility without the right to give orders to those who have the resources and need to

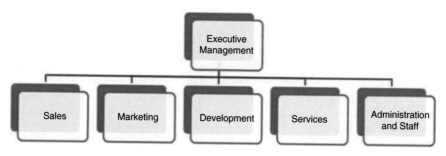

Fig. 2.13 Functional organization

contribute for success. If the company's culture is in conflict with non-hierarchical cooperation and any escalation to executive management is interpreted as a personal attack, as is common in many companies, the software product manager is in a losing position. SPM as a staff function can only work if executive management defines, communicates, and supports the software product management unit openly.

What are the alternatives? Let us first assume a functionally oriented organizational structure (see Fig. 2.13). Here, underneath the corporate executive management there are Development, Sales, Marketing, and Services plus administration and staff functions, e.g. Finance and Human Resources. The software product management unit could either be integrated with Development or Marketing. An integration in Sales is not recommended since the short term goals of Sales create too much of a conflict with the Software Product Management's goal of economic sustainability and frequently turn product managers into pre-sales engineers. Or software product management is a unit of its own in parallel to Sales, Marketing, Development and Services.

Integration into Development often seems more plausible. This approach is driven by the idea that Development can best foresee where technology is going. The experience of IBM that used this organizational structure for a long time shows disadvantages, however. Developers are typically far away from the market and the customers even when diverse initiatives support customer contact. Cultural differences between Development, Sales, and Marketing prevent a product management unit that belongs to Development to fulfill its role as mediator. It is not considered as (and probably isn't) impartial. The responsible Development manager will typically avoid being escalated by his Product Management unit. And Sales and Marketing—having been cut out of the requirements and implementation decisions—may well disavow the product after it is developed. When development makes decisions on product requirements, there may creep in an "I built it and by definition it must be great" mentality.

The same disadvantages appear in part when one considers making Software Product Management a part of Marketing. Marketing has the advantage of being closer to the market and the customers. Marketing is usually a smaller unit whose self-interest is better aligned with sustainable software product management, although its goals are more short to medium term. If the software product management unit is big enough we argue for it being a separate unit.

Many companies have migrated from a strictly functionally oriented structure to other organizational structures that are better aligned with the necessities of cooperation across the company. It is not the subject of this book to discuss the pros and cons of these organizational structures that range from matrix to business process orientation. However, we want to emphasize that, given the diverse forms of cooperation and communication within a company, no organizational structure—whatever it looks like—can make non-hierarchical, horizontal cooperation superfluous. The management of such horizontal cooperation is a major task of product management called orchestration.

Product Strategy

3

The pace of technological change in the past several decades has been faster in the software sector than in any other industry sector. This development makes it necessary for the organizations concerned, both software-intensive vendors and corporate IT organizations, regularly to make far-reaching decisions under uncertainty that have considerable financial and even survival consequences. Yet, in spite of the fast pace of change, companies with a clear strategic view are the ones that prove to be successful in the long term. In recent years, SAP, Apple, or PTC have been excellent examples. This does not mean that at these companies all product ideas are successful, or that every product strategy produces the desired results. It does also not mean that strategy definition is strictly top-down without experimentation. However, it does mean that these companies routinely manage to reach agreement on and consistency in their corporate vision, corporate strategy, product strategies (or product platform and family strategies) and more short-term implementation plans by means of iterative processes that sometimes require a great deal of time and effort. So the companies realize faster what works, and what does not work, can avoid waste, and move on in a more focused and more aligned way.

While a product vision gives direction for the future of the product in a condensed way (see Sect. 3.1), the product strategy provides the details by which to implement that vision. Normally a strategy covers a time span of about 1–5 years in the future, however this varies depending on the product's context, i.e. maturity, domain, technologies, and market segments. For consumer (B2C) products, it is typically shorter, for business-to-business (B2B) products, longer. Due to the increasing pace of change, a lot of companies have shortened the strategic timeframe that they look at, because specific strategic plans for the outer years have often proven to be obsolete by the time you get there. We consider this as a dangerous trend. In our view, companies as well as product managers need to know on a more abstract level where they want to go. Otherwise long-term decisions are made without any foundation which increases risks further. So having more abstract strategy goals for the outer years is better than no goals at all. In the sections of this chapter, we shall come back to this challenge.

© Springer-Verlag GmbH Germany, part of Springer Nature 2022
H.-B. Kittlaus, *Software Product Management*,
https://doi.org/10.1007/978-3-662-65116-2_3

In the startup world, the development of a product strategy is a highly iterative process that aims at finding and optimizing the product-market fit. The steps of an iteration are as follows: hypothesis—MVP—test—conclusion, where MVP stands for minimum viable product, which Eric Ries defined as "That version of a new product which allows a team to collect the maximum amount of validated learning about customers with the least effort." Since the aforementioned definition of an MVP lacks a customer value perspective, we prefer the following definition: "The minimum feature set of a new product that is derived through a learning phase and that some customers are willing to pay for in the first release." Through this iterative process, development and implementation of a product strategy are intertwined (see also the SPM for Startups syllabus).

When a product (and company) is successful and more mature, the product strategy tends to be more stable. An update of the product strategy is a more evolutionary process, and its implementation less intertwined. Since the elements of the product strategy cover all product-related functional areas of the software organization, all of them need to be involved in and contribute to its implementation.

The software product manager is responsible for defining the strategy for his product (or platform or family) and for supporting and updating this strategy using a standard process over time. The strategy should address the development or evolution of each of the items in the list shown in the Product Strategy column of ISPMA's SPM Framework (see Fig. 2.9) during the strategic time frame:

- Positioning and Product Definition: define scope, customer value, target market segments, channels of the product.
- Delivery model and tailorability: explain how the software product is made available to customers, and which options are given to customers for customer-specific adaptations.
- Service strategy: explain which professional services will be offered by whom as part of the whole product offering
- Sourcing: define where resources, in particular human resources and software components, are coming from.
- Pricing: determine how prices are defined and managed over time.
- Financial Management: plan and track financial aspects both from a short- and long-term perspective including business elements like benefits and cost, forecasts and the business plan.
- Ecosystem management: define the roles of the players in relevant ecosystems, and managing relationships with partners and other external stakeholders.
- Legal and IPR management: take care of all legal product aspects.
- Performance and risk management: define and take actions based on continuous business performance measurement and risk assessment.

These items are, of course, interdependent. If, for example, the available budget is smaller than originally assumed, it may only be possible to expand the product scope slightly or more slowly. If new segments are to be added to the target market within the strategic period, the product scope may have to be expanded.

Dependency on other products can also have considerable consequences, e.g., if certain functionalities or enabling code must be available in several products at the same time. In addition, the aggregate resource planning for all products needs to be coordinated with the resource planning for the company as a whole. As a rule, the larger a company is and the more dependencies of this type exist within a company, the more difficult, complex and time-consuming the entire alignment process will be, in particular for budgets, resources and roadmaps. The roadmap may be thought of as the bridge between strategy and implementation plan. Sect. 4.1 will cover this topic.

There are a number of models which may be used when defining parts of a software product strategy. One is Michael Porter's Five Forces [Porter79]. Another one is Alexander Osterwalder's Business Model Canvas ([OstPign10], see Fig. 2.2). Further variants of these models are also in use.

In Fig. 3.1, the elements of the Product Strategy column in ISPMA's SPM Framework (Fig. 2.9) are mapped to the Business Model Canvas and to the sections of this chapter which have a finer granularity in the areas of positioning and product definition.

In the last Sect. 3.14, we will discuss organizational aspects, tools and options for documentation in the product strategy domain.

Software is becoming a core element of the products of more and more industries, like automotive, manufacturing, and health. Therefore, software plays an increasingly important role in the product strategies of companies in these industries. To some degree, for them product strategy becomes software product strategy.

3.1   Product Vision

3.1.1   Overview

A strong product vision is often essential to engage and convince all stakeholders inside and outside of the company of the worth of a product. A vision describes what the future product will be, what needs it addresses, and why it will be successful (see [McGrat01, p. 1 ff]). The elements of the product strategy provide the details that turn the vision into a manageable and executable path into the future. In bigger companies a product vision needs to be aligned with the corporate vision.

The first version of the product vision is needed when work on the development of the product's first version starts. Over time, the product vision continues to evolve so that it always looks ahead at least to the end of the strategic time frame.

This section describes the contents of a product vision and outlines approaches how to get to a good product vision. The reader will understand the related process and the impacts.

Section in this book	Business Model Canvas	ISPMA SPM Framework, Product Strategy column
3.1 Product vision	./.	Product Definition
3.2 Product name	./.	Positioning and Product Definition
3.3 Customers	Customer Relationships Value Propositions	Positioning and Product Definition
3.4 Market	Customer Segments	Positioning and Product Definition
3.5 Product Definition	Value Propositions	Positioning and Product Definition
3.6 Delivery Model and Tailorability	Value Propositions	Delivery Model and Service Strategy
3.7 Positioning	Value Propositions, Channels	Positioning and Product Definition
3.8 Service Strategy	Key Partners	Delivery Model and Service Strategy
3.9 Sourcing	Key Resources	Sourcing
3.10 Pricing	Revenue Streams	Pricing
3.11 Financial Management	Cost structure Revenue streams	Financial Management
3.12 Ecosystem Management	Key partners	Ecosystem Management
3.13 Legal aspects	./.	Legal and IPR Management
3.14 Performance and Risk Management	./.	Performance and Risk Management

Fig. 3.1 Mapping of syllabus chapters, Business Model Canvas and ISPMA SPM Framework, Product Strategy column

3.1.2　Concept

Like product name (see Sect. 3.2), a product vision can be considered as an element that is referenced in a product strategy, but comes before it. The vision represents the objective that will be achieved with the ideas set forth in the strategy. There is no universally agreed definition of product vision to be found in the literature. We define.

Product vision = Conceptual description of what the future product will be at the end of the strategic time frame, i.e. high-level descriptions of a product concept and a corresponding business model.

The product vision is the "guiding star" or "North Star" for the strategy and the product team. It outlines in a condensed form:

- conceptual image of what the future product will be,
- the customer value proposition that says why the product is needed and cannot be replaced by an alternative, and
- the business value for the vendor, i.e., why it will be successful.

A product vision describes the future state of the product, to be reached by the end of the strategic time frame, or even later. It should be short, less than a page, preferably written in short, "punchy," marketing terms, in a style that has a motivating effect on stakeholders inside and outside of the company by painting a desirable, ambitious, but achievable future. The product vision is especially important in the initial conception and development phase for the first version of the product.If there is no final product name at that time, most companies work with an internal code name that is used in the product vision and in internal communication (see Sect. 3.2).

The term "product vision" is also used in connection with agile methodologies, in particular Scrum. While the Scrum Guide does not mention it [SchwSuth20], most Scrum consultants consider it as an important element of the Scrum approach. Originally that agile product vision was focused on the given development task. It was supposed to describe in a condensed way what the Scrum Team was to develop within a couple of weeks or months. Over time, some Scrum consultants, e.g. Pichler [Pichler10], have broadened the scope and use product vision in the sense we define it here.

3.1.3 Development of a Product Vision

A convincing product vision looks very straight-forward, logical and easy. However, developing it is more difficult and time consuming than most people expect. We suggest the use of a template that we have used in a number of software companies. It can support the development of a vision by focusing on the problem space and the solution space. The problem to be addressed by the product is described in a solution-neutral manner and explains the pain-points addressed by the solution as well as the criteria used for evaluating product success from the customer perspective. The solution is described in terms of use scenarios, features, benchmark, and unique value proposition. For the development of the vision, a combination of the product manager's draft as a synthesis of ideas and contributions solicited internally [GoFrPaKu10] and a workshop approach [Chesbrou05].

Problem statement	
the problem of	immense effort for reporting consumables
affects	nurses, and the clinic overall
the impact of which is	inefficient use of operating theaters
a successful solution	increase the availability of the operating theaters.
Position statement	
for	nurses and analysts
who	administer, assist in, and improve operations
the	**Consumables Tracking Solution (CTS)**
that	tracks the use of consumables in an operation, enables its analysis, and automates reporting
unlike	the current labor-intensive manual approach
our product	increases the efficiency of operations and delivers decision support for consumable planning and improvement.

Fig. 3.2 Example of a problem and position statement (source: EU FP7 FI-STAR)

Figure 3.2 illustrates the template. The example is from a product that tracks consumables in an operating theater. This template makes sure that relevant information is collected, but does not automatically result in wording that is marketing-oriented. So in a second step, this may need to be turned into a marketing statement, which transformation may be made by reordering the presentation of the vision statement:

> In order to significantly decrease clinics' effort and increase the availability of operating theaters, the Consumables Tracking Solution (CTS) reduces the nurses' and analysts' manual work by tracking the use of consumables in an operation, enabling its analysis, and automating reporting. It enables clinics to increase the efficiency of the operation work and deliver decision-support for consumable planning and improvement.

Often companies want shorter vision statements like:

> The Consumables Tracking Solution (CTS) increases clinics' efficiency and reduces cost by automating tracking, analysis and reporting of consumables in operating theaters.

In order to achieve the buy-in of the product team members, it can help to develop and evolve the product vision in workshops with the key team members.

3.1.4   Further Examples and Variations

While it should be relatively easy to come up with a convincing vision statement for a new product, it can be challenging to do that for a product in a later phase of the life cycle when investments are typically reduced. The following examples illustrate this dependency.

CRM SaaS product, early life cycle phase:

> For a mid-sized company's marketing and sales departments who need basic CRM functionality, the CRM-Innovator is a Web-based service that provides sales tracking, lead generation, and sales representative support features that improve customer relationships at critical touch points. Unlike other services or package software products, our product provides very capable services at a moderate cost.

Code Generator product, late life cycle phase:

> Current drivers of the Code Generator vision include:
> * Continued support of J2EE and .NET frameworks
> * Extending support of Web services
> * Infrastructure enhancements
> * Integration with our companies' systems management, security and application life cycle solutions

The Code Generator is a world-class enterprise application development environment that continues to deliver the core capabilities it has provided for two decades:

* Platform independence
* Application portability
* Productivity.

Some companies prefer not to stay so close to the product functionality and to be more "visionary" which translates into more abstract vision statements. Here are examples:

Salesforce started with "The end of software" as a vision which sounds a bit dramatic and is misleading since SaaS is based on software as well. What they meant was "the end of deployed software". They used this claim to justify their software-as-a-service approach.

SAS Institute's "Providing organizations with the Power to Know" fits the business intelligence market nicely promising the transformation of data into insight.

3.1.5   Outcome and Impacts

A compelling product vision can be a powerful instrument to keep the product team aligned and on track, especially during the development of the initial version of the software product. It can also be a good marketing tool during initial product launch and during later phases of the life cycle that communicates the core direction for the product.

A number of studies have documented the important role of product vision. Pearce and Ensley [PearEnsl04] looked at teams working on innovative development, shared vision and innovation effectiveness which they define as the speed at which innovation is developed, the magnitude of the innovation, and the productivity of the implementation. They found shared vision and innovation effectiveness to be reciprocally, positively and longitudinally related. This means they influence each other positively over time. Tessarolo [Tessarol07] looked at cross-functional teams working across internal and external organizational boundaries. He could show a shared clear product vision to be strongly correlated to speed of development.

Lynn e.a. [LyAbVaWr99] studied new product development projects in high tech industries. They showed product success to be most strongly correlated with vision and new product development process. In [LynnAkg01] Lynn and Akgün further detailed these findings by looking at four scenarios and three vision factors, vision clarity, vision stability, and vision support, i.e. how strongly the project team members shared the vision. They found that vision clarity correlates with success in evolutionary market and technical innovation and in revolutionary innovation, but not in incremental innovation. Vision stability correlates with success in incremental innovation and evolutionary market innovation. And vision support correlates with success in incremental innovation and evolutionary technical innovation.

3.1.6   Summary and Conclusions

Given the strong impact a good product vision has on product success and speed of implementation, it is worth investing some time and effort into creating the vision and revisiting it whenever the product strategy is updated. The proposed template can help with articulating a convincing vision. The product strategy must be tightly linked to and synchronized with the vision. So an update of the vision needs to be reflected in the product strategy.

3.2   Product Name

3.2.1   Overview

The product name is both the internal and external "face" of your product. So it should be chosen with a strong marketing perspective taking into account how the name as a term will be perceived literally, emotionally and psychologically by all the stakeholders. With software products, often numbers are added to the name to differentiate versions and releases of the product. Such an approach both preserves the product branding and conveys newness with a higher number. Combining the product name with a specifically designed logo may significantly increase brand recognition.

3.2.2   Concept

Product name is usually a tool to help accomplish product strategy but is not itself product strategy. If in the beginning phase when the first version of the product is conceived and developed, the product has not yet been named, most companies work with an internal code name that is used in internal documents and communication. It is in the DNA of any language that people need a name as an identifier for "a thing" when they want to talk about it. There are many studies that prove that a good product name has an effect on the buying decision of customers, more so in B2C, but to some extent also in B2B, e.g. [HiAlCeBa13]. The name, perhaps accompanied by a logo as a graphical representation, must have been chosen by the time the first version of the product launches, and it becomes the center of all marketing messages.

Naming a product works the same way for software as it works for other products. There are a number of criteria to be met for a good product name:

- Memorable, appealing and motivating for the potential customers in the target market.
- Distinguishing the product from competitive products.
- Legally on the safe side.

Naming is a major part of the branding of a product. Since software product managers are usually not experts on branding, it is advisable to involve such experts, in particular on the legal side (see Sect. 3.12).

The product name is what stakeholders identify a product by. As long as the name does not change, they consider it as the same product even though it may change significantly over time. For licensed software products, the legal and financial views often differ from this public view, i.e. a new version is internally formally considered as a new product even though the name stays the same.

For licensed products, it is common to denominate software versions (see Sect. 4.3) after a specific nomenclature, which is generally dependent on the vendor, however. Often, we find a three- or four-level hierarchy of software levels, for example:

- Version number
- Release number
- Modification or Patch Level

The version identifier is added to the product name. An example of complete product identification is Apache Http Server Version 2 Release 4 Patch Level 38 (in short Apache Http Server 2.4.38).

Some companies prefer to use the release date as the release identifier, e.g. SAP S/4HANA 1909 is the release made available in September 2019.

3.2.3   Process

Naming a product may sometimes be quite difficult. Everybody feels competent, everybody has an opinion. As the responsible product manager, you can leave the question to your executive manager who will dominate the discussion anyway, or you can organize a brainstorming or an internal competition with an award for the winner. A clearly articulated value proposition can inspire the name finding. The criteria to determine the winner are the ones listed above. A helpful discussion on project naming that is largely applicable to product naming can be found in [GausWein89, p. 128 ff.].

Finding an internal code name is not restricted by trademark considerations. For the official external product name, however, the trademark criterion can easily turn all the effort that goes into brainstorming to waste. You do not want to spend a large amount of marketing money on establishing a new product name in the market, and then find out that somebody else has a trademark on it and forces you to change your product name. So legal clearance and possibly protection is highly advisable before the money is spent. Often the investment in a trademark for the geographic target markets can make sense. Relevant internet domain names need to be secured as well. Since most descriptive names are legally protected somewhere by a third party, you can either buy the rights to the name from that third party, or go with some artificial word as name that may not be descriptive but is not already legally protected. If internal brainstorming does not succeed, specialized agencies can help who come up with proposals and take care of the legal clearance.

Once the name is set, the marketing activities should focus on making it known and creating a brand image in the target market (see Sect. 6.3). This usually means a significant investment.

Due to the significant branding investment, a change of the product name at a later point in time only makes sense in exceptional situations, e.g. when you are legally forced to change because some other party has the rights, or when the reputation of the product is so bad that you want to relaunch it under a different name, or when product names are aligned after an acquisition.

3.2.4   Summary and Conclusions

The product name is the label with which people identify the product. A good name can also have a positive effect on the motivation of people working on the product internally. While name finding is a hopefully rather infrequent task for a particular product, it requires and justifies effort and investment. Consideration of legal risks is critical.

3.3 Customers

Customers are at the core of any business. No customer, no business. So anybody who cares about the business must care about the customers. Creating and evolving products that meet the ever-changing needs of customers requires an excellent understanding of the problems they face and the environment in which customers operate. Product managers must therefore work towards such an understanding which we call customer insight (see Sect. 4.1).

We differentiate between customers as the ones who are the legal contractors and pay, decision makers, business users who work with the software product on a frequent basis, and IT specialists who work with the software product on a frequent basis. In the B2B area, customers are usually companies represented by select decision maker employees and/or interface with the software vendor, and are separate from users. In the B2C area, customers and users are often the same persons.

While the primary interfaces to existing and potential future customers are usually with Sales and Marketing units, the software product manager needs to be in touch with customers and users in order to better understand needs, usage of the product, and user experience with regard to the product. Every product manager has to find his own way of having frequent customer contacts without neglecting the wide spectrum of other tasks that are part of the product manager role.

In the B2B software business, it can make sense to maintain personal relationships with customer representatives whom the product manager can informally approach whenever he wants feedback on specific questions. However, these relationships must not fully replace the broader consideration of the target market.

In the B2C software business, there is usually a mass market with a high number of customers. Feedback from individual customers can be even more misleading than in the B2B market. A representative sample of customers promises more insight. Nevertheless, one-on-one contacts at fairs or similar events can add value.

In addition to direct contact with customers, data analytics methods play a more and more important role, in particular with SaaS products (see Sect. 4.2). However, collecting relevant customer data is only the first step to the creation of insights. Software product managers need to feed this data into discussions with stakeholders and use it for requirements analysis, as well as business modeling.

Customers of software standard products pursue conflicting objectives. They usually want the standard product to be a perfect fit for their needs and their environment, i.e. like a custom-made solution, but at the much lower price of the standard product. Finding a compromise between these conflicting objectives is a key success factor of the work of the product manager that touches on issues like customer value definition, product definition, customizing options, service strategy, pricing, or handling of customer-specific requirements. Conflicts can also arise between requirements benefiting existing customers vs. potential new customers, e.g. in different market segments.

The relationship with a customer can be considered as a "Customer Life Cycle", which consists of four phases that have some similarities to the product life cycle (see Sect. 4.4). Note, however, that the former life cycle describes how a customer

Phase of the customer life cycle	Appropriate activities
Customer initiation	requirements management information gathering consulting configuration
Customer acquisition	negotiation transaction processing financing delivery
Customer loyalty	customer service (Service Level Agreements) user behavior warranty, maintenance updates cross-selling
Customer recovery	new business resale secondary purchase upgrade/up-selling

Fig. 3.3 Phases of the customer life cycle

evolves. The latter describes how the product evolves. Figure 3.3 shows a simple customer life cycle.

In each customer life cycle phase the vendor, i.e. primarily the Sales and Marketing people, ought to define appropriate actions in order to optimize, maintain, and renew customer relationships.

It is in the interest of the software vendor, and therefore the product managers of the involved software products, to make the relationship with a customer, i.e. the "Customer Life Cycle", last as long as possible. We recommend establishing measurements for success for the different phases.

3.4   Market

3.4.1   Overview

The concept of a market is a central element of our worldwide economic system, and also a central term in economic theory. In general, it is the meeting point of buyers and sellers of goods and services where they can exchange offerings against some form of compensation. This exchange is called a transaction.

For a particular product, it makes sense to focus on the subset of buyers and sellers that are relevant for the product. This relevant market can be further broken down into market segments that differ with respect to certain criteria, e.g. B2B vs B2C markets vs multi-sided platforms:

- Business-to-Consumer (B2C): A software product is sold by a company to a consumer, e.g. online retail business.
- Business-to-Business (B2B): A company offers its software product to another company, e.g. companies handle transactions via an Internet-based procurement platform for an HR software product.
- Multi-sided platform: A company provides a transaction platform on which different parties do business or exchange information. In this case, the target segments need to be defined for all parties doing business or exchanging information through the platform.

The sellers in a relevant market can be competitors offering similar or functionally overlapping products, or players with offerings that are complementary. The latter players are candidates for partnership.

For a software product manager, defining the relevant market is a key part of the task of product positioning usually done in cooperation with Marketing. Once the relevant market is defined, the buyers in that market are the target customers for the product.

3.4.2 Concept

Since "market" is such a central concept in both the academic and the real world, there are many definitions from micro- and macro-economics, marketing, sociology, or anthropology. For this book, we use these definitions:

Market =
(a) The area of economic activity in which buyers and sellers of goods and services come together, and the forces of supply and demand affect prices.
(b) A geographic area of demand for commodities or services.
(c) A specified category of potential buyers.

Market segment (of a given market) = Market with a subset of the buyers, sellers, goods and services of the given market. The definition (a) above means that a market is a set of sets of potential buyers, potential sellers, goods and services, respectively, at a particular point in time. A market segment is homogeneous with regard to certain criteria.

As an example, we look at the market for weather apps worldwide. By using different criteria for segmentation, we can create different market segments of this weather app market:

- Free vs. paid apps: defines market segments that are restricted to the sellers that provide free or paid apps; with free apps, compensation is not monetary, but e.g. attention to advertisements. Some apps may be available with and without payment and therefore are part of both segments.
- Geography: restricts the market segment to the buyers and sellers active in a chosen geography and the products available in that geography, e.g. the UK.
- Functional scope: restricts the market segment to apps that cover the chosen functional scope, e.g. 15-day forecast in weather apps.

Sellers in a given market for software product A can be

- Competitors: they offer similar or functionally overlapping products; the buyer will either buy product A or the competitor's product, but not both,
- Potential partners: they offer products and/or services that are complementary to product A; they are members of product A's software ecosystem,
- Unrelated sellers: they are neither competitors nor potential partners; if there is a higher number of unrelated sellers in the market defined it is an indication that the market definition may not be sufficiently precise and narrow.

The group of buyers in a given market segment is often called customer segment, e.g. in the Business Model Canvas (see Sect. 2.4). Product managers need to be very specific about the customer segment(s) they are targeting so that they can develop a thorough understanding of customer needs. This understanding in turn is key to developing compelling value propositions that help sell the product (see Sect. 3.6).

A competitive advantage is achieved when the company offers a product that the competition does not, or when the company offers a better product than the competition. Competitive advantage comes from one of two sources:

1. Having the lowest cost in the industry (in combination with competitive functionality and quality) or
2. Possessing a product/offering that is perceived as unique in the industry.

Another contributing factor is the scope of product-market (broad or narrow). A combination of these factors provides the basis for the following three types of competitive strategies:

- Low cost strategy (be the cost leader),
- Differentiation strategy (be unique),
- Focus strategy (be the niche leader).

3.4.3   Determining a Product's Market

Determining the relevant market for a software product is by no means trivial. The most comprehensive definition of the market is the overall software market, which the software product manager can certainly use as a basis. However, as a whole, it is so huge and inhomogeneous that it is not really useful. The smallest conceivable market consists only of one product. This definition is not absurd if this product creates a new market without any competitors. In between these two extremes, of course, there are many ways to define the market that product managers play with in practice. If you want to point out the enormous sales potential of a planned product, for example, you select a broadly defined market segment with a correspondingly high volume. If you want to demonstrate what a large market share your product has, you choose a narrower definition of a market segment. There are no fixed rules for deciding which market definition is the best for a product. Market research companies that analyze software markets often divide the overall market into multilayered market segments by functions, geographic regions and customer groups (see Sect. 5.5).

There is a close connection between the market definition and the definition of the product scope which is part of product definition (see Sect. 3.5). The product manager must deal with this connection iteratively. On the one hand, the analysis of the market, market development and competition will influence the definition of the functional product scope. On the other hand, the product scope will determine in which segment of the market the product can successfully compete. What is needed, ultimately, is a time-related close correspondence between product scope, target market and business prospects. Planning the further development of such a correspondence over time requires coordination with the product vision, maybe also the corporate vision statement and strategy, and constitutes an essential aspect of product strategy.

The scope of requirements ensuing from the definition of the target market should not be underestimated. If the target market is the consumer market, the product must meet different requirements with respect to usability, packaging, pricing, sales channels, support structure, etc. than a B2B product. Some market segments are so special that they even require different approaches to development and requirements management. For games for example, development is often based on a story line rather than a technical specification, and developers typically have more freedom in the graphical design as part of an iterative prototyping approach [Waldo08] which requires some experimentation (see Sect. 4.2).

The requirements for a product to be marketed internationally are significant, e.g. in terms of product requirements, legal requirements and in the marketing and support structure. The resulting expenses will be offset by higher sales expectations. This relationship is discussed in detail by McGrath [McGrat01, pp. 235–255].

Part of forming a successful product strategy requires identifying competitive advantage. Providing an answer to the question "How can the product satisfy the needs of potential customers better than competition?" needs to be incorporated in the value proposition. The following two methods can be used alone or together to identify competition:

- Industry method: This method of identifying the competition is based upon an already established industry in which the business operates. The competition is identified as companies that produce the same or similar products. For example, a car manufacturer would identify other car manufacturers as competitors, and a mobile service provider would identify other mobile service providers as competitors. This method is particularly important to identify competitors if the company is planning to enter an existing market. The industry method also takes into account the level of competition within the industry. Some of the questions that can be asked to identify and characterize competitors in a given industry using this method are:
  - Who else differentiates like my company?
  - Who has entry and/or exit barriers like my company?
  - Who has vertical integration like my company?
  - Who is as global or as local as my company?
  - Who has cost structures like my company?
- Market method: The market method depends largely on how well the customer need is defined in the description of the target customer segments. The market method of identifying the competition can be established upon marketing products or services to customer needs. The competition is identified as companies that satisfy the same need. Market analysis is supposed to identify market forces, industry forces and key trends (see Sect. 5.5) which can be analyzed to identify competition. With the market method, a movie theater may identify entertainment as the customer's need. Substitutes like video rental stores, amusement parks, and concert venues could then be identified as competitors. The main question to ask in this method is
  - Who else can satisfy the same customer need?
  - Who pursues the same market segments with comparable value propositions?

The Market method can also be useful if a company wants to re-segment existing markets or create a new market. In that case the product offering may not belong to any existing industry (i.e. there is no direct "peer-group" of products) for comparison. Petal diagrams instead of traditional X/Y axis competitive analysis diagrams can be used in this case (see Fig. 3.4) as suggested by Blank [Blank13b].

In the petal diagram, the company is placed in the center. Next, the identified new market segments from where the customers will originate (can be taken from "Customer Segments") are plotted as petals. After that each petal (representing a market segment) is filled in with the names of the companies that are representative players in that market. Finally, the current and projected market sizes of the adjacent markets can also be shown to analyze and discuss "How big will our new market be?"

It is important to consider

- Direct competitors who produce a virtually identical product that is offered for sale within the same market (e.g. listed in the same product category by industry analysts or media)

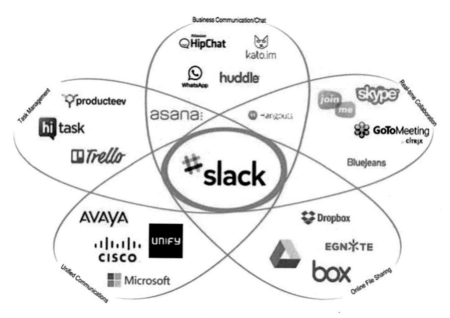

Fig. 3.4 Example for petal diagram, here for Slack (from http://cunninghamcollective.com/
insights/blog/2015/06/30/escape-the-box-three-great-ways-to-use-the-petal-diagram-for-strategy,
accessed on May 16, 2016)

- Indirect competitors who don't necessarily sell the same products, but offer
  different alternatives to satisfy the same customer need (different product category, solving the same customer problem in a different way)
- Other alternatives customers have, i.e. do-nothing, or do-it-yourself (manual
  process or home-grown software solution)

Once the alternatives have been identified, gap analysis (surveys with the customers,
distributors and partners) can be employed to analyze competitors, e.g. the strategic
groups method. Strategic groups are segments of an industry that group companies
with similar business models or business strategies [Porter98]. However, if the
companies want dramatically to improve their value proposition, they need to
identify offerings (not competing companies) that fulfill the same need (maybe in
a different way).

Unless there are specialists in the organization for market research and competitive analysis, these are part of the product manager's responsibilities (see Sects. 5.6
and 5.7). A product manager usually needs to cooperate with other roles like senior
strategy managers, marketing managers, or sales representatives to analyze competition and define competitive strategy for the respective product.

A competitive strategy is defined as a long term action plan that is devised to help
a company gain a competitive advantage over its rivals. It consists of business
approaches to attract customers by fulfilling their needs, withstand competitive

pressure, and strengthen market position. A competitive strategy exploits competitive advantage by identifying ways to use resources and capabilities to differentiate the product from its competitors [FleBen02]. It is always work-in-progress, i.e. over time the competitive strategy as well as the product itself need to be changed and adapted in order to maintain or gain competitive advantage.

Regarding competitive strategy, a well-known model identifies five forces that shape competition within an industry (Porter's 5 Forces model):

1. Threat of new entrants,
2. Bargaining power of suppliers,
3. Bargaining power of customers,
4. Threat of substitute products/offerings.
5. Rivalry among existing competitors,

According to Porter, when formulating a competitive strategy, two dimensions need to be considered

- the source of competitive advantage
  - cost leadership (cost! not price) or
  - differentiation
- scope of the target market
  - targeting the broad market or
  - focusing more narrowly on a niche of the market

By combining these two dimensions, there are three generic competitive strategies that can lead to success:

- Cost Leadership—addressing the broad market, while having the lowest cost base
- Differentiation—addressing the broad market, with product/offering that is perceived as unique in the industry (for example premium/luxury product)
- Focus strategy—be the niche leader, addressing the specific needs of the niche better than the products targeting the broad market

But while Porter's model is widely used, its focus is heavily on the costs of manufacturing products or costs of delivering human services. Therefore, for software markets that are fast-changing and where manufacturing costs are not an issue, other strategy models are needed.

More recent strategy models emphasize the ability of companies to actively shape market boundaries and thus, create new markets. For example the Blue Ocean Strategy approach [KimMaub15] asks vendors to:

- Create uncontested market space,
- Make the competition irrelevant,
- Create and capture new demand (innovations),
- Break the cost/value trade-off,

- Align the whole system of a company's activities in pursuit of low cost and differentiation.

However, the two approaches are not mutually exclusive and can be combined. For example, by slowing down profit erosion with an effective competitive strategy for an existing market, a company can increase the funds available for Blue Ocean investments and consequently increase its chances of finding an untapped, highly profitable market.

3.4.4 Variations

Customer segments do not always have to be very narrowly focused—according to Moore [Moore14, Moore04], it depends on the maturity stage of the respective market how broad or narrow the target segment can be. For example, when bringing to market a completely new type of B2B product—what Moore calls a new product category—it is often useful to kick-start mainstream adoption by focusing on a small, well-defined market niche (the beachhead segment). The strategy is to expand into adjacent market niches later—one after the other (bowling alley strategy). Once the new product category is better understood in the market, and broad adoption sets in at a fast pace (tornado phase), the vendor's top priority needs to be capturing market share. In this stage, a broader customer segment definition is preferable.

When using the Business Model Canvas as a tool for analysis, competition is not explicitly represented, but an important topic for product strategy. Some variations of the business model canvas address competition more explicitly. An aspect sometimes important to consider is the number of customer segments covered: in some types of business models, for example in multi-sided markets (such as eBay or a real estate market place) it is obvious that at least two customer segments need to be covered—for example buyers and sellers in a market place. Since these customer segments are highly interdependent, they should be covered in the same business model canvas. In other cases, the product is simply targeting multiple customer groups, potentially with different value propositions. It can make sense to cover these multiple segments in the same canvas, too, especially if—apart from the value propositions—the rest of the business model is the same for all target segments.

Another important consideration is the relationship between products and solutions (see Sect. 2.2): in an organization that offers both individual software products and solutions as products that include these individual products, separate Business Model Canvases should be developed for each individual product and for each solution. In that situation, it may happen that an individual product is sold stand-alone and also gets included into multiple solutions. In that case, the question arises how to address the multiple solution relationships in the Business Model Canvas for the individual product (not on the solution level). If the different solutions target different customer segments, it might make sense to list these solution-level customer segments separately on the product-level canvas, with a separate value proposition for each segment.

Finally, many software products need to get buy-in from multiple different constituencies, for example a smartphone app for kids, where parents might make the actual purchase or can veto the kid's purchase. In that case, it is often useful to include both the kids and the parents as separate target customer segments in the same canvas and to develop separate value propositions for these two segments. Other well-known examples for this are different roles that participate in the complex sales processes for large-scale enterprise software purchases.

Often the definition of the target market and its segments does not lead to a static result, but needs to be considered over the strategic time frame. In particular in the Powerboat or Icebreaker phase, the initial focus may be on a rather narrow market which can be widened over the strategic time frame. So it makes sense to look at the evolution of the market definition as part of the roadmap.

3.4.5   Outcome and Impacts

A good market and segment definition is of key importance for the product strategy. It is the basis for product definition, positioning and value definition, forecasting, channel and partner selection, and all the marketing work. At any point in time, there needs to be a clear definition that is accompanied by results from market analysis (see Sect. 5.5):

- Market scope and boundaries.
- Appropriate segmentation.
- For each segment:
  - Size (in annual revenue and/or annual number of licenses/customers).
  - Characteristics of customers.
  - Competitive situation.
  - Ease of adoption of your product by the segment in question.

Market and segment definition is tightly linked to product definition and positioning including customer value proposition (see Sects. 3.5 and 3.6) which are developed in an iterative process with market definition. It has an impact on requirements definition and selection (see Sects. 4.2 and 4.3) since the product contents need to be optimized for the selected market segments. Pricing is impacted by the competitive situation, and also by special characteristics and requirements in selected segments (see Sect. 3.10). And of course, the market definition is the basis for the work of Marketing and Sales (see Sects. 6.3 and 6.4).

3.4.6   Summary and Conclusions

The importance of the market, its definition, evolution and ongoing analysis cannot be overestimated. A market can be understood as a set of sets of potential buyers, potential sellers, goods and services, respectively, at a particular point in time. The success of your product depends on its fit to the target market. The better you understand the relevant market and its segments, the more you can improve that fit.

3.5 Product Definition

3.5.1 Overview

The product definition describes the product on a rather abstract level, i.e. what is it, and what it is not, over the strategic time frame. The product definition needs to define:

- Functional scope
- Quality scope
- Intended use and users
- User experience (UX) design scope
- Offering architecture (see Sect. 5.1)
- Business architecture (for application software) (see Sect. 5.1)

The definition may also address compatibility, technical constraints, and the whole product offering. All of them may change over time.

This section describes the contents of a product definition and outlines approaches how to get to a good product definition. The reader will understand the related processes and the impacts.

3.5.2 Concept

As part of product strategy, the product definition details the product vision without turning into a full-blown specification. It is intended to give guidance to the product team whenever decisions are required about what is inside or outside of the product scope, in particular with regard to requirements. It is also intended to provide a high-level product description that can be used as a basis for marketing material or for educating new team members.

"Intended use" and "users" provide rough descriptions of how and by whom the product is intended to be used. While the detailed definition of use cases is part of the requirements work, and the detailed definition of personas is part of UX design, here only high-level descriptions or lists of roles are provided. For example, when IBM defines a new database management tool, they can simply say it is intended for database administrators and system administrators and their administration tasks.

Functional scope describes which functional areas the product covers, and which functional areas are outside of the product's intended capabilities. The latter is very helpful in the area of product requirements management (see Sect. 4.2). For example, SAP started out with Enterprise Resource Planning (ERP) functionality, but added data warehouse, data analytics, or CRM (customer relationship management) functionality at later stages of its life cycle.

Quality scope describes in which ballpark the intended quality attributes of the product are to be. While the detailed definition of quality requirements is part of product requirements management (see Sect. 4.2), here the ballpark is often determined by listing comparable products or product areas. For example, when Microsoft defines a new version of Office, they can define the quality scope by saying that quality needs to be at least as good as with the previous version, but 20% better in the area of technical performance.

User experience (UX) design scope describes the intended ballpark UX. Similar to quality scope, the detailed definition of UX requirements is part of product requirements management (see Sect. 4.2) in combination with UX design work. Here the UX ballpark is often determined by listing comparable products or product areas. For example, when a company defines a new product, the product manager can define the UX design scope by saying that UX measures need to be at least as good as with a particular existing product in the company's portfolio, but 20% better in the area of subjective satisfaction, i.e. user happiness.

The offering architecture defines separately priced components of the product offering, and tailorability options in line with the tailorability strategy (see Sect. 3.6). The business architecture is relevant for application software, and is domain-specific, i.e. covers logical data model, process model, business object model etc. This is the responsibility of a business architect. For any architecture considerations, tight cooperation between product manager and architects is required (see Sect. 6.2).

When working on the product definition, the product manager has to take the company's compliance guidelines into account (see Sect. 5.5). The product manager might need to address product-specific compliance issues that are not covered by the company's guidelines, in particular, the areas of sustainability and ethics.

Compatibility scope is relevant for new versions and releases or follow-on products of existing products. It describes the level of intended compatibility. By upwards compatibility, it is understood that:

- In changing from software version n of a product to the next version n + 1, existing functions of version n continue to be supported.
- Data from version n can be transferred to and used with version n + 1 without changes.
- Interfaces of version n (APIs, Interfaces for other Systems/Products) remain unchanged.

Should only parts of these conditions be fulfilled, we speak of function, data and interface compatibility. Full upwards compatibility makes the customer's migration from version n to version n + 1 smooth and inexpensive. However, frequently with a new release of a product comes an expansion and change of the underlying data model which leads to changes to the data structures. In this case, data compatibility cannot be achieved easily. A separate data migration is required, for which the software vendor should preferably provide in the form of procedures and scripts. By downwards compatibility, it is understood that:

- Data from version n + 1 can be transferred to and used with version n without changes.
- Version n + 1 can communicate to version n, i.e. version n interfaces are supported.

In contrast to the upwards compatibility, downwards compatibility cannot always be expected or presumed. For example, when Microsoft introduced the new .docx format for Word documents with Word 2007, .docx documents could not be read with older versions of Word. In order to address that problem, Microsoft made a Compatibility Pack available for free which enabled some older Word versions to handle .docx documents.

Technical constraints are restrictions that require early decision. The technical constraints complement the quality scope of the software product from the technology, platform, and deployment perspectives. The term comes from requirements engineering, but these early decisions need making as part of the product definition. For example, a software vendor may decide that a particular software product will only run on Android and iOS as mobile operating systems, but not on any other alternative.

Whole product offering stands for the complete set of elements that are to be offered to the customers in order to provide a complete solution (see Sect. 2.4). This set can contain not only the software itself, but also additional software components and professional services from the vendor's portfolio or from other vendors. We have experienced situations where two customers bought the same product, but got different sets of components delivered. Therefore, we recommend that product definition encompass the definition of the whole product offering including a complete list of components that belong to the standard product offering and are included in its price. Since product-related human services are part of the whole product offering, the service strategy needs to be linked to product definition (see Sect. 3.7). For software components from other vendors, gaps in the offering need to be identified that can be addressed by those components. The selection of other vendors as partners has to be synchronized with ecosystem management (see Sect. 3.11).

3.5.3 Defining a Product

Product definition is an iterative process that seeks consensus between the relevant stakeholders, i.e. Product Management, Marketing, Sales, Development, Services, and executive management. The result is usually not static, but evolves over the strategic timeframe and beyond. The iterative process includes:

- Consultation of stakeholders and contributors.
- Development and testing of alternative product definitions with stakeholders and customers.
- Elaboration in cooperation with selected stakeholders.
- Roadmapping for refinement and buy-in (see Sect. 4.1).

The product manager needs to find a balance between continuous learning and improvement that translates into changes of the product definition, and some level of stability that provides a basis for customer communication and avoids wasted efforts.

There are a number of interdependent factors to consider: target market segments, customer value and positioning, service strategy, budget, pricing, and the product's life cycle phase (see Sect. 4.4). For new product development, i.e. in the Powerboat and Icebreaker scenarios, product definition means a rather dynamic learning process. During later phases of the product life cycle, the product definition tends to be more stable.

For new products, this is directly related to the minimum viable product (MVP, see Sect. 2.5) which Eric Ries defines as "that version of a product that enables a full turn of the Build-Measure-Learn loop with a minimum amount of effort and the least amount of development time" [Ries11, p. 77]. This focus on learning may be helpful for a startup, but from a business perspective, Steve Blank's definition of the MVP as the minimum feature set "that some customers are willing to pay for in the first release" [Blank10] seems more on the point. He sees the MVP as a tactic to reduce engineering waste and to get product in the hands of early adopters soonest. Of course, that will lead to learning. We define:

Minimum Viable Product (MVP) = The minimum feature set of a new product that is derived through a learning phase and that some customers are willing to pay for in the first release.

3.5.4   Outcome and Impacts

Product definition is an important element for positioning (see Sect. 3.6) and sets the scope and the boundaries of the product for the whole product team. It is usually documented as text, and when the organization decides to document the strategy in a formal product strategy document, product definition is part of it.

3.5.5   Summary and Conclusions

Product definition is an important activity for understanding what the product is about at any point in time, and how focus and priorities change over time. It covers intended use and users, functional scope, quality scope, UX design scope, compatibility scope, customization scope, and the delivery model. Individual products need to be viewed in the context of the Whole Product Offering, and developing the product definition requires an iterative process that involves all relevant stakeholders.

3.6   Delivery Model and Tailorability

3.6.1   Overview

Based on the product definition, the delivery model needs to address the following items:

- Licensed product vs. service offering (e.g. Software-as-a-Service (SaaS) or managed service)
- Degree of tailorability including tailorability strategy
- Mode of delivery (online access, online download, combination with services, etc.)

Tailorability means the enablement of the product for customer- or market-specific adaptations by providing properties that can be altered after system development.

3.6.2   Delivery Model

The delivery model describes in which way a vendor makes a software product available to customers. The alternatives are:

- On-premise, where the customer acquires a license for the software product and installs and runs it in his own operating environment.
- Cloud-based service, where—based on a service contract—the responsibility for the operating environment rests with the vendor and includes operations and maintenance. This can be SaaS/PaaS or managed service.

A mix of these is also possible. Historically, the standard delivery model for software vendors has been that when a customer buys a license for a software product, the software is transported to the customer on a medium like CD, the customer installs the software on his computer hardware (possibly with the help of the vendor) and runs it on his own. Today, it is usually downloaded over the internet, e.g. on markets for apps, components, or access to software or ICT services. Depending on the type of contract, the customer may be entitled to maintenance updates that he can install on his computer over time. Over the last 20 years, the Software as a Service (SaaS) delivery model (see Sect. 2.2) has become important with a market growth rate higher than for license products.

The decision on the delivery model has a significant impact on the specification and implementation of the software product. If SaaS is chosen as the delivery model it means that the software must be highly scalable and capable of multi-tenancy.

These are requirements that a lot of standard license software products do not fulfill. If a piece of software is not capable of multi-tenancy it may still be offered as a managed service, i.e. a separate instance of the software is operated for each customer. This leads to higher cost of operations compared to a multi-tenancy SaaS offering.

3.6.3   Tailorability

Well-designed flexibility is one of the key success factors of a software (-intensive) product, in particular in B2B. A software that can be tailored to customer-specific requirements can capture larger markets with diverse and dynamic customer segments. Being able to adapt a software without having access to the original, secret source code greatly increases the scalability of the business model by creating opportunities for third parties in the ecosystem to offer full-service tailoring and integration services on top. However, designing appropriate tailorability is one of the hardest problems in software product design, because of the need to balance many strategic, business and technical ramifications.The tailorability range goes from standard product as it is, i.e. no tailorability, to options for each and every element. With no tailorability, you run the risk that quite a number of your target customers will not buy the product because it deviates from their requirements in a few important areas. With too many tailorability options, you spend a lot of development effort on tailorability, and it may create a lot of effort and cost for customers before they can become productive with the software product unless defaults work in the majority of cases. With B2B products, tailorability options are typically more extensive than with B2C products. For example, most smartphone apps do not provide any tailorability options in order to keep things as simple as possible.

The categories of tailorability are:

(a) Configuration: setting or changing parameters
(b) Composition: adding or arranging components
(c) Customization: adding or changing program or descriptive code

The tailorability architecture defines these options in more technical detail as part of architecture management in Development (see Sect. 6.2). With SaaS, the tailorability options are usually more limited than with license products or managed services.

3.6.4   Mode of Delivery

Today, the standard mode of delivery for license products is the download of the object code over the internet. This comes with an automated installation procedure that ensures a fast and easy installation for the customer including steps that allow easy configuration and composition based on the tailorability options built into the software. Once the software is installed and running in the customer's environment, the vendor will offer new releases and bug fixes for the product (see Sect. 4.5) to the customer with maintenance contracts from time to time. With B2C customers, these new releases and bug fixes may be installed automatically unless the customer switches this feature off. B2B customers usually want full control which changes are made when in their runtime environments. A vendor may offer delivery services to B2B customers for the initial installation, tailoring, and later updates (see Sect. 6.5).

For the initial installation of a license product, vendors usually work with license keys which customers need to enter during the installation process. These license keys are a protection mechanism to ensure that third parties cannot make use of the software without paying the license fee. Within a product, the license key may also enable or disable the use of individual components or functionalities based on the offering architecture (see Sects. 3.5 and 6.2).

When the chosen delivery model is SaaS, the vendor usually provides access over the internet based on a password mechanism that again ensures that third parties cannot make use of the software without paying. Updates of the code in the runtime environment for new or changed functionalities or bug fixes are part of the vendor's responsibilities, with multi-tenancy installations usually without any control for customers. In case of managed service, customers may be provided more control.

3.6.5 Process, Outcome and Impacts

Decisions on the delivery model and tailorability options are highly strategic since they have significant long-term consequences for the product and often not only impact the product strategy, but also the company strategy (see Chap. 5). Therefore, a product manager will usually have to involve other stakeholders including executive management. Decisions have to be made early in the product's life cycle since they have a significant impact on the technical architecture and require significant implementation effort. Later changes, e.g. going from license product to SaaS or from single tenancy to multi-tenancy, are difficult and expensive to implement. Product managers and other decision makers have to consider many factors:

- Market situation, in particular the attitude of existing and target customers towards cloud computing,
- Revenue impact through different pricing approaches related to the delivery model: The dominant pricing models are one-time charge with license products, recurring charges with SaaS and managed service (see Sect. 3.10).
- Ecosystem impact of the selection of tailorability options: If the vendor wants to enable third party service providers to provide delivery services for the product customization options need to be provided with documented interfaces. If the vendor wants to provide all delivery services through the internal professional service organization, no customization options will be provided to customers and third party service providers (see Sect. 3.12).

It is the product manager's responsibility to prepare decisions by analyzing different alternatives and providing data, information and impact assessments for each.

3.6.6   Summary and Conclusions

Decisions on the delivery model are highly strategic since they cannot easily be changed later on and have a significant impact on the economic success of the product and the company, in particular the financial model, and the ecosystem and partner approach.

3.7   Positioning

3.7.1   Overview

Positioning is the definition of an approach to communicating a product to potential customers. This includes an analysis of customer value, often differentiated by target market segments, the selection of sales channels through which target customers may be reached in a profitable way, and the selection of partners and alliances. Where the product is in its life cycle will also affect positioning.

Concise, understandable positioning is a key product success factor. The objective is for the product "... to occupy a clear, distinctive, and desirable place relative to competing products in the minds of target customers." [KotArm15]. It makes it easier for sales and marketing to address customer groups with the right messages. It also helps internally in making all product-related decisions.

One of the important aspects of positioning is the question how a product differentiates itself in the market. This question is related to the concept of Unique Value Proposition which describes value elements that none of the available alternatives can provide. For proprietary products, the typical differentiating arguments have been better functionality, higher level of integration, performance etc.

In some markets, standardization is also important. But how can a product differentiate itself if it only implements a public standard? The vendors found this answer in the 1970s and still apply it: They implement the standard so that they can claim standard-conformance, and then they add useful proprietary features. Once a customer makes use of these features, he is tied to the vendor's product. So the features not only provide differentiation, but also the glue that makes a product more difficult to replace.

Positioning can also be relevant within the product portfolio of a software company, in particular when there are products with overlapping functionality. Such an overlap can easily create confusion for potential customers, the own sales force, and channel partners which needs to be addressed by clearly positioning the products against each other.

3.7.2   Customer Segmentation and Value Proposition

Once the market for the product is defined (see Sect. 3.4), the positioning must focus on describing the value of the product. Again this has to be considered over time since the value of the product will hopefully increase with each new version or release. The value definition needs to be approached from a customer perspective, e.g. what is the business value that the customer will get from using the product? When different customer segments experience different business values from using the product, it may be useful to segment and consider subsets of the total market.

The Business Model Canvas can be a helpful tool here. Whether evolving an existing business model or creating a new one, the business model generation process often starts with the two canvas segments called "Customer Segments" and "Value Propositions". These two segments are closely linked through the underlying concept of what customers need or want, specifically their pains, their desired gains, and their "jobs to be done".

Segmentation may be done based on end users or based on sales/delivery channels. Product managers need to be specific about the customer segment (s) they are targeting and build deep customer insight, understanding the problems and the environment in which customers operate (see Sect. 4.2). This customer insight is a prerequisite to create compelling value propositions. Here methods like the Value Proposition Canvas can help [OstPign14].

The customer needs in the value proposition canvas (see Fig. 3.5) decompose into: pains experienced, gains desired, and jobs to be done. Especially the "jobs to be done" angle [Christen13] can lead to a much more profound understanding of customer motivations and to a completely different view of

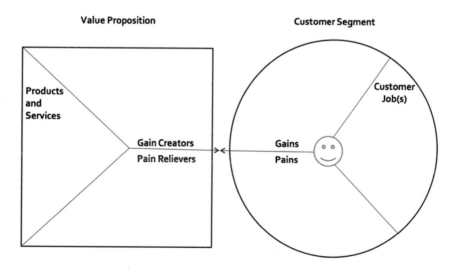

Fig. 3.5   Value Proposition Canvas [OstPign14])

competition that goes beyond direct competitors. This way, it presents an opportunity to develop much more compelling value propositions.

However, this does not mean that customer segments always have to be very narrowly focused—according to Moore [Moore14, Moore04]) it depends on the maturity stage of the respective market how broad or narrow the target segment can be. For example, when bringing to market a completely new type of B2B product— what Moore calls a new product category—it is often useful to kick-start mainstream adoption by focusing on a small, well-defined market niche (the beachhead segment). The strategy is to expand into adjacent market niches later—one after the other (bowling alley strategy). Once the new product category is better understood in the market and broad adoption sets in at a fast pace (tornado phase), the vendor's top priority needs to be capturing market share. In this stage, an undifferentiated strategy is suitable.

The customer understanding is translated into the value propositions that (hopefully) strongly resonate with the customer segments and help sell the products and services [OstPign10]:

- Pain relievers "eliminate or reduce negative emotions, undesired costs and situations, and risks your customer experiences or could experience before, during, and after getting the job done".
- Gain creators "create benefits your customer expects, desires or would be surprised by, including functional utility, social gains, positive emotions, and cost savings".
- Products and Services lists the products and services that together deliver the value proposition.

It is not easy to determine what the drivers of customer value are for a specific product category. Anderson and Narus [AndNar98] suggest generating a list of value elements and building customer value models. Almquist e.a. [AlmSenBl16] build an "Elements of Value Pyramid" based on Maslow.

Especially in B2B technology markets, including B2B software, it is very common that core products require add-on products, integration with partner products, and accompanying services as a minimum configuration to deliver a compelling value proposition. Geoffrey Moore [Moore14] emphasizes the importance of this— he calls this the whole product concept. Based on the value propositions, software product managers need to identify which additional products and services are required to deliver the whole product, and they must make sure these crucial whole product components are actually available to customers—either from the vendor itself or from partners. The Service Strategy needs to reflect this. Partners that contribute important whole product components need to show up in the canvas, either in the channels section or in the key partners section.

3.7.3 Go-to-Market Approaches: Channels vs. Product-Led Growth

Directly related to the definition of the target market (see Sect. 3.4), the product definition (see Sect. 3.5), and the positioning of the product is the question of sales channels. With a sales-led go-to-market approach, channels define the path through which goods and services as well as the compensation are transferred between vendor and customer. We define

Channel = A sequence of intermediaries through which goods and services as well as the compensation are transferred between a company and its customers.

With this definition, an internal direct sales force is included in the intermediaries. What is the best way to reach potential customers in the selected target market segments? That can be a direct sales force, and/or indirect sales through partners or the internet (see also Sects. 3.12 and 6.4).

There are two criteria that influence the channel selection the most. One is access to target customers, the other one is channel cost in relation to the financial picture of the product, in particular price which may be related to the selected delivery model (see Sect. 3.6). For low-price products, the cost of a direct sales force is usually not bearable. On the other hand, for high-price products in a B2B market, customers often expect a personal contact with a sales representative. In a lot of markets, software vendors cannot easily get direct access to target customers, but are dependent on partners who have established relationships with those target customers or the local proximity that allows less costly access. When a vendor uses multiple channels in parallel, there is the risk of channel conflicts, i.e. channels competing with each other. This needs to be anticipated and managed (see Sect. 6.4).

There are two main categories of sales channels for software products: The physical (human) channel and the virtual channel. In the physical (human) channel, direct sales means that products are marketed directly by the company to customers, eliminating the need for external intermediaries, such as wholesalers or retailers. An example is a direct sales force, where the company's sales representatives have in-person contact with customers.

In such a setup, the company will often assign key account managers to large existing customers. The key account managers are responsible for cultivating the customer relationship to drive repeat business with those customers. This is called "farming". For global players it can be useful to implement "global account management" to be present wherever the customer is.

In contrast, "hunting" is about recruiting new customers from the defined target market. Since the customers no longer seek information technology simply because it is new technology, vendors must provide IT solutions that improve the business and describe advantages and positive effects. Direct selling often requires IT sales specialists to communicate the resulting financial benefits to customers.

Another physical (human) channel is indirect sales which means that selling of products is conducted by partners, e.g., companies such as retail shops or wholesalers. For the different types of sales partners see Sect. 3.12. The advantage of the indirect sales channel is that more potential customers can be reached through the partners and their customer relationships. Decisions are required whether a one or multi-tier partner model is appropriate and how channel conflicts can be avoided with a multi-channel approach. On an operational level, the management of the selected partners is part of ecosystem management.

Telesales (or inside sales) means that a salesperson contacts customers to sell software products, either via telephone or through a subsequent face to face or web conferencing appointment scheduled during the call. Telesales is still being used, especially in B2B software sales, even though it has increasingly been considered as an annoyance by many customers.

Internet sales has become an important channel and belongs to the virtual channels. Here software products sell on the web through e.g. web-based apps, sales through app stores, in-app sales, etc. This works with license products, SaaS and advertising. Customers buy conveniently and easily from the comfort of their home or office at any time.

A further classification of channels differentiates

- Free versus paid: Free channels, e.g. social media or blogging, contain inherent costs (non-zero human capital cost). In contrast, paid channels like search engine marketing require explicit investment.
- Inbound versus outbound: Inbound channels rely on being discovered by the customer (pull messaging, e.g. blogs, e-books, and webinars), while outbound channels reach for customers (push messaging, e.g. trade shows, cold calling).
- Direct on the Internet, typically through the web page of the software vendor vs. indirect on the Internet, e.g. through a marketplace for software (such as STEAM for games), or through an app store (e.g. iTunes, Google Play).

Software companies must make fundamental decisions regarding channel mix: should the various sales channels be allowed to overlap and compete with each other or should each have a well-defined target market and objective? Sales distribution channels that are to overlap each other should be measured by common objectives in order to avoid channel conflicts as far as possible. This requires objectives which are higher to reflect the sum of what would have been the individual objectives. This may result in the individual channels all pursuing the large opportunities rather than going after the target markets which they were intended to pursue. The alternative, assigning specific target markets and objectives, may lead to some squabbles at the boundaries, but is often adopted in an effort to focus sales more strongly and avoid unnecessary overlapping. Channel conflicts are almost always counterproductive in practice.

The sales-led or marketing-led go-to-market approaches that we have described so far have traditionally been dominant in the software industry. An alternative go-to-market approach that is getting increasing attention is product-led, also known under the moniker "product-led growth" [Bush19] which is defined as a business methodology in which user acquisition, expansion, conversion, and retention are all driven primarily by the product itself. Here the product is used as its own sales tool by making it available to potential users who can try it out and purchase it from inside the product. The hurdle for initial use must be made as low as possible, e.g. in the form of trial-ware and upgrade-ware (see Sect. 2.4.5). As a consequence of this approach, sales-oriented product requirements from Marketing and Sales have to get high priority. Ideally the approach results in significantly lower cost of customer acquisition and retention. However, its applicability depends on the users' degree of influence on purchasing decisions for the product and the degree of dependency of customer value on the integration in the users' environment.

3.7.4 Process

Positioning is an iterative process that seeks consensus among Product Management, Marketing, Sales, and executive management. At the very least Marketing needs to participate in this work. The result is usually not static, but evolves over the strategic timeframe and beyond. There are a number of interdependent factors to be considered, in particular target market segments, product definition, and pricing.

Determining customer value and how they perceive it requires some in-depth analysis how and for what customers are going to use the product, and what their alternatives are. Alternatives can be competitive products, custom solutions, or doing nothing. If possible, it can be helpful to involve existing or potential customers in this analysis. The drivers or parameters need to be determined that influence customer value. Ideally, the relationship between the parameters and customer value is expressed in a formula. Customer value can be considered in absolute terms, or in terms relative to the identified alternatives that a customer has, or relative to the price of the product.

Each of the candidate channels requires analysis of the potential for access to potential customers in the target market segments and the resulting cost in relation to the financial model of the product. The results are the basis for channel selection.

Specific criteria should determine the sales channels a company uses for a particular product: Target market (segments) (see Sects. 3.4 and 3.6.2): Which channel has the highest potential to reach customers in the selected target market?

- Product definition (see Sect. 3.5) including the definition of the "Whole Product" and the delivery model: Can partners who provide components act as channels? Can candidate partners explain the product to customers given the product's complexity?
- Sales cost: What are the costs and benefits the selection of a particular channel entails.

Sales cost is a key criterion for selection of sales channels. Sales channels with human involvement are more expensive than the virtual (i.e. fully automated) sales channels.

The most expensive sales channel is usually the direct sales force of a software vendor. Therefore, this channel is only financially viable for software products in the high price segment. Software products at lower prices are rather distributed through indirect sales channels with human involvement, or through virtual channels (internet sales, fully automated) which requires that the product is adequately designed for the intended channel. A comprehensive channel strategy must also consider other factors:

- The relationship frequency: some channels are used systematically and repeatedly, others opportunistically (one-offs).
- The place of purchase (online retailer versus software retail store around the corner).
- The strategies in software ecosystems, i.e. niche players, keystone players, dominators (see Sect. 3.11).
- The purchase frequency or the degree of willingness to buy (impulse buyers versus regular customers).
- The purchase occasion, i.e. the situations in which purchases typically happen.
- The attitude towards the product or the service.
- The usage rate/frequency of the product.

The selection of channels usually results in a mix that can include direct sales including telesales and virtual sales, and partner sales. The terms and conditions for each channel needs to be defined so that channel conflicts are prevented. The operational responsibility of managing this marketing mix on an ongoing basis is with Marketing and Sales.

3.7.5   Outcome and Impacts

Customer value, the advantages that a customer experiences when using the software product, may be described in both absolute and relative qualitative terms. For example, we can identify a certain feature as highly valuable for customers in a particular segment and show this feature to be a differentiating factor compared to the alternatives. This qualitative description provides valuable input for the development of marketing messages by Marketing.

Simply evaluating the value as high, medium, low for the different market segments may be a good start that shows how well the product fits the needs of the respective market segment. This may also be used for a rough comparison with alternatives, but it is not good enough as input for marketing and pricing.

The vendor must identify drivers of customer value on a detailed level. These depend on the type of software. For transactional systems like an airline reservation system, the driver can be the number of transactions, i.e. flight reservations, or the revenue made through the system. For productivity tools, it can be the number of users or the usage time, or the savings in terms of time that employees need for particular tasks. The parameters identified to drive value are the ones that can be used to calculate the price in a value-based way (see Sect. 3.10). For a potential customer, the relationship between a product's value and its price in comparison to the alternatives determines the buying decision.

The definition of the channel mix may change over time based on experience, or when additional market segments are added to the original target market definition. For new product development, i.e. in the Powerboat and Icebreaker scenarios (see Sect. 2.5), positioning means a rather dynamic learning process. During later phases of the product life cycle, the positioning tends to be more stable.

3.7.6   Summary and Conclusions

Positioning provides important information on how the product will be described and communicated to its market(s). The core of positioning is the value proposition, and differentiation by customer segments may be required. In order to reach the customers in the segments in a cost-effective way, it is crucial to select and implement appropriate sales channels. Positioning is highly relevant for Marketing and Sales, but also for other product management activities like pricing or release planning.

3.8   Service Strategy

3.8.1   Overview

The software product manager is supposed to manage the whole product offering which includes product-related human services (see Sect. 2.4) even though the responsibility for the provisioning of these services may organizationally be separated from the software product organization. New customers may require services to become productive with the product as fast as possible and existing customers to stay productive as long as they use the product.

The service strategy needs to define the services that are part of the total offering and who is supposed to provide these services. If external partners are to provide services, this needs to be aligned with the tailorability strategy (Sect. 3.6.3) and ecosystem management (Sect. 3.12). This section describes the contents of a service strategy. The reader will understand the related processes and the impacts.

3.8.2   Concept

Product-related human services fall into two categories:

- **Delivery Services** mean all customer-specific services provided to customers to help them become productive with the initial software product or when a new version is installed. This includes installation and tailoring services. Tailoring based on the product's tailorability options is a customer-specific service that can mean a large project for configuration and customization.

- **Support** refers to all product-related services provided to existing customers such as maintenance, training, operations, user help desk etc. Support provides technical support to customers, usually covered by maintenance or SaaS contracts.

These services include education, installation, customization, operations, maintenance, technical support, and helpdesk covering technical and non-technical problems. Typically, these services are priced separately. Sometimes they are bundled with software product offerings.Details of these services are described in Sect. 6.5.

A software vendor needs to decide if and to what degree these services are provided by the vendor itself, and/or through partners. Resulting revenue from self-provided services and capacity considerations are important company considerations. Partners who provide product-related services may be motivated to sell the product to their customers. On the other hand, services can help the vendor to intensify the customer relationship, and to learn about the customer environment and how a customer uses the product. This information is valuable input for the positioning and evolution of the product. So the question who provides which services is clearly of strategic importance. Communication between the in-house service team and Product Management and Development is usually easier when they all belong to one product organization. Even companies that would prefer to relegate service delivery to partners can be compelled by customers to provide them as well as the customers expect a complete solution and may not want to establish an additional business relationship.

Although services can play an important role in providing maximum customer value, defining and managing services require knowledge and skills that are significantly different from those required to manage software products. While product managers should play a key role in identifying service opportunities relative to their product, i.e., service-related requirements, they should engage other professionals with the appropriate level of experience regarding detailed services definition, planning and delivery.

With enterprise software products, implementation often requires customization which means custom software development by which customer-specific functionality is added to the standard software product (see Sect. 3.6.3). This becomes relevant when a customer has requirements that the software vendor refuses to implement in the standard product because they are too customer-specific, i.e. not of value to other customers. When the vendor decides to offer this kind of custom software development, it needs to be clearly separated from the standard product both organizationally and contractually. The customizations, for practical reasons, should be done in such a way that future base product versions can be implemented and the customizations adapted with minimum rework, else the customer may become "stuck" on an old version or the vendor "stuck" with a huge unaffordable effort. In particular, for cost reasons this custom code must not be covered by the maintenance contract for the standard product. There can be additional customer-specific services like system integration.

For new product development, i.e. in the Powerboat and Icebreaker scenarios (see Sect. 2.5), services for the first customer are often provided out of Development since that first customer is intended to provide domain knowledge and the vendor organization needs to learn how to provide those services. The services for later customers, i.e. after the product is launched, needs to be done by the units declared as responsible in the Service Strategy including external partners. During later phases of the product life cycle, additional services may be identified and added to the service strategy. During the maturity and decline stages of license products, maintenance revenue usually plays an increasingly important role in the financial picture of license products.

3.8.3   Process

Ideally Product Management, Services, Marketing, Sales, and executive management all participate in the service strategy definition. At very least Services and Marketing need to participate in this work.

In order to define the whole product, product-related services need to be part of the product definition (see Sect. 3.5). For the service strategy, the product manager needs to take a number of aspects into account:

- Which product-related services are needed for offering a complete solution that satisfies target customers' needs, and that target customers are willing to pay for?
- Who can provide those identified services with regard to capacities, skills, and customer acceptance?
- What is the right balance between revenue generation and learning from self-provided services, and customer access and potential additional product revenue through external service partners who also act as sales partners?

Once the service strategy answers these questions, it is the task of either the internal Services unit or ecosystem management for partners to make sure that the identified services are available at the time when they are needed.

3.8.4   Outcome and Impacts

The service strategy is documented in text that is usually part of the product strategy document. It lists the services identified as part of the whole product offering and defines who is supposed to provide these services.

Product-related services can have a significant impact on customer satisfaction. They may also contribute significant revenue. The service strategy gives direction to Services as well as Ecosystem Management.

3.8.5   Summary and Conclusions

Product-related services are important for the business success of the software product. That is why the service strategy needs to be integrated into the product strategy and tightly linked with product definition. It looks at product-related services like education, installation, tailoring, operations, and maintenance that help a customer to become productive with the product. The service strategy answers the questions of which services are needed, and who is going to provide them. The product manager needs to manage the product-related services as part of the Whole Product offering.

3.9   Sourcing

3.9.1   Overview

Sourcing is the process of ensuring that the resources required to implement a product strategy are available whenever they are needed. Based on a corporate sourcing strategy that defines if, for what and to what degree external resources can be used, decisions on a software product level focus on human resources, make-or-buy for software components, and use of external services and data sources.

This section describes the criteria for sourcing decisions, related processes and impacts.

3.9.2   Concept

For sourcing, there are basically two options: Required resources can either be internal, i.e. come from inside of the company, or external, i.e. from outside of the company. Once the positioning and definition of the product for the strategic timeframe has been done, the activities need to be identified that are required to implement the product strategy including very rough estimates for efforts and skill and time requirements. These estimates can be refined on an ongoing basis, but initially they are usually good enough to develop a first idea of resource requirements.

For software products, the most important resource is skilled human beings. They can either be employees of the software organization, or professionals hired from outside of the company. In bigger organizations these decisions usually need to be aligned with corporate resource management (see Sect. 5.4), e.g. there may be a sourcing strategy on the corporate level that gives guidelines as to if, in which areas, under which circumstances, and to what extent the company wants to use external human resources. Under these guidelines, a product team can develop a product-specific sourcing approach.

There are a number of reasons why a software organization may want to work with external people, e.g. special temporary skill requirements, temporary capacity requirements, a general wish for resource flexibility in case of changes of strategy and plan, or cost considerations.

Since the mid-1990s, many companies have worked with external people in locations with a considerably lower cost level. This is known as near-shore or off-shore outsourcing. In the software area, some companies have managed to make this work and save money, but in a significant number of cases the hidden cost generated by communication overhead and lost time due to communication problems turned out to eat up the calculated savings. There can also be risks from skill dependencies. A lot of literature is available on outsourcing, e.g. [OshKoWil11].

In some situations, it can make more economic sense for a software organization to integrate a software component supplied by an external partner than to develop that component in-house. This is known as the Make-or-Buy decision. It may also apply to complete products. Reasons to buy can be faster time to market, improved quality, skills shortage, or resource shortage [BCWAGPSA19]. Aspects like interoperability, terms and conditions, cost, ongoing development and support, and setup of the cooperation need consideration. The product manager should not leave this decision to development since developers usually want to make and not buy. In case of a buy decision, it is of utmost importance to negotiate the contract with the partner that provides the software such that the dependence on the partner does not lead to a disaster like losing the right to use the software on short notice, or facing extreme price increases. There should also be consideration of what could happen in the longer term. Because IBM was not sure of the future of the PC, they refused to pay Microsoft for PC DOS and insisted on a royalty arrangement. The cash flow generated by that decision enabled the emergence of one of IBM's strongest competitors.

One option is the use of open source software which is very common in most of today's software organizations. Here, the product manager needs to assess the viability and ongoing support based on the level of activity in the respective open source community, and the legal risks due to the type of open source license (see Sect. 3.13.4). Again, we do not recommend leaving this decision to the developers alone since they are usually not aware of the legal implications.

Make-or-Buy decisions are also relevant in areas like infrastructure, or data. A good example is hosting for SaaS offerings. Reasons for partnering can be that a software organization has no experience with hosting for customers, or that there may be advantages in terms of price and scalability due to the economies of scale that a big hosting provider achieves. An example for sourcing data is stock market data.

3.9.3 Decision-Making for Sourcing

Given the business impact and risks that are associated with sourcing decisions, the product manager always needs to be involved in the decision making and selection of sourcing partners. Within the limitations defined by the corporate sourcing strategy, a product organization needs to decide if it can implement its product strategy with the available internal resources, or if and where external resources need to be added. That decision is usually not made by a product manager alone, but needs to be driven by Product Management. Once a decision for external sourcing has been made, an external partner has to be selected. Criteria can be financial stability and reputation of the partner company, skills of the available people the partner company can provide, cultural fit, terms and conditions, in particular price, or—in case of software components—functional and technical fit of the partner's component to the requirements. Contract negotiation may fall under a product manager's responsibility unless there are specialized units like partner management (see Sect. 3.12). Service contracts require the negotiation of service level agreements as part of the contract (see Sect. 3.13).

The selection of a partner company can be a trigger for analysis if the acquisition of that partner company could bring a strategic advantage, e.g. in terms of product set, skills, market share, risk reduction or financial impact, and is financially doable. However, the process of analysis, due diligence and acquisition is outside of the product management scope. Bigger companies have specialized merger and acquisition units for this (see [Popp13]).

The organizational unit whose resources are extended by the sourcing decision is usually responsible for the implementation. That can be Development for software developers or the integration of an externally sourced software component, Quality Management for testers, or Operations for a hosting partner. Though typically not responsible for the implementation and operational management, Product Management is well-advised to monitor the activities on a frequent basis in order to take corrective actions in case of negative business impacts.

3.9.4   Summary and Conclusions

Clever sourcing decisions can shorten time-to-market, increase quality and/or improve financial performance. However, external sourcing comes with dependencies and increased risk that need good oversight and management. Product managers' entrepreneurial responsibilities include driving these sourcing decisions, whether they concern human resources, or make-or-buy decisions for commercial software, open source software, infrastructure, or data.

3.10   Pricing

3.10.1 Overview

Software pricing means all activities required to set, communicate, and negotiate prices in a convincing way. The primary objective of software pricing is to find customer value propositions which align with product management's objectives, i.e. sustainable success of the software products across their life cycles. In the software business, cost-based pricing works for human services, but not for software products (see Chap. 2). For software a value-based approach is the way to go. Software pricing means finding ways to convert the value the software provides to a customer into economic value to the vendor.

This section describes the essence of software pricing. The reader will understand the concept, fundamentals from literature, the related roles and processes, and special considerations for subscription-based models. Software pricing is covered in much more detail in Chap. 5 of [KittClou09].

3.10.2 Concept

There are many approaches on how to design and systematize pricing. One of the first fundamental decisions of pricing is the choice of a pricing approach or strategy. It is common to distinguish between value-based pricing, market-based pricing, and cost-based pricing [BaGeBuBi14, WuBuRa20].

- **Value-based Pricing Strategy:** This pricing strategy is grounded in the value perceived by the customer. Perception-value is based on the customers' perceptions of what is expected compared with what is delivered. The necessity of evaluating this value and associated challenges make this strategy much more subjective in comparison with other pricing strategies. The common term of perceptive value is value for money, that is, the ratio between the customer value of a cloud service and the price. The main advantage of value-based pricing is its subjective fairness for consumers who can compare their expenses with the benefits gained. However, it is challenging to construct because the perceived value is primarily measured by the satisfaction of the individual customer—that is, there can be strong heterogeneity among customers, which may require additional segmentation.
- **Market-based Pricing:** This approach relies on analysis of market supply, demand and competition. Market-based pricing takes into consideration two factors that impact pricing—price sensitivity and market competitiveness for similar services. Some researchers and practitioners suggest the distinction between competitor-based pricing and premium pricing as separate approaches in market-based pricing.
- **Cost-based Pricing:** This pricing strategy derives directly from a vendor's cost structure. One of the primary reasons to adopt this strategy is that it is concrete and tangible. It can also be considered as "fact"-based pricing. Cost-based pricing can articulate a unit cost and provide a measurement for benchmark comparison. It is one of the managerial tools for many decision-makers to drive business performance.

Software product managers frequently do not relish the task of pricing their products. If they are lucky they have professional pricing managers by their side. But more often than not, they are on their own. So how does software pricing work? A cost-based approach works nicely for professional services. You calculate the cost per day of your programmers or consultants, add some percentage for general cost, down time and absence, add the profit margin, and voila—that is the price you offer.

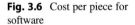

Fig. 3.6 Cost per piece for software

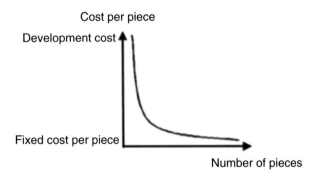

Unfortunately, this fairly easy approach does not work for software products. There is no significant variable cost, i.e. cost per license or per SaaS customer, that can be used as a basis of the cost-based price calculation (see Sect. 3.11.5). So the total cost per piece goes down significantly with a growing number of pieces, i.e. licenses or SaaS customers (see Fig. 3.6). This is much more drastic for software products than the economies of scale that are found in manufacturing industries.

So for software, the approach of choice is value-based pricing. That is described by Nagle and Hogan in their Strategic Pricing Pyramid (Fig. 3.7, [NagHog05]):

Strategic software pricing starts with a clear understanding of customer segments and value delivered to the customers (bottom layer of the pyramid).

Value Creation = The manner in which value is generated in a customer organization from using the product, including the metric that shows the impact of certain parameters on the value.

Segmentation may be needed if value creation is different in different segments. We analyze the value a customer realizes by using the product. Think of an airline reservation system. The value to an airline increases with each customer booking made through the reservation system.

Based on that value analysis, the metrics used in the price structure can be determined (compensator, effect, rating and charging from the model described in Sect. 3.11.5). We define.

Price Structure = The manner in which the prices for a given software product are offered, including the metric by which those prices may vary for the single product (e.g. one single price, price based on number of users, on capacity, on usage, or on volume of licenses acquired).

An important consideration is that metrics should mirror the generation of customer value which gives us a nice story how we can justify the price in relation to that customer value. We may decide to define the price structure as the number of bookings times a base price. Perhaps we want to add a fixed price component to this variable price; after all an airline cannot function without a reservation system and we may not want our entire business being dependent upon the variability in our client's bookings.

Fig. 3.7 Strategic pricing pyramid [NagHog05]

There is a wide variety of options available to define a price structure:

- One-time vs. periodic, also known as subscription-based pricing.
- Fixed price (one-time or periodic).
- Usage-based pricing (periodic), e.g. based on number of transactions, users or usage hours.
- Free, i.e. no charges, but revenue generation through advertising.

The resulting price structure may turn out to be quite complex, in particular with usage-based pricing when the actual price is calculated anew each month based on the customer's usage numbers of the previous month. In that case we had better make sure that our back-office systems are able to reliably handle the complexity and issue correct invoices. Otherwise we need to simplify the price structure so that we do not impact the customer relationship by frequent incorrect invoices.

Maintenance for license products is usually priced as periodic with an annual charge as a percentage of the list price. The percentage is typically in the range of 12–25%, depending on what is included in the maintenance contract, e.g. version upgrades, hotline for non-defects, or not. With SaaS, maintenance is not charged separately, but is included in the periodic charges of the SaaS offering.

In some product areas, e.g. airline tickets or rental cars, we see more dynamic pricing concepts where prices change frequently based on current demand, order inventory, etc. This is also known as yield management. These concepts can be applicable to human services. There are examples where yield management is also used for software, e.g. Amazon PaaS pricing.

The better value creation and price structure are aligned, the smoother is the communication of price to customers:

Price and Value Communication = The communication concept that is the basis for communicating price and value to customers by showing how reasonable the price is for the customer compared to the value he gets from using the product.

Strategic pricing also includes processes and policies to ensure the integrity of the price structure in the market, for example fences that prevent abuse of discounts (e.g. student discounts require proof of student status) or criteria for handling "exception requests" in price negotiations (discounting criteria as part of the pricing policy layer in the pyramid). We define

Pricing Policy = A formal definition of the manner in which prices may be altered, e.g. price level or price structure, by whom they may be altered, under what circumstances, and to what degree.

The policy sets governance criteria for the whole company regarding price. If the company has a separate Pricing organization, that organization usually gets a veto right to any transactions that do not adhere to the policy.

The top layer of the Strategic Pricing Pyramid is the price setting, i.e. setting of the price level. We define

Price Level = The actual amount of charge within the price structure. In our airline example, for an individual customer, we can calculate an upper limit of the quantified value by dividing the annual profit through the number of bookings which gives us the value per booking. Of course, the price level, i.e. the base price, needs to be considerably lower than the value per booking. Competitive analysis can further help to determine the price level. At what price are competitors offering their products? Does the product have competitive advantages/disadvantages that justify price differences? By carefully analyzing these elements, we can come up with the price level at which we want to offer the product. There are many pricing strategies to choose from:

- Premium price strategy (high price, high quality and image), often combined with a promotion price strategy (lower price, high quality, e.g. temporary special offers).
- Price differentiation strategy (same product, different prices, e.g. in different market segments—temporary, geographically, personnel, quantitatively).
- Price bundling (single pricing or product package, see also Sect. 3.11.7).
- Penetration strategy (low price with the introduction of a product in pursuit of rapid market share growth).

- Skimming price strategy (high price for innovative products for compensation of high investment).
- Life-cycle-dependent pricing strategy (situation-specific decision if, e.g. in the introduction phase, high or low prices are to be set).
- Non-linear pricing strategy (usage independent component, e.g. fixed charges, and usage based component, e.g. depending on usage).

The classic pricing theories of economic science like price elasticity usually assume a commodity market and a limited supply of goods. Since these elements don't exist for most software products, usual economic elasticity theories do not apply.

3.10.3 Fundamentals

Consolidating the variety of different definitions provided by scholars and practitioners [SiMoMeKa12, ÖzePhi12], pricing can be defined as the process of decision-making in determining the monetary compensation and related conditions of the goods and services the customer is offered. Pricing is an essential element of the business model and product strategy. In the industry, it usually has the additional more operational dimension of communicating and negotiating prices. Pricing requires close cooperation between different business functions (i.e., product management, revenue management, cost management, retention management) and business units (i.e., Development, Services, Sales, Marketing). Decision-making in pricing is based on an integrated analysis of different perspectives and streams of information. The primary objective of pricing is well aligned with product management's objectives, i.e. sustainable success of the software product across its life cycle. For standard software products, value-based pricing is the way to go. Software pricing means finding ways how to convert the value the software provides to a customer into economic value to the vendor.While price has been a central element of economic theories for centuries, the concept of pricing as a managerial discipline and business function dates to the late 1970s. It arose due to the deregulation of the airline industry, which provided flexibility for airline companies in defining prices for airline tickets [MorWin90]. Back then, pricing was considered as a part of revenue (or yield) management, defined as the processes and practices of selling "the right inventory unit to the right type of customer, at the right time, and for the right price" [KiPhSu12]. Efficient revenue management required comprehensive decision-making regarding these four "right" aspects, intending to maximize revenue streams.

The software industry has unique characteristics of revenue, pricing, and cost management. First, revenue management in the software industry is mostly about defining the "right pricing" and "right customers". The production, logistics, inventory—additional pillars of revenue management—are usually not relevant. Secondly, most software companies have a considerable disparity between fixed costs and variable costs, which creates supply-side economies of scale [HoRoPL00, KittClou09]. Thirdly, the software industry is often characterized by network effects that make perceived value and willingness-to-pay (WTP) contingent on the actual number of customers [KatSha94, Buxm01]. These three characteristics of software and software industry confirm the role of pricing as a key driver for market success and revenue growth for software companies.

While the commercial success of software companies depends on adequate pricing, decisions on designing and implementing pricing have always been challenging for software companies [BonChu00]. As a result, quite often, companies make decisions regarding pricing as a part of the last development cycles and launch software without fully activating its pricing potential. Achieving the "right pricing" in software companies requires a tighter alignment between pricing management and development processes than in any other industries.

For software products, many pricing experts emphasize the advantages of value-based pricing. The low variable costs for software products make cost-based pricing not directly applicable to software products. A monopolistic competitive market structure allows companies to move away from direct competition and avoid setting prices based on competitors and market equilibrium. However, many companies from the software industry still conventionally rely on cost-based and market-based pricing. The cost-based approach helps decision-makers set a baseline to charge customers for the minimum price so that they can at least cover their expenditures. While market-based pricing allows companies to rely on market forces and consider the current situation as an equilibrium. If there is a lack of focus in pricing at the strategic, tactical, or operational levels, the product and the company are likely to suffer or fail. Additionally, not all the discussed pricing approaches are mutually exclusive, and many companies use hybrid approaches that combine features of different models.

The servitization [Accenture definition: the shift from traditional business models to an outcome-based, product as a service (PaaS) model.] of software and transition towards a cloud-based model have enabled new opportunities for software companies in software development, delivery, and operations. These opportunities have implications for pricing. The SaaS transition twisted the overall focus of pricing from selling products to maintaining long-term relationships with customers through the triumvirate of customer acquisition, retention and monetization.

3.10.4 Roles and Decision-Making in Software Product Pricing

Larger companies often have a job role of pricing manager, which can be part of the Finance organization or reporting directly to the Executive level in order to achieve some level of independence with regard to the governance responsibility. Pricing specialists often have a Sales or Finance background. If a company does not have this role the pricing responsibility may be given to senior product managers if product management has a P&L responsibility. In smaller companies the pricing responsibility may be carried by executive managers themselves, e.g. founders in startups. Giving the pricing responsibility to Sales is not advisable for a standard software product business due to the inherent conflict of interests.

A product manager may have different roles with regard to pricing:

- Be the pricing manager, or
- Cooperate tightly with the pricing manager and define requirements regarding price structures and price policies
- Guide Sales regarding price structures, price policies and price levels for the product
- Support marketing regarding price and value communication for the product

It is imperative to keep in mind that price does not sell a product. The product must fit the customers' needs. Then, price can become the differentiator between doing nothing, buying a competitor's equally useful product, and buying your product. Pricing too low or discounting too deeply will lead to leaving a lot of "money on the table", particularly when this becomes predictable. Pricing too high will lead to a weak market share. Efficient pricing requires sophisticated decision-making and analytics, as well as coordination and finding compromises between the many business functions involved. Facing these challenges, large software and tech companies work with pricing specialists who cooperate with product managers to address all their products' pricing challenges [AthLuc19]. However, a wide range of newly established software companies, most of which are small- and medium-sized enterprises, do not have the resources and knowledge to make informed decisions on pricing strategy, tactics, and implementation operations. A patchy knowledge of pricing and complications in establishing and managing all pricing-related processes and practices results in a scattered and under-managed pricing process for many software companies. The Strategic Pricing Pyramid discussed above offers a systematic approach to value-based pricing. However, it might look too abstract for practical decision-making. Multiple more application-oriented decision-making frameworks were proposed by scholars and practitioners. Here we briefly introduce the approach offered by consulting company ACCION.

The decision-making framework consists of four sequential steps as follows (Fig. 3.8, [Accion15]):

1. **Define Your Upper Bound**

   Two significant factors that affect that upper bound for the software product are a competitive advantage and customers' willingness-to-pay for the product offered. At the most fundamental level, the pricing strategy hinges on how unique the product is and what the price customers are ready to pay for it, which is a derivative of the value you can convince a customer the product has for him.

2. **Define Your Lower Bound**

   The lower bound for the price is grounded into costs the price needs to cover to support profitability. Even if the software company can afford not to be focused on immediate profitability, understanding the revenue required to break even and become profitable is essential for long-term success. If covering the costs requires a price point that is above customers' willingness-to-pay, the company might need to reconsider the entire strategy for the product.

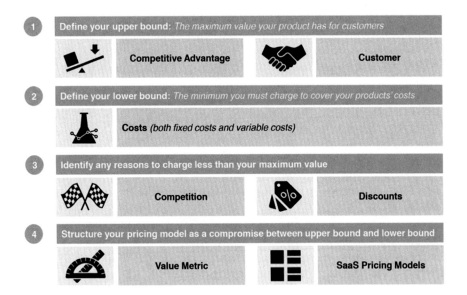

Fig. 3.8 Decision-making framework for pricing [Accion15]

3. **Identify Reasons to Charge Less than Your Maximum Value**

   At this step, pricing strategy meets pricing tactics. In most cases, the company has direct or indirect competitors, and competitors' pricing is an essential context for pricing decisions. Undercutting competitors' prices can be considered a strategic move, even when unique or superior features sufficiently differentiate the product. Additionally, effective customer relationship management might require tactical flexibility in pricing that can be achieved through personalized discounts.

4. **Structure Your Pricing Model as a Compromise Between the Upper Bound and Lower Bound**

   When it comes to transactional pricing, i.e. special bid pricing for larger customers, it can be tempting to divert from the standard price structure and pricing policies. However, with today's job migration and communication no one pricing products can assume that the knowledge of special pricing will remain secret, so companies need to ensure that they do not price even on a transactional level in such a way that they would not replicate that price for every customer. "Fencing" which is persuasive with a customer seeking lower price is very difficult even when legitimate. Special pricing should assume that the price will "bleed" to other situations, so it should not ever fall below the sustainable bottom limit.

3.10.5 Subscription-Based Models

It is hard to run a business based on one-off sales. Recurring revenue makes life so much easier. Once you have acquired the customer, you can be quite sure of a revenue stream over a longer period of time that covers your monthly cost and hopefully more. The insurance industry is built on this model. Employees are used to it with their monthly salaries. For customers, no upfront investment is needed, and the recurring payments are operational expenses.

The software industry has over time demonstrated the pro's and con's of each approach. In the 1970s and 1980s there used to be a price model called Monthly License Charge (MLC) for mainframe software products. It was the basis of IBM's wonderfully profitable software business. Of course, it means that revenue is deferred compared to a one-time-charge (OTC) model where the customer pays the full license fee immediately when the contract is signed. As a vendor, you need to be in a financial position to afford this deferral. When the PC software business started in the 1980's, the new players like Microsoft wanted the revenue quickly, so they chose the OTC model. They offered maintenance contracts to enterprise customers which generated at least some recurring revenue, but certainly less than the MLC model. It made Microsoft's financial numbers look great quickly. But over time, it meant that Microsoft could only generate additional license revenue from existing customers by charging for version upgrades. So Microsoft released new versions of Windows and Office every 2 or 3 years, not because customers wanted new functionality, but primarily for financial reasons. On top of that, Microsoft often did not care too much about ease of migration. So a large number of their customers resisted that approach and stayed on older versions as long as they could. As of March 2015, only 11.5% of Windows desktop/laptop users were on the latest Windows version 8.1 (according to Net Applications). This does not look good in the trade press, means maintenance efforts for 6 Windows versions in parallel, and results in relatively low upgrade license revenue. With Windows 10, Microsoft was trying something new by offering Windows 10 for free to all Windows 7 and 8 consumer customers in the first year. Did they give away revenue? Well, certainly some. But Windows 10 is the basis for an increasing number of Microsoft applications that come with subscription price models, e.g. the popular game Solitaire will have a Freemium model (use of the basic product is free, but you pay monthly for special features and ad-free use).

Another important aspect of periodic charges is that the pricing model lowers the hurdle for customers to stay current, i.e. frequently migrate to the latest version of the product. Depending on the type of software product these upgrades may happen seamlessly without the customer even noticing it.

The move to subscription price models has become a major trend in the software industry, in particular with Software-as-a-Service (SaaS). The SaaS model brought a radical shift in how software is engineered and developed as well as its product strategy and pricing, life cycle management, customer involvement, and relationship management [KittSalt22, StuSte12]. The price goes beyond the license fee for SaaS solutions and incorporates recurring service and maintenance fees [Cusuma07]. The transition towards SaaS created and magnified the number of pricing design, experiment, and control mechanisms available. Examples of such mechanisms include but are not limited to recurring subscription fees, new methods to ensure efficient price discrimination, and real-time usage tracking [DuJaKu18].

Subscription-based pricing can also be a model for all the other industries that embrace Internet of Things (IoT). Software is becoming a key component of their products. It opens the door to creative value propositions that will make customers pay for subscriptions on top of the OTC price of the base product. Think of software enhancements for entertainment components in the car, or a subscription for continuous high quality traffic updates. So there is lots of room for new ideas how to generate recurring revenue.

3.10.6 Summary and Conclusions

In this section, we have looked at the value-based pricing approach for software and at subscription-based pricing. There are many more aspects to software pricing than we can cover here. For a much more detailed discussion including considerations for corporate IT organizations, we refer to the pricing chapter in [KittClou09].

Pricing, and in particular the governance rules related to pricing, are an ongoing source of conflict. Sales has different, more short-term objectives than a Pricing organization, or whoever is responsible for Pricing. So the governance rules need to define clear responsibilities and escalation paths.

It is imperative to keep in mind that price doesn't sell product. The product must fit the customer's needs, then price can become the differentiator between doing nothing, buying a competitor's equally useful product, and buying your product. Pricing too low or discounting too deeply, particularly if this becomes predictable, will lead to leaving a lot of "money on the table." Pricing too high will lead to weak market share.

Since pricing has such a significant impact on the product's economic success over its life cycle, the task is always to find the approach which fits the market and optimizes the vendor's financial benefit over time. It can be quite hard to do a convincing customer value analysis. It can also be challenging, at least in B2B markets, to get accurate case by case information on competitors' prices (in some jurisdictions and with some vendor contracts, this may not even be legal to do). And a forecast always contains risk. However, if we want to optimize our business results there are no fundamentally different good alternatives to the value-based pricing approach for software products whether it is an on-premise license product or SaaS.

3.11   Financial Management

3.11.1 Overview

The primary objective of software product management is to achieve sustainable success over the life cycle of the product (or platform or family). This generally refers to economic success, which is ultimately reflected by the profits generated. Since profits lag behind investments, i.e., an investment phase involving no revenue and large development expense will be followed by an extended profitable phase, a longer-term perspective is appropriate. Therefore, the product manager has to plan and track financial aspects both from a short- and long-term perspective. This is called financial management and is tightly linked to pricing. It includes the representation of the product on the corporate level. Financial management is not limited to the product manager keeping track of the revenue numbers (see Sect. 3.14). It means a much more active role in shaping the parameters that are paramount for the economic success of a product or product family. The relevant topics are covered in this section, plus pricing in Sect. 3.10 and performance and risk management in Sect. 3.14.

3.11.2   Building and Using the Financial Model

The financial model, sometimes called a business plan, documents a complete picture of the financial numbers for the product over its strategic time frame. Business planning is a process that aims at getting the relevant stakeholders' consent to the model. The financial model is a forecast regarding cost and revenue that leads to a plan for resources and budgets. We look at forecasting in Sect. 3.11.3, at the cost side in Sect. 3.11.4, the revenue model in Sect. 3.11.5. Pricing was covered in Sect. 3.10.

Especially for a new product or when evolving the model for an existing product, the main purpose of the financial model is to answer the question: Under which conditions/assumptions can we achieve profitability? For this purpose, we recommend building a financial model that enables product managers to ask "what-if" questions, using the following practices:

- build a multi-year model that reaches beyond the break-even point (3 to 5-year models are common)
- model multiple revenue streams separately
- on the cost side, work closely with liaisons from the various company functions, including R&D and marketing, to build or leverage suitable models that describe costs over time.

For example, technical decisions on the R&D side may generate hidden costs or contingency costs later—and they can affect other areas (such as support).

- isolate underlying assumptions as parameters that can be changed easily, e.g. conversion rates from free to premium in a freemium business model
- build multiple scenarios

Once the model is built, it can be used to study the profitability of the product under various scenarios that use different assumptions. We recommend explicitly documenting any assumptions on which the financial model is based. Since it is critical to the product's success and usually gets a lot of attention and scrutiny from top management, product managers are advised to be prepared to explain each and every detail of the financial model.

3.11.3 Forecasting

Estimates and forecasts can be quite good under certain conditions: stable environment and historic data that can be simply extrapolated. However, extrapolation from the past only works when there is a past to extrapolate from, i.e. either for existing products, or if there is a very close analog that can be used. Note however, that any extrapolation from the past will miss dramatic changes in the environment that the past cannot forecast, much as a sharp curve in a road cannot be predicted by a glance in a car's rear view mirror. Classic cases are the demise of the buggy whip industry with the advent of automobiles or the failure to predict the growth of the PC and the internet. Unfortunately, we often have to come up with forecasts when stability is not present. That is what Philip E. Tetlock and Dan Gardner's book "Superforecasting—The Art and Science of Prediction" [TetGar15] is about. However, if you are seeking a recipe for reliable forecasts the book will disappoint you. The majority of the content concerns Tetlock's huge research studies and their findings. There is clear evidence that some people are consistently and significantly better than average at this kind of forecasting. And there is a section on more practical advice called "Ten Commandments for Aspiring Superforecasters", but it is only an appendix and comes more as an afterthought than as the climax of the book. It lists important factors that have an impact on the predictive quality of forecasts:

- Triage: Focus on predictable questions, not trivial and not unsolvable ones.
- Break seemingly intractable problems into tractable sub-problems.
- Strike the right balance between inside and outside view.
- Strike the right balance between under- and overreacting to evidence (when you adjust your forecast iteratively).
- Look for the clashing causal forces at work in each problem.
- Strive to distinguish as many degrees of doubt as the problem permits but not more: look at degrees of uncertainty.
- Strike the right balance between under- and overconfidence, between prudence and decisiveness: trade-off between accuracy and finite decision time.
- Look for the errors behind your mistakes but beware of rearview-mirror hindsight bias: do thorough post-mortems.
- Bring out the best in others and let others bring out the best in you: teamwork increases success statistically.
- Master the error-balancing bicycle: only forecasting practice and feedback loops can improve your forecasting ability over time.
- Don't treat commandments as commandments: There are no firm rules that apply to any case.

As you can see from the last bullet, this is half-hearted advice. We cannot do without forecasting, but it remains more art than science. Above all, be scrupulously honest in your assessments; do not allow either optimism or pessimism to shade objective conclusions.

3.11.4 Cost Structure and Management

For software products, development effort is usually the largest determinant of cost. So in order to manage cost, an upfront estimation of the development effort is essential. The discipline of software engineering has come up with a number of estimation methods over time, e.g. the more recent Cost Estimation, Benchmarking, and Risk Assessment (CoBRA method) described in [Trendow13]. These methods are usually targeted at custom software development projects, but can easily be adapted to software product development projects. However, all of them use historical data and experiences as a base to estimate a new undertaking. When there is no history the reliability of estimates is typically low (see Sect. 3.11.4). Planning Poker is a technique that works quite well for effort estimation which is a Development responsibility (see Sect. 4.4.3).

Cost management in mature software product organizations is usually done in a two-step process:

- The cost target is defined and is referred to as the budget. This can be defined in money, resource allocation (headcount), or a mix.
- Execution is expected to stay within budget. This is the responsibility of the line or project manager.

For a company or business unit in a mature state, the cost target for a product is defined as the affordable cost which can be estimated based on revenue and profit expectations for a certain period of time. If the company or business unit is in an investment phase, e.g. a startup, the cost target is usually defined by the available funds.

The financial model for a software product is typically structured similar to the income statement (also known as profit and loss statement, or P&L) for an entire company.

In particular, for software products, the income statement is often shown as in Fig. 3.9, with costs broken down into several categories. The first category, cost of revenue, is highly variable. Apart from cost of revenue, we usually distinguish between four other categories of operating expenses that are "fixed", i.e. they will not move immediately in synchrony with a short-term revenue spike or revenue decrease. These four fixed cost categories are: research and development (R&D), sales and marketing, general and administrative (G&A), and other operating expenses (such as asset depreciation).

Figure 3.9 shows the structure of a full income statement for a standalone software company, see for example the annual or quarterly reports of companies

Income Statement – Cost Structure

	Revenue	The "top line"
−	**Cost of revenue** or Cost of Goods Sold (COGS)	Revenue-related costs: parts, labor, e.g. support engineers
=	**Gross Profit**	
−	**Other Operating Expenses**	• Research & Development (R&D) • Sales & Marketing • General & Administrative (G&A) • Other operating expenses, e.g. depreciation of assets
=	**Operating Profit**	Profit from ongoing operations
−	**Non-Operating Expenses**	Interest paid or earned, taxes, ...
=	**Net profit**	The "bottom line"

Fig. 3.9 Income statement

like SAP, Salesforce, Adobe, Microsoft, or Google. For an initial assessment of the profit potential for a new product (e.g. for a startup) and for company-internal business cases, it is usually sufficient to stop at the operating profit. In the company-internal case, that's roughly equivalent to the contribution margin that the product contributes to the larger organization.

In most traditional "brick and mortar" business models, for example a manufacturing business or a retail operation, the cost of revenue (labor, parts, etc.) eats up most of the revenue, often in the 70% range. Only the remaining 30% of gross profit is available to cover the fixed cost listed above. This typically leaves rather small margins for operating profit and net profit. Service businesses, for example support or professional service organizations of software vendors, have a similar cost structure, since their main cost driver is the cost of people delivering the services, and this is classified as "cost of revenue" as well.

However, for pure software products, the income statement looks quite different: small cost of revenue often leaves a gross profit of 70% or more—and this is needed to cover high fixed costs, in particular in R&D. Usually, there are no expensive assets, so depreciation of assets is not a big concern either. Exceptions can come from investments in infrastructure and licenses from other vendors. In reality, many software businesses rely on a revenue mix that combines "pure" software revenue, e.g. from license sales, with revenue from support and professional services. Depending on the revenue mix, the structure of their income statement falls somewhere in the middle between the two extremes described above. There can be exceptions regarding low cost of revenue in the form of costs for embedded licenses or intellectual property, or profit sharing with partners.

Low cost of revenue also means low marginal cost, i.e. once the software has been developed and is up and running, it does not cost much more to serve an additional customer. This is a defining characteristic of digital business models and it gives software product managers a high degree of freedom in business model design and pricing, making it possible to stretch business models to an extent that is unthinkable in traditional industries, such as a freemium business model.

This choice in available business models and pricing strategies and the complexity that arises from combining multiple revenue sources makes a financial analysis mandatory for evaluating a software product strategy.

Due to the low marginal cost in many software products, the financial analysis often focuses mostly on revenue: costs are treated as unchangeable and the only question is: Can we find a price structure that enables the necessary unit sales in order to recoup our costs and generate a profit?

However, in more traditional manufacturing industries, this question is often approached the other way around: the target costing method starts with a desired competitive price point for a product and then sets a cost target that allows the company to manufacture and deliver the product and to generate a profit at the desired price. This approach may be useful for certain types of software products as well: for example if the potential market for a product is clearly limited, then development costs cannot be recouped through sales to more customers, and target costing can be helpful.

3.11.5 Revenue Model

Part of the business plan is the revenue model. According to [Popp11b], a business may combine multiple revenue models, and each revenue model can rely on multiple revenue streams (see Fig. 3.10). If multiple revenue streams are combined in a revenue model, this is called a hybrid revenue model. Hybrid revenue models are very common in the software industry: for example, the classic software license model often combines a license revenue stream with support revenues and revenue from product-related services, such as installation and customization services often called "delivery services".

Revenue streams are characterized by the following attributes:

- Compensator: who provides the compensation, i.e. revenue?
- Effect: the type of compensation, including—Payment.
  - No compensation, e.g. usage of open source software.
  - Compensation in other goods or services, e.g. a Google user compensates Google for its search service by providing information about his areas of interest.
- Rating: how is the consumption of goods or services measured?

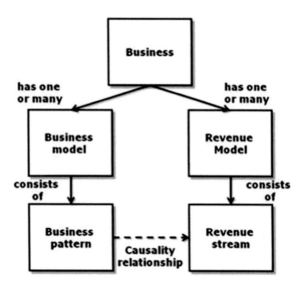

Fig. 3.10 Business Model
and Revenue Model
[Popp11b]

- Time-based, for example usage for 1 month,
- Usage-based, e.g. gigabytes of storage, number of unique or concurrent users that are permitted to use the product,
- Functionality-based, e.g. silver, gold, platinum editions with increasing functional scope.
• Charging: how is the compensation amount for a certain rating of goods and services determined?
  For example, charging a fixed fee per user per month for using the software.
    This also includes different options regarding the frequency of payment:
  - Recurring revenue from regular business: support services, rental models, IP [intellectual property] licensing.
  - One-time revenue types from regular business: perpetual license.
  - One-off revenue (not from the regular business): selling the IP, spin-offs, etc.

In order to come up with ideas for revenue streams, Osterwalder and Pigneur [OstPign10] suggest considering the following key questions:

• For what value are our customers really willing to pay?
• For what do they currently pay?
• How are they currently paying?
• How would they prefer to pay?
• How much does each revenue stream contribute to overall revenues?

Before building the revenue model, software product managers ought to work with Finance to understand which revenue recognition guidelines are applied in their organization: when exactly revenue can be recognized is especially tricky for software, varies somewhat between different accounting standards (e.g. IFRS which is heavily used in Europe vs. US-GAAP), and also depends on charging details (e.g. one-time license charge vs. recurring charges for a SaaS offering or a support contract) and bundling (e.g. pure software license vs. software bundled with professional services).

Product managers are typically in charge of building a revenue model that projects future revenue streams for their product, usually as a spreadsheet. There are two common approaches: extrapolation from the past vs. bottom-up. Both approaches use the established pricing strategy (see Sect. 3.10), as well as other input data, such as

- Current user and revenue base (in case of an existing product).
- Results from market analysis (market size, trends, growth rates, etc.).
- Planned sales channels.
- Planned investments in sales, marketing, customer acquisition efforts.
- Experience values regarding channel effectiveness, return on investment (ROI) of customer acquisition expenses, or historic sales ramp-up (adoption curves) for similar products.

Let's first look at the scenario of an enterprise software product in an established, "steady-state" market. The product is the market leader in terms of revenue share. The market itself has been growing at around 10% annually for several years, no major market disruptions are on the horizon and market forecasts from industry analysts agree that this growth pattern will continue for the next couple of years. The market has been very fragmented, but is consolidating, and the product has been gaining market share steadily, growing about 2% points above the market growth rate. The product still has "room to grow" by taking market share from its competitors, since its current market share is still well below 50%.

The company has managed to slowly drive up average deal sizes across channels, so that the historic revenue growth was achieved with only a small expansion in sales expenses. For the coming years, the company plans to continue on this trajectory regarding sales investments. The company will continue to update and evolve the product as it did in the past, and no pricing changes are planned.

Here we use the approach of extrapolation from the past. We may model future annual growth rates by taking future market growth rate projections from analysts and adding the 2% points that the product traditionally has "outgrown" the market. While building the revenue model this way is rather simple, note how many context factors from the past must continue to be true in the future for the revenue projection to hold water. If only one of these context factors changes, either in the market or company-internally (e.g. changes in sales approach and investment), the revenue model no longer provides plausible guidance.

Of course, that approach does not work for entirely new products where no historic data is available. We look at the scenario of a completely new product in a product category that does not exist yet. If successful, the product will establish this new product category. Here, it is tempting to start with the estimated market opportunity and to assume that the new product will capture a certain percentage of the market within a certain time period, say 1% in the first 3 years. This is called a "top-down" revenue model—a faith-based approach that does not enable any meaningful discussion, analysis, or planning. We prefer a bottom-up revenue model starting with projected customer base, which in turn is based on the sales and marketing strategy.

The model for the customer base may use the following inputs:

- Conversion rates along the customer acquisition process, for example for a web-based sales process.
- Other key metrics driving customer acquisition and retention, for example the "viral coefficient" where applicable (one new user on average draws in another x users (see [Ries11]) and churn rates (what percentage of the customer base do we lose in a given time period)).
- Planned investment levels in sales and marketing, e.g. number of sales representatives, online marketing budget, etc.
- Data on the effectiveness of channels, and of sales and marketing expenses, e.g. average revenue generated by a sales representative per year or effectiveness of customer acquisition efforts like online ads.
- Average deal size/order size (where applicable).

Once a customer base model is built, pricing information can be plugged in to create a revenue model. Since price structure and price levels are likely to change in the early phases of new product development, the model should accept pricing information as input parameters so that it can be changed easily.

Of course, when starting with a new product, all the inputs into the revenue model—from conversion rates to channel effectiveness to deal sizes—are assumptions. Historic data from comparable products may improve the quality of these assumptions, but they still remain assumptions. The Lean Startup movement emphasizes the importance of systematically validating all the assumptions that are critical to the success of a business model [Ries11]. As more and more inputs to the revenue model are validated, the plausibility of the revenue model increases.

Building a bottom-up revenue model requires more effort, but it provides a number of benefits: it can turn into a very helpful tool to assess viability of the planned sales approach, and to run what-if analyses for changes in pricing.

For example, for a product sold via the web channel, A/B tests may be used to study the impact of different price metrics, discounts, or price levels on buying behavior and conversion rates. Results from these tests can then easily be introduced into the revenue model to determine the financial impact of the pricing changes and changes in conversion rates.

Finally, the revenue model can also help detect inconsistent assumptions in the business model, especially regarding the interaction between sales channels and product structure: for example, in a B2B business model that relies primarily on license sales through a direct sales force with long sales cycles, each sales representative can close only a small number of deals per year. Therefore, the average deal size will have to be at least in the USD100,000 range.

3.11.6 Business Case

Since a product manager is responsible for the economic success of his product over its life cycle, business aspects play a major role in a product manager's tasks and activities, from the analysis and prioritization of individual requirements to the positioning of the whole product. We define

Business Case $=$ A decision support and planning approach for comparing the costs and benefits associated with a proposed initiative.

Depending on company rules, a business case may be required for each requirement within the requirements management process (see Sect. 4.4). At the minimum, a business case is required for any new release of a product: if an investment of $3M is proposed for a release there had better be a forecast of additional revenue from new customers or increased product usage which is sufficiently large over the vendor's return on investment (ROI) period to give the company their desired profit margin. The estimation of the cost side bears some risk, but is typically easier than the value side; for one thing, the costs all occur within the developing company's control. On the value side the challenge is threefold: often benefits and value are of a qualitative nature that is difficult to convert into actual earnings or savings; the monetary benefits may (and usually do) vary from customer to customer; and the benefits/value may be realized over an extended time period after the release is made available. A software value map to analyze value systematically can be helpful [KhuGorW13]. If benefits/value and costs are quantified, investment evaluation models such as NPV (Net Present Value), ROI (Return On Investment), or Pay Back Time can be applied to achieve comparability of alternatives.

To be effective, the business case should communicate the following information:

- The description of the undertaking (name, unique identifier, short text),
- The underlying assumptions,
- An estimate for the required investment (in absolute or relative numbers),
- The approach to generate business benefits with estimates for earnings over time (in absolute or relative numbers),
- A risk, sensitivity, and contingency analysis.

When business cases are used for selecting or prioritizing alternatives, relative numbers may be sufficient. When absolute numbers are used, there is considerable uncertainty and risk that needs to be addressed. This can be done by looking at different scenarios (e.g. best, median, worst) and analyzing the risks, the sensitivity of the estimates to the risks, and contingencies, i.e. possible actions to mitigate those risks. Given the high level of uncertainty, some people in the software industry claim that any business case is more a pseudo-scientific quantification of the gut feelings of the decision makers than a valid prediction. But even if this were true there is value, in particular from planning the approach to generate the identified business benefits and from the contingency planning. At the very least the exercise causes the product manager to think through and explain all the elements to decision makers.

A business case is credible when it is complete, balanced with important scenarios elaborated, and with underlying assumptions made explicit and accepted by all stakeholders. There is a lot of literature on business cases, e.g. [SheeGall15] or [Schmidt02].

With business cases, a continuous improvement process is highly recommended. Each business case needs to be revisited after an appropriate time so that actual outcomes can be compared to the business case and deviations can be analyzed. That helps the organization to learn, improve, and refine the business case.

For selecting or prioritizing alternatives, additional considerations can be helpful that consider what foregone when selecting a particular alternative:

Opportunity Cost = the comparative value of the next-best alternative when a decision is made.

Cost of Delay = the comparative value of earlier availability when a timing decision is made.

Lost revenue, lost opportunities or a worsened competitive position are all costs of delay.

When selecting or prioritizing alternatives as part of portfolio management, different financial management objectives can play a role dependent on where a product is in its life cycle (see Sect. 5.2).

3.11.7 Bundling

Another interesting business aspect is the bundling of products that can have an impact on the financial models of the individual products. We define:

Product Bundle = Set of products that is sold as one product with its own price.

A bundle can contain products from one or more vendors. There are different types of product bundles:

- Pure: The products are only sold as part of the bundle, not individually.
- Mixed: The products are sold as part of the bundle and at least some of them also individually.

There may be multiple motivations for bundling:

- The bundle makes it easier for the customer to buy a complete solution and signals that the vendor has already taken care of a tight integration of the involved products. The vendor hopes for increased revenue and profit or to exclude inroads of competition for part of a solution.

- The bundle is less expensive than the sum of the individual products and thus gives the customer the impression that he saves money by buying the bundle. Again the vendor hopes for increased revenue and profit since a percentage of the customers would not have bought all products in the bundle individually.
- The bundle combines market-leading products with products that are new or have strong competition. The vendor hopes for increased market share of the new or weaker products because for customers who buy the market-leading products anyway the bundled new or weaker products look like zero-cost add-ons.

The third case is a frequent cause for legal action if the vendor has a dominating position with his market-leading products. So Microsoft's plan to integrate Teams into Windows 11 bears a risk. In the second case, the price motivation has been analyzed scientifically (see [Biering04]), but unfortunately the results are often only applicable in special situations.

If a product manager is responsible for a product family, he may consider bundling within his family, but in most cases bundling means that several product managers have to cooperate, maybe even across multiple companies.

3.11.8 Summary and Conclusions

Product managers who have a pure technical background often struggle with the business aspects. However, these business aspects are of utmost importance with regard to the business success of the product over the strategic timeframe and the product life cycle. And in most companies the business aspects, in particular the financial model, are the number one driver for management decisions regarding the product. In this section we have looked at business case, financial model, forecasting, cost structure and management, revenue model, and bundling. In addition to these topics, we discuss Pricing in Sect. 3.10 and Performance and Risk Management in Sect. 3.14.

3.12 Ecosystem Management

3.12.1 Overview

Ecosystems have a significant impact on the work of the product manager. The product manager must conform to the role his company wishes to play in a particular ecosystem. The role has direct influence on the positioning of the product, the pricing strategy, the degree to which the product road map and requirements decisions depend on other players in the ecosystem. A product manager can influence the ecosystem strategy and its evolution.

This section describes the concept of ecosystems, partner programs and partner management, and the role of software product managers in that context.

3.12.2 Concept

Over the last 30 years the term "ecosystem" has found increasing usage. It is derived from biological ecosystems. The analogy expresses the interdependence of the players in business networks and was first drawn by Moore in 1993 [Moore93]. We define

Ecosystem = A set of businesses functioning as a unit and interacting with a shared market while maintaining beneficial relationships.

While ecosystems exist in all industries, they are especially important when it comes to software. There is no single vendor company in the software industry that covers the complete IT stack with its products. So if a customer wants to gain utmost value from a vendor's product he will almost always need additional products from other vendors. Only the combination will actually provide the value. So all vendors involved have dependencies on one another that need to be managed. This is typical for innovation platforms (see Sect. 2.2.1).

The situation becomes even more challenging when we look at multi-sided transaction platforms like internet marketplaces, or coordination platforms, e.g. in the area of supply chains (see Sect. 2.2.1). Here the platform company needs to define terms and conditions in a way that creates a balance so that the business models of the players on all sides are sufficiently attractive, the players stay on the platform and equity among stakeholders is ensured. An example is Uber who need to make their platform attractive for drivers by paying decent amounts of money, but also for passengers by ensuring high and fast availability of cars at relatively low prices. Work on the business model of a transaction platform falls under the responsibility of the platform manager. For more details on these scenarios see [ParAlsCho16] and [CusGaYof19].

We define

Software Ecosystem = A set of businesses functioning as a unit and interacting with a shared market for software and services while maintaining beneficial relationships.

These relationships are frequently underpinned by a common innovation platform (see Sect. 2.2.1) and operate through the exchange of information, resources, and artifacts.

The structural constituents of software ecosystems are stakeholders, relationships, boundaries, behavior, and strategies. Iansiti and Levien [IanLev04] define three principle roles participants in a business ecosystem can play:

- **Keystone**:
  A benevolent hub in the network that provides benefits to the ecosystem and its members. It usually provides the core of the innovation in an ecosystem. For technology-related ecosystems, this effect of keystone players is a key success factor for survival and adaptability of the overall ecosystem. Keystone players behave in favor of other players, especially by protecting niche players. The number and diversity of niche players determine the speed and diversity of innovation in an ecosystem, which is an important prerequisite for success. The

resulting distributed nature of the network makes it flexible and little vulnerable to external disruptions. Examples are Google in the Android ecosystem or Microsoft in the Windows ecosystem.

- **Dominator**:
  A hub that aims at controlling as much space in the network as possible. It leverages a critical position in the ecosystem to exploit or take over a large portion of the ecosystem. It is not interested in sharing value, but tries to capture most of the value itself. An example for a dominator is Apple who controls the IOS ecosystem to a large degree.
- **Niche players**:
  Most members of an ecosystem are niche players who do not try to compete with a keystone or dominator, but focus their business on critical competencies in narrow areas of expertise, if there is an opportunity to run a profitable business. They usually are smaller companies and outnumber keystone players or dominators. An example for niche players are app developers in the ecosystems of smartphone innovation platforms like Google's Android or Apple's IOS. Frequently successful niche players become acquisition targets of platform companies.

It is usually not part of the responsibilities of a software product manager to decide on the role his company wants to play in an ecosystem. This belongs into the realm of corporate strategy that is owned by executive management. Part of this decision is how proactively a company wants to influence the ecosystem and other players in it. Once these decisions are made, they have a significant impact on the work of the product manager, and he must conform to the role his company wishes to play in its ecosystem(s).

Among the niche players, there are different types of players in an ecosystem:

Development-related:

- Independent Software Vendor (ISV): Develops functional extensions, i.e. add-on or specific application as his product that uses the innovation platform product as a prerequisite and enhances its functionality. He is independent in the sense that he is not controlled or owned by the platform owner.
- Original Equipment Manufacturer (OEM): One company integrates the product of another company into its product offering.
- Technology provider: Provides relevant products and/or technology with interfaces to the platform product.
- Resource Provider: Provides code that is integrated in other players' products, or sends developers into other players' development teams, or provides operations services to other players.

Sales-related:

- Reseller: sells software products offered by a software vendor. The reseller has contractual relationships with the customers and with the vendor.

- Value Added Reseller/Remarketer (VAR): a reseller that offers a software product offered by a software vendor and adds components and/or services to them, e.g. customer-specific customizing. The VAR is helpful for better market penetration, and sometimes for enrichment of products with solution components.
- Intermediary: mediates between vendors and customers of software products, with the aim of them signing a contract, e.g. a provider of an internet marketplace.
- Original Equipment Manufacturer (OEM, see Sect. 2.2): An example is a database company licensing its software to a vendor of business application software to be included "under the hood" with the business application software. Here, the business application software vendor is the OEM whose brand name is visible, while the brand of the database vendor is less visible or entirely invisible. From the point of view of the database vendor, the business application vendor is one of their sales channels. The relationship may be considered as a type of sales and distribution outsourcing. The product integration can be visible to customers (black label approach) or invisible (white label approach).
- Value added distributor (VAD): is used for outsourcing of production and distribution activities, often for enrichment of products with solution components, for management of smaller partners and a better market penetration.
- Technological alliance: is often used as sales cooperation, for pre-installation of software on hardware, for completeness of solution offers and synergy in marketing.

Service-related (services to potential customers of products in the ecosystem):

- Consultants: Company or individual who offers solution definition (incl. product selection), business analysis etc.
- System integrator (SI): coordinates and performs the integration of software product components supplied by different vendors and customer-specific software. This includes the responsibility for the overall system design as well as the customizing and integration of product and service components and information management.
- Operations Provider: offers managed services like hosting, maintenance, etc.

Influencers:

- Consultants: may influence customers' buying decisions through their consulting work.
- Press: may influence customers' buying decisions through their coverage of relevant markets, products and companies.
- Market research companies: may influence customers' buying decisions through their coverage of relevant markets, products and companies.
- Customers: may influence other customers' buying decisions through their testimonials and their acting as reference customers for vendors.

An individual company can often be a player of more than one of these types. Competitors to the platform product or technology vendor of an ecosystem are usually not considered as part of the ecosystem unless there is a coopetition relationship, i.e. the same companies cooperate in one or more product areas and compete in other product areas.

If a company decides to influence its ecosystem and other players in it proactively it usually establishes some kind of partner program. We define

Partnership = Formalized relationship in a software ecosystem.

A partner program can be applied to all types of players in an ecosystem except influencers. For software more than for other products, a well-oiled network machine of diverse partners is a significant prerequisite for long-term success in addition to the traditional direct sales channels. For a software company, there are several good reasons for establishing and managing a partner network as part of a software ecosystem. Partners are needed in order to reach customers that could not be reached fast enough or at all with a direct sales force. To build up a sales organization is time and cost-intensive and requires significant revenue per person. A sales partner may be able to cover a sales area more easily and efficiently by combining products of several software companies and his own products and services. Moreover, many sales partners are already established in the market with customer contacts as value added resellers (VARs) or system integrators [Bech15].

Customers of business software are usually not interested in a particular software product, but in a solution for their business problems and an implementation of their business processes as efficiently as possible. Because of the complexity and interdependence of business software, the desired solution is typically not achieved by a single software product and requires significant tailoring and implementation effort. Customers frequently rely on qualified consulting and service companies that are contracted for the implementation and very often also for conception and design of the solution. This gives these companies a strong influence on the selection of software products, sometimes the decision is part of the contracted task. That is why partnering with these consulting companies can be more important for a software vendor than direct sales. This is valid for application software and especially for infrastructure software products. In many cases, the decision for a certain software technology or a software product is not made by the customer, but by the vendor of an application software solution who decides for a base technology, or by the system integrator who favors a technology or product and uses it as an integral part of his offer.

Last but not least, vendors whose products are not competitive, but cooperative, form technology alliances. These alliances are often created for the purpose of bundling sales resources. This can happen as sales cooperation, or by pre-installing software products on the hardware platform of another manufacturer. The advantage of pre-installation for the hardware manufacturer is that the additional software products make his product more attractive. The advantage for the software vendor is that this channel allows easy access to many end users that would otherwise fail to be addressed in the usual sales process. In view of the high sales volume, the purchase commitment, the negligible amount of time and effort invested in sales and distribution, and perhaps even the money saved on media and documentation, the software vendor will offer to sell his software on very favorable conditions. Technology alliances also aim at offering integrated solutions that the market requires by combining products and services of several partners so that the customer can assume a proven level of integration. Often partners want to benefit from the image, the brand or the market position of other partners.

In the end all partnering activities have one goal: faster growth and market leadership. A balance between growth and profitability needs to be found: The software vendor gives some part of the revenue and/or profit to its partners in order to grow faster and reach a leading position in the market.

A comprehensive discussion of business ecosystems can be found in [JanBrCus13]. Adnar and Kapoor [AdnKap10] look at what technology leadership and innovation mean in an ecosystem. [ParAlsCho16] and [CusGaYof19] analyze business models, in particular for multi-sided transaction platforms, and consequences for ecosystem management.

3.12.3 Partner Programs

Depending on the role that a company wants to play in a particular ecosystem, the company needs to be visible as an active member of the ecosystem and influence and support it. This work is typically split between Product Management, Development and Marketing. When larger partner programs generate a significant workload and require a uniform management of terms and conditions, a centralized partner management organization may be the appropriate organizational solution. But even then, product management needs to be involved on a strategic level. Software product managers are well advised to participate in, contribute to and try to influence the ecosystems important for their products. Partnerships and alliances that are required to actually provide a complete offering to the customer need special attention.

A partner program typically specifies:

- Structure of the partner program, e.g. different types and levels.
- The prerequisites that a partner must fulfill for participation.
- Contributions of the software vendor, e.g. for joint marketing, education, early technical information in case of changes, support, or platform for information exchange among members of the program.
- Terms and conditions, in particular with regard to sales.
- Additional rules, e.g. for joint marketing and sales activities.

When selecting partners, the strength and stability of a company, compatibility of business models, potential conflicts, market access, skills, and the level of commitment are important criteria (see also [FoFrFiLG14]). Partnerships only make sense when they are beneficial to both parties and the parties trust each other. This win-win-character needs to be ensured when designing terms and conditions of partner programs or negotiating individual partnerships.

An example of this not working well is IBM acquiring Lotus to take advantage of an established channel relationship and then putting complex products into that channel which was well suited to office and PC products but not at all for complex server products.

SAP is an example for a company that has an exceptionally strong focus on partner management with a partner management unit reporting directly to the CEO. Marketing is responsible for sales-oriented partner management (see Sect. 6.3). Here Product Management is involved in dealing with the partner's product requirements. Product Management takes care of product-related in-depth discussions with market research companies and journalists, the overall positioning within the ecosystem, and the selection of product-specific partners.

3.12.4 Summary and Conclusions

Software ecosystems have a significant impact on the business success of their stakeholders. In this section we have looked at the different roles and types of stakeholders. Companies can intensify cooperation within an ecosystem by establishing a partner program or joining other players' partner programs. While the big software companies invest a lot of resources in extensive partner programs in order to manage their ecosystems proactively, smaller players often do not give sufficient attention to this subject. In any case it is part of the software product manager's responsibility for product strategy to influence his company's approach to ecosystem management for the benefit of his product.

3.13   Legal Aspects

3.13.1 Overview

Software product managers are usually not legal experts. And they do not have to be. However, since legal risks can have a significant negative impact on the business success of a product, product managers need to be aware of those risks and take action to avoid or mitigate them. It is advisable to involve legal experts in these topics. But a product manager needs to know the important questions to ask the legal experts. That is what this section is about. We cover contracts, the protection of intellectual property, open source, and data protection in more detail.

3.13.2 Contracts

In this section the focus is on contracts between vendor and customer. The chosen delivery model, i.e. licensed product vs. Software-as-a-Service (SaaS) offering (see Sect. 3.6.2) determines the type of contract.

The term "license" is a non-technical legal term which is not described by statute. Therefore, the understanding of what a license is may differ, in particular it may denote the commercial license model, i.e. the way that license fees are calculated, or it may refer to the grant of rights of use under intellectual property laws, or under copyright laws, all of which may differ from jurisdiction to jurisdiction. In the latter sense, a license describes to which extent and under which conditions the licensee can use an item, e.g. software, which is subject to intellectual property rights which are usually protected by copyright or patent or other mechanism. These rights of use are granted by the licensor who may be the owner of all rights in such an item, i.e. the software company, or may be an entity authorized to grant the license, e.g. a reseller. The term "license contract" means an agreement between the licensor and the licensee about all terms in connection with one or more licenses. With software, the term "license" usually describes the scope of rights of use which the licensor grants to the licensee. Such rights may be exclusive or non-exclusive, perpetual or for a certain time period only, worldwide or geographically limited, or they may be limited in some other way, e.g. geographically or timely. Software licenses may also allow only a particular way of using the software, e.g. only on premise or also for Software-as-a-Service offerings. Please note that the EU Software Directive EC/2009/24 provides for certain legal rules on the protection of software for the European Union. For instance, under such Directive, the customer who has purchased software against a one-off payment is entitled to resell the software (even if such resale is prohibited by contract).

In case of SaaS or other software-intensive services, the customer does not acquire a license, but a service. The service provider needs to make sure that it holds the required rights of use, e.g. by way of license contracts with licensors of the software that is used as part of the service offering which explicitly allow this kind of use. Customers of such a service do not need license contracts, but only service contracts with the service provider, unless a proprietary client is required to be installed on the customer's system. In Infrastructure as a Service [IaaS]scenarios the license requirements may be different: the IaaS provider or the customer may need a license for the software installed that runs on the infrastructure provided by the IaaS provider.

The contract by which software or a software-based service is "acquired", may be negotiated individually or, particularly in the mass-market, based on so-called "standard terms and conditions," which describe the generally applicable legal terms.

The scope of the license or service describes the content of the agreement, i.e. the scope of software, documentation, services and hardware included. Vendor services (e.g. for custom modifications, initial migration work and for user training) and further services such as additional copies of the documentation are usually defined in a separate services agreement. It is worthwhile here to explain an accounting principle which will be important to the vendor (and which may explain certain vendor behaviors to the customer): in most countries, revenue for OTC software is generally bookable upon delivery of usable product and invoice to the customer. However, if there are services to be performed or an acceptance test following modifications or there is a right of the customer to cancel, then the revenue will not be bookable until all of the contingency conditions have been performed and are accepted. In today's frenetic scramble for more and earlier revenue, such contingencies will be very hard for a vendor to accept.

One of the peculiarities of software is that inherent in most contracts there is an assumption by both the vendor and the customer that the software contains errors (bugs). That is why the terms and conditions of the license must define how such bugs and any necessary modifications are to be dealt with. That is also why there is no guarantee with software except possibly a money-back provision if the customer is not satisfied; this generally takes the form of a trial period after which you must pay or you will no longer be able to use some or all of the functionality or a "pay now and we will refund your money within xx days if you are not satisfied". The "xx" usually ranges between 30 and 90, seldom longer. Both of these approaches, while helpful to the customer, raise revenue recognition issues for the vendor, as well as compensation issues to the selling organization or individual.

Warranty means that the vendor agrees to make the product perform as promised in specifications, advertising, or sales presentations during a limited time. The warranty period is typically 1 year, in some jurisdictions 2 years, unless specifically stipulated otherwise. Assistance with debugging and provision of fixes are usually free of charge during the warranty period, i.e. included in the license price. This situation may continue longer if maintenance is paid for the license. In the case of SaaS, maintenance is part of the scope of service anyway.

In this area the definition of a "bug" is always a critical item. A frequent matter of customer/vendor dispute is determination of the severity of a bug and whether or not it really is a bug or rather a request for product enhancement. IBM says that if the code does not do what the product specification says it does, that is a bug. However, on occasion, when a bug cannot be fixed, the specification is changed rather than the code. It may be impossible to achieve a legal definition that is absolutely airtight.

A part of every license will stipulate whether or not the licensee may transfer the license to another physical computer, how to proceed within a local area network, and how copies of the code are to be handled. Another critical issue is whether or not the licensee may transfer the license to a third party. In the European Union, there is a High Court decision that this kind of transfer is generally allowed. In other jurisdictions, the vendor may still try to prevent this.

Under type of charges one will not necessarily find the specific price, but possibly how the product is charged in terms of metrics. This is a candidate for a product specific addendum to a generic vendor license.

Vendors try to limit their liability as much as possible. Usually if a customer wants to continue to use the debugging service described under "Warranty" and have access to fixes past the end of the warranty period, he must acquire a maintenance contract. We recommend vendors to keep the maintenance contract separate from the license contract. In the maintenance contract, the vendor will define the entitlements being conveyed, charging and duration, and termination provisions. The vendor may also define a support escalation process which brings more resources to bear depending on the severity of the bugs. But see also under "Warranty" what a fix may entail. Some vendors also include upgrades to new product versions in their maintenance agreements. Various other aspects of the maintenance services may also differ from vendor to vendor.

In general, a vendor reserves the right to terminate maintenance for a software product or product version, the common practice being to give notice of this in advance. The vendor does this with the aim of reducing maintenance costs and motivating customers still using older product versions to migrate to new ones. The announcement that maintenance services are to be discontinued is usually not received very well by the customers involved. This regularly gives rise to fierce protests that are then settled by reaching a compromise if the protesting customers are important to the vendor.

Different geographies will have different views on this. Different product sets may attract different reactions. In Japan there is a tendency to stick with a product for a very long time, to the extent of being willing to pay extra for product "n" maintenance in order not to have to move to "n + 1". This is an extension of the adage "if it ain't broke, don't fix it." But this can also delay introduction of new technology. Microsoft recently experienced this when they announced the discontinuation of maintenance for Windows XP.

Then there are miscellaneous legal provisions that include the definition of the period during which one can make claims, governing law, and which courts will be used in case of dispute. Other legal provisions to be included pertain to the mutual handling of confidential information as well as to the rights and responsibilities entailed in terminating the license agreement, legal remedies and issues of compensation for damages and liability. A corporate customer in doubt about a producer's soundness may insist on a source code escrow (escrow service). This allows the corporate customer to access the source code in the event that the producer declares bankruptcy, thereby ensuring that maintenance can be continued. While customers sometimes ask for this, it is usually more a bargaining chip in negotiation than a practical request. The source code of an operating system, for example, would not be helpful for a customer. Some vendors like IBM even have large chunks of code in proprietary languages for which compilers are not commercially available. And where would the customer find the resource and talent to work on such code? Often customers lose interest in such a request when confronted by the cost of having an escrow agent keep a copy of the code.

Conflicts between vendor and enterprise customer generally arise in one of four areas:

- Whether the product is doing what the vendor claimed it would do and if not whose fault it is that it is not performing;
- The way in which the product is being used compared to what the vendor authorized; and
- The quantity of product in use compared to what the vendor authorized (for license contracts);
- Unused quantities of the product which the customer paid for but which he is not using, which is referred to as "shelfware" (for license contracts).

The license contract attempts to deal with most of these items. Examining the list of potential conflicts between vendor and customer, one can conclude that most of them arise because a software "purchase" typically does not mean that ownership or any proprietary rights are transferred as they usually are in the case of material products. Only a right to use is granted by the vendor, subject to various restrictions and often priced based on the scope of use or projected use. This circumstance gives rise to a legal complexity that results in similarly complex licensing terms and conditions, the details of which frequently differ from one country to the next, since the local legal requirements must always be taken into account.

Contrast the acquisition of software with that of a tangible widget: if you buy a shovel, you can use it 1 day to dig a trench, lend it to a friend the next day to mix cement, and your wife may use it to plant roses the third day. In fact, if one discovered that he had purchased too many shovels, he could try to sell his extras. Not so with software which will probably have restrictions on the purpose for which it may be used, the number and nature of the people who may use it, and possibly on where and how it may be used and/or resold. This difference has arisen in large part because of the relative ease of creating new software widgets from the original as opposed to a manufactured widget. A purchaser cannot create another identical shovel without incurring substantial cost, probably more than the cost of purchasing a new one, whereas a licensee can usually create another copy of a software product with a few clicks of his mouse. Because of this disparity software vendors have built in safeguards to ensure they receive revenue for all copies in use (or in some cases, installed). The wording of the terms and conditions of the license and related documents has by now become so creative that in some states in the USA, e.g. California, initiatives have (unsuccessfully) been undertaken calling for a law to regulate standard software license agreements, as the terms and conditions of license agreements now used by vendors can often no longer be understood by either retail or corporate customers nor on occasion by the vendors themselves.

SaaS contracts usually contain a service level agreement (SLA). SLAs stipulate which services a customer can expect to receive from a provider. In particular, this may include:

- Functional scope,
- Availability as an average as well as the maximum length of downtime,
- Quality in terms of absolute errors per time period according to degree of severity and maximum time for debugging according to degree of severity,
- Technical Performance, e.g. response time behavior or throughput rates,
- Scope and quality of user support, e.g. hotline, and maximum reaction time to operational demands, e.g. special evaluation of data on hand,
- Reaction time to new functional demands,
- Test options for new releases and versions including the scope of support and maximum debugging time according to degree of severity,
- Backup frequency and maximum restore time,
- Disaster recovery measures.

From a customer perspective, an SLA only makes sense if the contract includes penalties that must be paid by the service provider in the event of a breach of the terms defined in the SLA. The purpose of this is to motivate the provider and compensate for damage incurred by the customer in the event of a system failure.

A corporate IT organization acts as a service provider for the company's other business units. The services provided include further development and operation of the software and hardware used to support the business processes of the other departments. Whereas in the past the relationship between the in-house IT department and other departments was often informal, it has become common practice to use formal service level agreements (SLAs) to define this relationship, especially if the IT organization has been restructured as a legal self-contained corporate entity, almost like an outsourcer.

3.13.3 Protection of Intellectual Property

Introducing groundbreaking innovation with a new product or as part of an existing product can lead to a significant market differentiation and to major competitive advantages. The software product manager will then be responsible for finding a way to turn these competitive advantages into market success and safeguarding the competitive edge as long as possible.

There are a number of different legal constructs for the protection of intellectual property. From a macro-economic view, protection leads to more innovation since it increases the return on investments in innovation. On the downside the use of the innovative idea by others is delayed or made more expensive, since it cannot be directly copied. An example is a pharmaceutical company that develops a new drug and keeps the price high, thereby limiting its use.

On the micro-economic level, if a company seeks legal protection it needs to make a description of what it wants to protect public which makes it easier for competitors to understand it and duplicate it legally (and sometimes illegally). Since this can be difficult to prove with software, smaller companies sometimes avoid publishing their innovations, whereas larger corporations mostly prefer it. The advantages are the protection of competitive advantage, possibly an extra income through license fees, negotiating leverage in case of conflicts with other companies having similar software, and the marketing aspect of an innovative corporate image. Of course, there is no automatic correlation between the innovative capability of a company and the number of patents it holds, since the acceptance of a patent does not signify that the content is useful. So far, the general public does not seem to have realized this.

Software is primarily protected by copyright. The copyright protects the source code and object code in its given form. Copyright does not protect the underlying ideas, functions and algorithms and a copyright infringement thus presupposes an unchanged use of the software code. Product material such as manuals, brochures and product presentations are usually also protected. There are three more fundamental legal constructs which may play a role for the protection of intellectual property related to software:

- Trademark: Protection for the names of brands, i.e. brands do not apply to the software itself but only to the brand under which it is marketed.
- Trade Secret: Protection of company-internal knowledge (primarily against employees). This protection is exercised by restricting knowledge and access to a very small number of people and by using non-disclosure agreements. In most jurisdictions, trade secrets are only protected under unfair competition laws.
- Patent: Protection of the specific technical concept or idea. In most jurisdictions, patent protection can generally only be obtained for software which is integrated into a technical solution to a problem.

Traditionally, text has been subject to copyright law, technology to patent law. Since software became an issue, legal authorities and software developers, seeking protection for their intellectual property, have sought to choose existing recognized forms of protection under the law and have tried to press software into these existing alternatives [Klemens06] not accepting the fact that it does not really fit. This has led to continuous controversial discussions and country-specific regulations that are not aligned internationally.

In the US up until 1980, patent rights were hardware-oriented, i.e. it was hardly possible to have software patented. In response to pressure from software vendors, a Supreme Court decision changed the rules. Suddenly almost everything was patentable, even business processes. This resulted in a glut of patent applications, some of which seem rather useless or even ridiculous [Klemens06, p. 1 ff.].

As long as software patents refer to implementation details, they can be circumvented by implementing the functionality in some other way. This becomes more difficult if user interface elements that implicitly describe a business process are patented (see the Amazon example below).

Some years ago, conflicts arose regarding open source software and patents, as companies introduced patented elements into open source processes and subsequently requested license fees. All open source groups refused to accept this, arguing that using patents this way prevents progress. In 2002, open source guru Richard Stallman said that U.S. patent logic would have forced Beethoven to pay Mozart for the right to create a new symphony.

The monetary judgments that have been sought and sometimes granted in patent infringement cases in the US are increasingly seen as life-threatening for participants in the US software market.

The way that patent offices review software patents is also being criticized more and more. Officially, an application may not be accepted as a patent if its content already constitutes public property, i.e., whatever is already generally being used may not be patented. Unfortunately, there are good examples showing that patent offices were not capable of judging this. In [Besaha03] Besaha proposes measures for improving the patent process. In two ground-breaking rulings in April 2007, the US Supreme Court decided to lower the requirements regarding the non-obviousness test (Teleflex vs. KSR International) and restricted the applicability of US patent law to US territory (AT&T vs. Microsoft). The America Invents Act of 2011 brought some improvements, but no fundamental change.

Amazon is a widely discussed example of how patents can be used to safeguard the competitive edge of a product platform. Amazon had its one-click technology patented, making the ordering process extremely easy for registered customers. This discussion revolves around the issue of patentability. Opponents argue that, ever since the invention of the mouse, a click has always been used to effect a transaction. In their opinion, this technology is therefore not patentable. Proponents say that this special type of one-click technology used in connection with the online commercial transaction process for which Amazon has submitted a patent application did not previously exist in this form and can therefore be patented. In Alice Corp. v. CLS Bank International, the US Supreme Court decided in 2014 that an abstract idea cannot be patented just because it is implemented on a computer. Since then, hardly any patents on pure software or business processes have been granted in the US anymore.

This subject is being heatedly discussed in Europe, too. In compliance with the current European patent agreements, neither a computer program nor a business method can be patented as such. However, since it is not clear how a computer program differs from an invention that includes a computer program as one component among others, the European patent office has accepted software-related patents in the past few years. The urgency for a European patent law is obvious since the heterogeneous legal situation within the European Union means costs for patent applications are higher than in the US by a factor of 10. The European Commission has repeatedly started legislative processes in order to establish more explicit common regulations. The latest one is the European Unitary Patent law accepted by the European parliament in 2012. It only requires Europe-wide patents to be filed in three languages: French, English and German. Currently it is expected that the ratification process will be finished soon so that the European Unitary Patent law will come into effect in 2022.

Changes in the legal situation in both the USA and Europe regarding the granting of software patents can be expected on an ongoing basis given the discussions described above. Yet, regardless of how the legal situation develops, the software product manager will still be responsible for considering a patent application as a means of protecting intellectual property and safeguarding competitive advantages.

There are additional ways and means to do this. A key factor is assuring that valuable technical employees continue to be committed to the company. Studies show that typically $<10\%$ of the development staff actually possess the essential product- or technology-related skills. These are the employees that the company definitely wants to retain. This requires company-wide personnel retention programs that are generally not within the software product manager's scope of responsibility or authority. However, the software product manager needs to ensure that the employees relevant to his product are included in these programs. The competitive advantage can also be maintained by continuing to expand the differentiating elements through further product development.

   A major problem for all vendors selling software licenses is software piracy. IDC conducts studies for the Business Software Alliance (BSA) on global software piracy quite frequently. According to the latest study [BSA18] 37% of all software installations worldwide are not properly licensed leading to a total revenue loss of $ 46 billion in 2017. The piracy rate ranges from 90% in Libya to 15% in the US. Even if these numbers are a bit inflated there is no doubt that there is a significant problem and only slow progress. Many large software vendors now insist on the contractual right to audit customers as one way of curbing losses. That of course offers no protection for software usable by single clients, pirated versions of which are often available in Russia, China, and elsewhere for a fraction of the normal cost. Microsoft now checks routinely whether the requestor has a legitimate license before allowing downloads of maintenance and upgrades. There are quite a number of publications on what companies can do to prevent piracy, e.g. [CollThom02] and [GopSand97]. One of the attractive features of SaaS for vendors is that it eliminates the piracy risk.

3.13.4 Open Source

On the sourcing side (see Sect. 3.9), Open Source software is frequently an (important) part of software development projects and may help to reduce development cost and time [Popp19]. However, as all software, open source software may be subject to copyright protection. Thus, the developer of an open source software component is owner of any pertaining copyrights and offers modules free of charge under an open source license agreement. Consequently, a company which uses open source software for its own development processes has to comply with its license terms. An according license contract is frequently concluded (implicitly) when downloading or installing the open source component.

   A great variety of open source licenses is available [DeLaat05]. From the perspective of the user of open source, the so-called free licenses are not causing many problems. These licenses simply allow any kind of use of the open source software free of charge without stipulating any further restrictions, apart from uncomplicated formal requirements (e.g. Creative Commons' CC0, BSD License, MIT License).

   More difficulties can be caused by the so-called copyleft licenses which often-times govern the use of open source components [e.g. the GNU-Licenses (GPL, LGPL and GFDL)]. The underlying idea of copyleft licenses is that the open source software is made available free of charge and thus any further development of such copyleft software may only be distributed on the basis of the copyleft license. In practice, this means that the source code of software which was developed by using open source software must be offered free of charge—at least to anyone who acquires a copy of the machine readable code (object code), sometimes also to the general public. Dangerously, it does not matter how significant the open source code was in developing software. If only an open source code snippet is used, the respective copyleft license applicable to such snippet applies to the entire software (so-called viral effect). As long as such software is used for mere internal purposes of a corporation, the copyleft license effect does not apply. As soon as the object code is sold (stand-alone or as part of a hardware product), the obligations of the copyleft license apply, in particular the above mentioned duty to make available the source code, and formal requirements, such as the obligation to mention the applicable open source license in the source code. This may also apply if the object code is made available via a SaaS solution or the code is made available within a group of companies.

If open source code from various origins has been used, multiple open source licenses may apply in parallel—making it impossible to comply with all of them (in case of distribution). In case of an infringement, the owner of the rights (as a rule, the developer(s) of the respective open source code) has the right to request halting the use of the software and to claim damages. Damages may e.g. be calculated by the amount of profit made by distributing the software in violation of the open source license. Ruffin and Ebert [RufEbe04] look at the risks in more detail.

Companies which are developing software should implement an open source compliance process. In this process, a list of open source licenses which are compliant with the intended distribution model is set up and developers (employees, freelancers and subcontractors) are prohibited from using any open source software for which other than the listed licenses apply. If a developer requests the use of non-listed software, the pertaining licenses have to be checked by the legal department (or outside counsel). In case the respective open source license, e.g. copyleft, is not in compliance with the intended distribution model, the open source code should not be made part of the proprietary software to be developed. An option to nevertheless use the respective open source software, is to make it a part of a separate component which interacts through defined interfaces with the rest of the software. This approach may allow the software-developing company to avoid the obligation to make available the source code of the entire software free of charge, but limit such software to the component comprising of open source software.

A topic of some dispute is whether or not SaaS has to be considered as distribution under the copyleft licenses. Only a few open source licenses provide specific and clear rules in this regard, and in the absence of clear license clauses, the implications are unclear. It can be argued that SaaS is not distribution since the object code is not sold and not transferred to the customer. However, the purpose of copyleft licenses is to ensure free availability of the source code in case of commercial use. The Free Software Foundation, issuer of the most common copyleft license family, the General Public License (GPL), has expressed the view that distribution via SaaS does not equal distribution in the sense of the license. However, there are a number of open source licenses now, e.g. AGPL, that explicitly address the SaaS scenario.

3.13.5 Data Protection

European Union (EU) data protection law (primarily the GDPR—General Data Protection Regulation) applies to all companies and branch offices within the European Economic Area (EEA) and also to other companies to the extent they collect, process or use personal data with regard to services offered to or monitoring of means located in the EEA data subjects. The EU data protection law has served as a model for many other jurisdictions. Consequently, various other countries have enacted data protection laws which are meeting the EU data protection requirements, or are even more restrictive, e.g. Switzerland, Canada, Israel, Argentina, Australia etc. However, in many other countries, e.g. in the USA, the approach to data protection is fundamentally different. Whereas in the EU any kind of personal data (i.e. any data which relates or can be related to an individual) is protected irrespective of its sensitivity, in the US numerous special data protection laws apply in certain areas, e.g. for health data or credit card data; outside those areas the general principle of privacy applies which only grants protection to sensitive data from private spheres. As a result, e.g. personal data of employees is subject to the data protection laws in the EU, but not, at least in principle, in the US. However, the California Consumer Privacy Act (CCPA) now provides for some data protection rules similar to the GDPR.

Under the GDPR the company running software to process personal data, e.g. ERP software, CRM software etc., is responsible for data protection compliance as the so-called controller. Hence, the software-developing company is not directly in charge of data protection compliance. However, customers are, and will become more and more, aware of data protection issues and will thus likely request software which takes into account data protection principles and requirements, such as data minimization including pseudonymization wherever possible, access by users on a need to know basis only (roles) and data security. Moreover, GDPR establishes the principle of privacy by design and the right to be forgotten, among other regulations. Art. 25 GDPR codifies the principle of privacy by design/default. Such regulation requires controllers to purchase and develop software which is compliant with GDPR requirements.

The situation is fundamentally different if the software company runs the software and makes it available to its clients under a SaaS distribution model. In such cases, the client's personal data is processed on the company's server infrastructure. Nevertheless, the customer remains the controller of its data who remains responsible to ensure data protection compliance. As a rule, the SaaS provider is considered to be a commissioned data processor under Art. 28 GDPR. In such a case, the controller and the SaaS provider have to conclude a commissioned data processing agreement according to which the SaaS provider commits to comply with the directions of the controller, allows regular checks and controls and implements adequate technical and organizational measures for data security. Special restrictions may apply in certain areas, e.g. telecommunication, health data, insurance data, tax data etc.

To the extent that personal data is transferred from the EEA to recipients outside of the EEA, SaaS requires additional precautions if the recipient's country has not been approved by the EU commission as a safe country. The typical solution is that the controller and the SaaS provider agree on the so-called EU model clauses which oblige the data importer (i.e. the SaaS provider) to comply with the fundamental principles of EU data protection law. For recipients in the USA, the privacy shield safe harbor rules used to help to comply with GDPR requirements, but in 2020 the European Court of Justice decided them to be unlawful. As a consequence of this ECoJ decision (Schrems II), the EU Model Clauses alone are not deemed to be sufficient to justify a transfer of personal data to the US. The EU Commission and the US government are working on a new treaty that can provide a new reliable legal foundation.

The advantage of commissioned data processing is that the transmission of personal data from the customer to the SaaS provider (and back), which is triggered by the use of the software, is as a matter of principle not considered a transfer in the sense of the law. However, as mentioned above, this applies only provided that the SaaS provider has no discretion how to process the data and processes the data exclusively for the customer's purposes. If this precondition is not fulfilled each and every transmission of data between the customer and the SaaS provider needs to be based on the data subject's consent or a statutory permission.

3.13.6 Summary and Conclusions

Software product managers need to be aware of the legal risks related to their products which have the potential significantly to harm the business success of the product. And they need to address these risks in cooperation with legal experts. We have described risks and in the areas of contracts, protection of intellectual property, open source, and data protection. There are additional risks such as governance, finance, supply-chain, delivery commitments, laws on general terms and conditions, blacklisting of countries for specific software components etc. which are increasingly relevant (see for instance the growing impact of governance rules and transparency laws).

The term "compliance" is widely used now. It describes the goal that organizations aspire to achieve in their efforts to ensure that they are aware of and take steps to comply with all relevant laws and regulations (see Sect. 5.5). Software vendors can achieve competitive advantages in B2B markets by helping their customers to achieve compliance.

3.14   Performance and Risk Management

3.14.1 Overview

Once the product strategy is defined, business measures or key performance indicators (KPIs) are needed for continuous tracking and analysis of the business performance of the product. Ideally, these will address all elements of the product strategy. The measurement results help the organization to learn and improve, and to track whether the product is following or drifting away from the business model and targets and so as to take appropriate action.

As with any business activity, there are inherent risks that need to be identified and managed. Risk Management means the continuous tracking and analysis of risks identified in connection with the software product be it in development, sales, customer use or anything else. Again appropriate and timely action needs to be taken if needed.

3.14.2 Performance Management

Figure 3.11 shows examples for frequently used measures in four perspectives. Often the measures are standardized on the corporate level. If, however, the software product manager has the freedom to define them he must balance the trade-offs between what ideally ought to be measured and what can be measured in a relatively simple and cost-effective manner (see also Sect. 5.7).

An example of a comprehensive measurement approach is the Balanced Score Card (BSC) [KapNor96a, KapNor96b]. Balanced Score Card (BSC) defines a suitable framework for translating a product's strategy into a coherent set of performance measures. It complements traditional financial indicators with measures of performance for customers, internal business and innovation and improvement activities. Although a comprehensive framework, BSC needs to be carefully planned and implemented as it is complex, time consuming, and expensive to define and track relevant measures. Figure 3.11 shows a slightly different definition of perspectives.

The financial perspective (see Fig. 3.11) defines the long-term objectives of a product. While profitability is the most emphasized financial objective, other financial objectives are also possible depending on the life cycle stage of the product. For example, in the growth stage, sample measures are sales growth rate by segment, percentage of revenue from new product, in the maturity stage, sample measures are cross-selling, indirect profitability, cash-to-cash cycle, in the decline stage, sample measures are percentage of unprofitable customers, etc.

In the customer/market perspective, product managers identify the customer and market segments in which the product will compete and the measures of the product's performance in these targeted segments. Examples of such measures include new customer acquisition, customer satisfaction, and customer retention. Some of the measures will help the product manager to determine how well the product is performing in its target market, as well as in comparison to competitors.

In the internal business/organizational perspective, managers identify the critical internal processes in which the company needs to excel in order to deliver the product successfully. Sample measures include process quality, process cycle time, and other speed and cost measures.

The innovation and learning perspective identifies the infrastructure needed to create long-term growth and improvement. Sample measures include human capital

Perspective	Business canvas	Sample measures
Financial	Revenue streams and cost structure	Revenue (monthly recurring revenue (MRR), average revenue per user (ARPU) and customer lifetime value (CLTV)), profit and loss (P&L) metrics such as gross margin and EBIT
Customer / Market	Value proposition, customer relationships, customer segments	Customer satisfaction score (CSAT), net promoter score (NPS), customer perceived value, customer retention rate and churn rate, number of registered users; market share, share of (market) growth, share of (customer) wallet, customer acquisition cost (CAC), share of market spend
Internal business / Organizational	Key activities, key partners, channels	Process quality, process cycle time; speed metrics such as time-to-market, time-to-revenue, customer time-to-value (TTV); cost metrics such as cost of quality (COQ) and customer onboarding cost
Innovation and learning	Key resources	Human capital measures

Fig. 3.11 Mapping of four performance perspectives to business canvas segments and sample measures

measures (employee retention, employee satisfaction, employee skill, structural capital etc.).

Using all four perspectives together helps to reveal the existing gaps between people, systems and procedures that need to be bridged for delivering the promised value to customers and meeting the company's financial objectives. It is important to note that measures related to financial, market and customer perspectives are usually owned by the product managers; the process owner usually owns measures related to the internal business process perspective. However, the product manager can also use these measures for performance measurement of the product.

The choice of measures has to be a careful one since the chosen metrics should enable effective decision support and be simple to measure (see also Sect. 5.7). [FotrFric16] shows how analytics can help product managers with decision-making. While so-called vanity metrics make a company feel good, they do not provide actionable insight. Thus, a product manager needs to select actionable metrics (that provide insight and support decision-making). For example, during the growth phase of a paid web service, we recommend continued increases in budget for customer acquisition initiatives to take advantage of the growth opportunity. However, in that situation, focusing solely on the number of registered users in most cases is a vanity metric—what really matters in that situation is the number of users relative to effort/ acquisition costs. If the number of users is increasing by 50%, it might look good at first sight (vanity metric), but if the average acquisition cost per user shows a trend of increasing heavily over time, it is actually not a good development. There is a risk that the product will run into a situation where acquisition costs per user are getting higher than the average lifetime value of a new user. That is clearly not sustainable— every new customer will increase the company's losses. In this example, the standalone "number of users" metric is not really actionable for product managers, as it is not telling them whether their product is moving in the right direction or not. Here are some examples for actionable metrics:

- Split or A/B tests: a way of comparing multiple variants of a product to find out which one works best in terms of predefined objectives and measurements (see Sect. 4.1),
- Per-customer metrics: customer-centric measurements,
- Funnel metrics: measurements related to marketing and sales success,
- Cohort analysis: measurements focused on subsets of customers with common characteristics,
- Keyword metrics: measurements focused on search engine optimization.

With software product usage can be measured in ways that no other product area allows (see also Sect. 4.2). For a web-based environment the Lean Startup movement provides a lot of information on how to track users and develop meaningful metrics [CrolYosk13]. This data allows highly valuable insight into how individual product features are being used or not used.

Performance Management is tightly linked to Product Analysis (see Sect. 5.7) and Product Life Cycle Management (see Sect. 4.5), and Planning Processes and Tools (see Sect. 4.6). With Product Analysis, the organization ensures that the relevant product-related data becomes available in a reliable and frequent way. Market Analysis (see Sect. 5.6) does the same for market-related data. In Product Life Cycle Management, Product Management uses this product and market data to determine the positions of the product in its life cycle and of the market (product category) in its life cycle. Depending on these positions, prioritize different measures for Performance Management (see Sect. 5.7.3), allowing Product Management to track data continuously and take corrective action whenever needed.

3.14.3 Risk Management

Effective risk mitigation at all product management and development stages is critical for building a successful software product. There are three primary types of risks for which mitigation strategies need to be devised:

- Product risks: relate to getting the product right. Product risks relate to the unique value proposition, key activities and key resources, partners, cost structure (resources) and revenue streams (pricing),
- Customer risks: relate to building a scalable path to the customers. These relate to the customer segments and channels,
- Market risks: relate to building a viable business. They relate to business measures and intersection of cost structure and revenue streams segments (determining the product's margins).

Risks will differ depending on the product's life cycle stage. Addressing the right risks at the right time is important to minimize waste since incorrect prioritization of risks is one of the top reasons for waste.

When developing a new product, the customers' problems and existing alternatives need to be understood (problem/solution fit). From the risk perspective, aspects of the product such as value proposition and customer segments are the most important. A product manager is responsible for the risk-related activities identification, mitigation and contingency planning.

Then the product manager needs to make sure that the product being developed is what customers will pay for (product/market fit). From the risk identification and mitigation perspective, aspects of the product such as unique value proposition and pricing (segment: revenue streams) are the most important. It is a huge risk if one cannot identify whether customers will pay for a product or not.

In the growth phase (see Sect. 4.4), consider the risks associated with scaling channels and optimizing margins against competition.

Figure 3.12 can help to identify and document risks and how to triage them based on life cycle stage, risk level and uncertainty level. Once the risks are triaged, mitigation strategies against them can be devised

There is a large body of literature on risk management, e.g. [Pritch15].

3.14.4 Summary and Conclusions

Product management can become increasingly data-driven if the organization ensures the frequent availability of reliable relevant data. Performance management means the systematic continuous tracking of all business-related data, in particular

			High uncertainty
			Low uncertainty
Problem/solution fit			
	Low risk	High risk	
			High uncertainty
			Low uncertainty
Product/market fit			
	Low risk	High risk	
			High uncertainty
			Low uncertainty
Growth phase			
	Low risk	High risk	

Fig. 3.12   Technique for risks triage in new product development [BlanDorf12]

KPIs, analysis and appropriate action taking. Risk Management means the systematic continuous tracking and analysis of risks relevant to the product, and defining and implementing appropriate mitigation strategies.

3.15   Product Strategy Processes and Documentation

3.15.1 Overview

In this section we discuss a classification of the product strategy tasks based on frequency which can be used for a process view. We describe the structure of a product strategy document and look at tools.

3.15.2 Strategy Processes and Yearly Plan

The Merriam-Webster Dictionary defines a process as "a series of actions or operations conducing to an end". Since software product management is a continuous activity over the life cycle of a product the length of which is not predetermined, and it consists of a multitude of separate tasks, looking at software product management in total as one coherent process is not effective. That is also true when we only look at the combined set of activities in the product strategy column of the SPM Framework. However, it can be very helpful for product managers to classify the activities and map the periodic ones onto a yearly schedule. In that sense, we can consider the steps on the time axis as a process that aims at achieving consensus about the contents of the product strategy, even though they do not describe how the separate pieces of contents are developed or updated, and they do not cover all activities.

For classification we use the following categories:

- Continuous (C): done more often than once a month.
- Periodic (P): done monthly or less often, but with predefined frequency.
- Triggered (T): only done when a particular event or request happens, i.e. not with predefined frequency.

We can apply this classification to the product strategy activities listed in the SPM Framework (Fig. 3.13).

Strategy task	Continuous	Periodic	Triggered
Positioning and Product Definition		P for existing products	T if new
Delivery model and Service Strategy		P for existing products	T if new
Ecosystem Management		P	T if driven by ecosystem members
Sourcing		P for annual HR planning	T if driven by current situation
Pricing		P for structural changes	T if driven by current sales situation
Financial Management		P	
Legal and IPR Management		P	T if driven by Sales or Development
Performance and Risk Management		P (typically monthly)	

Fig. 3.13 Classification of strategy tasks

All activities classified as P can be mapped to a yearly plan which can be used as the software product manager's work plan. The mapping is usually dependent on the schedule of activities on the business unit or company level, e.g. the yearly business planning.

3.15.3 Documentation

The product strategy describes how the product is supposed to evolve over this strategic time frame. It should address the following items:

1. Positioning and Product Definition
2. Delivery model and Tailorability
3. Service Strategy
4. Sourcing
5. Pricing
6. Financial Management
7. Ecosystem Management
8. Legal and IPR Management
9. Performance and Risk Management
10. Roadmap (see Sect. 4.4).

The first elements, up to Sourcing, are often described in one cohesive product strategy document in order to emphasize the need for full consistency. The remaining elements, from Pricing to Performance and Risk Management, are also of strategic importance but are usually only included in a product strategy document on an abstract level. The details, e.g. price list or complete forecasting numbers, are kept separate. Producing documents like this is not very popular anymore, but our experience shows that consistency suffers when a document structure does not enforce and support it.

All these items are highly interdependent. If, for example, business planning results in an available budget smaller than originally assumed, it will only be possible to expand the product scope to a lesser extent or more slowly. If new segments are to be added to the target market within the strategic time frame, the product scope may have to be expanded. Dependency on other products can also have considerable consequences, e.g., if certain functionalities or enabling code must be available in several products at the same time. In bigger companies that have one or several product portfolios an individual product strategy needs to be aligned with the corporate strategy and portfolio. It should be observed that interdependencies can exist on different levels of abstraction, ranging from portfolio to product to feature to function to component and also covering management and business decisions included in the strategic concerns described above.

Another way of describing elements of the product strategy is the business model canvas that we discussed in Sect. 2.4.

3.15.4 Tools

Over the last few years an increasing number of tools have become available that are explicitly intended and designed for product managers. Some provide bi-directional interfaces to popular software development tools. While they are useful for the product planning activities (see Sect. 4.6.4), there are hardly any dedicated tools for product strategy. What product managers typically use for product strategy are Office tools and then business intelligence tools as the strategies become more data-driven.

3.15.5 Summary and Conclusions

Though it does not make sense to attempt to define a process that covers all of product strategy, a process view on the consensus building through periodic activities can be helpful. We recommend documentation of the product strategy in a cohesive document. There are hardly any dedicated tools that support the product strategy tasks.

Product Planning

4

The Software Product Management Framework describes product planning as a core software product manager activity. All product planning decisions should be based on deep customer insight (Sect. 4.1).

The last few years have brought increased heterogeneity in approaches and techniques used in product planning based on a number of factors. The different approaches are discussed in Sect. 4.2 including the subject of Product Requirements Engineering, i.e. the collection, analysis, and documentation of the software product's requirements.

Section 4.3 covers Release Management. Section 4.4 discusses Roadmapping, i.e. the strategic and long-range planning for the evolution of a software product. From an execution perspective, Product Requirements Engineering is a continuous activity while roadmaps and release plans are revised at discrete points in time.

Product planning links to the company's planning activities, in particular to portfolio management (see Sect. 5.2). Each product that is part of the portfolio will be in its own specific life cycle stage requiring specific management and investment focus. We discuss product life cycle management in Sect. 4.5.

The chapter concludes with Sect. 4.6 which gives an overview of software product management performance measurement and how to improve it.

4.1 Customer Insight

The meaning of the term "Customer Insights" has evolved considerably in recent years. Typically, it is attributed to data analytics methods used by customer insight managers or data scientists. The term "Customer Insights", as used in this book, refers to a deep and always up-to-date understanding of customer context, problems, and their dynamics. We use the term "customer" for all types of customer-side stakeholders, like user, buyer, IT manager, owner, operator, etc. (see also Sect. 3.3). Although software product managers increasingly use data analytics, experience shows that it is equally important to spend a significant amount of time in direct

© Springer-Verlag GmbH Germany, part of Springer Nature 2022
H.-B. Kittlaus, *Software Product Management*,
https://doi.org/10.1007/978-3-662-65116-2_4

contact with customers to gain a deep understanding of their "jobs to be done" and the problems they encounter.

Ideally, product managers are the subject matter experts for customer problems. This enables them to relate the product direction outlined in roadmaps to existing or upcoming customer problems. Basing product goals on customer data adds credibility for the product manager and therefore helps to get buy-in to the plans from the team.

The following list describes typical direct customer contact opportunities:

Customer Visits: Product management should visit key customers on a regular basis. Such events can be organized by local sales or key account managers. During such visits, the product manager gains first-hand insights into the existing and changing use of the product. This helps to strengthen the product manager's empathy with the customer.

Meeting Customers at Conferences, Workshops, and Events: Conferences and events provide product managers with a cost-effective opportunity to speak with several select customers. No extra time or budget is required, as the customers are on site anyway.

Organizing Customer Round Tables (focus groups): Selecting key customers who represent the target market for the product enables discussion and exchange of ideas about the product. Needs that only a few customers have are quickly identified. Product progress over the years can be reflected with representatives of the target segment. Focus groups are usually organized with representatives from marketing, sales, and product management. To be effective they must be well-planned and presentations or lists of questions well-thought through ahead of time.

Design Sprints with Customer Participation: In agile development design sprints offer the opportunity to explore problems and solutions jointly with customers. This allows the customer not only to articulate their problems directly, but also to create a shared understanding of the customer's problem with the team. Selection of customers to participate must be done with care, as such customers will have major influence on product direction.

Supporting Selected Pre-sales Activities: Since product managers are subject matter experts on the product, they are sought-after by Sales to support pre-sales activities. Product management can learn from these events about sales-inhibitors. E. g.: Which aspects of the product make it hard to sell, which features are missing that would close deals. Pre-Sales engagements are an essential tool for product management to understand the mindsets of Sales and buyer personas.

Participating in Support Escalations: Support escalations are another opportunity for in-depth experiences with customers. Product management gains a deep understanding of current product use and their own product company's support staff.

Participation provides insights into how product support analyses problems and how customers can quickly identify a problem area.

Participating in Online Forums: Product-specific online forums provide a very efficient way to get in touch with customers and hear about their problems and wishes. However, since these forums are usually public, participants may not be totally open, and there may be participants who make negative statements intentionally.

Regular participation and engagement helps to keep abreast of issues and trends facing existing customers. Direct product manager contact with customers not only provides an analytical understanding of their problems, but may also create empathy. Given the many opportunities to interact with customers, effective time management becomes an essential skill of good product management. Product managers should have a plan for allocation of time among the various opportunities throughout the year.

In recent years, data analytics are providing more and more insights into customer needs (see also "The Data-Analysis-Driven Approach" in Sect. 4.2). Data analytics methods are:

- Monitoring online reports of market research agencies, blogs and trade press for customer information
- Monitoring, measuring, and analyzing of user behavior while they use the product
- Using data analytics software that retrieves information about customer behavior throughout the internet

A third category of customer insights gathering techniques are hybrid techniques. Three widely used techniques are:

Customer Observation Watch customers working with the product. The focus is not only on the specific tasks performed with the product, but also which actions trigger these tasks and what happens before and after. Observations may be video recorded to share with the product teams. Customer observation is usually carried out by UX specialists. Some companies have specialized usability labs for this.

Split or A/B Testing Two or more different functional implementations are offered to selected customers. This technique can determine which solution is better accepted or suitable for solving a particular problem. A/B tests are usually carried out by UX specialists, product owners or product managers. They provide first-hand insights (see also "The Data-Analysis-Driven Approach" in Sect. 4.2).

Launching a Beta Version or Minimum Viable Product (MVP) for evaluation: Early product versions that may not be fully ready for release may be provided to selected customers. Product management selects the right customers, establishes a relationship with them as well as the beta or MVP contract terms. To achieve meaningful results, early access programs require substantial time commitments from product management. The selected customers must be notified early of the availability of the early access program, the scope and expectations of the test scenarios must be defined, and after an agreed period of time, customers must provide feedback. Early access programs not only help to reduce risk of product defects, but also provide valuable first-hand insights about product use as well as potential future sales references from influential customers.

Collecting relevant customer data is only the first step in developing product insights. Software product managers need to feed this data into discussions with stakeholders and to use it for requirements analysis as well as business modeling.

4.2   Product Planning Approaches

The applicability of product planning approaches and techniques depends on the degree of vendor control of the runtime environment(s) in which the product runs, and on the product's phase in its life cycle. This is the way in which we created the four software product scenarios described in Sect. 2.5.1. While roadmapping is important in all scenarios, release planning and product requirements engineering work differently in the four scenarios:

- **Powerboat**: New products for vendor-controlled environments (such as Amazon before its initial launch): SPM focuses on defining the minimum viable product (MVP) for the first customers by evaluating the product idea. The definition of the MVP requires a close link with development for extensive prototyping.
- **Speedboat**: Evolved products for vendor-controlled environments (such as Google Docs): SPM focuses on extending the product scope and thereby increasing the target market. Scaling of the product requires ongoing analysis of the actual usage of the product, of the market, and of competition, e.g. by monitoring customer feedback and product use. The release frequency may be high, and updates to the software product tend to be automated.
- **Icebreaker**: New products for customer-controlled environments (such as Docker before its first release): SPM focuses on defining the MVP for the first customers by analyzing the customers' business processes. SPM's role is to ensure that requirements remain broad enough for the target market and not specific to just a few customers.
- **Cruise Ship**: Evolved products for customer-controlled environments (such as Oracle database): SPM focuses on extending the product scope and thereby increasing the potential market. This scaling of the product requires ongoing analysis of requirements, market, and competition, e.g. by directly collaborating with customers. Since existing customers will not want to test and install new releases often, the frequency of releases is rather low, often one or two per year.

Fig. 4.1 Examples for most
applicable product planning
approaches

Component	Most applicable approach
Back-end	Requirements-driven
Front-end	Data-analysis-driven
AI/ML	Data-input-driven

Real-world situations may be of hybrid character. An organization may decide to offer both a licensed product and a SaaS product with a largely overlapping code base. Also, a product may consist of a cloud component and an on-premise component. In these hybrid scenarios, organizations often follow the different pure-scenario approaches in parallel for the different components but need to take care of resulting conflicts.The standard approach for software product planning and development is **requirements-driven**. This approach is broadly used for legal and regulatory requirements, commodity functionality requirements, and technology requirements. Hypothetical customer needs, often referred to as "problems", and potential solutions may be evaluated through qualitative and quantitative validation with customers, users, and other stakeholders to define additional important requirements. The requirements-driven approach is described in detail in Sect. 4.2.1.

There is a second approach called **data-analysis-driven** where the product team experiments with different implementations of design and product concepts, and makes decisions based on the analysis of performance statistics or usage data. Data may also come from the (potential) user side covering how they behave in certain situations, or what their Jobs To Be Done (JTBD) are, or how much time they spend on which tasks. Such experimentation is a good approach when the focus is on innovation and optimization under uncertainty. A third approach is called **data-input-driven**. It applies to artificial intelligence/machine learning (ML) where data is used as input for an ML engine.

These three approaches are not mutually exclusive. In many real-world situations, we recommend that they all be used in parallel for different parts of a product and/or different types of requirements in order to achieve optimal results. For example, a software product may have three different components for which different approaches are most applicable (Fig. 4.1).

4.2.1   The Requirements-Driven Approach

Overview

The requirements-driven approach continues to be relevant to all scenarios. Requirements engineering is the process of eliciting needs and expectations from stakeholders, identifying concepts to satisfy these needs, and validating whether these concepts satisfy the needs. The methodology identifies requirements with appropriate notations which are then communicated to the staff or vendors who implement the requirements, and used later to check that the delivered product conforms to the requirements. The alignment between product concepts and stake-holder needs is essential for a product's value creations and to win the support of the stakeholders.

This section introduces important requirements engineering concepts, describes requirements engineering methodology for the four important product scenarios (see Sect. 2.5.1), outlines how to document requirements and how to manage the requirements engineering process.

Concepts

The IEEE standard glossary of software engineering terminology (IEEE 610.12–1990) defines a requirement as "(1) a condition or capability needed by a user to solve a problem or achieve an objective and (2) a condition or capability that must be met or possessed by a system or system component to satisfy a contract, standard, specification, or other formally imposed documents." Applied to product management and stated in simpler terms, requirements are characteristics of the software product that are (a) needed by stakeholders of the software product and (b) agreed with the product team or supplier. Requirements may also be imposed by market or industry regulations. The requirements definition will guide the activities to be performed in the requirements engineering work.

For a software product, a **stakeholder** is a person, group of people, or organization who influences the product. Product stakeholders include parties outside and inside the product organization. Outside are customers and users as well as channels used to deliver and service the product. User profiles are often characterized by so-called Personas [PruGru03]. Inside are corporate management and the company functions that depend on the product, including marketing, sales, distribution, service, and support. Stakeholders are also representatives of dependent systems and other products with which the product interfaces. Regulatory bodies that the product must comply with are also stakeholders. Even though the number of stakeholders is high, the product manager does not need to involve all of them in requirements engineering. The involvement of stakeholders who have the knowledge to make the product attractive and stakeholders who have the power to implement or stop the project are both critical to the process.

Software requirements are **functional** if they define what the software does in reaction to inputs. Functional requirements are often described as user stories. A **quality** requirement, sometimes called non-functional requirement, defines a quality property of the entire product or of a product component. Quality requirements can come from a user perspective or development perspective [Wiegers03].

Quality requirements from a user or customer perspective:

- Availability: concerning the percentage of time or duration that a product is available for use and fully operational.
  Example: The system must function in a 7×24 mode.
- Efficiency: referring to how efficient the product is in using resources as processor time, memory, or communication bandwidth.

Example: The system must fully function over an internet connection with 16 Mbit/s.

- Flexibility: indicates how easily a product can be extended with new functionalities.
  Example: The product must provide best-in-class APIs.
- Installability: refers to how easy it is to install the product initially or product updates later on.
  Example: Product updates can be installed fully automatically based on the customer's settings.
- Integrity: concerning protection against unauthorized access, data privacy, information loss, and infections through maleficent software.
  Example: The system must apply a checksum mechanism to ensure the integrity of all exchanged documents.
- Interoperability: referring to how easily the product can exchange data or services with other systems.
  Example: The system must exchange documents with other systems only in pdf format as described in ISO standard 32000-2:2020.
- Performance: indicating speed or capacity of the product.
  Example: The system's response time must not exceed 0.1 s.
- Reliability: indicating how long a product can be used without failure.
  Example: The system must have a mean time between failures of at least 7 days, i.e. 168 h.
- Robustness: the degree to which the product or product component continues to operate correctly when confronted with invalid inputs, defects in connected systems, or unexpected operating conditions.
  Example: The system must not terminate in case of invalid API requests, but reject those.
- Safety: indicates how well the system, its users and its data are protected against unintended usage or external impact.
  Example: The product must ensure that the system's data is fully recoverable after power outage.
- Security: indicates how well the system, its users and its data are protected against intended mal-usage or internal and external attacks.
  Example: The product must ensure audit logs that are verbose enough to support forensics.
- Usability: refers to the effort that is needed of the user to prepare input for, operate, and interpret the output of the product.
  Example: The system must be designed such that 95% of all users are able to perform an international bank transfer the first time without assistance.

Quality requirements from a development perspective:

- Scalability: refers to the range of workload scenarios in which the software can run with satisfying performance

Example: The system must be able to support between 100 and 10,000 concurrent users while maintaining the performance requirement of a 0.1 s response time with the runtime cost per user per month not exceeding $10.

- Maintainability: indicates the effort it takes to correct a defect or make a change in the product.
  Example: 90% of the defects found in the system must be fully fixed (analyzed, code changed, tested) with a development effort of less than 4 person hours.
- Portability: indicating how easy it is to migrate a product or product component from one operating environment to the other.
  Example: A new release of the product developed for Android must be fully ported (analyzed, code changed, tested) to IOS with a development effort of less than 200 person hours.
- Reusability: referring to the extent to which a product component can be reused in other products.
  Example: The components and/or modules of the product must be designed, implemented and documented in a way that they can be successfully reused in other products without the original developer being involved.
- Testability: indicates the ability to test all parts of the product and the effort the test takes.
  Example: For a new product release, a test coverage (percentage of code executed at least once during the test) of at least 90% must be achieved with a test effort lower than for the previous release.

Requirements about product packaging, licensing, delivery, and service requirements complement the product requirements. For many of the requirements, tests will be developed to verify that the developed software product indeed meets the required characteristics.

A possible product characteristic is only a requirement if at least one influential enough stakeholder needs it. Otherwise, it is merely an idea. This differentiation between requirements and ideas has important implications on the requirements process: the results from creativity workshops and related activities should only be considered as product requirements when enough stakeholder support has been gained. If the need for an idea is not confirmed by stakeholders, the idea should be treated with caution.

> Let's use the Samsung Health app product[1] to exemplify the concepts. A functional requirement of such a lifestyle application is to provide the user with the ability to count steps. In response to movements of the smartphone, the app increases the step count that it measures. A quality requirement is the precision of the step-counting. That precision could be measured, for a given

(continued)

---

[1] https://www.samsung.com/global/galaxy/apps/samsung-health/

movement sequence, in terms of correct, wrong, and missed step counts and the quality requirement expressed in those terms.

A common quality requirement is interoperability with other applications. In the case of Samsung Health, interoperability is implemented via the Samsung Digital Health SDK API with functions that offer access to health data and Samsung Health services. Other product requirements refer to the contents and design of the product home page used for product documentation.

The integration with an electronic patient health record is an idea that many vendors of health and lifestyle applications are discussing. This idea should only be considered as a requirement for implementation, however, if support from medical personnel and patients can be obtained that require the integration.

Product managers not only manage requirements but also inputs on other abstraction levels, such as goals and constraints for product design [GorsWohl06]. The IEEE definition is useful for differentiating between these concepts. Requirements are characteristics of the product. A **goal** describes the desired impacts of the product. Goals are as important as requirements because goals describe the value proposition of the product. According to ISO/IEC FDIS 25010, common goals include desired usefulness, trust, pleasure, and comfort for users, effectiveness, efficiency improvements, freedom from risk and flexibility for customers, and compliance with regulations. Requirements engineering is concerned with eliciting the goals that the product should achieve and the requirements the product should implement to satisfy the product goals. The explanation of how requirements will allow achieving the goals is called **vertical traceability**.

Product managers are not only confronted with requirements and goals, but also with **constraints** for product design. Design differs from requirements in that the design decisions are characteristics of the software product that are not visible for a stakeholder. Usually, design does not need to be agreed with stakeholders but is under the responsibility of the product organization. Still, for some design decisions, negotiations cannot be avoided because stakeholders impose them as constraints on the software product.

For Samsung Health, one of the goals is a "healthy lifestyle" for the user. The goal is not a requirement because it describes the impact of product use on the user. The adoption of a healthy lifestyle is clearly a characteristic of the user and not of the product. The Health app product will contribute to achieving that goal by encouraging the user to adopt such a lifestyle.

In the example of Samsung Health, a constraint may be raised by the Cloud operations group of Samsung that requires the use of Docker for flexible deployment of the Health app backend. That constraint is justified by

(continued)

efficiency and flexibility goals of the Cloud operations group and the ICT technology stack on which the Health app backend is deployed. Again, the arguments of how design decisions are connected to requirements and goals are called vertical traceability.

Requirements may originate from different sources:

- Stakeholders, e.g. customers, users, user groups, business experts, executive management, partners, internal stakeholders like Development, Marketing, Sales, Services etc.,
- Data sources, e.g. literature, social media, market analysis, product strategy, company guidelines, analytics, standards and regulations,
- Systems in operation, e.g. other existing software products, competitive analysis.

The goal of product requirements engineering [RE] is continuous identification and management of requirements needed to implement the product strategy and address stakeholder needs. These requirements are called "product requirements" and cover requirements for the whole product (such as requirements for the business model, pricing, or marketing aspects). In contrast, the requirements of the stakeholders are called stakeholder requirements. We differentiate:

Stakeholder requirements express individual stakeholder's needs. One very important stakeholder is the customer. Their requirements are typically under Sales' or Technical Support's responsibility as part of their Customer Relationship Management mandate.

Product requirements address no individual customer, but rather one or many markets which consist of any number of customers that may have similar needs, but with high variability. This market focus influences and impacts all other aspects of product RE, especially elicitation of requirements, innovation candidates, decisions, and management. Product RE is part of the software product manager's responsibilities, and tightly linked to specific SPM activities needed in a market-driven context, such as creating a product vision, strategy definition, roadmapping, innovation, and release planning. Product requirements often result in requirements for development, but there are also product requirements that address other areas, e.g. bundling, new pricing models, new delivery processes, or improved support.

Detailed requirements which further refine product requirements that are selected for a particular release and require implementation in the software code. Detailed requirements can also address internal development needs that are raised during development activities. Detailed Requirements are under Development's responsibility.

These three types of requirements can be understood by looking at the flow of information about needs and expectations from the stakeholders via the product manager to development.Stakeholder requirements express needs and expectations of a stakeholder towards a software solution. In customer-controlled installations, customer requirements are engineered in customer-specific projects that deliver a software system integrated, deployed, and configured specifically for that customer. Such a project uses the customer requirements to tailor the vendor's software product and integrate it with other systems of the customer. In vendor-controlled installations, the customer uses the provided software service largely as-is and uses his customer requirements for configuration.

Product requirements represent a consolidation of the requirements of individual customers. With product requirements, the product manager considers the needs of a market from the perspective of the product strategy. When consolidating customer requirements into product requirements, the product manager looks for generalization across customers, "which requirements are common enough to be considered for the product?", and alignment with strategic objectives, "which requirements can be justified with the product vision and strategy?" The link between the product requirements and the customer requirements that the product requirements originate from is called **horizontal traceability**. The product requirements represent the pool of requirements that a product manager considers for release planning. The more the markets have been served with the product, the more product requirements are available to the product manager.

Product requirements become detailed requirements when they are selected for implementation in a product release. Development takes responsibility for the implementation of the selected requirements and—dependent on the chosen development methodology—translates them into a specification of a new software release. In contrast to the product requirements, that specification is detailed and precise enough for implementation and testing. The link between the detailed requirements and the product requirements that the detailed requirements originate from is called horizontal traceability again. In an agile environment, these are the requirements in the teams' backlogs for which the respective product owner (in Scrum terminology) is responsible.

> A hospital that is interested in using Samsung Health for lifestyle measurement of patients may request the integration of Samsung Health measurements with the patient records stored in the hospital information system. This request is an example of a customer requirement. A recurring need of integrating the Health app with various hospital information systems would encourage the Health app product manager to look for standards that can be used to specify and offer a generic application programming interface (API) that eases such integration.[2] A decision to build such an API is an example of a derived product

(continued)

---

[2] Samsung offers such an API on http://developer.samsung.com/health

requirement. Once a decision is taken to implement the product requirement, the API becomes a detailed requirement. The development project for Samsung Health v4.4.0.0119, for example, included requirements for a new cycling speedometer and requirements for connectivity with the Garmin Bike Sensor.

Requirements Engineering Methodology

Requirements engineering is the systematic process of aligning a software product with stakeholder needs. Without such alignment, the software would be a mere collection of bits and bytes that would likely not create identifiable value, thus would not generate sales. We consider the alignment as a process of seeking inputs from the market to understand needs, adjusting the product to meet the needs, and checking whether the changed product leads to improved satisfaction. The better the alignment is, the better the business performance of the product will be.

One of the product manager's core tasks is the management of product requirements. The product manager is responsible for the following tasks continuously and before release development starts:

- Consultation with experts and employees, creation of ideas for the product, validation of these ideas by exposing them to stakeholders in discussions or via prototypes.
- Collection of requirements from diverse sources. Customer projects and ideas from development constitute important sources. Other inputs can come from user representatives, market research, and developers, legacy and competitors' systems, laws and regulations, and previously used requirements specifications.
- Functional analysis, including clarification and consolidation of the requirements and estimation of value. Such analysis is particularly important when products do not stand alone but form part of a larger offering.
- Technical analysis to describe how the requirements may be met and what the estimated effort and costs are of doing so.
- Documentation of the results of the functional analysis with an appropriate level of detail as a base for development.
- Go/no-go and make/buy decision according to the company-specific decision processes.

During the development of essentially every product, there will be the need to change initial requirements or add completely new ones. Such changes may pose a risk for development execution and may cause conflicts among Sales, Marketing, Development, and Product Management, which the product manager will need to resolve. It is important in this context to understand how requirements management and the development process interconnect, since different development methods also differ in how easily they can accommodate requirement changes. The product manager—usually in cooperation with whoever is responsible for detailed requirements, e.g. product owner, project manager, etc.—is responsible for the following tasks in the implementation of a product release:

- Implementation management by tracing the individual requirements, i.e. by documenting where and how each requirement is met; this documentation can then be used for customer feedback,
- Change management by deciding on change requests that lead to changed, dropped, or new requirements and documenting of the rejection or acceptance of each change request with the rationale for the decision,
- Quality assurance, if possible through an independent QA organization, to verify that the implementation is consistent and complete with respect to the original requirement.

The product manager may choose between two tactical approaches for requirements engineering. The traditional approach involves **inquiry cycles** [PohlRupp11] with the following elements:

- **Elicitation** is the systematic application of methods such as interviews, focus groups, workshops, observation, creativity, surveys, and artifact analysis to understand the application domain and to identify stakeholders with their objectives and expectations. Important sources of requirements are internal; in particular research and development can ensure innovation. The resulting requirements need to be properly documented, either in natural language or model-based. Elicitation techniques based on Artificial Intelligence, in particular natural language processing and machine learning, are making the transition from research into practical application (see [DaFeFrPa18, Rietz21]).
- **Triage** means a first analysis and determination of whether a given requirement is inside or outside of the product scope. This might include bundling of small low-level requirements in order to increase the productivity of the process. The product manager will typically maintain a backlog with a significant number of requirements that are inside the product scope, but not yet in plan for implementation, need more detailed analysis, or need periodic reevaluation.
- **Analysis** of the remaining requirements aims at matching the elicited information with appropriate solution concepts by applying specification, modeling, and prototyping methods to help determine inclusion/exclusion from the release.. It also must include estimates of cost and required resources.
- **Selection** means the decision making which requirements are implemented in a particular product release, i.e. selection includes prioritization and is part of release planning.
- **Validation** involves the application of methods like reviews, inspections, and simulations to ensure that the proposed solution adequately takes the problem context into account and is acceptable to stakeholders. The result of successful

requirements engineering is a specification that documents agreement between stakeholders and development or suppliers of what will be delivered in the developed product.

There are several requirement life cycle phase models. Examples of phases that might be used are:

- *New*: the initial state of a requirement.
- *Approved*: the requirement is approved and ready to be analyzed.
- *Specified*: the requirement has been analyzed with regard to implementation concept and cost and impact estimates.
- *Rejected*: the requirement is already accounted for, a duplicate, or out of scope.
- *Selected*: the requirement has been selected for inclusion with a given priority.
- *Implemented*: the requirement has been met, i.e. development is finished with a solution to the requirement.
- *Tested*: the necessary tests have been carried out in order to ensure an adequate level of quality.
- *Released*: all activities for the product release have been completed.

Naming and number of phases may vary depending on the preferences of the organization and the product scenario.

Internationalization

The decision to sell a product internationally will usually entail additional requirements compared to a purely domestic product. One common additional requirement is the support for multiple languages. If a product is first released in a local language and subsequently translated into another language to make the product available in another country, retrofitting the new language is often time-consuming. National language support enablement should be considered early in the product specifications and design. Such an approach requires the language-dependent parts of the product, the user interface, screen masks, messages, help functions, and online documentation, to be separated from the business logic.

When scaling a product to a global market, there are regulations, standards, certificates, and permits that need to be catered for, met, or obtained for each specific country. Many customer environments and product domains are subject to such national regulations. Currency is obvious. Another widely known example of a regulation that applies to customer environments is the American Sarbanes-Oxley act. It regulates financial practice and corporate governance and contains requirements that affect a company's business processes and the software products that support these processes. Another example is the European GDPR (General Data Protection Regulation, Sect. 3.13.5). In the medical industry the medical device directive is a pervasive example. It regulates all products including the software and hardware which affect the well-being or life of humans. In Europe, products that comply with the directive gain market access and obtain the CE mark.

A global product must consider cultural issues and local usage. Seemingly trivial but potentially crucial examples are date format and numeric decimal and thousands separators. In Europe dates are invariably dd/mm/yyyy; in the U.S. mm/dd/yyyy; meanwhile for proper date sorting some organizations prefer yyyymmdd. In the U.S., the period is used as a decimal separator and the comma as a thousand separator, while in Europe and much of the rest of the world, the roles of those punctuation marks are reversed. Getting such points right may be crucial to the success of products in specific countries. Even in the case of purely functional requirements, countries have different priorities, often due to cultural differences. And there are certainly differences in the legal aspects like sales laws or warranty. As all these cases show, internationally oriented product management which considers these aspects and prioritizes them properly is crucial to successful international development and sales.

Documentation of the Requirements

Requirements must be documented to be useful for building a shared understanding, planning the product, and coordinating the development. How requirements are documented does not matter [Fricker14]. Aggregated over more than 400 projects, no evidence could be found that requirements engineering success was influenced by decisions about templates for requirements phrases, box-and-line drawings, or even formal specifications. The way requirements are stored did not have any influence on requirements engineering success either. Specifications may be saved with documents, spreadsheets, Wikis, or requirements databases. What is important is the right methodology for building a strong business case and aligning the software product with the needs of the product stakeholders.

To be efficient, requirements engineering practice should comply with policies on the development side. These policies include standards for requirements specification, the toolchain in the company, and the needs of those who are working with the requirements.

The software development methodology chosen by the development organization determines how to document requirements and ensure that the requirements are addressed, solutions implemented and tested appropriately.

With agile development, requirements are planned and coordinated with backlogs rather than with specification documents. A backlog is a list of coarse-grained features that are refined into fine-grained requirements. Features are called Epics; user stories are fine-grained requirements. Epics should be used for documenting a shared understanding of the meaning of the feature that the product manager had in mind. For both epics and user stories that represent functional requirements, the user story template can be used. It has the following format [Cohn04, LuDaWeBr16, Lucassen17]:

- Specification: a sentence that follows the structure "As a <user in the role X>, I want to <use the functionality Y of the software> so that <the benefit Z that shall result from using Y that I as a user am interested in>."

- Comments added as the user story is being discussed: any information important to correctly interpret the user story. The comments may include constraints that must be considered for implementation.
- Tests added as the definition of "done" are discussed: exemplary scenarios of how the system is used and test data defining how the software will react to user inputs. The tests may be further formalized with the Behavior-Driven Development approach [SolisWang11].

With more traditional development methodologies like Waterfall, the upfront planning of the system development is important. Requirements specification documents created before development starts drive the development plan. Requirements management is a document-centered task. All requirements are combined into a document, the high-level specification of a product. This becomes the main working document of product requirements management. The early requirements specification defines the technical specification. The ISO/IEC/IEEE 29148:2011 and IEEE 830:1998 standards describe common templates for requirements documents. In a public tender context, the V-Model XT and Hermes processes provide good templates.

Whether the development proceeds in an agile or Waterfall fashion, the product manager is expected to decide about quality requirements that complement the functional requirements. He will decide quality characteristics, prioritizations, and define expected quality levels. Types of quality requirements are discussed in the speedboat and icebreaker subsections.

Finding the appropriate quality levels is difficult in practice, and may affect development cost and customer experience in dramatic ways [RegnBSO08]. Too much quality will force development to choose architectures that may be an order of magnitude more expensive than if less quality can be afforded. Too little quality will lead to bad quality experience for the customers and users that interact with the product. Customers will often choose competitive products that deliver better quality in areas that are critical to them. To determine appropriate levels of quality, the product manager needs to understand the customers' priorities in terms of product quality attributes, competing products' respective performance from the customer perspective, and technical options and associated costs for building useful or competitive quality while avoiding quality excess. This work proceeds best in focused collaboration with Marketing and Development. Workshops with experiments to understand the effect of product quality on the user's quality of experience may be useful [FoFrFi14].

Many software organizations want traceability among requirements artifacts, in particular between stakeholder, product and detailed requirements (see above). That means the ability to follow the path from the original requirement to the software implementation and back. They often implement an integrated tool chain for managing these artifacts. An integrated tool chain will allow the product management organization to establish horizontal traceability from stakeholder requirements to the product implementation and vertical traceability from strategic objectives to design decisions. The traceability connections are created by giving each artifact unique identifiers that could be referred to in the same way as web pages link to each other with URLs. Standardized notations and traceability give transparency about development plans and progress, thus allow rapidly introducing or reacting to changes. In regulated markets, such traceability may be a requirement for placing a product on the market. In some environments the introduction of traceability has enabled systematic reuse of requirements, code, and tests to the extent that the time-to-market for a new product might be accelerated by 90% in a product line environment.

A Siemens unit, for example, has established the following tracing capability and toolchain [ClSeRBC07]:

- Stakeholder requests (documented with text documents) traced to features (managed in a requirements database).
- The features (managed in the requirements database) refined into system use cases (managed in a modeling tool).
- The use cases refined into requirements that describe concrete system capabilities (both managed in the modeling tool).
- Documentation of product releases (managed in a document versioning system) defining when the concrete system capabilities would be implemented (managed in the design modeling tool).

Some organizations have introduced alternative and enhanced forms of requirements documentation. Storyboards, whether hand-drawn or assembled with photographs, may make descriptions of product use more intuitively understandable than just abstract specifications. Videos showing the use of the product and how stakeholders react to such use may further enhance the storyboards [FricSFT16]. Such rich-media documentation is useful in situations where the product organization needs to be convinced about the product context, where development work needs to be precise, and where there is a need for knowledge transfer and learning. In addition to their use for requirements documentation, photos and videos may serve to advertise products, to educate users about how to use the product, and to capture experiences of these users in support of product evolution.[3]

Whatever approach is chosen to document requirements, a product manager has to decide about the depth of the requirements specification. This depth, or the level of detail, should be adapted to the maturity of the requirements understanding and the knowledge of the requirements receivers. A hint about a possible solution may be enough for an experienced subject matter expert that the product manager has collaborated with over a long time. In contrast, junior developers may need to learn about many details before they can interpret the requirements correctly. For planning the appropriate level of detail, a simple test exists for testing requirements understanding: ask how the recipient will implement it. If you agree: fine. If not: change the understanding by adding detail or seek another team [Condon02]. Also, keep in mind that requirements tend to be vague and abstract early when product

---

[3] https://youtu.be/CBsOiabbNIc shows an example of such a product video.

concepts are being explored and evaluated. Later when the product concepts have been chosen and solidified, the requirements must be detailed enough to facilitate planning, product development, and testing.

Managing Requirements Engineering

Requirements are used to justify decisions among architectural options, to estimate and schedule work, to facilitate quality assurance, and to coordinate among different products. Like all business processes that are cross-organizational and require the cooperation of different organizational units, the requirements management process is a big problem in a lot of companies.

The knowledge of who will implement a given requirement and when it will be implemented avoids redundant activities and allows planning of dependent work. An assigned and scheduled requirement can be reviewed, followed-up, and changed if necessary. The following paragraphs describe measurements that companies may use. The measurements make sense especially in the speedboat and cruise ship scenarios as the measurements are particularly useful for mature products where there is a desire to improve the requirements engineering process.

One essential measurement is **time-to-market**. This measurement tells how fast and flexible the product organization is to react to market changes and to implement strategic decisions. If time-to-market is too slow, development capacity may need to be increased, product development focused, and the release frequency increased. The time-to-market measurements can be refined with measurements that reflect how fast and thoroughly requirements are addressed, e.g. the average time from the initiation of a requirement to the point of decision on implementation and to the availability of the product release that contains the implementation.

Another essential measurement is the **size of the requirements backlog**. This measurement tells how much work is pending. If based on a clear definition of the organization's requirements process steps, the measurement gives confidence that the flow of requirements through the process is not constricted at some point. Requirements' flow is made visible by measuring backlogs at different locations in the organization. This also helps identify and eliminate bottlenecks and overcapacity. Ericsson, for example, applied such value stream analysis systematically to improve and balance the overall productivity of their product organization [PetWoh10].

A third measurement that is useful, particularly during requirements triage and scope definition of a development project, is the **degree of confidence in requirements decisions**. Common confidence issues concern the linkage of requirements with business strategy, seeing the big picture of the offering, understanding the planned product's value, and knowledge of customer problems [KKTLD15].

Measurement of how well the end-to-end process works is a key success factor. The role of the process owner is necessary, even though it is not always pleasant. The management board needs to support him and give escalation rights to him. The following would constitute good assignment of process ownership to functional areas:

- Stakeholder requirements: business development, customer management.
- Product requirements: software product management.
- Detailed requirements: development.

Stakeholder requirements management can be tightly linked to product requirements management. Detailed requirements management is closely linked to development work. The connection of detailed requirements management to stakeholder and product requirements management is usually looser.

4.2.2 The Data-Analysis-Driven Approach

Overview
Insight into how users work with the software product has always been of utmost interest to product managers. However, with the on-premise delivery model of licensed products, customers—in particular enterprise customers—have been reluctant to give vendors access to their runtime environments. So user-specific measurements and tracking of behavior in the runtime environment has usually not been an option. Some vendors tried to do something similar internally, e.g. in usability labs with test users, but that could never really fully mirror real-world customer usage. The situation is different in the SaaS/PaaS delivery model where the vendor is in control of the runtime environment.

Concepts and Techniques
Particularly in the Speedboat scenario, the vendor has a plethora of options—except for some legal restrictions with regard to personal data—to measure and track usage. A great deal of data can be generated and analyzed on a continuous basis to answer detailed questions on what to build, which is known as **product discovery** or customer discovery, e.g.

(a) which code paths are most heavily used and offer the strongest leverage with regard to improvements of technical performance,
(b) which parts of the code are hardly used, may stand for functionalities that users are not interested in, and may be candidates for code reduction,
(c) where do users spend a lot of time in a workflow which may be an indication for a usability problem,
(d) which of two or more alternative implementations works best (A/B testing), e.g. which design of a web page results in the highest conversion rate on an e-commerce transaction platform.

Example (d) stands for an approach based on experimentation which can be highly valuable, in particular in the area of UX Design. **A/B testing** works like this:

Design:

1. What is the hypothesis that we want to verify/rule out?
2. Which measurable key indicator(s) can be used to do that?
3. What are the statistical requirements, e.g. sample size etc.?
4. Is our software + infrastructure prepared for these measurements? Can we get access to the measured data? Are there any legal restrictions?

Implementation:

5. Preparation of software + infrastructure + data access (if required) + legal clearance (if required)
6. Execution
7. Data analysis
8. Conclusion

An example for a hypothesis and a measurable key indicator is: New implementation B improves conversion rate by 20% compared to current implementation A on an e-commerce transaction platform.The design and execution of these experiments is usually done by product owners who need to have good skills in the area of statistics. Often there is a trade-off between statistical validity and time-to-conclusion. This approach helps with "local optimization" but does not replace product strategy which is the product manager's responsibility.

Additional data-analysis-driven techniques are:

• Monitoring online reports of market research agencies, reviews, tweets, blogs and trade press for customer information
• Using data analytics software that retrieves information about customer behavior throughout the internet

4.2.3   The Data-Input-Driven Approach

Overview

While many artificial intelligence (AI) technologies continue to be in the research stage, progress in the area of machine learning (ML) has recently been so significant that components based on ML are more and more frequently included in standard software products. The most common approach uses an ML engine, which is the software implementation of a neural network, in combination with domain-specific data structures. The data-input-driven approach is applicable in this situation, i.e. relevant data sets are used as input into the ML engine as part of the learning process. This approach can be relevant in all four product scenarios.

Concepts and Techniques

A product manager whose product includes such an ML-based component needs to deal with the situation that the functionality of this component is no longer exclusively implemented in software code based on requirements, but emerges from feeding data into the engine. Organizations usually introduce a new role called data scientist in these situations. Data scientists are experts in statistics, data quality, data modeling, and data cleansing. Organizationally they can be close to product management, development, or in a unit of their own. In any case, the product manager needs to work closely with the data scientist who is—at least initially—not a domain expert, not experienced in acquiring relevant data or getting legal clearance for this data. The data scientist needs to learn about these aspects, but the responsibility for these tasks is typically with the product manager who needs to have a basic understanding of the AI technology used, its data requirements and its possibilities and impossibilities.When relevant data which describes outputs to particular inputs is used as input into the ML engine, the neural network goes through a learning process. The combination of inputs and outputs can come from

- human labeling or tagging, e.g. with image recognition,
- real world data, e.g. with credit defaults.

Thereby the outputs of the ML engine to particular inputs are getting "better" over time, i.e. the accuracy rate increases. This approach has proven to be powerful in a lot of application areas from chatbots and image recognition to credit default prediction and automated driving.The product manager must make sure that the focus is on the customers and their business problems, not primarily on the technology. This includes the definition of personas and use cases. He must take care in defining the input training data and ensure that all types of customers are adequately represented and no minorities are excluded. The data-input-driven approach is dependent on the application area. In some areas, in particular with a broad spectrum of consumers, data-pooling can work, i.e. the use of input data from different sources. In other areas that are very customer-specific, only data from the individual customer can be used as input for the learning process. In the latter case, the product needs to provide an easy-to-use interface that enables the customer to feed the system with his data on a regular basis.

Vendors tend to use a classic release concept for the standard product that includes the ML engine, software code around it, the data structures, and the generic data model inside the engine if applicable. In the early phase of an ML-based product, vendors usually work with an MVP (Minimum Viable Product) approach. This works best when the first customers have some "skin in the game", i.e. pay for the value that they get from the product.

4.2.4   Product Planning in the Four Product Scenarios Techniques

Given product scenarios will determine which product planning approaches and techniques are most applicable. Product planning may be performed at the level of the whole product, at the level of features, or at the level of a software release. The product level is essential in the powerboat situation, where the product manager uses experimentation to align a minimum viable product with market needs. The feature level is essential in the speedboat situation where the product manager uses experiments for identifying and defining complements to the minimal product that is frequently released. These complements are intended to make the product attractive to new market segments. The release focus is essential in the icebreaker and cruise ship situations, where the product manager decides about a well-designed scope of a product that is released comparatively rarely. The data-input-driven approach can be applicable in all scenarios whenever AI components are part of the product.

The following subsections present common product planning techniques in the product management scenario (see Sect. 2.5), into which they fit best. However, each method may be used in any of the situations if it leads to desired knowledge about product-market alignment.

Powerboat

The Powerboat scenario is the typical startup scenario, characterized by a lack of knowledge about customer needs and how a product might satisfy those needs. We only present a summary here since we cover this scenario in much more detail in [KittMang22].

In the Powerboat scenario, the product manager has the role of the creative researcher. The Early Stage of a startup is focused on finding the right Problem-Solution Fit which aims at deriving a minimum feature set which can be launched as a minimum viable product (MVP, see Chap. 3). The Growth Stage focuses on finding and optimizing the product-market fit using an iterative approach.

The learning process in these early stages can sometimes result in dramatic decisions, so-called pivots, that change the course of the product and startup. Pivots can be of three types:

- Product Pivot: When the startup learns that one or some parts of the product are much more beneficial to customers than the rest of the product and the customers care more or are willing to pay more for those.
- Customer Pivot: When a startup learns that there is a new segment of customers willing to pay more for your product than your present customers.
- Problem Pivot: While talking to customers and doing the research, a startup discovers that the customers have a much bigger problem than the one the startup is trying to solve.

The Powerboat situation calls for creativity, knowledge, and ways to make the product sufficiently tangible to obtain meaningful feedback. Techniques that are suitable for this situation are prototyping and workshops. We outline these techniques in the next few paragraphs.

Product ideas are created by encouraging people competent in the product domain to think outside of the box. A really new idea solves problems that have not been solved so far or solves a well-known problem with a new concept much better than previous products did. Good ideas are often relatively inexpensive to implement for the product company and generate a "wow" for customers and other stakeholders. Good ideas may be created by combining for the first time a well-known problem with a well-known solution. Brainstorming workshops may identify such recombinations [MaiGiRob04]. Many creativity techniques have been developed to support such workshops, including the 6-3-5 technique, where six participants handing off three ideas each to each other five times, the analogy technique where solutions from one domain are transferred to another domain, and the Six Thinking Hats technique that allows evaluating ideas from the perspectives of facts, value, risk, emotions, possibilities, and structured reasoning [PohlRupp11].

Large companies may have research departments to produce innovations. Alternatively, a software vendor may work with universities. Researchers can offer a product manager important ideas and direction, especially for product strategy and further technological development. Even if many research results cannot be directly converted into products, research can provide insight into new developments which can be expected in the next 3–5 years, and to think about how current products can be positioned accordingly and early enough. Also, many innovations can be implemented faster and with better quality if they are initially prototyped and tested in a research environment. To enable such a pre-product-development phase, researchers will have knowledge of relevant product technologies and of experimentation methodologies that product development departments often do not have. Someone outside the product organization may view the whole set of potential customer problems in a fresh light and develop new approaches.

Prototypes may be created at varying levels of real-world fidelity. Important for a good prototype is that the idea becomes clearly visible and that the relevant stakeholders can give feedback on the implemented idea once they have experienced it.

- Early-phase low-fidelity prototypes: user interfaces are approximated by drawing the wireframe of the graphical user interface [MivBen14]. Such drawings may then be combined into a sequence of screens that show the appearance of the application for a scenario using the application. Products that involve hardware can use existing devices that have the intended functionality but may not look exactly as intended or vice-versa. The key is rapid development and not fidelity. Such early-phase prototypes make a software solution tangible; their low fidelity encourages feedback and discussion.
- Mid-fidelity prototypes: for maturation of the early prototypes, tools may provide interfaces that the user can interact with by clicking on the GUI components (click-dummy prototype). Hardware may approximate a final look-and-feel with

the help of 3D printers that have become capable of creating a large variety of shapes and functions.

- Late-phase high-fidelity prototypes: as a next step, the target development technology implements the look and feel with an early version of the final functionality. These late-stage prototypes are useful for letting users explore the use of an application. The high fidelity enables validation of the ideas it implements in realistic conditions experienced using the prototype.

Product ideas may be validated in workshops that involve a review of the vision by the stakeholders affected by the product (especially customers and users), roleplaying the product, and debating the benefits, limitations, and risks of the product. Such focus groups produce valuable inputs for the design of the software product because they elicit knowledge and experiences about the use context of the product from the perspective of the future customers and put these results into the perspective of other customers that may modify their importance or interpretation [KruCas14].

For role-plays to be effective, it is critical that the participants be true customers and users, that the role-play take place at the location and setting where the product will be used, and that the moderator help the participants to walk through the intended usage process. The role-play will generate emotions about the product, both positive and negative, and discussions of how to exploit the product and how to solve problems that have not been considered during ideation and prototyping. This feedback can be used to create a backlog of adjustments to the product to make it more attractive or into criteria for selection of user and customer groups to whom the product should be offered. If video-recorded, the workshops also generate ample footage for requirements communication to developers who cannot participate [FricSFT16] and for early marketing and publicity with product videos.

Kano Model: Attractive Attributes (Delighters)
Powerboat product ideas are intended to be innovative. Customers often did not anticipate such solutions, thus were not seeking them in advance. Innovative products themselves generate desire for the innovation and the impetus to take advantage of the new product. The Japanese researcher Kano suggested that such products or features are called "delighters" or "attractive attributes" [KaSeTT84]. The implementation of a delighter leads to a "wow" on the customer side because it can result in great satisfaction. No one will notice the lack of a delighter. But the determination that a delighter exists can be elicited from a product survey with very positive answers to a question like "How would you react if you could obtain a product with capabilities X?" and negative answers to a question like "How would you feel if our product did not have capability X?" The product manager benefits from such customer surveys by obtaining information about a market. For example, if customers were indifferent to the first and second questions, the specific product idea is apparently not attractive and not worth implementation.

Speedboat

The Speedboat scenario is one in which there is a first product aligned with market needs which the product organization wants to grow. How to achieve that growth is unclear, however. The product manager has been working with a few enthusiastic or visionary customers and may not yet understand the needs and expectations of the large majority of pragmatic more conservative customers that represent the mainstream market ([Moore14], see also Sect. 4.6). Product realignment that some call "growth hacking" may be exploited by scaling up Powerboat activities: to reach new customers, the product manager changes the positioning of the now growing product and thereby accepts new requirements.

The Speedboat situation requires ideas for new product features and feedback from the market about how attractive they are. Under the Data-Analysis-Driven Approach (Sect. 4.2.2), we have already described applicable techniques, in particular in the area of experimentation. Additional techniques that are suitable for this situation are idea castings, market research, user groups, input from development, Hackathons, and "growth hacking." These techniques are outlined in the next few paragraphs.

New ideas for evolution of the product are important inputs in the Speedboat situation. Market growth requires new features which make the product attractive to customers that have not previously shown interest in the minimally viable product. At the same time, many people have developed product expertise and should provide inputs and implementation ideas for product changes. Idea castings are one approach to harvesting ideas from those people [GoFrPaKu10]. A casting involves calls for ideas in the organization, convening meetings where employees share their ideas with product management, and combining the ideas into a product concept with a strong business case. Such idea castings are especially effective when the successful idea owners are rewarded by becoming part of the product organization, for example with leading positions in product development.

To obtain inputs from the market side, market research and user groups play an important role:

- Market research (see Sect. 5.6) offers aggregated market analysis with feedback on product strengths and weaknesses and trends of how the markets and technology develop.
- User groups, by comparison, provide a primary source of individual inputs. A user group focuses on exchanging information between its members and the software vendor. That exchange permits members to influence the vendor's product development. For the product manager, this is an excellent tool for obtaining first-hand feedback about the strengths and weaknesses of his product from the perspective of the users and customers. Customers who perceive their ideas and inputs have been incorporated into products will become future ambassadors and customer sales people and advocate adoption of the product. Most major software vendors have user groups or, the larger variant, conferences at the international scale. For example SAP runs its SAPphire conferences each year in collaboration with local SAP User Groups.

A phenomenon that is difficult to manage in this context is the tendency of executives to match or just outdo the competitor of the moment. Such "shooting behind the duck" will fail utterly to consider that the competitor will move while development takes place. A product manager must anticipate what customers want beyond that current competitor offering and get there before the competition.

To obtain technology-oriented inputs, product management must collaborate with the development organization. No other unit has a deeper understanding of the technical details. Technical necessity will dictate the implementation of numerous requirements. One example is changing to a new operating system or database release—something that may not add value to the product solution per se but may be necessary because maintenance for the old version is terminated, because the new version offers better performance or flexibility, or because the entire potential customer base is moving to the new platform. When considering inputs from development, however, the product manager needs to be aware that sometimes a simple technical solution that is available in a timely fashion is often better than a technically interesting, and in some sense perfect or "gold-plated" product.

An increasingly used approach to explore technology are hackathons, events in which developers meet with peers, technology suppliers, and other stakeholders [RaaMoBia13]. For the organizer, the goal of the event is an efficient assessment of the requirements and design of products and platforms that guide future development. Participants benefit from belonging to a community formed through collaboration, inspiration for product development, and motivation to drive the personal work forward. Hackathons are particularly well suited for exploring products, platforms, and standards that target developers and depend on interoperability.

Looking outside the company, social media have become an important source for identifying topics and influential individuals or organizations that should be involved in requirements engineering. Twitter, for example, has several hundred million users that are active at least once per month. To support social media analysis, there are applications which can detect emerging topics and trends [MathKou10]. Social media further may identify interesting individuals and organizations which can connect important topics that are otherwise unconnected. Filling those so-called structural holes have been shown to generate great product opportunities [LinWuWen12].

A related set of techniques has started to establish itself under the term "growth hacking." Startups use this term to refer to a combination of creativity, analytical thinking, and social metrics to improve product exposure and sales. Techniques aim at improving product sales and obtaining feedback at a low-cost, and may include search engine optimization and content marketing. A variety of techniques may also be used to monitor product use and obtain feedback from customers to guide product evolution:

- Analytics [CrolYosk13]: the collection of measurements about the use of a website or application screens. Particularly interesting are frequencies of page or screen use, click-trails, and measurements of performance, reliability, and related product qualities.

- Experiments [McFarland12]: selective presentation of content variations to learn about user preferences. A widely-used approach is A/B testing, where two alternatives are compared with each other.
- Micro surveys: the presentation of forms that allow users to provide feedback. Commonly, these ask questions about the user's quality of experience, bugs encountered, and ideas for improving the application. An interactive chat between the user and the vendor's sales staff or help desk may enhance a survey and the knowledge obtained from it.

No matter the source of inputs, the product manager must view the received inputs in an overall context. He must determine how representative the suggested ideas and needs are. The most vehemently presented inputs are not always the most important to promote or secure the product in the market in the medium and long term. Given the finite resources to develop and improve his product, the product manager will need to be careful in choosing the requirements.

Kano Model: One-Dimensional Attributes (Satisfiers)

The product features that are elicited, tested, and implemented in the speedboat situation represent characteristics of software products for which better fulfillment leads to an increment of customer satisfaction. Each customer segment expects such characteristics to be present in the product; the absence of these characteristics in the minimal product variant developed in the powerboat stage was one reason to forgo the procurement of the product. Kano suggested that such product characteristics are called "satisfiers" or "one-dimensional attributes" [KaSeTT84]. The more comprehensive the implementation of satisfiers, the more attractive the product is to target customers. The fewer the satisfiers, the less attractive the product.

A satisfier X may be identified through product surveys with positive answers to questions like "How would you react to a product with capability X?" and negative answers to a question like "How would you feel if our product did not have capability X?" Satisfiers give the product manager information for prioritizing development. Strong negative reactions to the absence of features paired with strong positive reactions to the presence of these same features indicates where to set priorities for product enhancements. Similarities among respondents point to customer segments eager for a product release containing those features.

Icebreaker

The icebreaker scenario refers to new product development of a software product intended to run under customers' control. In companies employing a professional services business model, the decision to develop such a product offering may result from an insight that the vendor's customer-specific projects have significant potential for reuse. To exploit that potential, a company may engage in a stepwise productization process [ArWeBriFi10]. The first step is identification of standard features in the customer-specific solution, then management based on proactive development planning. Further standardization and packaging of features may build upon the first reuse step to create a general product. The customer projects use that product as a platform to develop customer-specific solutions. The last step of productization is the definition of a release train that offers a predictable agenda of updates to the product and minimizes the need for custom development.

As an alternative to product conceptualization in customer projects, a software product may be conceived by developing early versions of the product in the laboratory in intensive collaboration with a small set of selected pilot customers. Interviews or workshops provide customer input. To guide the prototyping, large companies tend to adopt technology readiness levels such as the ones suggested by the European Commission. TRL1–6 are usually research-oriented. Starting with TRL4, product management may take over the lead and bring the product to the market.

TRL 1—Basic principles of the idea observed
TRL 2—Technology concept formulated
TRL 3—Experimental proof of concept
TRL 4—Technology validated in the laboratory
TRL 5—Technology validated in a relevant environment
TRL 6—Technology demonstrated in a relevant environment
TRL 7—System prototype demonstration in operational environment.
TRL 8—System complete and qualified
TRL 9—Actual system proven in operational environment

Depending on the customer contact person, it may be sensible for the product manager to engage members of the sales and marketing staff and have them attend the events with the pilot customers. To avoid confusion and customer dissatisfaction, a vendor must be careful to provide consistent, positive messages to the customer representatives in the various meetings and prototype demonstrations. For example, it is better to express a statement like "well, yes there are several problems now but those will be eliminated when you install the new code release when it is available next year" as "the product is excellent now, and we are continuing to invest to make it even better." If the communication is not under control, the enthusiasm of a lab developer for the next release can easily leave the impression that the current release has numerous problems and that any implementation ought to be delayed—the opposite of what sales would like the customer to take away from the session.

Kano Model: Must-Be Attributes (Dissatisfiers)
The third category of requirements that Kano suggests is called "dissatisfiers" or "must-be attributes" [KaSeTT84]. Dissatisfiers refer to attributes of a

(continued)

software product that have been considered state-of-the-art for an extended time, characteristics that will be missed by a stakeholder if they are not implemented. In contrast to the satisfiers, the dissatisfiers do not generate excitement or delight if implemented. But a missing dissatisfier may lead to a "no" from procurement and to rejection of the product.

Dissatisfiers are of importance in the icebreaker scenario, where the software product is deployed into the customer's premises. Here, the integration of the software product into the chain of tools that are used to support the customer's business process will not excite the customer. However, the absence of such integration will disappoint the customer. One of the common integration concerns for many enterprise systems is for user account management. Lack of support for relevant account management standards, e.g. for single sign-in, may lead to rejection of the product in a customer's environment even if the product satisfies the core stakeholder needs.

In a survey, a dissatisfier X can be identified with negative answers to a question like "How would you feel if our product did not have capability X?" paired with a neutral answer to a question like "How would you feel if you obtained a product with capabilities X?" These negatively formulated questions can be used to discover minimal product requirements.

Cruise Ship

The cruise ship scenario is characterized by the presence of a product that has been installed by a number of customers and needs evolution. The product is deployed at customer sites by professional service staff—the vendor's own or partners'—who use the appropriate product versions to develop and deploy customer-specific solutions by using the tailorability options the product provides.

A factor that makes the cruise ship installation complicated is that customers use different product versions. Since these versions need to be supported, homogenization is an important concern of the product manager who needs to convince resisting customers to install updates and upgrades. Customers are often not interested in updating as each update involves cost of adaptation, deployment, conformance checking, and training. Updates also introduce uncertainty about the proper functioning and stability of other customer systems. Microsoft, for example, struggled to convince customers to adopt the most recent version of Windows, with the effect that versions need to be supported that are more than a decade old. In recent years they have evolved their strategy by providing no-charge upgrades and more backward compatibility.

The cruise ship scenario usually confronts the product manager with a stream of bug reports and feature requests from a variety of sources (see Sect. 4.2.1.2). They may originate from customers' requests for proposals that sales staff provide, customer requirements from customer delivery projects, or customer support incidents. Marketing, customers, sales channels, and development may supply additional requests.

Marketing teams may provide valuable inspiration for the design of a software product. Marketing is likely to supply information about what the product must be able to do so that it is successful and which features could make the product more attractive. The way in which a product is presented on the internet, is packaged for sale, or advertised often plays a major role in the sale of consumer products. Marketing staff may also provide valuable information regarding licensing terms and conditions, pricing, etc.

At any company the sales and fulfillment team has the most—and hopefully the best—customer contacts. This is reason enough for it to be an important source for gathering requirements. Due to their broad scope of responsibility, however, many sales people have trouble precisely defining requirements for a single product—unless the person concerned is a product sales specialist.

The requirements obtained from the sales and fulfillment staff are often vague or express the opinion of just one or a few customers. Yet, this information is important for the product manager, particularly as an "early warning system." The sales channel is often the first point of contact for a customer who is dissatisfied with a product or product service. The product manager should respond appropriately before the customer switches to a comparable competing product. Meeting with the customer together with a development representative or organizing a requirements workshop often does wonders. The effect of this is that the customer is more satisfied—feeling that the vendor has taken his problems seriously—and that the sales specialist feels upbeat, having been able to define his fuzzy requirements more precisely together with the customer.

A company needs to exercise caution when developers meet customers, however. The very act of bringing a developer in to talk to a customer may convey an expectation that the requirement will be addressed even if the vendor has other intentions. Any invitation to such a meeting must make clear that the meeting is to gather information and that there is no commitment to development. One must also guard against an excess of candor if it takes the form of "that is the silliest requirement I ever heard!"

Because there are varied inputs from multiple sources, a successful product manager must develop a good instinct for identifying the real problems and saleable solutions. Members of the sales and fulfillment team—with motivations focused keenly on the next sale—tend to present their customer's requirements as the most important of all. This will often create a conflict for the product manager. On the one hand, he should always work in close collaboration with the sales unit, and on the other, he must prevent the sales staff from distorting product requirement prioritization or sidestepping him and submitting requirements directly to development.

Software products may be sold and distributed through sales channels like retailers, partners, value-added resellers (VARs) (see Sect. 3.12) If the product is sold and distributed by third parties, the in-house sales department has limited direct customer contact and thus has difficulty in obtaining information pertinent to making product decisions. In this case, the retailers and partners are an important source of information for obtaining suggestions for new products or feedback on existing products. Such business partnerships work well if both parties benefit from them. A retailer or partner must be positive about the vendor's products, regardless of whether he makes money out of the license or product consulting and implementation services. The reseller will be as keen to remove inhibitors to sales as the vendor and is a good source of such information. Retailer and partner events organized in cooperation with the partners' sales department are—like the user meetings discussed above—a good forum for the exchange of ideas.

Internal staff or external consultants who execute customer projects are a valuable source for gathering new requirements, especially for commercial software products that require a great deal of consultation, tailoring, and implementation services. External consultants are interesting for the product manager because they are independent, are often familiar with products in various customer environments, and have usually already worked with similar competing products.

There are cases of customers developing a product "add-on" that may be interesting to include in the product offering. In such a case, the vendor needs to decide whether the "add-on" should remain customer-specific, should be integrated into the product, or should become part of an ecosystem strategy where the "add-on" is managed by a third party as an independent product on top of the vendor's product. It is advisable for the product manager to meet with the customer together with a development manager or a system architect. Another proven forum is a "customer advisory council" of carefully selected and representative users to review plans and comment on these plans before investment in new functions. However, such a dialogue-oriented approach only works if customers are representative of the target market and insightful about the underlying product technology.

Ideas about product enhancements and technological improvements generated by product development may constitute a further source of product requirements. These ideas often have a long-term perspective and tend to be justified with cost-saving arguments, while requests from the customer side tend to follow business development arguments. The product manager needs to balance these long and short-term needs and consider both aspects in roadmapping and release planning decisions that follow product requirements engineering.

Also, the support team can be a helpful source of information for requirements management. The support department knows well the problems customers have—no other function receives as many customer complaints. It is worthwhile for the product manager to monitor and evaluate the problem database. The support function is also a good partner with whom to collaborate in conducting customer satisfaction surveys. These surveys may not result in detailed requirements but can provide valuable pointers to product-related areas that need improvement.

The costs generated by support may be significant. Call center studies have shown that 80% of all calls concern the same 5–10 problems. In many cases, these problems involve installation, documentation errors, or problematic workflows. Improving the installation procedure, documentation, help functions or user interface can drastically reduce support costs as well as increase customer satisfaction.

The process of collecting, evaluating, and prioritizing the stream of requests obtained from the many sources in the cruise ship situation goes through a series of steps. The first step is called triage which is a fast decision if it is a "must" requirement, a "never ever" requirement, or a nice-to-have that needs more in-depth analysis. Then, nice-to-have requirements are collected and evaluated based on strategic relevance for the product [GorsWohl06]. Selected requirements are then evaluated from the perspective of market value and development cost [KarlRyan97]. We will elaborate on the evaluation and selection for implementation in the release planning chapter.

Kano Model: Indifferent Attributes (Non-requirements)
A fourth category of features useful to consider in the context of the Kano model [KaSeTT84] may be called "non-requirements" or "indifferent attributes." These features are those that the product manager should avoid including in his product. They are attributes of a software product that neither generate positive emotions when implemented nor negative emotions when not implemented. The indifference of the customers implies that development resources should not be wasted on implementation on those requirements. By definition, a product which lacks the features is just as attractive as one that has them implemented.

In the cruise ship scenario, the product manager may face a stream of requests from various company functions. The filtering out of indifferent attributes from this stream is important. A requirement that is perceived as critical for one customer may not be perceived as important by other customers. A requirement that may be considered exciting by some sales staff may not deliver any increase in product sales.

Some features may not be interesting to some customer segments and, at the same time, be important toother segments. Market segments indifferent to potential enhancement features may receive a high priority for early product releases. Offering them product versions which have a limited scope, i.e. that do not include enhancements that must be gotten right for other segments, may offer early core product feedback.

Non-requirements can be identified with the same questions as satisfiers: "how would you feel about a product with capabilities X?" and "how would you feel if our product did not have capability X?" The non-requirements are those for which no strong positive or negative answers are received.

4.2.5   Summary and Conclusions

This section has outlined three product planning approaches: requirements-driven, data-analysis-driven, and data-input-driven, and how they can be applied in the four different product scenarios. The powerboat scenario features a lightweight, flexible experimentation process; the speedboat scales creativity supported by user feedback and data analysis; the icebreaker follows a product development process that generalizes from individual customer projects; and the cruise ship has a continuous inflow of requirements for evaluation and transformation into product requirements. The data-input-driven approach is applicable in all four scenarios whenever AI components are part of the product.

4.3   Release Management

4.3.1   Overview

Release management refers to the management of the contents and schedule of an upcoming product release. With the requirements-driven approach, the content of a release is the result of a selection of requirements. With the data-analysis-driven approach, experiments are prepared, usually in a requirements-driven way, and tests undertaken. Once relevant data is generated from experiments, the results of data analysis determine the final release contents. With the data-input-driven approach, releases are defined based on the data sets being input into the AI/ML engine and the resulting quality of the system behavior [ISTQB21].

In the customer-controlled scenarios, the release frequency is relatively low, usually two to four releases per year, since most customers are not willing to install more than that number of releases. Each release provides significant changes, i.e. new or changed code. This requires release planning in order to define the content and schedule of product releases to maximize product value over its life cycle. The software product manager needs to make sure that the release plan is synchronized with the product roadmap and matches the organization's capability for delivery. Release planning may occur for several versions of the product in parallel.

Usually, development resources are not sufficient to implement all the identified requirements for the product. Therefore, the product manager must prioritize product requirements to determine which ones will be delivered in the forthcoming release. Requirements prioritization is the focal point of release planning decisions as it allows focusing on the most important functional or quality requirements and their timely delivery to the potential customers.

For market-driven companies, prioritizing requirements is challenging because of the number of candidate requirements suggested and a lack of direct customers to validate the importance of those requirements. Thus, balancing market pull and technology push as well as resolving conflicts between Marketing and Development becomes an integral part of requirements prioritization negotiations [RegnBrin05].

In vendor-controlled scenarios, the release frequency is usually much higher. Product functionality is delivered often and in small increments. An agile methodology is frequently applied in these scenarios, often combined with continuous deployment and a DevOps approach. The team selects a small number of items from the backlog for implementation and deployment. Each increment delivers some quantifiable value to customers. Feedback after each increment helps to maximize the customer value and satisfaction. Vendor-controlled environments enable product managers to experiment and apply a data-analysis-driven approach (see Sect. 4.2.2). More systematic release planning is only used for larger requirements that need changes in different parts of the code with dependencies, or span teams or delivery cycles. Techniques how to address these issues are described in the methods for large-scale agile development, e.g. SAFe [KnasLeff20].

4.3.2 Releases with Continuous Development and Deployment

Vendor-controlled environments may use a continuous development and deployment approach to shorten time to market. This usually comes with agile methodology and a DevOps approach (see Sect. 6.2) that ensures a high degree of automation. In this environment, individual requirements are selected for implementation, picked up by the development team from the backlog, then implemented and deployed by going through the DevOps process. When Amazon claims that they do more than 1000 releases per day, the term release means the deployment of such small changes in the runtime environment, thereby making the changes quickly available to the users of the system, i.e. the software product.For a product manager, it can be challenging to avoid conflicts between his own prioritization decisions and the development team's decisions. For larger requirements that require changes in different parts of the software, or for more complex dependencies between requirements, systematic release planning (as described below) is also applied in this environment.

4.3.3 Systematic Release Planning

Software products that run in customer-controlled environments, i.e. the Icebreaker and Cruise Ship scenarios, require systematic release planning. In the Powerboat and Speedboat scenarios it is relevant for complex subsets of changes (see above).

Concepts
The Release Concept
A software product evolves over time and thus exists in different releases. Releases have different amounts of new and/or changed code and visibility external to the product organization. According to the ISPMA glossary, releases offered to customers are called product releases, while releases only visible within the product organization are called pre-releases. Releases with more significant changes may be called versions, while releases with less significant changes are called minor releases or increments. Figure 4.2 gives an overview of these terms.

A variety of labeling schemes for the released software is practiced by vendors. Depending on the type and amount of change, releases are called major, minor, update, and service or patch release. Other names may be invented for marketing

Term	Definition
Release	An instance of software made available to stakeholders.
Pre-Release	A result of development activity that is testable, e.g. the result of a sprint in Scrum.
Product Release	An instance of the product delivered to customers, and maintained as part of product maintenance.
Major Release	The release contains significant new or changed functionality compared to other releases. Such a release might be referred to as a new version for marketing or business reasons.
Increment or Minor Release	A minor release that contains less significant new or changed functionality compared to other releases.

Fig. 4.2 Release planning definitions

reasons. To use a widely-known software product as an example, Google numbered a release of the Android Gmail application "version 5.10.112808100" to reflect that the Gmail app release was the update "112,808,100" of the tenth increment of the fifth version of the product.

The hierarchy of new functionality within a product is: version, essentially a product with a planned set of functionality over time, release of a product, i.e. it is an instance of that product version with new and/or changed functionality. With licensed products or managed service offerings, multiple versions and releases of the product may be used by customers in parallel, when the vendor cannot convince all customers to run on the latest version. In this situation, the vendor may have to provide new releases and maintenance for multiple versions or release levels in parallel. This can also happen when a vendor offers an older version at a considerably lower price to address price-sensitive markets. However, the support of multiple product releases in the market generates cost, diverts resources to maintenance, may generate significant complexity to support, and thereby reduces the organization's capacity for developing new releases. For that reason, product organizations typically try to keep the number of concurrently maintained releases small.

The Release Planning Process
With the requirements-driven approach, releases are planned by selecting requirements for implementation. Requirements can come from a variety of sources (see Sect. 4.2.1.2). With the data-analysis-driven approach, experiments need to be prepared by implementing code which can also be done as pre-releases that need planning.

To achieve short time-to-market, a first version of a new product should be small, yet still viable for the first customers. Later releases enhance that minimally viable scope and make the product attractive for customer segments that were not addressed with the first version. When a product achieves maturity, release decisions aim at keeping the product competitive and interoperable. At the end of life of a product, release

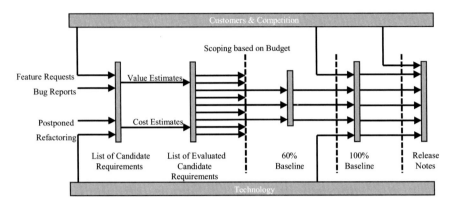

Fig. 4.3 Requirements flow and selection for a mature product, adapted from [Davis05]. Vertical gray bars stand for requirements baselines. Vertical dashed lines stand for selection decisions

plans may contain features that help customers to migrate to replacement products. Section 4.5 describes how the product life cycle affects product planning.

Figure 4.3 shows how inputs obtained from the market and technology perspectives are used in step-wise refinement and selection processes to decide content for a mature product release. Specifications are developed for candidate requirements which are then evaluated in terms of value and cost. Once the requirements to be included are decided, based on selection, available budget and development resource, a release plan is laid out. The selection of requirements to be implemented is called the scope of the release. As the analysis and development unfold in the release projects, release plans are reviewed and adjusted until a dependable commitment can be given for what the exact scope is that is about to be released. Each published instance of the release plan is called a baseline.

Release Trains, Staging, and Product Variants

To minimize the time-to-market and utilize specialist capacity efficiently, software organizations work with parallel development activities resulting in releases. A heartbeat is used to define a schedule of releases that is called a release train. Figure 4.4 shows such a schedule. The release train below shows clearly how this development plan allows compact utilization of requirements engineering and development capacity. Management and other company functions are involved on a regular schedule for scoping and product release. Notice that the term "release train" is a central term in SAFe [KnasLeff20], but defined differently. Here an "agile release train" is the team of agile teams working together.

In many situations, the release development work is based on a staging process that aims at delivering software product releases that are attractive, mature and high quality. As the staging evolves, the implementation of requirements must meet a series of quality gates. Development creates a pre-release for each quality gate.

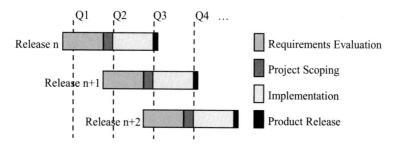

Fig. 4.4 Parallelization of release development with a release train, based on [RegHNBH01]: shown is an extract with a series of 3 releases over four quarters (Q)

When product families, lines, or platforms are involved, release planning becomes a complex multi-dimensional problem. Versioning across product variants adds complexity to the time-oriented versioning described above. If the same product is offered in different industry-specific incarnations or on multiple platforms the product manager must deal with horizontal versioning, adding yet more complexity. Vertical versioning is the term for product variants with differing functionality and price points. An example are Microsoft's Enterprise, Professional, Home and Student editions of Office. When a product portfolio comprises a bundle of separate products with dependencies on each other and individual release plans, release planning and execution for the bundled product can become a nightmare. Hence, the product manager must do as much as possible to simplify the portfolio of variants and the release planning process.

Release Planning Methods

Various methods exist to answer the following questions: when and what should be released? The release planning decisions that drive the answers must balance many sometimes conflicting forces. On one side, the selected requirements need to satisfy business objectives and real customer needs while leading to a recognizable advantage over the competition. Such value consideration needs trade-off between technology push and market pull, i.e. between innovative technology-driven features and customer requirements. The organization's strategy may guide this trade-off and determine to what degree the company is reactive to its markets by giving priority to customer needs or pursues a proactive innovation strategy by pushing new technologies to the markets. On the other side, the selected requirements need to take into account the capabilities and capacity of the product organization, while being compliant with time and budget constraints and architectural considerations. Other influencing factors can be release themes, customer commitments and sales and marketing activities like a product presentation at a trade fair.

Deciding on a Release Plan

Academics have done interesting work considering release planning as an optimization problem. Major factors considered in such release plan optimization are the

Objective: agree with stakeholders on the scope of the next release project.

Steps:

1. Understand the product and organizational environment
2. Understand the parameters of development
3. Understand product life cycle dependencies that influence release decisions
4. Prepare draft release plan
    5.   Execute release plan by generating, evaluating, and negotiating possible release plans, and making decisions
6. Analyze and reflect on the release planning experience
7. Package experience documentation and results to make the experience available to others

Fig. 4.5 Generic approach for deciding about a release plan

value and effort estimated for individual requirements. Other factors are marketing themes attached to new releases or versions, dependencies between requirements and other products, customer commitments, and risk. Formal optimization approaches easily deal with value, effort, and dependencies. Other factors are more difficult to account for in an optimization model. Consequently, the optimization of release plans has been called the "Art and Science of Software Release Management" [RuheSal05]. The difficulty of formalizing a release planning equation is a reason that many product managers do not use mathematical optimization.

In practice, release planning involves negotiations and setting priorities to resolve conflicts between stakeholders about release objectives and contents. An approved release plan is one that all stakeholders agree to, and conflicts are inevitable. Typically, a multi-stakeholder agreement is an iterative decision-making process of requirements elicitation, concept validation, and decision-making. Software development methodology will also affect release planning. Agile and lean approaches allow frequent consideration and re-consideration of requirement priorities, thus support a trial-and-error learning process of what is acceptable to the stakeholders. In contrast, waterfall development freezes project scope and formalizes change management early. Hence, this latter development methodology requires more upfront thinking and, consequently, more firm agreements including a willingness to freeze requirements for periods of time.

Figure 4.5 shows a generic decision-making process for a software product release. Even though presented in a linear fashion, the process is highly iterative because the value of a release is hard to judge [Carlshamre02]. The evaluation criteria can often not be defined in advance. Judgments are highly subjective, and the grouping of requirements and features affects the value and cost of their implementation. As a consequence, it is difficult to assess whether a release content is good enough.

Release planning work requires significant preparation. In relation to step 1, a solid understanding of the product and organizational environment helps the product manager in the execution of the release planning process. Knowledge of the stakeholders, requirements, preferences, constraints, and cost constraints allows the product manager to conceive tactical options for alternative release plans and streamlines the release planning process. The preparation concludes in step 4 by selecting analysis and visualization approaches and defining a schedule of stakeholder workshops.

The step 5 is iterative and involves discussions between the stakeholders concerned with the release. The critical stakeholders are product management, engineering, marketing, and executive management. Scoping of the release requires consensus concerning the evaluation and prioritization of requirements as well as skillful visualization of the results among the important stakeholders.

Release planning work concludes by analyzing the process and the achieved outcome. The analysis aims at identifying opportunities for improving release planning. It involves investigation of the stakeholders' satisfaction with the release planning process and the appropriateness and stability of the release planning decisions. These outcomes should flow into the preparation of subsequent iterations of release planning thus avoiding unnecessary problems proactively while achieving an efficient and flexible process.

Evaluation Criteria
The evaluation, prioritization, and packaging of requirements into releases require creativity and experience. The ideal release, of course, is well-balanced, perfectly timed, and contains the most significant requirements which are of value to customers, which are required to fulfill the organization's strategic initiatives, and which satisfy the need for quality improvements. Obviously the release must be accepted by all product stakeholders. This ideal will rarely be achieved in practice. Usually focus areas must be defined for a release, e.g. making it a release for a new customer segment, a release focused on quality improvements, or a migration release that supports, for example, a new database system.

There are always more requirements than can be implemented within the given resources and budget. Also, time considerations may be important, e.g. to meet the deadlines of trade fairs or answer announcements of competitive products. Some companies perform a business evaluation of each individual feature. That means that a business case is calculated that considers the cost side, in cooperation with development for the estimation of effort, and the value or benefits that an implementation of the requirements would bring. Other potential release influencers include product dependencies, the grouping of requirements to optimize implementation thus reducing effort and cost, or coherent content to ease explanation of the release to customers and stakeholders. Also, the resolution of conflicts between marketing and development are an integral part of requirements prioritization negotiations. Based on this evaluation, the product manager needs to decide what is best given the resources, budget, and time restraints.

Requirements evaluation from the perspectives of the business, management, and system uses various criteria [WohAur05]. Business criteria are based on the product strategy. They include marketing concerns, e.g. release themes and dates, the

---

Prioritization criteria for value
- Priority of stakeholders: prioritize by the beneficiaries of the requirements.
- Priority of customers and users: prioritize the requirements of prioritized customers.
- Competitors: prioritize requirements that allow equalizing or gaining sales advantage over competitors.
- Urgency: prioritize requirements by considering the product's release date.

Prioritization criteria for cost
- Effort: prioritize requirements that require little implementation effort.
- Development cost/benefit: prioritize requirements with high expected benefit and low cost.
- Staff: prioritize requirements for which the right knowledge and skills are available.
- System operation: prioritize requirements based on the expected cost of system operation.
- Availability of support: prioritize requirements for which technical support and training can be provided.

Prioritization criteria related to the development of the technical solution
- Complexity: prioritize requirements that avoid architectural degradation of the systems.
- Evolution: prioritize requirements that bring flexibility for system evolution.
- Dependencies: group requirements that should be implemented together and prioritize them by technical and marketing-related dependencies.
- Volatility: prioritize requirements that should be stabilized or isolated.

Fig. 4.6 Common prioritization criteria based on [WohAur05]

competitive situation, stakeholder priorities, and requirements volatility. Management criteria include value, cost, and risk of the development, the need for resources and competencies, the delivery date and calendar time in relation to the roadmap, and the availability of support for education and training. System criteria include system impact, complexity, requirements dependencies, evolution, and maintenance. Requirements dependencies increase the complexity of release planning and require additional analysis as the removal of any prerequisite requirement for the release affects the dependent requirements. Requirements which span teams or delivery cycles need extra care. Figure 4.6 gives an overview of the most common prioritization criteria.

The products' position in its life cycle affects the selection of release planning criteria. In the early phases of the product life cycle, a high degree of uncertainty characterizes release planning. The product is not yet completely shaped, and the product use cases are evolving. Release planning focuses therefore on the most important requirements needed for onboarding of the next customers and learning by the product organization. To ease change and evolution, a minimum viable product (MVP) approach is pursued (see Sect. 3.5.3).

The growth phase calls for releases which extend the MVP with features to satisfy interesting market segments and counter competitive threats. In this phase, interoperability is a key concern as it allows a product to be integrated into the customers' environments and increases the customers' difficulty of switching to alternatives.

Because of the many additions, the product evolves rapidly, and complexity becomes an issue.

In the maturity phase, release planning no longer focuses primarily on the addition of new functions. Instead, requirements are prioritized that support new environments, improve user experience, and increase performance and reliability. Since the product architecture and constraints are well known, requirements can be estimated more precisely than in earlier phases, which leads to improved release planning outcomes.

Towards the end of the life of a product, requirements are prioritized that help to retain customers with minimal investment or help them switch to a replacement product that has hopefully been added to the company's portfolio. Large and disruptive improvements are implemented only in the new replacement product to motivate customers to migrate.

Prioritization Techniques

Several requirements prioritization techniques are commonly used. Simple techniques which can be employed ad-hoc are used to evaluate requirements in workshops with the concerned stakeholders. More advanced techniques, based on mathematical optimization, require tool support and generate and analyze options for release plans off-line in the preparation of decision-making workshops.

Figure 4.7 gives an overview of the techniques adapted to a workshop setting. In such a workshop, a moderator prioritizes requirements together with stakeholders according to chosen evaluation criteria. To ensure the credibility of the results, the workshop must involve stakeholders who have the best possible knowledge about the concerned requirements and estimates. Market representatives should evaluate requirements value, and developers requirements cost. The prioritization is repeated for each prioritization criterion. When stakeholders are confronted with many requirements, the requirements are aggregated, e.g. into features, before prioritization.

Especially in agile settings, the Planning Poker technique is used for estimating effort. The technique is efficient and leads to reliable estimates [KarTRBW06]. The technique also permits the differences between estimates to be used as uncertainty indicators and disagreements can be resolved through dialogue among the participants. These two aspects expose and control risk, thus building participant trust in the prioritization results. In addition to effort estimation, the technique can be used for evaluating requirements based on other criteria as well.

Selecting requirements for implementation requires sensible aggregation of scores against multiple criteria. Wiegers suggests combining benefits from need satisfaction, the penalties of need dissatisfaction, cost of requirements implementation, and risk into an aggregate score [Wiegers03]. The requirements selection problem then becomes the problem of selecting the best-scoring requirements. Also, Ruhe and his colleagues consider requirements selection as a multi-criteria optimization problem. A further approach is the Analytical Hierarchy Process that allows defining weights for criteria in addition to evaluating the requirements with the criteria. While providing fine-grained rankings and supporting sensitivity

Top-10
1. Prepare: the moderator introduces the requirements and the prioritization criteria.
2. Evaluate: each participant selects the ten most relevant items privately, without sharing the results with any other participant.
3. Aggregate: the moderator counts the number of votes for each requirement. Success enhancer: in step 2, 10%-30% of the requirements should be selected.

Numerical Assignment (Grouping)
1. Prepare: the moderator introduces the requirements and the prioritization criteria.
2. Evaluate: each participant privately partitions the requirements into three groups, for example, into "critical" (weight 9), "important" (weight 3), and "optional" (weight 1).
3. Aggregate: the moderator calculates the weighted sum of votes for each requirement. Success enhancer: in step 2, each group should have approximately the same size.

Ranking (Sorting)
1. Prepare: the moderator introduces the requirements and the prioritization criteria.
2. Evaluate: each participant privately sorts the requirements so that the highest-ranking requirements is at the top and the lowest-ranking at the bottom of the list.
3. Aggregate: the moderator calculates the median rank (more robust) or average rank (enables many statistical tests) of each requirement.
Success enhancer: allow participants to sort visually, e.g. with a spreadsheet.

100 Dollar (Cumulative Voting)
1. Prepare: the moderator introduces the requirements and the prioritization criteria.
2. Evaluate: each participant privately invests a total of 100 points (or dollars or euros) into the set of requirements, proportional to the perceived worth according to the criteria.
3. Aggregate: the moderator sums the number of invested points for each requirement. Success enhancer: vary the number of points to be invested as necessary.

Planning Poker for Effort Estimation (Consensus Seeking)
1. Prepare: the moderator introduces the requirements and the procedure.
2. Evaluate: each participant privately estimates the effort for implementing the requirement.
3. Aggregate: each participant shares his estimate and, if it is the highest or lowest estimate, provides a justification for it. The group discusses the estimates and justifications.
4. Seek Consensus: go to step 2 if no consensus has been reached. If the differences between the most optimistic and pessimistic estimates are small, select an estimate in the middle.
5. Repeat the Planning Poker for all requirements to be evaluated.
Success enhancer: make estimates based on a Fibonacci-like series of numbers. A commonly used series is 0, ½, 1, 2, 3, 5, 8, 13, 20, 40, 100, ?, and Coffee. "?" reflects the inability to estimate. "Coffee" reflects a need to take a break, e.g. for private discussions.

Fig. 4.7 Prioritization techniques for workshop settings, in the order of increasing complexity

analyses, these approaches suffer from a dependency on tools and from giving the impressions of being black boxes. They deliver results in ways that are not understood by the stakeholders. Also, the estimates of value and cost are often questionable even if sophisticated estimation approaches are used. Accordingly, the simpler techniques are much more frequently used.

Quality Performance (QUPER) Approach

1. Prepare: define the type of quality requirement to be defined.
2. Evaluate benefit: estimate the breakpoints of useless, useful, competitive, and excessive quality from a user perspective.
3. Evaluate cost: estimate barriers for quality levels that require a significant change of the technical approach.
4. Analyze market: estimate the product's current quality and the current and expected quality of the competing products.
5. Propose releases: estimate quality targets for coming releases that reflect technical feasibility and the product's competitive strategy.
6. Repeat by extending the analysis with other important quality characteristics.

Success enhancer: measure the users' perceived benefit with a Mean Opinion Score "MOS." The MOS is on a scale from 1-5 and may be determined experimentally [empirically?] by letting users use the concerned features and asking them for feedback [FoFrFi14].

Fig. 4.8   QUPER technique for planning quality levels, based on [RegnBSO08]

The Pareto principle is often used for release planning. Pareto analysis is a technique to match the most important requirements with the given delivery capacity. The technique is based on the 80:20 principle that says that 20% of the work will generate 80% of the value. This approach selects the top 20% of the analyzed requirements. Davis recommends starting development with a requirements baseline that represents 60% of the capacity available in development [Davis05].

While the techniques discussed thus far work well for functional requirements, they are of limited use for quality requirements. The definition of quality requirements, such as performance, usability, and reliability is often a problem of defining appropriate levels of quality, rather than defining whether to add or remove a quality requirement. Regnell and his colleagues proposed the quality performance QUPER approach that determines quality levels based on competitive analyses and architectural barriers [RegnBSO08]. QUPER is a simplified form of the more elaborated Quality Function Deployment approach [SchoHerz17]. Figure 4.8 gives an overview of the QUPER technique performed by a team of analysts who are competent in technology and have market knowledge.

Visualizing and Agreeing on Prioritization Results

Visualization makes the requirements evaluation results accessible for the decision makers. It is a tactical tool that can be employed during the release negotiations. Visualization can be used to underline how collected evidence supports or speaks against the arguments that are used when deciding about a proposed release plan.

Either text or graphical format may be used to present evaluation results. A widely-used approach is to use sorted requirements lists or tables that indicate selection and discarding of requirements. In an agile context, the sorted requirements lists are called requirements backlogs. In a product line context, often tables are used that show the matching of requirements to product variants. Both visualization

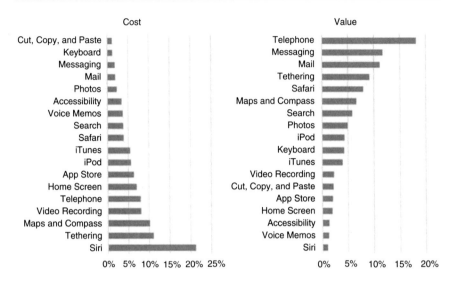

Fig. 4.9 Visualization of evaluation results for smartphone features with bar charts

approaches may be enhanced with information about ratings and rankings, by adding columns with the respective information. When used for supporting decisions, text-based visualizations offer insights both into the evaluation results and the detailed data.

When estimates are on a proportional scale, graphical representations are attractive. Their advantage is that they can express patterns and relationships better than text-based formats. A simple approach is the use of bar charts, illustrated in Fig. 4.9 that shows evaluation results of smartphone features. Bar charts can also be visualized as stacked bars, e.g. to indicate the contribution of individual stakeholders to the total estimate. Graphical formats can indicate the estimated spreads. For example, frequency distribution charts show the spread of values [RegHNBH01] and box-plots aggregate information about these distributions [McGiTuLa78]. These are common tools used by statisticians to give an overview of estimates.

When relationships between estimates are of interest, scatter plots become a useful visualization tool. In comparison to one-dimensional graphical representations, scatter plots make interesting data points, e.g. outliers, and clusters of data more visible. In release planning, scatter plots may be used to show the cost/value relationship of requirements. Figure 4.10 shows a cost/value diagram of the evaluation results shown in Fig. 4.9. Each point represents a feature: the x-axis the relative cost and the y-axis the relative value of a feature.

Figure 4.10 illustrates the use of a cost/value diagram for selection of features with a dashed line. If all features above the line are implemented, the selection implies the creation of 83% value for 46% cost by a development project in comparison to implementation of all requirements. Such selection of features leads to a large return on investment. Similar diagrams and similar analyses can compare

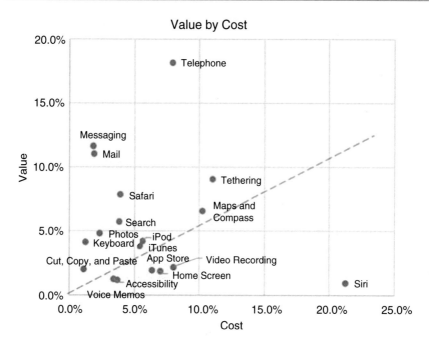

Fig. 4.10 Visualization of evaluation results as a cost/value scatter plot. Dashed line selection

features based on other combinations of evaluation criteria, for example, the criterion of risk.

More advanced charts have been proposed by Regnell and colleagues who suggest the use of disagreement charts, satisfaction charts, and influence charts [RegHNBH01]. The disagreement chart shows how much stakeholders agree or disagree on the priority of each feature. It allows identification of problematic features. The satisfaction chart shows how much each stakeholder's priorities agree with the overall priorities. The influence chart, finally, shows the weight given to each stakeholder. We refer to Regnell's publications for the details of how to construct these diagrams. What is important is that the product manager knows who disagrees, who is satisfied, and who has what kind of influence. That knowledge allows acting based on a full understanding of the decision-making.

To get to agreement when multiple stakeholders are involved, it is not enough to use the analytical approaches discussed thus far. Reaching agreement depends on the skillful use of evaluation results, the development of convincing arguments, and the willingness of all involved to adjust their position to reach an agreement. This readiness for a successful dialogue requires trusted relationships among the involved parties, having prepared alternative proposals for release plans, and in-depth understanding of the impact of these plans on stakeholders.

It is also important to know that a product manager does not need to obtain the support of all stakeholders [FricGru08]. An alliance of stakeholders suffices if the allied stakeholders have enough power to make the decision. If an agreement is not possible, the product manager may propose a middle way between the stakeholders' positions to reach consensus. If conflicts persevere, the product manager may initiate an escalation of the decision to an authority with power stronger than the involved parties, for example to the head of the business unit or company to which the product belongs.

The Release Plan

In comparison to a roadmap, the release plan focuses on the short-term, a single release. The results from release planning are documented in a release plan which defines the core product in terms of functionality, quality, and constraints (see Sect. 4.2.1.2). Release plans are important because they define the way the organization balances its capabilities for short-term goal achievement and long-term investment by adding, changing, and removing or re-focusing resources. The software product manager needs to make sure that the release plan is synchronized with the product roadmap and matches organizational interests.

The release plan is used by the development manager to scope product development. Often, development resources are not sufficient to implement all the identified requirements for timely delivery, implying a need for prioritization and debate between stakeholders to reach an agreement about trade-offs. Since such detailed planning leads to new insights, release planning may imply changes in the product roadmap which affect stakeholders other than just product development.

Release planning may occur at regular intervals or at moments that are important for the product organization. Companies may synchronize development activities with a heartbeat to achieve consistency across multiple software systems. The heartbeat determines when release development activities start and when resulting product releases become available to customers. The frequency of the heartbeat varies, from one release per year to one release per few weeks.

Release planning should be supported with tools for managing requirements backlogs to handle the often large amount of detail. Tools, discussed in Sect. 4.6, give transparency to pending and completed work and may be as simple as a spreadsheet or as advanced as issue trackers that interoperate with project, test, and knowledge management tools. This transparency, reflected in changes to the backlog, gives an indication of remaining time-to-complete and of whether the right amount of development resource is available.

There is no standard format for a release plan. The development and release process will guide how a release plan is documented. The simplest versions of release plans often appear in agile development projects, the most elaborated versions in product line or systems-of-systems environments with staged releases of the product under development. The product manager needs to understand this product development context and adapt the format and contents of his release plan.

Minimal elements of a release plan include:

- A definition of the software version,
- The release date,

- Resource assumptions, and
- Selected requirements.

Many release plans include additional information:

- The intent-summarizing theme of the release,
- Supported stakeholders, and
- Traceability to the sources of the selected requirements.

A release plan may be even further enhanced with the following information:

- The customers or beneficiaries who are the targets of the software release,
- The budget, capacity, and staffing for the development work,
- How the release supports the implementation of the product strategy,
- Assumptions, dependencies, risks, and other issues

Traditionally release planning documents the scope of a release in a succession of requirements documents. The marketing requirements document (MRD) describes the market opportunities to be addressed with the release. It is the first document to capture the list of evaluated candidate requirements. The product requirements document (PRD) consolidates relevant customer requirements into a coherent vision of the planned product release that considers the budget that is available for the release project. The technical requirements document (TRD) is a low-level specification of functional requirements, quality requirements, and constraints for the software to be developed. It defines the full scope of the software product.

Agile approaches to requirements specification derive from backlogs used to manage software development. These approaches are also frequently used in the powerboat and speedboat constellations. Rather than writing requirements documents, Wikis and issue tracking tools are used to define plans and monitor progress. The plan that historically has been defined by the documenting requirements in a document is here defined by allocating the requirements to a release. The progress that was historically visible by the progressive document updates is here managed by defining and following the life cycle of individual requirements.

During the implementation of the release, the product grows and matures. Upon conclusion of the implementation, the documentation of the release must reflect any updates to the original documentation of the product. At this stage, the release notes replace the earlier release plan with a description of the implementation requirements together with an overview of known issues and bugs for the release. The internal product documentation also includes technical artifacts, including architecture, development environment, code, test environment, tests, and test reports.

Frequently, part of the product manager's release responsibility is the final release decision, i.e. if the new release is ready to be made available to customers. A number of criteria will be relevant to this decision [AlNaPfRu17] with the value of new functionality and achieved quality being the most important.

4.3.4   Summary and Conclusions

This chapter has given an overview of the concepts, process, and techniques for release management in different scenarios. With a requirements-driven approach, release planning often requires an evaluation and selection process, in which requirements from market pull and technology push undergo analysis and are allocated to release development lined up in a release train. To decide on the scope of a release, the product manager seeks agreement and support from important stakeholders with proposed plans developed by prioritizing requirements according to criteria like value, cost, and risk. The chapter described the generic release planning process and gave an overview of the many techniques that are available. The chapter has concluded with suggestions for documenting the release plan, both with backlogs in an agile environment and as a series of documents with more traditional methodologies.

4.4   Roadmapping

4.4.1   Overview

Product roadmapping is a flexible technique for strategic and long-range planning of software product evolution [PhaFarPr04]. A product roadmap describes what the product organization intends to deliver and achieve with the product over time. Roadmapping can apply to a single product, a portfolio, a product line, or to a family of products. Roadmaps are a structured and often graphical means for exploring and communicating the relationships between evolving and developing markets, products, and technologies over time. The roadmap translates the product strategy into an implementation action plan over the strategic timeframe.

Roadmapping assumes that a product is in a changing but reasonably predictable environment where markets, technologies, and products come and go. The company will evolve the product with the necessary development, marketing, research, or procurements. The roadmap describes the planned results of these activities. A roadmap is a means of documenting predicted or planned changes, agreeing with key stakeholders on the timing and scope of change activities, communicating the agreed plans, and monitoring the implementation of the plans as the activities of the roadmap unfold.

A roadmap depends on corporate and product vision, on product, market, and technology research, and on product strategy. The technique assumes that the product organization has a good understanding of the company's position and the company's strategic direction For example, product management should have a good understanding of target customers, user personas, and market trends. Marketing should have a good understanding of the current state of target markets, important events that the company needs to react to, and of trends and target customer problems that should be addressed. Research and Development need to understand the capabilities and limitations of their own software, technical contributions available from third parties, and any competitive or alternative solutions.

When we use the term "roadmap" in product management, we mean a strategic roadmap that describes on a higher level of abstraction how and when the elements of the product strategy are intended to be implemented over the strategic timeframe. A description on a feature level does not make sense, in particular for the outer years, since the product manager does not know today which features will be implemented in a release 4 years from today. In agile environments, the term "roadmap" is often used as a plan for features the development team is supposed to implement over the next couple of months. This has the character of a development plan, and as such makes sense, but is clearly different from the strategic roadmap that we are referring to. In some companies, these two meanings of the term "roadmap" can get mixed up, e.g. when a long-term roadmap is filled with feature descriptions. These companies usually realize sooner or later that feature planning does not make sense for long timeframes like 5 years. Unfortunately, the conclusion is frequently not to use a higher level of abstraction for the contents of the roadmap, but rather to shorten the timeframe that the roadmap covers. While we agree that for the near-term the roadmap can be more detailed down to a feature level, we do not recommend shortening the time frame. Successful technology companies like Amazon may look at strategic timeframes of up to 10 years.

Roadmapping is best as an iterative process, where a roadmap is proposed and agreed, activities launched to implement the roadmap, the achieved results and outcomes reviewed, and the roadmap revised. The contents of a roadmap derive from exploring alternative approaches to creating value with a product and by involving the product stakeholders in decision-making. The roadmap is then used to focus requirements engineering, plan release implementations, and handshake with development. Deviations from the roadmap are investigated to understand their causes and the roadmap adapted to ensure relevance and feasibility. The roadmap is updated at regular intervals, before the launch of large initiatives, or upon release of software products. A product manager must ensure that a roadmap continues to be up-to-date, since roadmaps are frequently used as a fundamental means of strategy communication in both internal and external presentations.

This chapter introduces the basic elements of roadmaps, describes the major sources of inputs needed to build a roadmap, and describes approaches for building and communicating roadmaps. At the conclusion the reader will understand the structure and form of software product roadmaps and how to implement roadmapping.

4.4.2 Concept

Roadmap, in the most general sense of the word, is a plan to guide progress toward a goal (from the Merriam-Webster dictionary). The term originating from automotive travel has found increased acceptance in other areas such as science, technology, industry, and business planning to refer to a description of past events and a plan of how the future will evolve [KostScha01]. In software product management, a product roadmap is a document that describes contents and/or outcomes of the product releases planned over the strategic time frame. In other words, it is a plan of how to implement a product vision and strategy by building and evolving one or multiple related software products over a series of releases.

The purpose of the roadmap is to provide in bold strokes an overview of how a product will develop over several releases, how the product is used to serve important markets, and how technology will be used in building the product [Groenv97], in short how the product vision is going to be turned into reality during the strategic time frame.

A product roadmap usually has the following basic elements:

- Timescale
- Releases and versions
- Release themes and main features
- Target markets
- Product dependencies
- Ways in which technology may impact product or implementation

Roadmaps are most often presented graphically to illustrate dependencies between their elements. Figure 4.11 illustrates the key elements of a layered product roadmap used for product planning [PhaFarPr04]. The vertical axis describes the layers that are relevant to achieving the product vision. The layers used for roadmapping are selected to suit the product planning needs. The horizontal axis indicates the time. For software products with frequent releases this timeframe is up to 1 year [LeKaVä07]. Products with hardware tend to use longer timeframes [Groenv97].

A layered roadmap contains the following elements: The markets layer defines the milestones to be achieved in the product markets. Milestones refer to

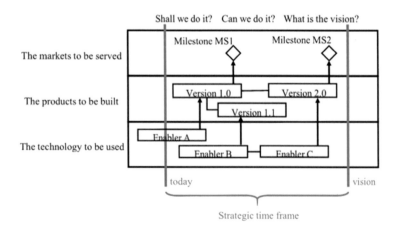

Fig. 4.11 Layered product roadmap based on [PhaFarPr04]. The time flows from left to right

achievements that are important to the product's bottom line. The milestones can refer to targeted segments, to differentiation versus competitors, to target market share, to target installation base, to contracts to be won, or other drivers used to judge product success. During the later requirements engineering, each milestone will be refined by specifying customers and stakeholders, rules and regulations, and requirements to be fulfilled.

The products layer describes development in terms of product versions and releases. A coarse-grained roadmap indicates the timelines, themes and intended outcomes for the software product. The themes guide the scope of product versions. A fine-grained roadmap indicates the main content elements to support the themes and to reach intended outcomes. Product development rollout of releases intended to achieve market-level milestones reflects the strategy that the product manager has chosen for product success.

The technologies layer contains important technological enablers to be incorporated and implemented in the software product. Such enablers may comprise components, frameworks, standards, or ICT services. Enablers may be developed in-house, developed in collaboration with an open-source community or partners, or procured from suppliers.

In Fig. 4.11, the horizontal sequences indicate the role of the created assets for enabling future assets [KhuFrGor15]. For example, product versions and releases may replace earlier product versions and releases, and thus are dependent on them. The vertical cross-layer arrows indicate the value impact of created assets: the use of the assets as means to achieve the ends at which the arrows are pointing.

Some product roadmaps can be as simple as having just a single product layer. Such roadmaps imply roadmap users already have knowledge of product impact and product technology. Other product roadmaps indicate additional dependencies and drivers for product development and release. To depict such dependencies and drivers, additional layers may be introduced or existing layers enhanced with additional information like:

- Events of relevance for marketing such as conferences, fairs, publicized launch dates,
- Events of relevance for sales such as customer contracts or projects,
- Use scenarios and pilot projects used for product validation [FricSchu12],
- Distribution, service, and support services,
- Heartbeats with regularly spaced releases, for example monthly, quarterly, or half-yearly [RegHNBH01],
- Need for and availability of experts and capacity of product development staff [VähRau05],
- Dependencies with other product, technology, organization, or industry roadmaps, and
- Risks which require monitoring and mitigation.

The definition of product roadmaps requires simultaneous consideration of technology push and market pull. Technology push should be used to exploit assets and capabilities other companies will find hard to copy or imitate [Teece10]. These assets should be used to facilitate and accelerate the development of products and features that provide a strategic advantage in the markets. Market pull should be used to exploit opportunities for the company such as important tenders, cooperation with partnering customers, or synergies with marketing and sales initiatives.

Completed roadmaps show the way in which companies address and respond to technology pushes and market pulls over time. The near-term roadmap addresses the question "shall we do it?" This part of the roadmap is used for obtaining stakeholder commitment, launching development activities, and allocating resources to these activities. Its contents should thus be reliable and indicate what the product stakeholders have agreed to do. The mid-term roadmap addresses the question "can we do it?" It is used for launching feasibility studies. Its contents should be attractive and indicate what the product stakeholders have agreed to explore with market analyses, technology evaluations, and prototyping. The long-term roadmap addresses the question "what is the vision?" It should express what the stakeholders perceive to be attractive goals in terms of market, product, and technology development. The path chosen from today into the future should enable the creation of the right market, product, and technological assets to achieve these goals.

4.4.3   Graphical Representations of Roadmaps

The format of roadmaps may vary [PhaFarPr04]. Figure 4.12 gives an overview of common variations.

The *tree-shaped roadmap* allows expression of multiple alternative time axes by depicting the growth of a tree from the root into leaves. Another name for such a tree-shaped roadmap is the feature tree. It is a way to define alternative or complementing options for the evolution of a product. The stem represents the product's core, the branches and leaves enhancing features. A branch indicates dependencies among the nodes. The tree-shaped roadmap may later be transformed into a linear roadmap by deciding on an implementation order of the nodes while respecting the dependencies that are implied by the growth metaphor of the tree [FricSchu12].

Vector-shaped roadmaps are used to express quality or performance. The vector-shaped format works well to define performance improvements achieved with a planned sequence of product releases. The horizontal axis represents time, the vertical axis performance. A vector represents a platform or technology that gives rise to a series of product versions with increasingly better performance. After some steps in the product evolution, the many changes may have led to so much architectural degradation that the product cannot be evolved anymore with reasonable effort and needs replacement. At that moment, a replacement product with at least comparable functionality and performance must be available to replace the old product. Vector-shaped roadmaps are also useful to analyze innovations by depicting the impact of new technologies that replace older ones. In this context, vector roadmaps are called S-curves.

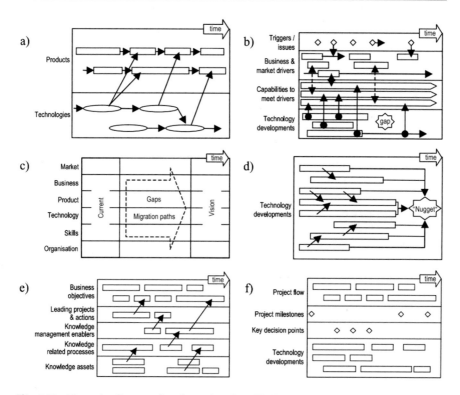

Fig. 4.12 Alternative formats of roadmaps based on [PhaFarPr04]

The *bar-shaped roadmaps* represent a third important format, typically used for technology roadmapping. Each row corresponds to an important capability of the product and contains a description of the technologies available for implementing that capability. Such information is essential for planning improvements to the evolving product, particularly when technology determines the improvements rather than the way the technology is incorporated into the product. Such bar roadmaps may be created during technology evaluation and used as one of the important inputs to product roadmapping workshops.

Examples (a)–(f) show how different graphical representations may be used in roadmaps. Example (c) is frequently used in external roadmap presentations without any timing information.

4.4.4   Roadmapping Process

Product roadmapping is a creative, expert-based approach for understanding, planning, and managing product development and evolution. Product management drives the activity, supervised by senior management, and involves representatives of the product organization's areas like development and marketing. Important criteria for selecting the representatives are knowledge and authority in each area the participant represents. Product management must have understood the products it is responsible for, marketing its markets, and development the software and the technologies depended on.

During the roadmapping, the parties work together to build a shared understanding of how to implement the product vision and strategy and to agree on how and when they contribute to the implementation. Product management then uses the resulting roadmap to launch and supervise projects and to determine and monitor key performance indicators (KPI). Figure 4.13 gives an overview.

The first step of the roadmapping process identifies and evaluates options for implementation of the product vision and strategy. Each option is a building block which may be added, removed, or changed as the product evolves. Options may also be defined as alternative product concepts or complementing features used to enhance a base product. Options may depend on each other or be mutually exclusive. Roadmaps with a tree structure, as opposed to layered roadmaps, may be used to give a visual overview of the foreseen combinations and structure alternatives, complements, and dependencies.

Each option requires impact evaluation. On one hand implementation of an option requires appropriate design of software architecture and processes; on the other, each implemented option creates value by satisfying needs and expectations of stakeholders, by generating customer and user desires, and by establishing assets useful for building enhancements and future products. Each option requires time, staff, capacity, and financing to implement and deliver it to customers. Options may also create social capital by building knowledge, skills, and relationships [KhuGorW13].

A pragmatic way to evaluate options is to discuss them with the stakeholders. Such a dialogue can happen during planning meetings [Pichler10] or in a more elaborate handshaking process to define implementation proposals [FrGoBySc10]. Figure 4.14 shows a lightweight template of how such discussions may be documented and agreed with marketing (value attribute) and development

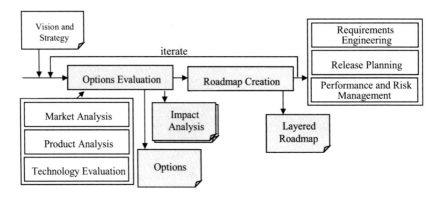

Fig. 4.13 Roadmapping process. Grey: core activities, white: dependencies

Attribute	Description
Title	Name of the option (product concept, feature, or theme).
Description	Specification of the concept, feature, or theme.
Value	Supported market needs, stakeholders, and elements of vision and strategy.
Concept	Specification of planned implementation, including components, frameworks, services, and knowledge needed for implementation.
Evaluation	Strengths, limitations, and risks of the choices documented above.
Alternatives	Alternative concepts that have been dismissed and why they were dismissed.
Estimates	Value and cost estimates.

Fig. 4.14 Documentation of an option [ClaHeyScho08, FrGoBySc10]

(design attribute). Some organizations implement such handshaking as a continuous process.

The second step of the roadmapping process is the creation and agreement of the roadmap itself. A layered roadmap helps to define when and how each option will be realized or whether an option is discarded in favor of others. This step should be undertaken as soon as the options and their impacts are sufficiently understood. The step may be effectively implemented with a workshop approach where decision makers of product management, marketing, development, and other product stakeholders participate [PhaFarPr07].

During the workshop, the roadmap is built and reviewed by roughly following the following agenda:

- Introduction: introduce workshop objectives, participants, and agenda.
- Strategic landscape: discuss the product vision and strategy, the situation, opportunities, and issues of the company, markets, and technology. The aim is to build a shared understanding of product context. Important events, issues, and activities are shown on the product timeline.
- Options: discuss and prioritize the known product concepts and features to achieve a shared understanding of options, dependencies, and impacts.
- The way forward: use the roadmap to explore possible sequences of product development and to review dependencies with Marketing and Development. Conclude with an agreement on actions regarding imminent projects and what to explore with feasibility studies.
- Consensus: agree on actions and assess satisfaction with the workshop results.

The roadmapping workshop delivers a plan of product development and evolution and a forecast of what will happen in a wider company context and the role of the product team going forward. Careful selection of the workshop participants ensures that the company uses best-possible knowledge for doing these predictions. The contributions of the key product stakeholders in the joint decision-making ensure

understanding of the roadmap and commitment to implementing the actions necessary to realize the roadmap. For product development, the roadmap is a means to
facilitate technology push. For marketing, it is a means to respond to market pull.

The results of the roadmapping workshop depend on the knowledge of the
participants. Much that is discussed and agreed may not be feasible or may not
generate the desired impacts. Technologies may not be as effective as anticipated
and have undesirable side effects. Customers may not accept a product, for example,
because base factors such as security, privacy, quality of service, or the user
experience turn out not to be as good as needed. It is thus essential for the product
manager to evaluate product use, product design, and market acceptance early.
Lessons-learned from ongoing projects, feasibility studies, product monitoring,
and customer feedback are key inputs for the next roadmapping iteration.

4.4.5   Variations of Roadmapping

Product managers may use roadmapping as a tool not only for product planning but
also for other purposes. Product roadmaps may be tools to achieve synergies in a
portfolio of products for cost reduction and for the convincing and coordinating of
parties external to the company. The former type is called cross-product roadmaps,
the latter external roadmaps. For each alternative purpose, the product roadmap
sketched in Fig. 4.11 is used as a starting point and adapted.

Use cross-product roadmaps when several products are released with the same
technological base within a product line. The product line, as defined in Chap. 2, is a
form of reuse that focuses on identifying the common and variable parts between
multiple related products. The common part is called a product platform (see Sect. 2.
2.1) and is shared by the products. To plan reuse of the platform, a feature tree is
created for the set of products contained in the product line [SchoHeTB07]. The
feature tree describes the options available for building the products for specific
markets or customer segments. In a second step create a layered roadmap to define
timing of platform and derived product development. A cross-product roadmap
differs from the basic already introduced product roadmap in that it contains multiple
products and is used to analyze the opportunities for planned reuse among the
products. Once created, the roadmap may be used to coordinate actions and
responsibilities between teams.

Cross-product roadmaps may also be used by organizations that offer a portfolio
or family of products but are not interested in systematic re-use. In this situation, the
cross-product roadmap defines how products complement each other. Use it also to
ensure that the products contained in the family are non-overlapping and that the
family does not have any gaps in its product offering.

Finally, cross-product roadmaps may also be used to plan and manage the
evolution of a software ecosystem. Such use of roadmapping has similarities with
an industry-level roadmap [KostScha01], where multiple organizations convene and
agree on how to cooperate to address important industry-wide problems. Such use of

roadmapping requires a joint objective and willingness of the companies participating in the roadmapping effort to share knowledge and to cooperate.

External roadmaps, in contrast to the roadmaps used internally in a company, are used to allow customers, market research agencies, suppliers, and other stakeholders external to the organization to understand the product vision and strategy and the approach being used to implement them. Such sharing of a roadmap allows positioning a product and eliciting feedback that is useful to validate the plans for product development and evolution. External roadmaps also play an important role in demonstrating the viability of a product. They build trust in the commitment of the company to long-term continuous investment in the product. Influential customers or partners may want to see a product roadmap, against the signature of a non-disclosure agreement, before they make a significant investment decision or decide about continued cooperation. Similarly, press and market analysts base their judgment of where the company is headed on how convincing a story about future product(s) as expressed in the roadmap is. External roadmaps are derived from internal roadmaps and contain just enough information to fulfill external information needs without disclosing too much of the company's confidential internals. To influence external stakeholders, the external roadmap requires information sufficient for competitive analysis including the targeted vision, current and announced products, differentiating features, supported applications and solutions, and sometimes early pricing information. Company robustness can be communicated through an overview of the customer base, market share, distribution channels, capabilities that are hard to copy or replicate, and important partnerships. The goal of such information is to allow customers and partners to build trust in the viability of product and company and to encourage others to refrain from competing. However, revealing too much, particularly extolling the virtues of future enhancements, can lead customers to postpone the investment and wait for the next release or version. And it can over-promise, leading to disappointment later if development plans change.

External roadmaps should include legal disclaimers which explain the confidential and legally non-binding character of the information. The former contributes to the credibility of the roadmap. The latter allows product management to retain flexibility while protecting the company against litigation. Such flexibility is important when the roadmap has become invalid, and changes are necessary. Companies have to decide how they want to deal with the confidentiality of a roadmap. Some companies require external parties to sign non-disclosure agreements before the roadmap is presented to them. Other companies make their external roadmap freely available on their web sites.

External roadmaps can also help coordinate product development with customers, partners, and other external stakeholders. When an external roadmap is used for that purpose, the involved external parties should be involved in its creation. The external roadmap is then used to constrain the internal roadmap. Such roadmap creation follows a process like the one outlined in Fig. 4.13. It leads to the same benefits of tapping into the knowledge of all involved participants and committing the partners to joint actions. The external roadmap then has the character of an industry roadmap centered on the development of the product's ecosystem. The cooperating partners are responsible for keeping their internal roadmaps consistent with the jointly agreed external roadmap.

Agile development methodologies use the term roadmap, but with a different meaning. In SAFe [KnasLeff20], it stands for a near-term plan of deliverables, e.g. what Development will produce over the next 6 months.

4.4.6   Summary and Conclusions

This section has given an overview of the roadmapping concept and how to use it for product planning. We have described the layered roadmap concept for product vision and strategy implementation and introduced additional forms of roadmaps useful for defining planning options and analyzing them. The section has also described a workshop-based roadmapping process for developing an internal roadmap and explained the relationship of internal to external roadmapping.

Once created, the roadmap is a tool for communicating how the product vision and strategy will be implemented. In comparison to an early vision statement, the roadmap is more detailed, describes the impact on development and marketing, describes intended outcomes and specific actions to be performed by important product stakeholders. The short-term roadmap provides justification for commitment of resources to activities needed to develop and evolve the product. The mid-term roadmap captures the technology push and market pull ideas of the product stakeholders. It defines the research questions that need feasibility studies. Finally, the roadmap specifies the sequence and scope of releases in coarse-grained terms. This information helps the product manager to launch the right activities, orchestrate the parties that need to cooperate, and monitor the progress of the developing and evolving product. The elements of the roadmap refer to the goals and outcomes to be achieved, the milestones for goal achievement, and the dependencies affected when milestones or goals are not met.

Completed roadmaps provide inputs for dependent product management activities. Identified activities provide the basis for forecasting, budgeting and the instantiation of activities for the development of specific product releases. The scope of the planned releases provides information about what kind of requirements engineering is necessary, including user interfaces requiring interactive user design, interfaces to external software systems, and other features that require refined alignment between markets and technology. The roadmap is also a starting point for detailed planning of upcoming software releases. Release planning will complement the roadmaps with detailed prioritization and selection of features. Roadmaps may also provide essential information for defining or refining key performance indicators such as the timing and quality of the product versions and the impact of these versions on the market. As for any other decision-making activity, the relationship between roadmapping and release planning is neither top-down nor bottom-up. Instead, one influences the other. Thus, roadmapping should always be thought of as an iterative process and roadmaps reviewed whenever important insights are gained from dependent activities.

4.5 Product Life Cycle Management

4.5.1 Overview

Product management is responsible for a product throughout its entire life cycle, from conception and introduction through growth and maturity to decline and end-of-life. Each product life cycle phase affects the product manager's focus and how he does product planning. In the early stages, experimentation with the product concept and with new features is important. In the later stages, maintenance and replacement take center stage.

Not only the product, but even product categorization goes through a life cycle. In the early stages of product categorization, the technology adoption life cycle applies. Enthusiasts and visionaries become excited about the new capabilities and try to build new business(es) using the technology. That phase is followed by the Chasm, a stage in which success in market niches determines the survival of the technology. A successful product category will continue to grow one niche market after the other until a widespread appeal has surfaced and a viable market created. That market grows, matures, and eventually declines. The category life cycle affects product planning as well. Each product categorization phase has a predominant type of new customer who is receptive to the product category and needs to be addressed if a product is to be sold successfully.

This chapter introduces the concepts of product life cycle management. The reader obtains an understanding of the three relevant life cycles and their stages, and recommendations about common tactics to implement product planning. Our primary focus will be on new products for immature markets and product evolution for mature markets.

4.5.2 The Product and Product Category Life Cycles

Product management must have a solid understanding of the various phases of a product and the product category to which it belongs. The development of appropriate strategies and actions to suit a product's position in its life cycle require such understanding. The product manager must also ensure that the right knowledge for building and maintaining the product is available in the product organization. Finally, a product manager must analyze how well the product is performing by monitoring product profitability, actual versus planned revenue, customer satisfaction, and market share (see Sect. 3.13). If necessary, corrective actions must be initiated, and the concerned product team must be supported and given the competencies necessary to implement those actions.

Life Cycle Model for a Software Product

The importance of the product life cycle for a company is evident when looking at the product portfolio and how that portfolio evolves over time (see Sect. 5.2). Portfolio evolution may be measured by recording the number of new product sales or active licenses. The recording of new product sales is common for products in an early life cycle phase where the growth of the business is of key interest. The recording of active licenses is common for license products in a late life cycle phase because that record allows knowing who is still using the product.

The growth and decline of business volume for a product version over time reveals the different stages in its life cycle. We see a product moving through six life cycle phases: the product is conceived and created, introduced to the market, grows, matures, declines in use, and is finally withdrawn. Each phase of the life cycle has its individual characteristics, business aims, and focus areas for the product manager's attention. Figure 4.15 provides an overview.

A product organization pursues different business aims depending on the product life cycle phase. The first three life cycle phases of a product are investment phases. Investments in the product are necessary to develop, test, and market the product. Products in later phases serve as cash cows and generate significant revenue with relatively little investment. The resulting profits may be invested in other promising products or new ventures. Often, the product manager will minimize the need for additional investments in a product, maximize the revenue generated, and achieve break-even as rapidly as possible. Agile approaches combined with a minimal viable product strategy and rapidly released product versions may yield quick return on investment by generating positive cash flow much earlier than a waterfall-oriented approach [DenCle04].

Figure 4.15 shows the product life cycle phases. During conception and creation, the product manager assesses market opportunities for product ideas, aligns a winning idea with company strategy, positions the product, then develops and tests the product [SongMon98] by going through experimentation and feedback loops. This progression is described in more detail in [KittMang22]. Market introduction includes the validation of the product with customers, testing of the marketing and advertising programs, and coordination, implementation, and monitoring of

Business outcome	Phase
Investment	Conception and creation
	Market Introduction
	Growth
Cash Cow	Maturity
	Decline
	Withdrawal

Fig. 4.15 Life cycle model for a software product

the new product launch. During growth, the product manager markets, extends, and evolves the product to win new customers, gain market share, and fight against competitors who do the same [Moore14]. In the maturity phase, the business aim changes, and the product assumes the role of a cash cow. The product manager starts limiting investments in the product and evolves it only as much as necessary to maintain the installed base [RajlBenn00]. When product sales decline, a limited servicing of the product with minimal bug fixes replaces the previously more extensive product evolution. To account for the declining income within the decline phase, a product manager seeks ways to reduce cost, e.g. by moving support services to a low-cost country. With the final phase of withdrawal, the product manager prepares the product's phase-out and manages its closedown.

The life cycle phase also influences maintenance. A vendor may introduce variability into the product to address diverging needs of different market segments, especially during the growth phase of a product. Later, the product organization will recognize a need to minimize the number of parallel versions of a product that require discrete maintenance. Excessive parallelism produces portfolio and organizational complexity, and each version must be separately updated and tested incurring cost and resource use. Therefore, the maintenance of older versions is frequently decommitted with some lead time to motivate customers to migrate to newer versions. These migrations are often a point of conflict between vendor and customers that vendors try to mitigate by offering discounted upgrade prices. Challenging decisions are thus required when moving from one phase to another. Approaches that worked well in one phase may need to be changed to prepare for the next phase, even when the changes create irritation and resistance.

In practice, the life cycle of a product is hardly as stepwise and linear as Fig. 4.15 suggests. While the markets for B2B license products may be slow, internet-based B2C markets tend to be turbulent. Consequently, product development and evolution are often iterative and confronted with much trial-and-error and failures. Also, a product organization may discover that a product is in a different life cycle stage than initially thought. For example, a product believed to be mature may be changed and evolved to address a newly discovered growth market. The lengths of a product's life cycle and its phases are unpredictable and can vary significantly.

The iterative nature of the early product life cycle phases is particularly important until a product is on the market that satisfies customer needs, is well differentiated, and is technologically viable [KhuFrGor15]. Only successful products undergo all life cycle phases; unsuccessful products should be withdrawn rapidly.

The product organization utilizes measurements appropriate to a product position in its life cycle to support product life cycle management. Data from product analysis and market analysis will determine the current product life cycle phase. Other measurements monitor and control the life cycle-specific work and the outcomes that are achieved with that work. Section 3.14.2 offers more details on these measurements.

Life Cycle Model for a Product Category

Products compete within product categories which Moore defines as "A term used by customers to classify what they are buying and distinguish it from other purchasing choices". Examples are smartphones, or ERP software. Such product categories either already exist in the market or a vendor might research or leverage new technologies to establish a new category. The product category also follows a life cycle. For the early stage, Moore coined the term "technology adoption life cycle", which he defines as "A model that describes how communities react to the introduction of a discontinuous technology, consisting of a progression through five adoption strategies: technology enthusiast, visionary, pragmatist, conservative, and skeptic". The later stages are called "category maturity life cycle" defined as "A model that describes the rise, duration, and decline of a category of product or service". The combination is named "market development life cycle" [Moore08, Moore04a]. Figure 4.16 provides an overview.

The life cycle of a product category reflects how the market reacts to that category. Most customers will be resistant to new types of products and will only adopt what has already been proven. Technology enthusiasts and visionaries will be more welcoming early on. So in order to make decisions about whom to market a product to and how to market that product at a given point in time, it is important for product managers to understand the current category phase of their product. Spending money in the wrong area would be a waste, and highest potential target customers change from category phase to category phase.

An idea for a new product category is often developed in collaboration with enthusiasts that are willing to try and to explore new technologies with little proven evidence of success. Examples might include the first automobile manufacturers or the first banks to install ATMs and issue bank cards. These innovators are few in number. A product needs to address the next class of customers: the visionaries to grow product sales. Visionaries are often interested in a potentially risky product because of the potential it brings to build new business. While working with the visionaries, a product manager must manage to adapt the product to the needs of the first big category of customers: the early majority. If not successful, the product will be trapped in a "Chasm" seeking and not finding new customers and not able to achieve significant revenue growth.

Customers in the early majority adopt a product on pragmatic grounds. The product should be well established, deliver expected value, and be of high quality. Moore has characterized a product category at this stage to be first in a Bowling Alley, then a Tornado, and finally the Main Street. Each Bowling pin in the Bowling Alley corresponds to a market niche that may be convinced of the category with the help of another already won niche. The Tornado and Main Street represent the transition to the mass market that offers attractive growth rates with few threats by competitors.

When a product category further matures, the conservative customers become important. They invest in products that are mature and convenient to use. Also, they are price-sensitive. If multiple competitive products exist in the same space, fierce competition may characterize the mature product category because the market

Phase	Constellation	Dominant New Customer Type
Early Market	Testing and early adoption of a new product category by a market.	Enthusiasts and visionaries
Chasm		Niche market
Bowling Alley		Increasing number of niche markets
Tornado		Pragmatists
Main Street		
Growth Market	Large-scale adoption of the product category.	
Mature Market	Growth flattens, and competition is noticeable.	Conservatives
Declining Market	Technologies for new product categories emerge.	Skeptics
End of Life	A new product category is in the Tornado stage.	-

Fig. 4.16 Market development life cycle model for a product category based on [Moore08, Moore04a]

growth has flattened. A strategy which relies on competitive replacement is essentially always a losing proposition since cost of sales goes through the roof and revenue expansion is modest.

A market starts to decline with the emergence of and experimentation with technologies for new product categories. In this stage, the only source of new revenue for the aging product category may be the skeptics who have resisted so far. Skeptics may be persuaded to adopt if the product is integrated into other products or services. As soon as a new product category is in the Tornado stage, according to Moore, the declining market should be exited. However, as long as the business is still profitable based on ongoing revenue from the existing customer base, it may make sense to continue.

Shipments of Digital Still Cameras

Figure 4.17 shows how successions of product categories imply changes in the markets, and how each category evolves measured in units shipped. We chose here the camera market because it is well documented and an interesting example of how the inclusion of software into a product category can replace categories based on other technologies. Growth and decline are clearly evident as one category replaces a previous category. The growth of the digital camera category puts an end to the prospering film camera category.

Following Moore's model, sales to early adopters drove growth. The early adopters followed the latest technology with a good reputation. Once compact digital cameras were sufficiently reliable, early adopters shifted from buying analog cameras to digital ones. The products based on the previous technology were mostly

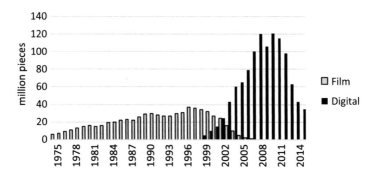

Fig. 4.17 Example of how product categories affect markets: Camera market (Source: CIPA)

sold to a declining number of conservatives. The graph also illustrates the decline of the digital still cameras category.

The relative maturity of technology for a product category and Moore's market maturity life cycle model affect a product's value focus and proposition as well as the product planning priorities. Figure 4.18 gives an overview. These recommendations apply to competitors who address a specific market with the corresponding product category. The value proposition characterizes the type of message to which new customers will be receptive. The product planning priorities indicate what the product organization must do to grow and sustain business in the market.

A product manager has to understand to which category his product belongs and the phase of this category to select appropriate options for product planning. In combination with the product life cycle phase, this information will influence product planning.

Managing products within the "technology adoption" phase involves not only intense communication with early adopters, but also development and deployment approaches that allow rapid evolution of the product. Such a product planning option is facilitated by the Powerboat scenario. A product manager in the Icebreaker scenario should also strive to find ways to evolve and adapt the product to market needs. Alternatively, a product manager should evaluate whether and how the Icebreaker approach may be converted to a Powerboat approach.

Creating a new product for a mature market requires the selection of approaches to take away market share from existing products. The options correspond to the following four types of incremental innovation [Moore08]:

- **Product line extension** broadens the product offering by specialization. Variants of the product are created which target specific businesses and provide a better fit for that group.
- **Enhancement innovation** optimizes the product offering from a user experience perspective. Product features of this innovation type do not change the core product, but optimize existing features.
- **Marketing innovation** positions the more or less unchanged product for new markets.

Phase	Value Focus	Value Proposition	Product Planning Priority
Early Market	Curiosity of enthusiasts	New technology to try and explore	Identify most attractive use cases for the product
	New opportunities for visionaries	New means for business development	Mature the product and reputation to win trust of niche market
Chasm, Bowling Alley	Value for pragmatists (narrow niche)	Practical, value creating product with low risk	Increase convenience and win trust of new niches
Tornado, Main Street, Growth	Value for pragmatists (broad market)		
Mature	Convenience for conservatives	Established, cheap standard with reliable support	Develop products for new product categories
Decline	Necessity for skeptics	Product integrated into other offerings	Phase-out the product, and replace by new product category or exit the market

Fig. 4.18   Implications of the product category life cycle for product planning

- **Experiential innovation** modifies the customer's end-to-end experience from initial encounter to ultimate disposition.

Marketing and experiential innovation do not require changes to the core product. These innovation types give innovation options to the product manager that are independent of development resources. The interplay between product life cycle and market category life cycle depends largely on the strategic planning within an organization. Based on portfolio considerations there may be situations where strategic planning decides to move a product to its end-of-life phase, even if the product is still in its growth phase.

4.5.3   Product Planning Tactics

Product and category life cycles influence product planning priorities and focus areas. The development of a new product for a new market will require a planning approach that completely differs from the evolution of an existing product in a mature market. We offer here a discussion of three important constellations. Other constellations are possible and may be addressed with a combination of the three we present here.

Innovating with a New Product in an Immature Product Category

When developing a new product for a new market, the product manager finds himself in the product life cycle stage of product conception and in the early product category cycle stage where a new technology is becoming interesting for enthusiasts and visionaries. This situation is covered by our Powerboat or Icebreaker product scenarios. The product conception phase implies substantial investment in development and testing of the new product. Since there is no established market for the chosen technology yet, much work goes into trials in collaboration with the enthusiasts and visionaries to identify the most attractive use cases for the product.

Many startup companies may be working in this constellation. As a result, approaches that facilitate flexible trials and learning must influence product management thinking. Even established organizations may use such approaches, usually by putting the innovating team in a separate organizational unit. The separation ensures that the team is not concerned with the daily business operations of the rest of the larger organization and that the team's goals and measurements suit the innovation situation. At some point in time, the new business needs to be integrated into the established organization, but not too early. Graveyards are filled with the corpses of products which died because the product or product line was "mainstreamed" into the regular business too quickly and where loss of independence thwarted its market entry.

In both the startup and the separate unit cases, the product team benefits from business and technological background, either developed at universities or reused from previous products, to accelerate product development and market introduction [KhuFrGor15]. This scenario is described in more detail in [KittMang22].

New Product in a Mature Product Category

When developing a new product in a mature product category, the product manager is in the Powerboat or Icebreaker product scenarios. He finds himself in the product life cycle stage of conception and creation. The new product will address a market in which pragmatic customers expect more value and conservative customer prospects expect more convenience. The mature product category implies that competitors exist and have well-established ties with important customers.

New products in a mature product category unavoidably implement a follower strategy that copies or imitates a successful product concept. The product addresses already known needs that are relatively easy to elicit because of the previously existing products. Important for the success of the follower strategy is that the product is more attractive to the targeted customers than the competing products. To achieve this aim, the product manager may adapt a broader product concept to the specific needs of a narrow customer segment or offer a comparable product at a lower price and greater convenience.

Evolution of an Existing Product in a Mature Product Category

When evolving an existing product in a mature product category, the product manager is in the Speedboat or Cruise Ship product scenarios. He finds himself in the product life cycle stage of growth, maturity, or decline, and in the category life cycle stage of the mature market.

The mature product life cycle stage implies that the product is being used as a cash cow to invest in new products. Only a limited part of the product's revenue is used to extend the product's scope and increase the target market. The conservatism of new customers implies that the feedback obtained from the large customer base should be used to make the product easier to use and to integrate it as a standard into other offerings.

When companies have existing products in mature product categories, product management thinking is usually influenced significantly by methods or approaches that facilitate collaboration with many company-internal stakeholders, use of feedback about existing products, and structured decision-making with staff that has in-depth product knowledge. Product management will follow structured processes that reflect the way in which highly mature companies work.

We have discussed the benefits of simplifying products and services offered to customers. To accomplish this, product lines and ecosystems become attractive ways to manage the increasing diversity of the customer base and new markets. The product organization may utilize product lines as a structured approach to reusing components across a set of product variants, embedding them in a common product platform, and specifying the selection of features that are offered for each variant [PohlBoLi05] (see definition in Sect. 2.2.1). The product organization may decide to turn the product platform into an innovation platform product and allow other companies to use this product as a common platform for the development of their own value-adding products and services. This ecosystem approach allows sharing risks and efforts with specialized companies against a share of the possible revenue ([JanBrCus13], see Sect. 3.12).

4.5.4 Summary and Conclusions

In this chapter, we have discussed product life cycle management by looking at the product life cycle, the technology adoption life cycle and the category maturity life cycle. We have analyzed the ways in which these life cycles affect product planning. The product life cycle describes the six phases of a product in a company's portfolio. The first three phases are investment phases. In the following three phases, the product serves as a cash cow to generate profit and finance the investment in new products. With the increasing maturity of a product category, a series of new customer types appear whose specific needs must be addressed if a product moving into that category is to be successful.

The phases in these life cycles relevant for a particular product affect the product manager's focus and product planning tactics. The development of a new product in a new category differs substantially from the evolution of an existing product in a mature category. The approaches described in this chapter are prototypical approaches. In real-world situations, our discussion is the starting point for an essential specific analysis, which may lead to conclusions that differ from what theories suggest.

4.6   Process Measurement and Improvement

4.6.1   Overview

Many software organizations must balance release schedules, cost control, and product release content to meet market expectations. To improve organizations, assessments are used to evaluate the practices in use by the organization and to compare them with those of other organizations or frameworks. Similarly, assessments may be compared with benchmarks, quantitative data about work and achieved outcomes within the same or another company or even within the industry. The benchmark allows comparison of the assessed organization with an earlier situation or 'best practice.'

This section gives a brief overview of product planning processes, how product management performance may be measured, which frameworks are available to improve software product management practice, and which tools may facilitate product management productivity. The section adds the process performance perspective to the product performance perspective that we discussed in Sect. 3.14. The section also relates to Sect. 5.7 which explains how to obtain performance indicators to assist in managing performance.

4.6.2   Product Planning Processes

For classification of product planning tasks, we use the categories introduced in Sect. 3.15:

- Continuous (C): done more often than once a month.
- Periodic (P): done monthly or less often, but with predefined frequency.
- Triggered (T): only done when a particular event or request happens, i.e. not with predefined frequency.

We apply this classification to the product planning activities listed in the SPM Framework (Fig. 4.19).

Most software organizations define and implement a process for product requirements engineering in order to stay on top of the usually high number of requirements to be managed. Such a process is typically supported by an appropriate tool (see Sect. 4.6.4). In mature software product management organizations, processes for release planning and roadmapping are often defined in a more formal way.

Strategy task	Continuous	Periodic	Triggered
Product Life Cycle Management		P for existing products	T if new
Roadmapping		P	T if changes need to be reflected and a presentation is required
Release Planning		P	T if changes need to be reflected
Product Requirements Engineering	C		

Fig. 4.19 Classification of planning tasks

4.6.3   Improving Product Planning Performance

Product planning performance may be measured in terms of process and outcomes. Common process measurements are: size of the product backlog or number of pending product requirements, average and peak durations for requirements to be decided upon, time and money spent on product planning, and confidence in product planning decisions. Changes in the number of pending product requirements and duration required for requirements decisions will reveal bottlenecks or overcapacity in the product organization [PetWoh10].

Intel and Google popularized the OKR approach (Objectives and Key Results) which focuses on outcomes [Doerr18]. Outcome measurements include those related to product development, such as planning accuracy [HerrDan08], and those related to how well requirement cost and value were predicted during the release decisions [KaReTh06]. A root-cause analysis of the major deviations between prediction and realized results should guide future product planning decisions. Examples of causes that lead to deviations are under-estimation of development effort, acceptance of too many change requests, orders issued by a specific customer, actions from competitors, or the lack of availability of a good solution to a design problem.

Once a product vision has been defined, product management is in a race to bring the product to market. Time-to-market is critical to positioning a product in the market before competitors do. Even if a product has already been released, existing features must evolve and new ones be rapidly developed. Product extensions may make the product attractive to additional segments of the market which were insufficiently addressed before and more satisfying for existing customers.

Time-to-market also influences the value created by the product [DenCle04]. It influences the timing of revenue creation from the developed product which in turn affects return-on-investment. The earlier a product is released the earlier revenue is generated. That revenue can fuel further investment needed to build the product. Earlier product availability may allow penetration of the available market segment and make it harder for competitors to realize revenue in the segment, and early revenue shortens the time to reach break-even. Earlier installations allow revenue to be accumulated over a longer time than if product management waits with product releases.

Once a product is established, efficiency and adherence to plans become increasingly important. The product management organization must be structured and processes designed to optimize the relationship between value created and effort invested. Release plans are a frequent focus for improvement. They require revision whenever schedules are not met, whenever a product dependency or its schedule changes, and when product releases do not perform as expected. Release plans revised outside of the corporate planning cycles must be formally synchronized in the next corporate planning cycle.

The product organization should prioritize product development work with regard to value impact and cost [KarlRyan97].

As soon as a product is released there will be feedback from actual and potential customers. Accuracy of feedback prediction before the release of the product can provide a measure of confidence in the product planning process. Often, confidence issues may be identified that allow proactive risk management. Common issues concern the linkage of requirements with business strategy, seeing the big picture of the offering, understanding of the planned product's value, and knowledge of customer problems [KKTLD15].

After release, customer feedback is essential to determine whether the product design was appropriate to the target market. If interest in the product is mediocre, the product strategy, in particular scope, positioning, or target market may have to be changed. Outcome measurements include those related to product development, such as planning accuracy [Ebert07], and those related to how well requirement cost and value were predicted [Karlsson06, HerrDan08]. The better the original assumptions were, usually directly related to early product validation, the less requirement volatility and the more product stability. A root-cause analysis of the major deviations between prediction and realized results should guide future product planning decisions. Examples of causes that lead to deviations are under-estimation of development effort, orders issued by a specific customer, actions from competitors, or the lack of availability of an effective, validated solution to a design problem. Any critique that is received as feedback should be evaluated and the product definition or positioning adapted.

Figure 4.20 summarizes these aspects of product management performance and offers suggestions for relevant measurements, to be used as a starting point for product management performance measurements and assessing how performance evolves over time. A root-cause analysis of major deviations between prediction and realized results should guide future product planning decisions.

Performance Aspect	Selected Measurements
Time-to-market	Duration between product or feature definition and release.
Value	Return-on-investment, revenue, market share, customer feedback
Efficiency	velocity in value per time unit, amount of work remaining (backlog)
Predictability	Confidence, adherence to plans
Quality	Requirements volatility, number of problem reports

Fig. 4.20 Aspects of product management performance and corresponding measurements

Process improvement programs follow the assessment and benchmarks [Jones08]. Various frameworks have been developed for improving product management practice in the product organization. Section 2.5 gives an overview of software product management frameworks that are useful for assessing software product management practice and for planning improvements.

The frameworks are useful for assessing the as-is situation and should be used for planning incremental improvements that are effective but do not overwhelm the product organization. Apply guidelines in these frameworks judiciously, reflecting on what works well and what not in the organization's practice.

It is effective to elicit experiences from product managers on a continuous basis and to use feedback for bottom-up improvements of product management practice. Of greatest importance are patterns of recurring practices that work well and are effective. These should be documented and spread throughout the organization as organizational "best practices."

4.6.4 Tool Support

Product management is such a multifaceted, data-driven, and decision-oriented work that it would not be possible without tools. A product manager documents ideas, analyzes data to answer questions about the product, leads the product organization through important decisions about the product, and orchestrates the functional areas of the organization like product development and operations. Documentation tools are used to make ideas available throughout the organization. Modeling tools are used to analyze situations and reduce complexity. Prototyping tools may be used to allow stakeholders to experience possible products. Communication and tracking tools will serve to win stakeholders and to orchestrate their work. Figure 4.21 gives an overview of important tool categories.

The market for product planning tools is quite young. Historically, product managers have used development tools like Jira even though they are not ideally suited for product management work. At least the use of development tools ensured that there were no data synchronization problems between Product Management and Development. The newer specific product planning tools try to address that requirement by providing interfaces to popular development tools like Jira. Examples are

Aha!, ProductPlan and ProdPad. The requirements management tools category is much more mature. IBM Rational Doors succeeded in establishing itself as a requirements management tool. It has become a standard in the automotive and aviation industries. For markets that are not required to comply with comparable regulation, a new market leader, Atlassian, has emerged. Atlassian offers cloud-based products for Wiki-based requirements definition and requirements management.

Tools from domains other than software have not been successful in capturing the market for software product management. For example, there are components in Enterprise Resource Planning (ERP) software offerings called product life cycle management (PLM). These were designed primarily for manufacturing companies where product life cycle has a meaning very different from software. We expect new categories of tools to become important in product organizations, including product usage monitoring tools and collaboration tools that allow developers, supporters, and users to interact with each other. Among these new tool categories, there is no dominant tool yet, and we expect that more tools will be released and disappear again.

Since product management works intensively with other units within the company, it can be helpful for a product manager to get access to these units' task-specific software systems. The granting of such access will depend on the company's culture, the organizational structure and defined role of product management, as well as the personal working habits and reputation of the product manager. Development project management and issue tracking tools, support tools, customer relationship management tools from marketing, and company-wide or unit sales planning and control tools of the company or individual units may all have potential uses. What is important is that the product manager has timely access to all factual data that he needs for his work. If that can be achieved without giving him access to task-specific software systems, everyone will likely prefer that.

The use of tools can significantly improve productivity. McKinsey has shown that tool support of software-related activities has a significant positive correlation with the business success of a company [SrTrWaWa20, GnJiSrWa21]. At the same time, there is no guarantee that the use of tools will generate productivity improvements. The effect of a tool on productivity has been shown to differ significantly depending on the context in which the tool was used [BrMaJaHe96]. A tool may increase the productivity for some products and projects and, at the same time, decrease the productivity for other products and projects of the same organization. The processes of the organization and the complexity of the products will affect the impact of a tool.

Conversely, the choice of an inappropriate tool can have devastating effects on an organization. Employees blocked in their work due to an inappropriate tool will do everything they can do to circumvent the tool [Farmer06]. Use a systematic tooling process to avoid such problems proactively [GoWoGL06]. The tool selection process should select tools which address the right problems, are better suited to managing those problems than other tools, can be implemented in the organization, and are accepted by the users that interact with the tools in their daily work. To avoid

Category	Benefits	Examples
Product Planning Tools	Direct support for planning tasks like roadmapping, release planning, and requirements engineering, some extended into product strategy tasks	Aha!, Product Plan, ProdPad.
Experimentation Tools	Direct support for design and execution of experiments in the runtime environment including statistics	Amplitude, Optimizely, VWO.
Documentation Tools	Documentation of ideas and decisions and visualization of concepts. The tools should allow collaborative editing of the documents.	Word processors, presentation tools, e-mail, Wikis like Atlassian Confluence, and shared repositories like Dropbox.
Modeling Tools	Structuring and analysis of data, information, and knowledge in preparation of decision-making. Some of the tools allow informal modeling without any constraints, while others implement standard languages.	Mind-mapping, roadmapping, and system modeling tools, e.g. with UML or SysML. Stackoverflow ranks UML tools.
Prototyping Tools	Approximation of systems, their user interfaces, and their use for discussion and testing with stakeholders.	GUI design tools, e.g. for creating wireframes.
Communication Tools	Communication with stakeholders. These tools are usually used in conjunction with documentation tools.	Phone, e-mail, messengers, and conferencing tools, such as Skype or GoToMeeting.
Tracking Tools	Enactment of workflows, usually to manage requirements, issue, and task backlogs.	Spreadsheets and issue management tools.

Fig. 4.21 Categories of tools for product management

manual, clerical work all tools should be integrated into the organization's toolchain and find a permanent home in the organization [Farmer06]. Only once tools fulfill these requirements and lead to desired productivity improvements should they be rolled out organization-wide.

4.6.5   Summary and Conclusions

This chapter has given an overview of indicators for measuring the performance of the product management process and how the performance may be improved. The indicators reflect the important primary concerns of a product manager: time-to-market, value, efficiency, predictability, and quality. Frameworks for process improvement and software tools are instruments to improve the performance of product management. These become effective when the product manager knows how to integrate them into an appropriate methodology—knowledge that may be obtained by education such as defined by the ISPMA syllabi.

Process improvement frameworks and classroom training need to be accompanied by practical experience gained through actually practicing product management and learning from others. Observing and reflecting on one's practice, attempting to generalize from the observations, and testing the learned lessons in new situations provides relevant improved understanding and abilities [Kolb14]. Communities of practice (like ISPMA) allow practitioners to develop relationships with experts, peers, and stakeholders, share ideas, set standards, and establish tools to solve problems [WenSny00]. Such learning enables product managers to improve as individuals, as a community, and as effective employees of their companies.

Strategic Management

5

Strategic Management is an activity within an organization whose objective is to define, plan, agree, implement and evaluate the organization's strategy. Strategic management falls under executive management which can delegate preparatory work to staff functions. It includes a number of elements related to software product management (see the ISPMA SPM Framework in Sect. 2.5). Software product managers are typically not responsible for any of these activities, but they either participate in them, e.g. portfolio management, provide inputs, or make use of their outputs, e.g. product analysis.

Of course, it is not the objective of this book to provide a handbook on executive management. This is covered by a huge spectrum of publications. However, since a software product manager has responsibility for his product(s) and thereby partial responsibility for the success of the whole company, he is very directly involved in some aspects of executive management.

A software product manager often spends some of his time with the task of representing his product in the internal strategy and planning processes of his company. This includes marketing and sales plans, budget, and resource planning. The underlying question is which resources will be dedicated to the product in the short, medium, and long term. This decision is based on market and revenue forecasts, the positioning of the product in its life cycle, and the dependencies with other products. From these elements, the product manager puts a "story" together that is used to "sell" the product within the planning processes.

The company's culture influences how these planning processes work and what is expected from the product manager. Ideally, all involved parties should have a common goal of getting to an agreed result that is good for the company. Often, however, these processes degenerate into a competition that the players try to use for their personal advancement. The "winner" is the one who gets most of the resources for his product. Only executive management can prevent this degeneration. The individual product manager will have to play his role according to the company's culture, for the good or for the bad.

© Springer-Verlag GmbH Germany, part of Springer Nature 2022
H.-B. Kittlaus, *Software Product Management*,
https://doi.org/10.1007/978-3-662-65116-2_5

Typically, the corporate strategy and planning process is a mix of bottom-up and top-down planning. Bottom-up means that each product manager develops a plan from his product perspective. Top-down means that executive management, typically under the lead of finance, looks at the aggregated bottom-up plans and cuts them down to what seems affordable. Since the assigned budget and resources have their consequences on the revenue side, this process is iterated until an agreement is reached. This process serves as a synchronization point at which the plans on all levels and of all products are synchronized. Executive management usually defines the schedule of this process. IBM, for example, has gone through two cycles per year, the Spring and the Fall plans, for a long time.

At this point we want to examine the elements of the corporate strategy and planning process and the role that the product manager plays in them.

5.1   Corporate Strategy

5.1.1   Overview

Formal corporate strategy processes are a phenomenon that entered the scene in the 1960s. Since then, many different approaches and tools for strategic management have been developed and are used across industries. These approaches and tools can be traced back to different schools of thought that evolved over time. Some of these tools and approaches are frequently used in modern software organizations. We will focus our discussion on these frequently used tools.

In addition to industry-agnostic approaches to corporate strategy, there are also tools and approaches that have been developed specifically for high-tech markets, including software markets. They have been designed to address the specific strategic challenges of markets that are based on quickly evolving technology, resulting in fast value erosion for products.

Software product managers may have to provide input whenever the corporate strategy is updated or revised, and they need to ensure that product strategies stay consistent with corporate strategy. To achieve this, software product managers should understand the tools and approaches used in higher-level strategy processes in their organization. Understanding key ideas, assumptions, and process underlying high level strategy development helps product managers improve their contribution: they can both provide more useful input into strategy development and better understand and use the guidance they receive from the organization's higher-level strategy.

5.1.2   Concept

Corporate strategy considers a timeframe that is at least as long as the strategic timeframes of the individual software products. Therefore, the time frame considered may be up to 5 years, or even longer, depending on the domains covered.

Fig. 5.1 Elements of corporate strategy with their equivalents on the product level

Elements of Corporate Strategy	Comparable Elements on the Product Strategy Level
Corporate vision, mission, values and goals	Product vision
Corporate positioning	Product positioning
Business model(s) and financial plan	Business model(s) and financial plan
Product portfolio(s) and their evolution	Product Roadmap
Market trends and competitive strategy	Market trends and competitive strategy
Technology trends and innovation strategy	Technology trends (from market analysis)
Resource and competency evolution	–
Policies and governance	–

Strategy processes on the corporate level can happen on a periodic schedule or be triggered by major changes in the environment, for example substantial regulatory changes, unexpected major strategic moves by competitors, or technology disruptions. Updates to an existing strategy are typically conducted periodically—tied to an organization's regular planning and reporting cycle, for example preceding the annual planning cycle.

A corporate strategy process includes development of or updating of strategy elements: corporate vision, mission, values and goals; corporate positioning, business model and financial plan; product portfolio and evolution; resource and competency evolution; technology trends and innovation strategy, market trends and competitive strategy; policies and governance.

Many of these strategy elements are comparable to corresponding elements on the product strategy level. Figure 5.1 compares the elements from these two different levels of strategy process.

However, there are key differences between corporate and product strategy. The corporate vision is typically a very short statement, often just one very high-level sentence about a desired future state that the corporation wants to help create. This describes why the company exists. Typically this is elaborated on by a corporate mission statement that describes on a high level what the company is doing to achieve the vision, and a statement of the company's values and goals.

Unlike a product roadmap, the corporate strategy process will look at entire portfolios of products and set goals and boundary conditions for the evolution of these portfolios.

Finally, corporate strategy addresses areas that do not have a direct equivalent on the product strategy level: Innovation strategy (see Sect. 5.3), resource and competency evolution (see Sect. 5.4), compliance management (see Sect. 5.5) and policies and governance.

5.1.3 Process

Corporate strategy processes are often based on industry-agnostic tools and approaches which can be traced back to different approaches to planning that have evolved over time.

In [MinAhlLa08] Mintzberg, Ahlstrand, and Lampel provide an overview on strategic management approaches, identifying ten underlying schools of thought in corporate strategy. They further classify those ten into three major groups: prescriptive, descriptive, or integrative.

Figure 5.2 provides an overview of the schools of thought and their associated tools, based on [MinAhlLa08].

Strategic management processes frequently use the tools and approaches highlighted in the rightmost column of Fig. 5.2:

- SWOT Matrix: maps the internal Strengths and Weaknesses of the organization against the Opportunities and Threats presented by the external environment. Individual products frequently use SWOT analysis as well, as part of market analysis (see Sect. 5.6).
- Scenario Planning: aims to broaden the view of decision makers by developing several alternative long-term scenarios, where each scenario describes a possible future state of the organization's external environment. Then, the impact on the organization and possible responses are elaborated for each scenario. This is especially suitable in volatile times and fast-moving markets—a reason for software organizations to use this strategic tool. Product managers may contribute to the development of scenarios or contribute to developing the strategic responses due to their understanding of the markets.
- Porter's 5 Forces: Michael Porter in [Porter79] and [Porter08] identifies five forces that characterize the nature of competition within an industry, also called the industry structure. The five forces are: threat of new entrants, bargaining power of customers, threat of substitute products or services, bargaining power of suppliers, and rivalry among existing competitors. In [Porter85] he described that firms can choose only three classes of strategies—what he calls generic strategies. These are cost leadership strategy, differentiation strategy, and focus strategy (niche strategy). The 5 Forces model and the generic strategies are routinely taught in management education and are broadly known and used, especially in industries where the costs for manufacturing and delivering products are

School	Key assumptions	Authors	Examples of key approaches & tools
Design School	"Establish fit" – between internal capabilities and external possibilities; Design several alternative strategies (a creative act) and choose the best .	Kenneth Andrews	**SWOT matrix** (internal Strengths & Weaknesses, external Opportunities & Threats)
Planning School	"formal procedure, formal training, formal analysis, lots of numbers" replace the creative act of strategy design	H. Igor Ansoff, George Steiner	Elaborate planning cycles and schedules, **cascading systems of plans**; **Scenario planning**
Positioning School	Impact of industry structure on strategy: only a few positions in the market are desirable, and there are only a few generic strategies to select from	Michael Porter	**Porter's 5 forces** - for competitive analysis **BCG growth/share matrix** – for portfolio management (problem child, cash cow, star, dog);
Learning School	Strategies emerge as people (individually or collectively) learn about a situation as well as their organization's capability to deal with it. The leader's responsibility is not to preconceive deliberate strategies, but to manage the process of strategic learning.	Brian Quinn, C.K. Prahalad, Gary Hamel, Peter Senge, & many others	**Internal corporate venturing**
Power School	Strategy formation is shaped by power and politics, both inside the organization and outside. The resulting strategies take the form of positions or ploys more than perspectives	Many, including Michael Porter	**Strategic alliances** **Strategic sourcing** - incl. make vs. buy and vertical (dis-) integration decisions;

Fig. 5.2 Schools of thought in strategic management

non-negligible, for example for software-intensive products that include hardware.

- The BCG Growth/Share Matrix: the Boston Consulting Group in 1970 introduced a methodology which classifies products according to their success in the market vs. the attractiveness of the market in which they participate. The methodology is frequently used in portfolio management as well (see Sect. 5.2 for a more detailed discussion).
- Internal Corporate Venturing: an approach in which larger organizations encourage employees deeper down in the corporate hierarchy to come up with new product initiatives. These initiatives then compete for corporate funding, similar to startups working to raise venture capital. This is usually part of an organization's innovation management strategy (see also Sect. 5.3).
- Strategic Alliances and Strategic Sourcing: in today's markets companies typically act within a complex web of relationships, for example with suppliers, channel partners, and other partners. In that situation, strategy needs to be developed collaboratively with partners, always with a view that there may be multiple relationships with a single entity. For a deeper discussion of partner relationships, see Sect. 3.12.

5.1.4   Examples and Variations

So far, we have looked at industry-agnostic approaches to strategic management. In addition to those, software organizations may use approaches and tools developed specifically to address challenges of fast-moving high-tech markets:

- Category Maturity Model for high-tech markets: This model described by Moore in [Moore08] helps determine strategic focus areas depending on the maturity stages of the product categories relevant to the organization (see Sects. 4.4 and 5.3).
- Strong focus on innovation management: Software markets are often fast-moving, with the potential for rapid value erosion—this usually leads to a strong emphasis on innovation management (see Sect. 5.3) and on ensuring the product portfolio stays fresh (see Sect. 5.2).
- Ecosystem strategy: Software organizations often need to maintain a complex web of relationships with other players in their ecosystem(s) . Determining the role the organization wishes to play in the ecosystem—keystone, dominator, or niche player—is typically part of Corporate Strategy (for more on these roles and the associated strategies, see Sect. 3.12).
- Big data and analytics: in many cases, in particular with SaaS software, software organizations can obtain detailed information on usage patterns and user behavior that helps in making strategic decisions (see Sect. 4.1).

5.1.5   Outcome and Impacts

The outcome of corporate strategy processes is typically comprehensive documentation which describes conclusions and next steps, as well as the rationale behind the conclusions, i.e. the process used and more detailed information that led to the conclusions. These will be presented in some level of detail to key decision makers of the organization. A simplified subset of the results, focusing on key messages and required changes will typically be circulated at lower levels of the organization.

Software product managers need to understand their organization's corporate strategy as well as the portfolio strategy so they can ensure their product strategy aligns with these higher-level strategies.

5.1.6   Summary and Conclusions

Corporate strategy processes often consider a timeframe of 5 years, or even longer, depending on the domains covered. A wide range of strategy elements will be developed or updated to cover the strategic period: from very high level elements such as corporate vision, mission, values and goals, down to policies and governance. Strategy development at the corporate level may result from major external events, or happen simply on a periodic schedule, for example preceding the annual planning cycle.

Software product managers may have to provide input whenever the corporate strategy is updated or revised, and they need to ensure that their product strategies stay consistent with the corporate strategy.

To achieve this, software product managers must be familiar with all the strategy tools and approaches used in their organization. Tools and approaches that are frequently used across industries include Porter's 5 forces, SWOT matrix, BCG growth/share matrix, strategic alliances and strategic sourcing, internal corporate venturing, and scenario planning. In addition, software organizations frequently use tools and approaches developed specifically for fast-moving high-tech markets: Moore's category maturity model, a strong focus on innovation management, ecosystem strategy, and leveraging big data and analytics to support strategy decisions.

5.2   Portfolio Management

5.2.1   Overview

In any product organization, leaders need to ask themselves regularly: Do we have the right products for future business success? Portfolio management addresses this key question, looking both at the existing product portfolio, and at plans for product evolution and new product development. Software product managers often represent their product(s) in the update cycle for the product portfolio.

Portfolio management is a well-known technique in the financial services industry. An investor or fund manager invests the available capital in a diversified way, i.e. in different stocks, securities, real estate etc. The total collection of these investments is a portfolio. Portfolio management is the management of these investments over time following profit and risk criteria. This same approach is applied to a set of investment opportunities in both existing and new software products, deciding which products and product development initiatives will receive how much investment over the strategic time frame.

Since the portfolio management process is concerned with investment allocation, it is typically tied to the regular planning and budgeting cycle of the software organization (periodic activity). In practice, this is usually on an annual basis.

In the software business, it is especially important to evaluate the portfolio on a regular basis, for the following reasons:

- Market needs can change rather quickly: software markets are fast-moving, definitions of market segments can shift over time with new market segments forming, and well-established market segments may become less attractive.
- New competitors may enter the segment: software markets typically have low barriers to entry and the boundaries between market segments are often fluid, so that vendors in adjacent markets can enter "your" markets, for example by extending one of their products.
- Software is malleable, so even existing products can evolve in many different directions—which can easily lead to uncontrolled growth and lack of alignment between portfolio products, which may in turn create portfolio gaps or unintended overlaps between products that result in positioning and sales problems within the portfolio.
- Software organizations need to ensure they have a balanced portfolio of products in different life cycle stages—in particular, they need to ensure that there is always sufficient investment in new products.

The last bullet results from the unique economics of software products. Software has relatively low variable costs (cost of goods sold) and high fixed costs. Consequently, it typically takes several years for new software products to become operationally profitable, i.e. before product revenue covers ongoing product-related expenses, unless customers are willing to pay for part of the development cost (see also Chap. 2).

Therefore, software organizations need to make sure they invest some of the revenue surplus of more mature, successful products into new product initiatives. They need to make these investments early enough—so that the new products mature in revenue terms as revenue from older products stagnates or declines. On the other hand, a successful mature software product is usually highly profitable, with high profit margins (profit as percentage of revenue). Its high overall revenue will make it an indispensable source of profits for the organization. Therefore, the organization needs to allocate sufficient investment to mature products to keep them competitive, so as to exploit the associated revenue and profit opportunity as long as possible.

5.2.2 Concept

The portfolio management process should review the product portfolio to ensure it still meets corporate objectives and guidelines, covering both existing products and proposed new product initiatives.

The review evaluates the product portfolio from several angles, asking the following questions:

- Do portfolio products meet their respective measures of business success, such as profitability, market share, numbers of active users?
- Is the portfolio innovative enough: are we maintaining our market position with existing products and do we have enough new products in the pipeline?
- Are we satisfied with our evolution plan for the portfolio: are there new opportunities that we would like to take advantage of—with new products or major extensions of existing products? Are there gaps in our portfolio, for example due to a new emerging market segment?

Software product managers typically must provide the following product-specific information as input into the portfolio review process:

- Product roadmaps
- Forecasts of relevant business metrics, for example a multi-year revenue forecast
- And the investment requested for the product.

In addition, product managers are typically asked to provide a summary of the product-specific market analysis, covering market sizing, trends, and competition (see Sect. 5.5), as well as a summary of the product analysis, describing where their product stands against plan (see Sect. 5.6). The product-specific analyses may be used by the portfolio management team to complement and extend the market and product analysis created at the portfolio level.

5.2.3 Process

Portfolio Management for software products follows the same basic methods and processes as any portfolio management. Based on a structured and transparent process, it balances limited resources in order to maximize benefits.

Figure 5.3 shows the three steps of portfolio management, i.e. extraction of information, evaluation of business and context, and execution of decisions. These three steps for software and IT portfolios are adapted—depending on whether the software products are stand-alone products (e.g. ERP system) or elements to be embedded into other products (e.g. automobile). Often specific aspects of IT and software are insufficiently aligned with business needs, and products fail due to priority conflicts, insufficient budget allocation, and continuous changes. A key success factor for portfolio management in this context is to focus on

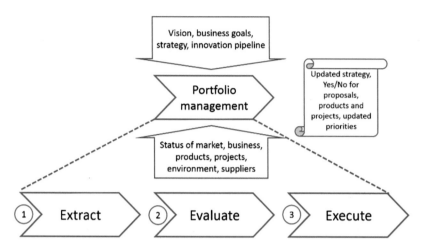

Fig. 5.3 Three steps of portfolio management [EberDumk07]

software-specific aspects, while not ignoring the overall business environment in which the software is embedded or used.

We have already emphasized that in fast-moving software markets, innovation must be a key component of software portfolio management. To ensure a focus on innovation, software portfolio management often uses the concept of three time horizons that Moore applied specifically to fast-moving high-tech and software markets [Moore14].

According to Moore, "Horizon 1 corresponds to managing the current fiscal reporting period, with all its short-term concerns, Horizon 2 to onboarding the next generation of high-growth opportunities in the pipeline, and Horizon 3 to incubating the germs of new businesses that will sustain the franchise far into the future."

To ensure long-term success of the organization, portfolio balance consists of having all three time horizons adequately covered.

Moore contends that Horizon 2 initiatives are the most challenging ones: Horizon 1 covers existing products which usually have been allocated sufficient resources across the organization. Investments made in Horizon 1 typically deliver a return in the same reporting period. Horizon 3 initiatives are usually addressed by separate lab or research organizations with their own separate funding.

In contrast, Horizon 2 initiatives are somewhat lost in the middle: they still need nurturing and investment to become successful products or new businesses, and this nurturing is not part of the research lab's agenda, it needs to come out of the established businesses. However, the full financial benefits from these investments will be realized in the future, typically several years out, and not in the current reporting period.

Therefore, organizations frequently fail in creation and nurturing of Horizon 2 initiatives. To address this problem, portfolio management processes typically look at investment proposals for each time frame separately, and with a special focus on Horizon 2 initiatives. It can be helpful to allocate budgets to the three horizons top-down upfront, and then do portfolio management for each separately.

To achieve an adequate balance between timeframes, organizations may start with a top-down split of the total investment budget between the timeframes, see also Sect. 5.4 on Resource Management.

5.2.4 Examples and Variations

A key challenge in portfolio management is the need to look at many different products at once, to put them in context, and to prioritize them. To help deal with the complexity, product classification into a matrix provides an overview of the portfolio. These matrixes typically describe two attributes that are relevant to portfolio decision making.

A popular example is the Growth-Share matrix. It was introduced for corporate portfolio management by the Boston Consulting Group in 1970 [Hender70] and is still widely used today. It classifies products according to their success in the market vs. attractiveness of the market in which they participate. Relative market share is used as the measure of market success, i.e. market share relative to the number three player in the market. Market growth is used (High/Low) as the measure of market attractiveness.

The result is a two by two matrix. According to Henderson [Hender70], the four quadrants of the matrix carry the following meaning:

- "Products with high market share and slow growth are cash cows. Characteristically, they generate large amounts of cash, in excess of the reinvestment required to maintain share.
- Products with low market share and slow growth are pets. They may show an accounting profit, but to maintain share the profit must all be reinvested, leaving no cash throw off. The product is essentially worthless, ..." Today, these are often called dogs.
- Low market share, high growth products are the question marks. They almost always require far more cash than they can generate.
- The high share, high growth product is the star. "... If it stays a leader, ... it will become a large cash generator ... The star eventually becomes the cash cow, providing high volume, high margin, high stability, security, and cash throw off for reinvestment elsewhere."

The resulting matrix may resemble Fig. 5.4. In this example, the matrix represents the entire software portfolio, the colors indicate different product families, and the size of the circles represents investment planned for the current year.

In fast-growing and fast-changing markets, portfolio management needs to ensure the portfolio always has cash cows and stars, it needs to critically evaluate the potential of the question marks, and aggressively to exit the pets or dogs.

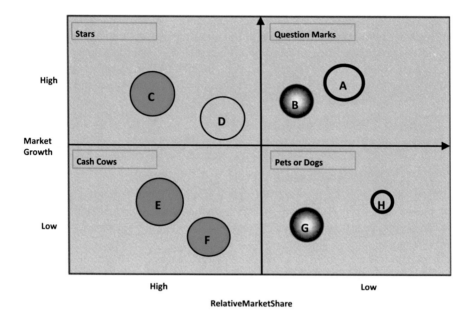

Fig. 5.4 Growth-Share Matrix for existing product portfolio

Portfolio matrices may use several different attributes. [Cooper00] suggests the following attribute pairs:

- Risk vs. reward
- Technical vs. market newness
- Technical feasibility vs. market attractiveness
- Competitive position vs. attractiveness
- Cost vs. reward
- Cost vs. time to implement.

Another pair used to compare new product initiatives only (Horizon 2) is the Oyster-Pearls matrix classification of new initiatives by probability of success vs. expected profit. An example might look like this (Fig. 5.5):

Based on this representation of new product initiatives, the portfolio management process would want to ensure investment in the white elephants was curbed: these are new product initiatives that are not likely to succeed, and even if they were to succeed, they are not likely to generate significant profits.

Portfolio management looks forward to current and arising opportunities and challenges. It relates closely to innovation management (see Fig. 5.6) where proposals are made and eventually implemented—given positive analysis by portfolio management.

While in project-oriented organizations, portfolio management is often applied to the project portfolio, we do not recommend it to product organizations. When you

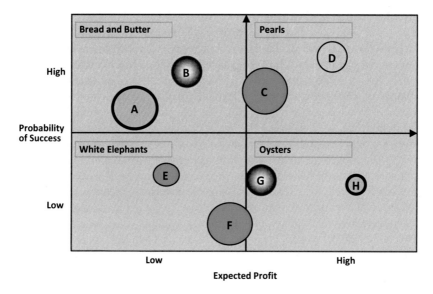

Fig. 5.5 Oyster-Pearls Matrix for new product initiatives

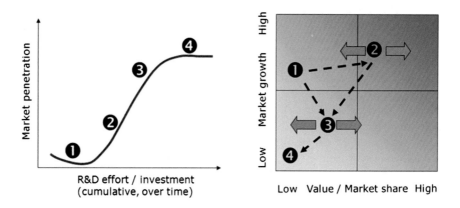

1. Experiments (learning, investment, no payback, go/no-go)
2. Growth (value is growing fast, market positioning, invest)
3. Saturation (adapt / reduce investments, cash in profits)
4. End of life (high maintenance, decide / communicate end of life)

Fig. 5.6 Product life cycle stage vs. BCG growth-share matrix [EberDumk07]

have applied portfolio management to the product portfolio, there is no need to do portfolio management for the projects in which new releases and versions of these products are developed.

5.2.5 Outcome and Impacts

On a portfolio level, one of the desired outcomes is an investment strategy that minimizes risks at the portfolio level and balances the need for short-term profit maximization with the requirement to invest for future success. Another desired outcome is alignment between portfolio products so that synergies may be exploited, for example by optimizing products for upsell and cross-sell opportunities between adjacent products.

Overlaps between portfolio products—in terms of multiple products offering similar value propositions to the same customer groups—need careful management. It's a matter of careful balance: while it may make sense for adjacent products to have some overlap in their value propositions so that each product is complete and can be successful on its own, portfolio management usually tries to avoid full, direct competition between products within the same portfolio.

The results of the portfolio update cycle define boundary conditions for the products: In addition to the investment level that will be allocated to each product, product managers will also receive key business goals and business measurements, for example revenue or growth targets. Finally, the portfolio management process may define portfolio themes to be factored into release plans and roadmaps for the products. These boundary conditions, as well as the investment levels allocated to each product may have significant consequences for individual product strategies.

5.2.6 Summary and Conclusions

Portfolio management uses a structured and transparent process to allocate limited resources to maximize benefits across existing products and new product initiatives. A key outcome of the process is investment allocation among competing initiatives, so portfolio management is typically tied to the regular planning and budgeting cycle (periodic activity, often performed annually).

In the fast-moving software business, critical periodic portfolio analysis is essential to ensuring the portfolio is aligned with market developments, meets organizational goals and objectives, and is balanced across the life cycle stages of products.

Software product managers typically represent their product(s) by providing inputs such as: product roadmaps, forecasts of relevant business metrics, for example a multi-year revenue forecast, and the requested investment. In addition, product managers typically need to provide a summary of the product-specific market and product analysis.

Portfolio management frequently uses matrices to classify products and to derive appropriate strategies for each class of products. A popular example is the BCG Growth-Share matrix.

One of the outcomes of portfolio management is an investment strategy that minimizes risks on the portfolio level and balances the need for short-term profit maximization with the requirement to invest for future success. Another desirable outcome is alignment between portfolio products so that synergies can be exploited, while overlaps between portfolio products are managed carefully.

5.3 Innovation Management

5.3.1 Overview

Software markets tend to be fast-moving with low barriers to entry. Therefore, they are often highly competitive. Differentiators of software products tend to have a short lifespan, as competitors are often quick to catch up.

The result is quick value erosion for software products: delighter features (from the Kano model, see Sect. 4.2) quickly become standard, are taken for granted, and turn into performance or even must-have features. Competitive advantage of a software product needs to be constantly re-created—and innovation is one way to address that challenge.

That is the reason software organizations typically put a strong focus on innovation, and why software product managers need to understand key innovation concepts so as to ensure product benefits from innovation initiatives of their organization.

5.3.2 Concept

Innovation can occur in many shapes or forms: There can be innovation in product marketing, in expansion of current business models, or improvement of organizations or processes. Product managers often focus on product innovations that result in new features, new quality aspects, or improved user experience.

Innovations also have different levels of market impact, ranging from incremental improvements of the current product offering to disruptive innovations that create new product categories and new markets, replacing incumbent products in the process.

With such a wide spectrum of innovation types to consider, software product managers must focus their energy and the available investments on most effective innovations. [GoFrPaKu10] describes an innovation process which works well in software environments.

The suitability of an innovation depends not only on the life cycle stage of the product itself, but also on the maturity stage of the product category (see also Sect. 4.5). Geoffrey Moore in [Moore08] identifies 14 different types of innovation useful to product managers of high-tech products—including software. He presents a model suggesting which innovation types to use at a given category maturity stage. For example, application innovation—finding and exploiting a new application or use for an existing technology—is necessary for a new technology product category to achieve initial penetration into the mainstream market. Line extension innovation—creating a new sub-category to engage new customers or to re-engage old ones—helps maintain and even grow revenue in a mature product category.

Since software organizations put a strong focus on innovation, we may find innovation initiatives at different levels of the organization. For example, a large organization might fund a corporate research initiative with the charter to work on "horizon 3" innovations (see Sect. 5.2), which require several years to turn into viable products. It might also fund "horizon 2" innovations that can be productized faster, but still require more than 1 year to pan out. These might be funded through the portfolio management process. Finally, the individual product level may fund "horizon 1" innovations which require less than 1 year to become products.

Even with adequate funding of innovations software organizations often find it difficult to derive business benefit from these initiatives. A famous historic example is the failure of XEROX to benefit from the groundbreaking innovations of its horizon 3 research lab XEROX PARC: these innovations included the windows-based graphical user interface (GUI) and desktop paradigm and the computer mouse.

Therefore, success requires continuous alignment of innovation management with corresponding elements of the corporate strategy. Alignment is required in both directions: When innovation management leads to significant results these need to be incorporated into relevant corporate, portfolio, and product strategies so they may be transformed into competitive advantage. On the other hand, innovation management needs to align agendas and resources promptly to changes in corporate strategy.

5.3.3 Process

Creating innovation is a process of understanding problems, available technologies and developing good ways of applying the technologies to the problems. It is extremely difficult to order or formalize innovation processes.

However, innovation can be fostered by creating an environment conducive to it. An important prerequisite is the organization's culture: an innovation-friendly culture needs to be established and nurtured from the top down, one in which employees are encouraged to come up with ideas, are allowed to test and validate them with potential customers, where it is acceptable for innovative attempts to fail without punishment or critique of the employees, and instead learn from failure. The organization must establish processes which allow for the testing and tweaking of innovative ideas.

While it is important to create an environment that fosters innovation, it is also important to have process gates to select the most promising ideas, to put focus and resources on them, and to reject ideas which don't align with company strategy. These might include those for which the company does not have the right competencies and is unwilling to invest in building up the missing skills. Overall, this is a challenging task within a company. On one hand, it is desirable to generate many ideas and give them a chance; on the other hand it is important to focus on a few to bring them to success.

A great idea is normally never perfect at the beginning and requires many improvement and testing iterations before it matures. This refinement and testing process involves iterations of discussions with customers and the R&D team, creating incremental improvements applied in prototypes, re-testing the concepts, and challenging the value. This process typically combines an agile development process with customer collaboration.

While creating the innovative environment as well as deciding which ideas to realize is the responsibility of management, software product managers should take advantage of such an environment, spend time on their research in terms of opportunities, come up with ideas together with their team and prepare them well to increase the chances of receiving funding and support for a project. This includes understanding and describing the big picture of benefits post-implementation but also requires preparing an initial business case describing potential financial impact. Other benefits may need to be enumerated and accounted for, perhaps user experience, customer satisfaction or customer retention. A good selection methodology is the software value map [KhuGorW13], as it incorporates many different value aspects allowing a structured decision.

Gathering this information supports management in making a decision, and also helps validate that the proposed innovation project fits into the overall corporate strategy. Once a project is approved or proceeds to the next gate, it is the product manager's responsibility to select the right users/customers with whom to collaborate. Such collaboration drives development teams to work iteratively on the project and get quick feedback from real users. These many validation steps ensure quick feedback and needed corrections before significant investments are made. At every stage gate the progress should be documented, presented, and predictions updated. The further advanced a project is, the more reliable the predictions of business impact will become. This process ensures that should things turn out differently than projected, a decision can be made to either stop the project, re-align the project with the corporate strategy, or even to expedite the project.

5.3.4   Examples and Variations

Lean Startup

We have already emphasized the importance of refining ideas through an iterative process that relies on fast feedback loops with customers. This is especially important for innovations that seek to establish a new product category. An approach to address this special situation was developed in the Silicon Valley—and the term Lean Startup was coined in 2011 to describe it (see [Ries11, BlanDorf12, Blank13c]). Despite its name, this approach works not only for startups but for corporate innovation projects as well.

Product managers drive the customer iterations. They bring customer demands together with developers' solutions and refine each until value and user experience are optimized. Requirements triage (see Sect. 4.2) is a simple yet efficient tool for understanding which of the suggested ideas are the most suitable and promising. In

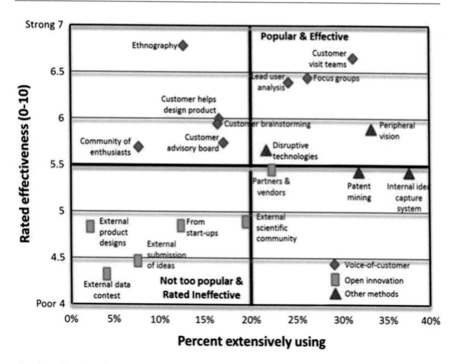

Fig. 5.7 The effectiveness vs. popularity of ideation techniques [CooEdg09]

this phase, it may also turn out that the chosen strategy to achieve the vision is not appropriate. This leads to pivoting, which means the vision remains but a completely different strategy to get there is required.

Idea Generation

There are many methods that support idea generation. Among them, Cooper and Edgett [CooEdg09] have done research on the effectiveness of different idea generation methods.

Figure 5.7 visualizes their findings, mapping idea generation methods by effectiveness vs. frequency of use. The method rated most effective is ethnography, which means in this context that users of a product are observed while performing their respective jobs. The results show their challenges and possible improvements they experience.

In general, the most effective methods involve customers, through interviews, for example. The most frequently used method is internal idea creation, probably because it is the easiest to execute as one only has to think of an idea without the effort of involving customers. However, as the table shows, it is not the most effective idea generation method.

5.3.5 Outcome and Impacts

We previously noted that innovation initiatives can typically be classified based on the time horizon at which they look. Horizon 3 initiatives are often driven in some type of corporate research lab, while horizon 2 initiatives may be executed within a business unit and funded through the portfolio process. Horizon 1 initiatives are often driven on the individual product level—although they may affect multiple products and may be "imposed" on individual products as part of a portfolio theme (see Sect. 5.2).

Innovation management affects strategy on all levels of the organization: corporate strategy, portfolio strategy, and product strategy.

On the product level, the responsibility for aligning with innovation efforts falls on software product managers—they need to ensure that their products benefit from innovation initiatives. Again, this is a bi-directional process: on one hand, software product managers need to understand their organization's innovation initiatives to determine whether in-plan innovations might be used to benefit their products. On the other hand, they may seek to influence the agenda of innovation initiatives so that they address actual product use cases and customer problems: sponsors of corporate innovation initiatives are often quite interested in leveraging the deep market insight and customer understanding of product managers to help inform their agenda.

5.3.6 Summary and Conclusions

Since software markets are fast-moving, software organizations typically put a strong focus on innovation so their products and product portfolios stay competitive.

Larger software organizations often establish different types of innovation initiatives that work on different time horizons: from corporate research initiatives with the charter to work on "horizon 3" innovations, to "horizon 2" innovations that can be productized faster, and "horizon 1" innovations which typically are driven on the level of the individual product.

Software product managers are responsible for ensuring that their products benefit from the innovation initiatives of their organization. To do that effectively, they need to understand key innovation concepts, such as

- The three horizons framework.
- The category maturity model that suggests which types of innovations are most critical depending on the maturity stage of the market.
- Approaches for iteratively improving innovations through iterative processes that rely on fast feedback loops with customers, combining an agile development process with customer collaboration and using Lean Startup techniques.
- Idea generation methods, in particular voice-of-customer methods, such as ethnography.

5.4 Resource Management

At the corporate level, resource management needs to ensure that resources are available in the required quantities and qualities and at the required time so that the company is able to implement the corporate strategy and the aligned product strategies. This applies to human, physical, financial, as well as information resources. For software, human resources are the most important, both in terms of numbers and skills. A software product manager, usually in close cooperation with the responsible line managers, needs to ensure that the resource requirements called out in product strategy and plan can be fulfilled, i.e. are aligned with corporate resource management. This includes identifying resource gaps and constraints and predicting upcoming resources shortages, so that timely actions may be taken.

A product manager's life would be easier if he could make any sourcing decisions by himself based on the product strategy and the annual budget allocated to the product (see Sect. 3.8). However, that is not the way it works in most companies. Decisions on hiring new employees or making investments in IT equipment or real estate or renting space in different locations are considered as long-term commitments that cannot be made solely based on short-term resource needs. So companies usually establish corporate decision processes for these resource aspects in which the individual product manager is a requestor, but not the decision maker. When there are corporate guidelines for sourcing, a product manager may be a bit more empowered within those guidelines. As an example, when external human resources are needed for capacity or skill reasons (see Sect. 3.8), additional corporate rules may apply, e.g. procurement processes optimized to keep external spending as low as possible. The efficiency of all these processes can differ significantly from company to company. In other words, it can eat up a lot of a product manager's time and energy to "fight the system".

If portfolio management not only allocates budgets, but assigns human resources to product teams as well, that can improve efficiency. For strategic and/or successful products, the core product team should stay quite stable over long periods of time to keep productivity high and reduce resource management overhead. Human resource skills are as important as their numbers. When the product manager can see that certain skills will be needed to implement the product strategy, the skills can be temporarily sourced externally, or can be hired as new internal employees, or existing employees can be educated and trained.

If a software product has a very long life people will retire or leave the organization for other reasons. It is part of the product manager's life cycle responsibility to keep an eye on the continuous availability of skills needed to keep the product viable even if the direct management responsibility for this is with other units, e.g. the development manager.

5.5 Compliance Management

Compliance means the act of obeying an order, rule, or request, in more detail:

| On the legal side: | implementing any relevant legal or regulatory requirements |
| On the non-legal side: | acting in accordance with any relevant external or internal standards and guidelines, e.g. in the areas of sustainability or ethics |

Compliance management means controlling the decision process of selecting which legal and regulatory requirements are relevant and with which non-legal standards and guidelines the organization wants to comply. It also includes governance to ensure that the defined compliance requirements are consistently implemented and audited in the organization. It may include participation in and/or influencing of the definition of external rules, standards, and guidelines.

Section 3.13 outlines the legal requirements that are often relevant to software. To define their sustainability goals, organizations may use the "The 17 Goals" of the Division for Sustainable Development Goals (DSDG) of the United Nations as a starting point [UN15].

There has been renewed interest in ethics related to software since the mid-2010s. Such topics as the impact of social media on the well-being of individuals and on the outcome of elections and political decisions have stimulated increased focus. There is concern in some quarters over the increasing use of algorithms and Artificial Intelligence (AI) for making important decisions in business, like loan or hiring decisions, and in government, for example within police forces.

Bowles [Bowles18] provides a comprehensive overview of areas where those who shape software products, including software product managers, need to consider and answer ethical questions. Key areas where software ethics plays a role include:

- Algorithmic bias,
- Use of "persuasive" mechanisms, nudging, or approaches to make software more "sticky" (i.e. to increase user engagement),
- Fairness in utilization of user data, including new types of personal data generated through computer vision and listening, e.g. from voice assistants or cameras embedded in cars, or from smart devices in the home, or health and fitness trackers,
- Moderation and free speech, e.g. on social media platforms,
- Ethics in conducting A/B tests, e.g. using children as subjects of study, or running studies to measure the impact of changes in the software on the well-being of subjects,
- Environmental impact of software, e.g. taking carbon footprint into account when deciding between different solutions to a particular requirement.

The black box nature of many recent artificial intelligence (AI) technologies raises specific ethical questions—even more so when AI is used in autonomous systems. Therefore, organizations developing AI-based software need specific AI ethics guidelines. In 2020, Balasubramaniam et al. [BaKaKuHi20] conducted a case study with three companies from Finland that already had established AI ethics guidelines. The authors identified the following common ethical issues of AI (in alphabetical order): autonomy, anonymity, fairness, privacy, safety, security, transparency, and trust. They researched to what extent and in what way the AI guidelines of the three case study companies addressed each issue. The authors suggest that "... organizations develop and use ethical guidelines to prioritize critical quality requirements of AI."

It is the responsibility of the software product manager to ensure their software product aligns with company compliance guidelines. This alignment may have significant consequences for the software product, for example impacting product definition or creating additional product requirements.

In 2019, Duboc et al. [Duboc19] presented the Sustainability Awareness Framework as a tool for requirements engineering. The framework consists of a diagram to highlight the potential effects of software systems on sustainability (Sustainability Awareness Diagram, SuSAD), and a questions framework to guide semi-structured interviews. The SuSAD represents the impact of a software system on five sustainability dimensions: social, individual, environmental, economic, and technical. The questions framework provides interview instructions and question sheets with targeted questions to address each of the five dimensions. There is special emphasis on eliciting chains of effects and using imaginary extreme scenarios to make interviewees consider long-term, compound impacts of the proposed software system.

Beyond simple alignment with company guidelines, compliance and ethics also present opportunities for differentiating software products. For example, a product manager may exceed minimum legal and regulatory requirements in the areas of data protection or protection of minors, or may choose to be more transparent than competitors regarding the inner workings of sensitive product algorithms.

5.6   Market Analysis

5.6.1   Overview

The goal of market analysis is to determine the characteristics of both current and future markets by researching customers, competitors, relevant technologies and economic developments.

Organizations evaluate the attractiveness of a future market by gaining an understanding of evolving opportunities and threats as they relate to their own organization's strengths and weaknesses.

5.6.2   Concept

It is of utmost importance for a software organization to have deep insight into trends and developments in relevant markets: the markets in which it is already engaged, markets which it wants to enter, markets which might be the source of new competitors, and newly emerging markets or market segments.

Market analysis is typically performed on all three levels we discuss in this section: on the corporate level, the portfolio level, and the individual product level. Unless the company has a dedicated market analysis unit, software product managers are responsible for the product-level analysis and provide their results as input into portfolio or corporate strategy.

To conduct a market analysis, software product managers or market research specialists will typically look at the following areas:

- Market Forces
  - Market issues: Identify key issues driving and transforming your market.
  - Market segments: Identify major market segments, describe their attractiveness and seek to spot new segments.
  - Needs and demands: Outline market needs and describe how well served they are.
  - Willingness to pay: Identify and describe the features for which customers are willing to pay.
  - Switching cost: Describe the cost factors customers are facing when they switch to/from a competitive product.
- Industry Forces
  - Competitors (Incumbents): Identify incumbent competitors and their relative strengths.
  - New entrants (Insurgents): Identify new, insurgent players and determine whether they compete with a business model different from yours.
  - Pricing: Identify price structures and levels prevalent in the selected market segments.
- Key Trends
  - Technology trends: Identify technology trends that can threaten your business or enable it to evolve and improve.
  - Regulatory trends: Describe regulatory trends that may influence your business.
- Quantitative data about the market to support the qualitative analysis
  - Market size.
  - Competitor's revenue, profit, market share (e.g. analysis of the annual reports, if available).

When collecting information for market analysis, the following information sources may be useful:

Primary Research   Simply doing one's own research, using:

- Direct contacts inside the organization, for example colleagues from marketing, sales, support, other services, and development.

- Direct contacts outside the organization, including ecosystem participants like partners, media contacts, and customers who may also provide valuable insight into competition.
- Systematic industry studies, which might range from conducting a survey to commissioning a custom study with an industry analyst or market research agency.

Secondary Research This means using research done by others, for example industry analysts or market research agencies.

Industry analysts play an important role in IT markets: they are a valuable source of quantitative information, for example current market (segment) sizes, growth rates, market shares. They also provide qualitative information, for example market segmentation, technology and business trends, and newly emerging opportunities.

Internal Market Research Department Organizations often have specialized market research departments acting as internal service units which product managers should make a point of leveraging. These departments conduct their own research and collect, evaluate and aggregate information from industry analysts and market research agencies, and provide regular updates to their internal audiences, in particular to product managers. Often, they also control access to the services of industry analysts. If no such market research department is available, software product managers may need to perform the market analysis on their own.

For competitive analysis we need to go beyond simple feature-by-feature comparisons of existing products. We also need to understand the strategies of competitors, their product and portfolio strategies, and their vision. All the information sources listed before as well as the website, documents, and events of competitors may provide relevant information, as may their annual or quarterly reports, materials for investors, product brochures etc.

5.6.3   Examples and Variations

Defining the Addressable Market
Defining the product market is central to market analysis and helps better to understand customers. Several different segmentation models are available, one of them is the Three Level Model proposed by Weinstein [Weinst04].

This list explains how to define the levels:

- Level 1—Relevant Market (see Fig. 5.8)
  - Define Geographic Trade Area = current market served.
  - Define Product Market = current products offered (myopia).
  - Define Generic Market = mass marketing definition (mass market).
  - Relevant Market = Larger than Product Market/Smaller than Generic Market.

Fig. 5.8 Example for definition of level 1—relevant market: achieving balance between going too narrow nor too broad

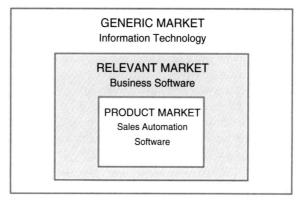

- Level 2—Defined Market
  - Defined Market = Relevant Market segmented into penetrated market (existing customers) and untapped market (non-customers).
- Level 3—Target Markets
  - Apply Segmentation Dimensions to Defined Market.
  - Identify Multiple Segments within Defined Market.
  - Select Attractive Segments within Defined Market.

A key benefit of this model is its ability to find the balance between myopia (too narrow segment definitions) and mass market (too broad definition).

Industry Analysts
Industry analysts are a valuable source not only for quantitative market information, like size of market segment and market shares of players within the segment, they also provide qualitative information, for example technology and business trends, changes in market segmentation, and newly emerging opportunities.

There are many smaller boutique analysts that specialize in certain geographic or functional segments. The worldwide leaders conduct qualitative and quantitative analyses on a larger scale, like IDC, Gartner, and Forrester Research. In selecting analysts, consider their different strengths in conjunction with your information needs to find the best candidate(s).

What they have in common is relatively high prices for the use of their research results. Their primary target customers are usually corporate IT organizations who use the research results as input for investment decisions. Industry analysts stress their independence, although, in fact, they are forced to cooperate with software vendors to some degree to obtain the information they need. In addition, over time, analysts expanded their business models to include consulting services, regularly used by vendors and corporate IT organizations alike; these may lead to a conflict of interest. They also sell research results to vendors who want to use them for marketing purposes.

Results provided by the market research companies are nevertheless a useful source of information, even if one should not rely on them unquestioningly. Always bear in mind that market research companies do not merely penetrate vendors' marketing hype and conduct serious analyses, but that they also produce their own hype to promote their business. Like tabloid newspapers, this may take the form of exaggerating conflict or finding perceived contradictions in marketing statements vs what a software vendor is actually doing. Product managers need to assess all inputs available to them, use their own judgment and make business assessments and decisions in consultation with colleagues, superiors, and their company-internal market research department (if available).

Market research can also be useful for marketing, as CRM software producer Siebel (since acquired by Oracle) demonstrated in the spring of 2003 when it published the results of a CRM market analysis conducted by Gartner in worldwide full-page advertisements. The advertisements displayed, among other things, the "Magic Quadrant," a Gartner evaluation of companies and their products based on a system of coordinates with a "completeness of vision" axis and an "ability to execute" axis. There is no better advertisement for a vendor than to be located in the "Leaders" quadrant, as Siebel was in the majority of the analyzed CRM segments in the above example. IT industry analysts generally impose very strict limitations on what kind of information may be used in which context: for example, they might allow a software company to use approved quotes in marketing materials or refer to their position in the magic quadrant.

Figure 5.9 shows the Magic Quadrant's skeleton, in which companies are positioned. Gartner describes in [Gartner22] how a magic quadrant is to be read. The axis "Ability to Execute" summarizes factors such as the vendor's financial viability, market responsiveness, product development, sales channels and customer base. The axis "Completeness of Vision" reflects the vendor's innovation, whether the vendor drives or follows the market, and if the vendor's view of how the market will develop matches Gartner's perspective. Figure 5.9 also shows how Gartner indicates the individual quadrants should be interpreted.

Gartner also regularly publishes the Gartner Hype Cycles, another qualitative market analysis tool that is quite influential in the IT industry. A Gartner Hype Cycle (Fig. 5.10) describes the response to new technologies. Gartner defines the terms used as follows (see [FeRaBu17]):

- Innovation Trigger (formerly called Technology Trigger): The Hype Cycle starts when a breakthrough, public demonstration, product launch, or some other event generates press and industry interest in a technology innovation.
- Peak of Inflated Expectations: A wave of "buzz" builds and the expectations for this new technology rise above the current reality of its capabilities. In some cases an investment bubble forms, as happened with the Web and social media.
- Trough of Disillusionment: Inevitably, impatience for results begins to replace the original excitement about potential value. Problems with performance, slower-than-expected adoption or a failure to deliver financial returns in the time anticipated all lead to missed expectations, and disillusionment sets in.

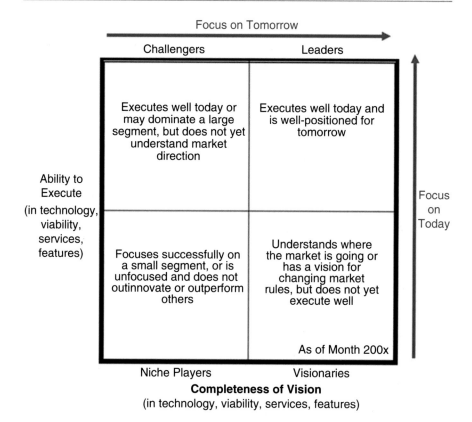

Fig. 5.9 Gartner magic quadrant (Gartner, Inc. 2021)

- Slope of Enlightenment: Some early adopters overcome the initial hurdles, begin to experience benefits and recommit efforts to move forward. Drawing on the experience of the early adopters, understanding grows about where and how the technology can be used to good effect and, just as importantly, where it brings little or no value.
- Plateau of Productivity: With the real-world benefits of the technology demonstrated and accepted, growing numbers of organizations feel comfortable with the now greatly reduced levels of risk. A sharp uptick ("hockey stick") in adoption begins, and penetration accelerates rapidly as a result of productive and useful value.

New technologies positioned on the Hype Cycle do not move at a uniform speed through the cycle. When discussing a new technology, Gartner also provides their estimate how long it will take the technology to reach the plateau of productivity.

This is important information that product managers need to consider in their planning activities.

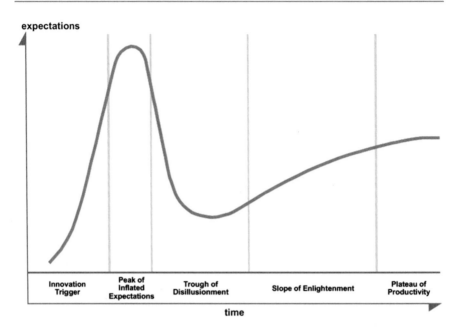

Fig. 5.10 Gartner Hype Cycle [FeRaBu17]

5.6.4 Outcome and Inputs

A large part of market analysis results are graphics, such as market size and market share diagrams, visualization of trends and their impact on markets and on the competitive landscape. Therefore, market analysis is often documented in slide decks, accompanied by spreadsheets providing more detailed numbers and the foundation for charts.

Market analysis results are used in a number of activities of software product management, in particular product positioning, business aspects, ecosystem management, and roadmapping.

5.6.5 Summary and Conclusions

The goal of market analysis is to determine the characteristics of both current and future markets, researching customers, competitors, relevant technologies and economic developments.

Sources for market research can be classified into primary research, secondary research, and the company-internal market research department (if available).

Market analysis also includes competitive analysis. Here, it is important to go beyond simple feature-by-feature comparisons of existing products and to understand the strategies of competitors, their product and portfolio strategies, and their vision.

Industry analysts play a very important role in the IT industry, providing both quantitative market research data, as well as competitor information and qualitative insights into market and technology trends.

5.7 Product Analysis

5.7.1 Overview

Businesses are becoming more and more data-driven across all industries. Product Analysis defines the data relevant for the management of a product, locates or generates it, accesses it reliably and regularly, aggregates it based on agreed definitions, and makes it available in an appropriate way to everybody who has a need to know. Product managers will use such data for performance management (see Sect. 3.14) and product planning (Chap. 4), executive management as input to portfolio management (see Sect. 5.2) and for operational business management.

5.7.2 Concept

With more and more data available to companies, presenting the data in a way that is germane to and useful for making high quality decisions is increasingly challenging. This is what product analysis is about for product-related data. We differentiate hard measures, a.k.a. key performance indicators (KPIs), and softer measures.

KPIs lend themselves to four different areas. Often used examples:

- Financial KPIs focusing on the history, current state and plan for:
  - Cost of the product (development, maintenance and support, third party license fees, patent license fees). This information usually comes from the finance and controlling organization.
  - Current revenue and the pipeline of potential customers (license, subscription, maintenance and support revenue). This information comes from the sales and finance and controlling organizations. It can be subdivided by time period, by product version, etc.
  - Profitability, for which product-related costs are subtracted from product-related revenue.

Period accounting rules apply to all the financial numbers which means that the numbers from the books may not fully reflect the complete situation. So internally, it makes sense also to look at contracted revenue.

- Customer-related KPIs focusing on the history, current state and plan for:
    - The number of licenses ordered, installed, new, total etc. (for a licensed product).
    - The absolute number of active customers and end users including growth rates and market shares (from Market Analysis) (for SaaS, internet platforms etc.). This information may be useful for analysis of customer retention in the later stages of the product's life cycle, but the definition of an active customer may be highly political.
    - The maintenance status in terms of total number of customers, number of releases in maintenance and number of customers per release. This information usually comes from the support organization.
    - The quality status in terms of the numbers of support incidents and customer escalations per release. This information usually comes from the support organization.
    - Customer satisfaction may be assessed by examining pre-defined metrics or based on qualitative analysis. Customer satisfaction is difficult to quantify. Often companies conduct customer surveys on a frequent basis. But satisfaction is generally not determined on the basis of a single factor, but rather as a group of up to 20 variables regarding a range of topics, such as reliability, documentation, usability, service quality, sales coverage, etc. [JohGus00, Myers00].
- Development-related KPIs focusing on history, current state and plan for:
    - Quality during the development process and its relationship to customer-perceived quality (see above).
    - Productivity of the development team.

Some development organizations tend to consider this data as internal, but a product manager needs to look at this data at least on a summary level.

- Product-usage-related information and KPIs:
    - For licensed software products where the runtime environment is under customer control, runtime measurements are usually limited and may require the customer's agreement.
    - In an internet environment like Software-as-a-Service (SaaS) or a (self-developed) e-commerce transaction platform, measurement is easier, since software and runtime environment are both under the same company's control. This includes measurement of web analytics, click rates, numbers of visitors as well as detailed monitoring of the ways in which users interact with the software [CrolYosk13]. Some internet companies use customer discovery to test the user acceptance of new features (see Sects. 4.1 and 4.2).

Product managers will find these data helpful in assessing requirements (Sect. 4.2).
    All the measurements need to be considered over time, i.e. not only current actuals, but also in comparison to the history, the plan and budget, and possibly

the market (with data from market analysis, see Sect. 5.5), as many times trends are even more important than point in time static numbers.

Customer satisfaction is one of the softer measures, as is qualitative input like feedback from market analysts, trade press articles, individual customer feedback, information from the sales channels (like win/loss analysis or opportunities), information from the support and service functions and more.

5.7.3 Implementation

When an organization has more than a few products in its portfolio, we recommend using common definitions for the selected measures so that numbers are comparable.

Then productivity may be optimized by establishing a central data analyst or team who collect the data reliably and regularly, aggregate them, and make them available in a way that is effective for decision makers, be they product managers or executive managers. Standardized graphical representations can also add value here.

When there is no central product analysis, this analysis becomes the responsibility of each product manager or product management team. In that case, the product manager can focus directly on those measures that are selected and relevant for a particular product (see Sect. 3.14). This selection can change depending on the phase of each product in its life cycle (Fig. 5.11).

Even if there is a central data analysis function responsible for product analysis, product managers must fully understand measure definition, data sourcing, and measure aggregation. This may require some in-depth investigation. When a product manager does this for the first time, he may find surprising and unexpected results. For example, he may see product revenue that is accounted for as service revenue

Phase	Focus of product analysis
Conception and creation	Financial KPIs for planned data, Development-related KPIs
Market introduction	Product-usage-related KPIs based on planned and current data, Financial KPIs for planned and current data, Development-related KPIs
Growth	Customer-related KPIs, Financial KPIs, Product-usage-related KPIs, Development-related KPIs
Maturity	Financial KPIs for current data, Product-usage-related KPIs, Customer-related KPIs, Development-related KPIs
Decline	Customer-related KPIs, Financial KPIs, Development-related KPIs
Withdrawal	Financial KPIs for historic and current data

Fig. 5.11 Key Performance Indicators (KPIs) in product life cycle phases

(from combined product-service deals), or costs charged against the product that have absolutely no relationship to the product. Those findings require correction.

Product analysis results are used in many aspects of software product management, in particular business aspects, performance management, product life cycle management, roadmapping, release planning, and product requirements engineering (see Chap. 4).

5.7.4 Summary and Conclusions

For a software product manager, it is of key importance to have reliable product-related data updated frequently as a basis for decision-making. Company-wide standards regarding the selection, definition, data sources, aggregation methods and graphical representation help understanding of and comparing between product results significantly.

5.8 Corporate Strategy Processes

On the corporate and/or business unit level, strategy processes are usually governed by a yearly calendar that ensures that business planning is finished in time for a new financial year. The financial year may not be identical to the calendar year, e.g. Apple's financial year starts on October 1. At the beginning of the financial year, all stakeholders within the organization need to know what the objectives, allocated resources, and budgets are within which they are expected to operate. Corporate business planning needs to be aligned with an updated corporate strategy which in turn needs to be aligned with updated product strategies. All of these updates should be scheduled on the yearly calendar as well (see also Sects. 3.14 and 4.5).

Documentation of corporate or business unit strategies can differ significantly from company to company. Some companies go through the annual update cycle rigorously, in particular publicly traded companies. They usually document the results internally, and publish a subset externally. A documented corporate strategy is very helpful for product managers since they can align to it and use it for justification of their respective product strategies.

Unfortunately, there is a surprisingly large number of companies that do not update their corporate strategies yearly. There may be no need for an annual update (which would be a rarity for software), executive management may be hesitant to document a strategy because they are unsure where they want to go, or there may be political reasons for not documenting the corporate strategy. This last situation occurs frequently in companies where owners and customers overlap and have inherent conflicts of interest that executive management does not want to address explicitly. All of these situations make life more difficult for a product manager.

Orchestration of an Organization's Functional Areas

6

An "enterprise" is, essentially, people with different abilities, experiences, and skills working together as employees to reach common goals. Once an organization has left its startup stage, a company defines and assigns work (tasks) to the individuals whose skills and strengths can best handle them. This requires cooperation amongst the people and functions towards common company goals. The disparate work efforts and roles need management to ensure harmonious operation and synchronization of efforts. We will use the language and metaphor of a musical orchestra to describe these tasks. Management must define and communicate goals—strategic to operational—then establish organizational structures that: create and support cooperation, check progress towards goals frequently, and intervene whenever necessary to correct problems. In this sense, software product management is a comprehensive management task focused entirely on one or several software products.

The division of work for a software company usually means that there are separate functional units. The ISPMA SPM Framework identifies four key functional areas that a software product manager usually needs to orchestrate: Development, Marketing, Sales and Fulfillment, and Delivery Services and Support. The framework lists the core tasks that each of these functions performs in the respective columns of the framework. If an activity in one of these four key areas is outsourced to an external partner, the product manager needs to include this partner in his product orchestration as well. He may need to include other areas, in particular, the SPM units of other products within the company, Finance, Human Resources (HR), Legal, and Research. Here, the product manager's orchestration responsibility includes the alignment of product strategies and plans, functional and technical research and innovation initiatives, resource management, and correct and timely measurements.

More and more, corporate IT organizations are organizing themselves like software companies, often without differentiating between Sales and Marketing. In such organizations, whether there are HR and Legal functions will depend on the degree of independence from the parent company.

© Springer-Verlag GmbH Germany, part of Springer Nature 2022
H.-B. Kittlaus, *Software Product Management*,
https://doi.org/10.1007/978-3-662-65116-2_6

Whether Software Product Management is a separate organizational unit or not, product managers collaborate with a wide range of stakeholders from both outside and inside their organization. Inside the organization, they work together with other business functions in a cross-functional product team that ideally stays in place for the long term, i.e., not merely for a single release. The purpose of this team is "... to manage all the elements needed to achieve the financial, market, and strategic objectives of the product as a business" [Haines21].

The cross-functional product team has members from different departments in the organization and may often be virtual, with members from different geographic locations or cultural backgrounds. In this setup, the challenge for product managers is to achieve "influence without authority, accountability without control" ([Hall13], p. 1). This task is conflict-laden in several dimensions. Orchestration challenges typically exist:

- Between product managers for different products in the organization's portfolio due to resource allocation, budget allocation, positioning of products against each other within the portfolio, functional scope, interfaces, release dates, and larger requirements that require parts of the implementation to be implemented in different products with attendant dependencies,
- Between sales and development unit due to short-term goals and individual customers versus long-term more abstract goals,
- Between product manager and development unit due to release scope and dates, resource allocation, and planning of development activities (overall project portfolio, not details of each project),
- Between product manager and marketing unit due to brand marketing versus product marketing, and
- Between product manager and sales and fulfillment unit due to discounting, the reliability of commitments regarding the sales volume of the product, reporting granularity, customer commitments and realistic function delivery versus everything that customers want.

Units like Sales and Development differ in their cultures in all industries, but nowhere as severely as in software. While sales people usually have an orientation towards short-term goals and individual customers, developers tend to have a long-term abstract perspective. Denning and Dunham state in [DenDun03], p. 141: "Information technologists are trained to view worldly objects as potential abstractions to represent inside a computation. Customers collapse into abstractions in this world. Abstractions do not have concerns or make assessments." On the other hand, sales people tend to make a sale at almost any price even when customer requirements have to be committed that endanger the focus and consistency of a software product.

Condon talks in his book [Condon02] about software product managers having to act as mediators in conflicts like this one. Very rarely has a software product manager the right to give orders to all relevant organizational units. Typically, he needs to sell and persuade. Such persuasion may be easy if he is considered competent in the subject under discussion. But since nobody can be equally competent in all areas, leadership in a non-hierarchical sense is required. However, often the product manager does not act as leader, but as Jack of all trades. In such companies, executive management, as well as the managers of the other organizational units, tend to misuse the product manager as caretaker for any problem that comes up and does not clearly belong to one of the units. As a consequence, the product manager is forced to give higher priority to the urgent tactical problems than to the important strategic ones which often means that he cannot deal with the important ones that influence the mid to long term success of his products at all. Executive management should not allow such situations. What can help are clear mandates that include the following:

- Clear definition and separations of concerns, responsibilities and competencies, and clear definition of accountability,
- Delineation of responsibility between product managers and development managers,
- Definition of release planning, requirements management, and quality assurance processes, and
- Establishment of clear channels of communication between product managers and different organizational units (for example Sales).

In addition to those mandates, roadmaps are also important tools to support collaboration with and between the various company functions.

To achieve excellence in orchestration, software product managers need to drive process excellence in terms of working with other functions. Excellent software product managers do not just react to operational challenges. Instead, they proactively foster better relationships and drive the best processes for collaborating with other functions.

In this chapter, we look in more detail at the orchestration tasks required to harmonize Development, Marketing, Sales and Fulfillment, Delivery Services and Support, and then we describe associated skills requirements.

6.1   Role and Processes

The role of orchestrator is one of the central tasks of SPM. It aims at optimizing the cooperation of all units for achieving product-related goals. Each unit is expected to contribute to product success in the best possible way. Conflicts of interest are bound to exist among the units and sometimes even within the product management organization. This task calls for successful negotiations in case of conflicts of interest [FrGoBySc10, Thomp14].

Conflicts may surface when implementing certain product strategy decisions. For example, a change in pricing that affects the pricing metric may impact development by requiring implementation of changes in license reporting or enforcement, support to update support pricing, marketing to update the price list, license key generation, the training of Sales, and to communicate the change to customers.

Conflicts may also surface in operational tasks. For example, resolving an escalated customer problem may require the product manager to change a roadmap to provide a good longer-term solution. He may also need to coordinate activities between support, development, and sales (account management for the customer) to find an acceptable workaround for the short term.

The SPM Framework can show which activities of other functions—represented by cells in the orchestration columns—are affected by a decision or problem at hand. This knowledge can help identify the stakeholders that need to be involved.

Once the right stakeholders have been identified, the software product manager needs to use his understanding of the other functional units to map out a suitable approach for addressing the situation. Such an approach may include establishing role clarity and defining a process to use to address the situation at hand. Then, the product manager can exercise his leadership skills to work through the agreed process with the stakeholders.

Software product managers typically do not have the power to direct other members of the cross-functional team. To achieve a constructive, successful collaboration with these other functions, software product managers can use two levers: First, they need to exercise their leadership skills (see Sect. 6.6). Second, they need to achieve a common understanding of roles, responsibilities, and contributions of each member of the cross-functional product team.

A comprehensive process model is the ideal vehicle for setting expectations and achieving role clarity. Process models can be characterized by

- Their scope regarding the business functions they cover and
- Whether they explicitly recognize different stages of the product life cycle.

The ideal situation from an orchestration perspective is an up-to-date process model. That process model should take a holistic product view and cover all business functions involved in taking a software product to market. The model should also encompass life cycle stages and cover the entire life cycle of a software product from inception to withdrawal, i.e. be a product development life cycle (PDLC) model. The coverage of the life cycle is important because the different stages of a product's life cycle require vastly different contributions from the various business functions.

Unfortunately, few software organizations have implemented such a comprehensive process model. Instead, many process models are established that only cover development activities—a software development life cycle (SDLC). These types of process models are often based on the chosen software development methodology, Scrum for example, and do not distinguish between different stages of the product life cycle. SDLC models may be helpful for clarifying roles and responsibilities when collaborating with the development team, but from a software product manager's perspective, they are incomplete since they do not address other critical functions required to take a software product to market.

In all cases where the product manager cannot lean on an up-to-date, comprehensive PDLC, product managers need to negotiate rules of engagement, deliverables, and timelines individually with the other business functions represented on the cross-functional product team.

A RACI matrix [Haines21] is frequently used as a tool to clarify roles and responsibilities. A RACI matrix defines who is Responsible, Accountable, Consulted, and Informed for each activity or deliverable within a process. The RACI matrix may be used to establish functional support plans (FSPs): "FSPs are created as action planning, horizontal contracts across the cross-functional product team's memberships. FSPs describe the activities, deliverables, dependencies, and schedules for each team member across the entire life cycle ..." [Haines21]. Most companies today handle this in a more informal way.

In the long-term, it makes sense for software product managers to push for the development and introduction of a suitable PDLC. The PDLC will reduce the effort involved in negotiating FSPs with multiple different business functions.

6.2 Development and UX Design

The development unit is responsible for all technical software aspects including the implementation of extensions and changes to the software. The development function exercises a strong influence on the product's functional capabilities and qualities, as well as the user experience. Therefore, successful collaboration with Development and User Experience (UX) Design is a key success factor for software product managers—and there are many possible areas for conflict. The Development column in the SPM Framework details the tasks of the Development functional area.

Product Architecture Management addresses all aspects of product architecture. Product Architecture has a significant impact on a software product with regard to evolution and flexibility. We covered two architectural dimensions, offering architecture and business architecture, under Product Positioning (see Sect. 3.5.2). The more technical dimensions of product architecture fall under Development's responsibility (see Sect. 6.2.2).

Development Engineering Management addresses all development considerations relevant across and above product-specific development activities. These include development processes and tools, configuration management, knowledge management, resource and skills management, development sourcing, and estimates.

Development Execution addresses the execution of the actual software development work. The chosen development methodology to do this has an impact on the way SPM and Development cooperate (see Sect. 4.2). Development may work based on a project structure or in a continuous mode. Development is also usually responsible for writing internal documentation and contributing to software-related external documentation.

Development organizations use a variety of methodologies. The chosen development methodology will impact on the work of the software product manager and on the interface between SPM and Development. Specifically it will affect the way requirements are submitted for implementation and the way acceptance of project deliverables is managed. Most companies use a mix of different methodologies, be they agile, iterative, or stage-gate, often called waterfall. Popular agile and lean methodologies include Scrum, Kanban, and eXtreme Programming (XP).

At a high level, both agile and iterative development are driven with small, controllable steps or iterations. With most agile methodologies, every iteration consists of analysis, design, coding, and testing. With iterative, coding and testing are done in iterations while analysis and design are done upfront. With stage-gate, or waterfall, there are no iterations, but one stage or phase is done after the other. So, with stage-gate and iterative, requirements are handled early whereas with agile, requirements usually need to be handled in each iteration.

In agile projects a specific role deals with requirements. In Scrum, the Product Owner fills the role. In smaller agile environments, the SPM may assume the Product Owner role, but that construct does not scale up [Kittlaus12]. In larger environments, additional team members who cooperate tightly with the SPM will fill the Product Owner role. The Scaled Agile Framework (SAFe, [KnasLeff20]) offers an approach for scaling agile in larger organizations.

With agile methodology and continuous integration (and even continuous deployment), new functionality can be delivered daily if customers can deal with such a high release frequency (see Sect. 4.3). The SPM challenge is to focus on the strategic and important items in such a high-paced environment.

Detailed requirements engineering is part of Development Execution and follows a process like the product requirements engineering process (see Sect. 4.2). Once the release contents are defined, corresponding product requirements are submitted to Development and further refined. Detailed requirements may also include development-internal needs identified within the Development organization. Continuous tracking of detailed requirements and synchronization with product requirements are required. With agile methodologies like Scrum, much of the requirements analysis is done by the product owner.

User experience (UX) design addresses every aspect of the users' interactions with a software product or component (see Sect. 6.2.3). UX Design may be part of Development's responsibilities, organized as a separate shared-service organization, or be part of the Product Management organization. The UX design scope and product expectation are described in the Product Strategy under Product Positioning (see Sect. 3.7).

Quality Management addresses the technical quality of software. It encompasses test strategies, infrastructure and plans, technical support strategies and structure (together with the Support unit), a historical quality database, quality forecasting, and the execution of tests.

The product manager's orchestration responsibilities include agreements on release scope, schedules, estimates, tracking of the execution, tracking of project vs. product requirements, acceptance of results based on tests, and negotiations and adjustments of plans including scope changes if needed.

6.2.1 Organizational Setup, Roles, and Processes in Development

The organizational structure, job titles, and processes used by the development function depend on several factors. These factors include the type of software product and the development method, e.g. waterfall, iterative, or agile, and the process chain from code development to product delivery.

The typical setup in a traditional software development organization using a waterfall or iterative development process includes the following roles:

- Development team, including developers, architects, and development managers: This team may be relatively stable with developers working on the same product for many years. In that case, the development team has deep and highly relevant product knowledge;
- Separate QA team—by intent, members of this team often are different from the developers with a specialization in quality assurance.
- Engineering support teams: e.g. roles for maintaining development and test environments, configuration management, etc.

An agile development organization that uses Scrum, for example, has the following roles as part of a Scrum team that is supposed to have ten or fewer people [SchwSuth20]:

- Product Owner
  The Product Owner is accountable for maximizing the value of the product resulting from the work of the Scrum team and for effective product backlog management, i.e. taking care of detailed requirements.
- The Scrum Master is accountable for establishing Scrum as defined in the Scrum Guide and for the Scrum Team's effectiveness.
- Team Member doing development and testing
  In contrast to the typical setup for waterfall development, testers in agile development are often part of the agile team.

A software organization may introduce additional coordination layers and functions to scale the development organization beyond a small number of Scrum teams. For example, a release management function may be established, as suggested by the Scaled Agile Framework (SAFe, [KnasLeff20]).

Some agile gurus tend to be dogmatic, arguing that the role of product owner covers everything needed for product management and the role of SPM is superfluous. We disagree. In our experience, the operational character of the product owner role does not leave enough time for the strategic tasks of product management. Often the combined workload is too high for one person, and the job profiles are hard to reconcile. Therefore, we feel a separate SPM role is needed. Our view is also described in SAFe [KnasLeff20]. If the roles of software product manager and product owner are assigned to two different people, they need to be closely aligned. Organizationally product owners may either be part of the development organization with a strong dotted line into product management, or they are part of the product management organization and assigned to the development team. Both cases result in a matrix structure [Hall13]. In a smaller environment, it may be possible to assign both the SPM and the product owner role to the same person, this person needs to cover all SPM tasks as described in the SPM Framework and this book [Kittlaus12].

Continuous Everything and DevOps
Software organizations increasingly automate the processes that lead from finalized code changes to the deployment of new software in production environments.

The software product manager needs to understand the technical capabilities of the development organization and to make sure that the actual delivery to customers aligns with business needs: the best use of these capabilities must be a business decision, based on what the market can absorb.

The processes that lead from finalized code changes to deployment in production environments include:

- Continuous Integration: automated integration, build, and test in the development environment,
- Continuous Deployment: automated push of software into the production environment, and
- Continuous Delivery: automated delivery of software to customers.

If continuous integration, deployment, and delivery capabilities are in place, the organization can choose how frequently to deliver code changes to customers. Continuous deployment can result in multiple production deployments per day, for example in a SaaS delivery model [HumFar10].

To implement continuous deployment and delivery, Development needs to collaborate closely with other functions. If the software vendor also operates the software, for example in a Software as a Service (SaaS) delivery model, tight integration with the Operations function is required. This integration is called DevOps: "DevOps is about aligning the incentives of everybody involved in delivering software, with a particular emphasis on developers, testers, and operations personnel" [HumMol11].

DevOps is a development methodology aiming for a tighter cooperation between Development and Operations to achieve better quality of software products, shorter time to market, and improvements in operational efficiency. It is primarily applicable to the Speedboat scenario. At the core of a DevOps setup is a collaborative culture. To strengthen this culture, product managers need to build a clear and common view for the product vision, strategy, and principles across the functional units involved. They can form the basis for daily decision-making and execution. Once a DevOps approach with elements like automated testing and a seamless tool chain is established, product managers not only benefit from improved time-to-market, but also up-to-date product status insights that enable fact-based discussions with the functional units [BasWebZh15, JabiPeTa16, EriAmrDa17, ForJumKi18, LuPiBo18, LRKMM19].

In a DevOps context, it can be beneficial to establish a "release heartbeat" where new functionality is released to the market at regular intervals, e.g. once every week or every 6 months. The heartbeat drives alignment and efficiency within the software organization and properly sets expectations of the market.

Typical Areas of Conflict: Development
Typical areas of conflict between SW Product Management and Development include:

- **Release Planning: Disagreement About the Priority of Requirements**

Disagreements may relate to individual requirements or features or to classes of requirements: for example, SPMs often focus heavily on functional requirements, while Development may push to spend more effort on architectural improvements, code cleanups, reduction of technical debt, or on addressing non-functional requirements.

- **Release Planning: Development "Does What They Want" Instead of Executing the Release Plan**

As an example, Development might consider the list of requirements to incorporate in the next release or the planned release date as unrealistic considering existing resource and schedule constraints—and simply execute based on priorities they set themselves.

- **Detailed Requirements Engineering: Disagreement About the Meaning of Requirements**

The software product manager does not agree with the way Development has interpreted and refined certain product requirements.

- **Requirements Management: Changing Requirements**

From a development perspective, it would be ideal if all requirements were completely and precisely defined at the beginning of the implementation of a new release without any subsequent changes. From a business perspective, however, changes in the market, in customer situations, or on the legal side can lead to changes in requirements at any time. In these situations, Product Management and Development need to ensure timely decisions. The additional efforts in development that are caused by such changes depend to a certain degree on the type of development process employed. The waterfall model assumes a strictly sequential process and cannot cope well with late changes. Iterative or Agile models are better suited to handling change. Also, iterative and agile models provide early indicators of customer acceptance of the results.

- **Agile Development: Misalignment of Sprints with Product Strategy**

Over multiple sprints, the product increasingly evolves in a direction that is not in line with the release themes and epics defined by the product manager.

- **Continuous Deployment: Disagreement About Deployment Frequency**

Once continuous deployment capabilities have been set up, Development and Operations may want to use these capabilities to their full extent. However, the software product manager may want, e.g. for marketing reasons, to group changes, delay deployment of certain changes, or simply control the timing of new functionality.

- **DevOps—Quality Problems from Imperfect Implementation**

DevOps requires smooth automated process execution from the time the developer commits a piece of changed code to the code database until that code is actually deployed in the runtime environment. Quality problems can result from insufficient process design, technical problems during execution, insufficient coverage of automated testing, etc.

Giving Product Management the role of internal client can help to ease or avoid these conflicts. The client role includes responsibility for budgets, contents, and acceptance of the results of the development activities. Budgeting will be ensured in the planning process (see Sect. 5.2), content managed in the release and requirements management processes (see Sects. 4.2 and 4.3), and acceptance of development results is based on reviews and tests that are part of the development process. The software product manager must rely on qualified internal or external reviewers and testers, e.g. a Quality Management unit, who provide a reliable basis for his acceptance decision.

The software product manager may find it difficult to initiate a strict separation of client and contractor since the developers tend to see this more as an annoying control than as help whereas people on the business side often feel forced into sharing responsibility for the results of development. If these initial difficulties can be overcome, the separation usually turns out to be helpful. It makes the role definitions more precise and leads to better cooperation. The separation does not prevent all conflicts between Product Management and Development, however. It simplifies and clarifies the rules of conflict resolution.

The Capability Maturity Model Integration (CMMI, [CMMI18]) of Carnegie Mellon University describes an ideal of Software Engineering: the "perfect" software organization can work with all types of development processes in the same reliable and masterful way and selects the optimal type at the beginning of each project following certain criteria. Few development organizations are perfect in that sense. Most are glad when they master one process type in a reliable way. We do not recommend the software product manager enforce any process type that the development team does not master. An unsuitable process would increase the probability of project failure. Rather, the product manager should motivate Development to adopt more flexible process types depending on the type of software. For example, the development process for software games is highly prototype-oriented and seems to be closer to the production of a Hollywood movie than to traditional commercial software development [Waldo08].

The software product manager is dependent on being able to predict if Development can meet the plan in terms of time and quality. Once a plan is agreed upon, the product manager is advised to follow the progress of the implementation with respect to the plan. He must ensure that Marketing and Sales are ready for the launch of the new product or release. Mistakes in the prediction can result in significant cost, bad press, and revenue loss. Since these mistakes happen within most software organizations, many software companies do not publish fixed dates. Instead, they start with limited availability for pre-selected customers before the product becomes widely available. Internal IT organizations may follow the same model by introducing new applications for a small number of users first. However, this approach is often impractical for company-wide applications without building extensive interface code—e.g. payroll. With agile methodologies, often part of the defined release contents is sacrificed in order to meet the planned date.

6.2.2   Product Architecture Management

The chief architect of a software product, sometimes supported by a team of architects, will design, maintain, and manage the product architecture. Product Architecture has a significant impact on a software product with regard to evolution and flexibility. It consists of a number of dimensions listed in Fig. 6.1 and needs close cooperation between product manager and architect. This table suggests a division of responsibilities. The aspects that fall under the responsibility of the software product manager are part of the software product strategy.

Business Architecture needs to be defined by modeling experts in cooperation with domain experts. With software vendors they may be part of the SPM organization, for corporate IT organizations they are usually on the business side.

The product architecture can serve as an enabler for competitive edge and market differentiation over time. One method to ensure this is to have a defining technology for the software product. These become core technology assets that may be used in multiple components, products, and offerings, which must be difficult to copy and which are the basis for significant customer value in a way that creates sustainable differentiation. Both the product manager and the architects must pay attention to the continuous improvement and protection of the defining technology of their software product.

One of the hardest problems in creating and developing a software product is to design an architecture that balances flexibility and cost of implementation. Changing requirements over the life cycle of a product may require changes to architecture, which in the worst case can mean a full re-implementation of the product code.

Architecture dimension	Software Product Manager	Technical architect
Offering architecture	Lead – define separately priced components of the product (suite, platform) offering, and tailorability options.	Ensure technical feasibility including access management, support for licensing and pricing approach, etc.
Business architecture (only for application software)	Lead – define domain-specific architecture, i.e. a logical data model, process model, business object model, etc.	Ensure that technical architecture supports the implementation and change management of the business architecture.
Technical architecture	Define the relevant strategy elements such as the delivery model, pricing approach, release approach, quality scope, and IT stack constraints.	Lead – define the technical architecture in line with the business architecture and strategic and technical requirements, e.g. IT stack, programming languages, etc.
Tailorability architecture	Define the tailorability strategy as part of the delivery model in line with the ecosystem strategy and sales and marketing strategies.	Lead – Define the tailorability architecture as part of the technical architecture in line with the tailorability strategy.
Governance	Ensure that development activities remain consistent with the planned offering, business architecture, and compliance goals.	Lead – ensure that development teams implement in line with the defined technical architecture, and that the technical architecture is only changed based on a well-defined and controlled process.

Fig. 6.1 Software architecture dimensions

6.2.3   User Experience (UX) Design

The SPM Framework places User Experience (UX) Design in the Development column from a functional perspective. Organizationally, it can be part of Development, a unit of its own, or close to Software Product Management. UX Design can be a key factor for differentiation and competitive strength. It addresses every aspect of the users' interactions with a software product or component with the purpose of shaping the user's behaviors, attitudes, and emotions about that product or component.

UX is a broad term covering and interacting with disciplines like graphic design, information architecture, Human-Computer-Interface (HCI) design, interaction design, and usability engineering [ShPlCoJa13]. UX addresses every aspect of the users' interactions with a software product or component with the purpose of shaping the user's behaviors, attitudes, and emotions about that product or component. Emotions include delight and annoyance about the product [LeCBölPe13], excitement and fear in games, and a feeling of being in control when using decision-support software. UX must consider human-system interaction, user interfaces, device and workplace ergonomics, service and content offered by the product, the context of product use, and standards like ISO 9241 [ISO98]. UX also needs to consider the various standards and user expectations, which may vary widely across types of software and market segments.

Cagan distinguishes four UX design-related activities that are critical to the success of software products: interaction design, visual design, rapid prototyping, and usability testing. These four roles need to "[...] work closely with the software product manager to discover the blend of requirements and design that meet the needs of the user." [Cagan08].

Startup communities have developed a variant of UX, Lean UX, to "[...] break the stalemate between the speed of Agile and the need for design in the product development life cycle." [GotSei13]. Lean UX is based on three foundations: design thinking, agile software development, and the Lean Startup method. All three methods emphasize experimentation, rapid iterations, and deep customer and user involvement. The principles and techniques of these underlying methods are then applied to the design process. "[...] this is the essence of the Lean UX approach. Only design what you need. Deliver it quickly. Create enough customer contact to get meaningful feedback fast." [GotSei13].

Typical Areas of Conflict: UX Design
Due to the objectives of UX Design, there is a significant overlap with the product manager role, especially in the following areas:

• Developing a deep understanding of customers' true needs.
• Understanding intended product usage.
• Developing product scope and product definition.
• Eliciting product requirements.

In these areas, software product managers may find that UX designers are powerful allies that help them define a product that serves customers and users even better. Alternatively, they might be in stark conflict, quarreling over decisions and accountability.

A software product manager is well advised to channel the creativity of UX designers into the refinement of early product concepts and utilize their experimentation skills to get evidence that the product concept works for the intended users. If the UX designers discover significant problems in user acceptance and product effectiveness, the product manager may have to pivot the product concept.

6.2.4   SPM's Focus Areas for Orchestrating Development and UX Design

An SPM needs to focus on the following areas when orchestrating development and UX Design:

- Product architecture that balances flexibility and cost of implementation.
- Acceptance of results based on verification and validation tests.
- Release scope and dates, planning of development execution.
- Execution of plans.
- Synchronization and tracking of detailed vs. product requirements.
- Estimates.
- Resource, knowledge, and skills management.

The less experience a development organization has with software product development, the more they will underestimate the extra effort that comes with a marketed product vs. software that just runs in one customer environment. This situation needs an SPM's special attention regarding estimates and the execution of plans.

6.3   Marketing

Marketing is a top priority for a software company. Successful software companies spend a relatively high percentage of their revenue on sales and marketing. There are several reasons for this:

- Software is an intangible commodity that is not easy to describe. The intangibility makes it more important and time-consuming to give the customer an "idea" of the product by way of marketing measures.
- Gross software sales margins are very high due to low variable costs. The high margins can pay for expensive marketing measures, boost sales numbers, and thus create a yet higher profit margin, even after marketing expenses are deducted.
- The law of increasing returns (see Sect. 2.3) in the software industry challenges every vendor to have his products achieve market leadership. Sales numbers and market share are therefore crucial for every software company.

In this book, we assume that software product management and marketing are two separate tasks assigned to two separate units within a company. However, in cases when a company does not have a separate marketing unit, the software product manager often must take care of some or all of the marketing responsibilities and may get the title "Product Marketing Manager" [Weber17] or similar.

Marketing is responsible for all aspects of preparation and support of the product sales activities of a company, including the creation of product awareness and communication of product positioning in the market. The actual split of responsibilities between Marketing and Sales may differ from company to company. Typically, companies establish a company-wide marketing strategy within which the marketing activities for individual products are defined and executed. The Marketing column in the SPM Framework describes the main Marketing tasks.

Marketing planning addresses the development and negotiation of plans for all marketing-related activities during a given time period, often a year, including budgets. Plans can be product-specific, or for groups of products. They need to synchronize with corporate and product strategies and plans, and the sales plan.

Channel optimization means the selection, implementation and management of channels appropriate for a product. Management of marketing partners within the product ecosystem can be part of the marketing responsibility unless there is a dedicated partner management organization. Both require tight cooperation with SPM and alignment with the corresponding product strategy.

Value communication is the process of connecting defined customer values with identified target markets for the product and accomplished via relevant communication and engagement tools conveying the value messaging in formats, content, and channels adapted to the customer's buyer journey.

Product launches mean the introduction of a new product, version or release to the market.

Marketing needs to orchestrate all activities that serve to create attention from existing and potential future customers, in the trade press, with market research agencies, and so on. Typically, SPM, Development, Sales, executives, partners, and sometimes customers are involved. SPM plays a key role in agreeing target effects of the launch. These should include marketing targets, sales, and customer satisfaction as well as desired effects on user adoption, user behavior, or scalability metrics.

Opportunity management means the continuous pursuit of identified business opportunities with the objective of turning those opportunities into concrete product success. This may include the formulation of product requirements, development and implementation of new product marketing and communication approaches, and tight cooperation with Sales. New business opportunities will surface through customer analysis, i.e. the frequent analysis of existing or potential customers or groups of customers with regard to new business opportunities.

Channel preparation means that the selected channels (see Sect. 3.6.3) are enabled in time to sell a new product, version, or release. It includes skills management and the provision of materials, web site, and customer testimonials. Sometimes this responsibility is assigned to Sales.

Operational marketing means execution of the marketing plan, tracking of relevant measures, and correction and optimizing of the marketing plan and channel mix based on tracking measurements or as new insights and opportunities arise. The product manager's orchestration responsibilities towards marketing are a core driver for continuous development of product value. Based on the defined value proposition, the orchestration includes the positioning of the product in the marketing strategy and marketing plan, and the cooperation around execution and optimization of the marketing activities, product launches, channel and partner management. The orchestration of marketing is also an important source of input to product management. Opportunity management, customer analysis and direct customer marketing activities can feed into product planning. Selective participation in industry, customer, and marketing events is a source for qualitative validation of the value proposition. Marketing performance measurement also enables quantitative validation of values. This may be especially efficient for digital marketing channels, and digital tools used at events with many participants, where analysis of actions and reactions from the audience may help to evaluate the relevance of different value proposition messages and even product concepts.

The product marketing department of a software producing organization is responsible for all aspects of preparing and supporting product sales. Their goal is to craft an effective marketing and sales funnel: attracting as many prospects as possible, turning them into leads that are interested in the product, converting them into paying customers, and ultimately turning them into promoters of the product.

This product marketing goal closely aligns with essential responsibilities of a software product manager as identified by Ebert [Ebert07]: to conquer markets and grow market share. Because of this, effective collaboration with and orchestration of the product marketing department is a core determinant for creating a winning product [GriHau96]. Nevertheless, the core activities of product management differ from those of product marketing. Product management defines the product to be built, while product marketing defines how to communicate the product to the market.

Note that selling a product is not the most important part of marketing. Although sales is a closely related discipline, the goal of marketing should be to make sales unnecessary by developing the right product and communicating it to the market in the right way [Druck73, KotArm15]. Marketing achieves these goals by effectively creating value propositions for specific personas in cooperation with product management. A value proposition is a promise of value to be delivered for a customer segment (see Sect. 3.7). Personas are fictional characters that represent an archetypical customer.

There are many different templates for defining a value proposition. Both Winer [Winer99] and Moore [Moore14] offer a simple and strong one:

- For (target customer) who (need statement), the (product/brand name) is a (product category) that (key benefit statement/compelling reason to buy)
- Unlike (primary competitor alternatives), (product/brand name) (primary differentiation statement).

6.3.1 The Marketing Organization

Marketing a software product needs to address the following three challenges [KotArm15]:

- Strategic marketing: defining an overarching strategic direction for marketing that accords with the corporate strategy,
- Product marketing: translating the marketing strategy to the product level
- Marketing communication: executing the marketing strategies to create tangible deliverables such as promotional materials or event booths with a strong focus on value communication.

Depending on the size and design of the organization, these challenges may be addressed by a single person, a team, or even multiple teams. The three challenges are highly interdependent. The marketing strategy influences the marketing goals that the product marketing team pursues. Similarly, the product marketing decisions affect marketing communication (MarCom). The success of the MarCom activities, then, affect the key performance indicators (KPI) of all three marketing disciplines. The MarCom KPIs inform the product marketing KPIs, which in turn inform the strategic marketing KPIs.

Strategic Marketing
The goal of strategic marketing is to create a recognizable brand. Together with the Board, the Chief Marketing Officer formulates, analyzes, and evaluates a marketing strategy in accordance with the corporate strategy for positioning and presenting the company or products in the market. They define a clear message that the other marketing disciplines embed in their activities. For example, upper management may make a strategic decision to focus marketing investments more on the company's brand or on specific products.

Especially for software, which is a product type that is difficult to describe and to communicate, the creation of a strong brand is essential for successful market recognition. In the software industry, the marketing expenses compared to revenue are higher than in most other industries. It can be observed that a software vendor spends 5–6% of its total revenue for external marketing programs. This spending does not include personnel expenditures and other internal expenses.

There are various qualities that characterize a successful brand, of which a software product manager must be aware:

- Brand reputation rests on an identity that has gradually developed, namely the corporate identity, which consists of company-specific competence coupled with the experience and culture of the company.
- Brand core values need to be outlined as clearly as possible and easy to understand. Focusing on only a few dimensions constitutes a key success factor.
- A strong brand develops its own "ecosystem" as described in Chap. 3. Such an ecosystem is decisive in determining how a brand and a company develop, thus

has a restrictive character. An ecosystem does not permit arbitrary diversification attempts, as these could be detrimental to the brand.

- Strong brands require publicly visible profiles. These may be created based on technological leadership or the fringes of a niche market and are difficult to develop in a mainstream market.
- Strong brands owe their existence to a convincing core element, namely company-specific competencies, or to their fascinating aura. The addition of an emotional desire to the brand's core creates the ideal situation. In the IT market, Apple is a good example of generating such an aura.
- Particularly in difficult times or in intensely competitive saturated markets, strong brands have a clear advantage and tend to improve their market position in comparison to weaker competitors.

In multi-product companies there is always conflict between brand marketing and product marketing. The software product manager advocates that Marketing makes his product known and understood by specific target groups or boost product sales. If Marketing is intent on establishing a brand, however, it will invest its limited resources in establishing and maintaining the publicly visible brand profile.

A brand is a valuable asset for a company. A product marketed under this brand name will benefit from the brand recognition. Oracle, for example, consistently markets all its products using the corporate name. They use the brand name consistently for their diversification strategy and to market Oracle database products and other products, such as financial applications or application servers.

A company such as IBM, on the other hand, would have difficulty marketing all its products using the corporate brand name IBM. IBM offers a too wide range of products and services. The brand is still valuable, but its breadth makes it difficult to evoke the associations desired for specific software products. Particularly in the software market, where IBM is traditionally not recognized as a major player, brands need to be differentiated. IBM, therefore, continued to use the brand names "Lotus," "Tivoli," and "Rational" after the acquisition of these companies to achieve better recognition in the respective market segments and to prevent losing the intrinsic value of these brands. At the same time, immediately after acquiring Informix or Sybase, IBM merged these brand names with its own IBM DB2, which never attained the same brand status as Oracle. We can see here the conflict between corporate brand and individual brand names for products or product families, reflecting the conflict of interests between corporate marketing and product marketing. IBM has never succeeded in establishing "IBM Software" as a distinct brand despite attempts to do so, perhaps because these attempts were not consistently pursued and implemented.

An effective marketing strategy influences the end results of the MarCom activities. Therefore, popular strategic KPIs will include both strategic and tactical result metrics:

- The Net Promoter Score for a brand is a method to measure customer loyalty by asking a single 0–10 scale question: "How likely is it that you would recommend the brand to a friend or colleague?" The promoter score is the percentage of customers who answer 9 or 10 less those who answer 0–6.

- Brand Awareness, typically expressed as a percentage of a target market, is a measure of whether potential customers correctly identify a brand. The measure indicates whether a customer responds to the brand after viewing its logo or packaging.
- Return on Marketing Investment (ROMI)—a simple Return on Investment (ROI) formula calculated as follows: [Incremental Revenue Attributable to Marketing (€) × Contribution Margin (%) − Marketing Spending (€)] / Marketing Spending (€).

Product Marketing

Product marketing starts with market and customer analysis. Marketing opportunities are identified by analyzing relevant market segments, understanding their respective needs, and defining the appropriate communication approach for each segment. Marketing is responsible for this process in close collaboration with product management based on the product strategy. For a new product release, Marketing prepares the release launch by preparing the appropriate marketing communication deliverables and possibly by organizing events.

The KPIs for product marketing are roughly those of strategic marketing, but on a product level instead of brand level. The product-level KPIs need to be aligned with corporate objectives and used to inform the strategic marketing KPIs. The product-level KPIs should include at least:

- The Net Promoter Score for a product by asking a single 0–10 scale question: "How likely is it that you would recommend the product to a friend or colleague?" The Net Promoter Score is the percentage of customers who answer 9 or 10 subtracted by those who answer 0–6.
- The Product Awareness is comparable to the brand awareness measurement but also includes whether the product evokes the brand and the brand, the product.
- Conversion is a measure of how many potential customers converted into paying customers.
- Cost per Lead is a measure of how much, on average, had to be invested to acquire one new lead.
- Return on Investment is the average revenue per lead divided by cost per lead.

Marketing Communication

Marketing communication, MarCom, or operational marketing, is the execution of the marketing plan and results in concrete marketing outputs with a strong focus on value communication. Traditionally, this activity focused on producing print media, television, and radio advertisements. Now, marketing communication also includes the use of the brand language, public relations, sponsorship, social media, trade shows, and in-product communication. Within a software product organization, Marketing takes ownership of these activities and discusses the deliverables with the software product manager. The software product manager should only be actively involved in marketing communication activities in exceptional situations.

The marketing communication plan for a product derives from the marketing strategy and defines objectives for individual marketing measures. Besides advertising, important measures are public relations, online marketing, telemarketing, and sales support. A special case is the launch of new products, new versions, or major releases of existing products. Best practice is a launch plan for each product launch, developed, implemented, and integrated into the overall MarCom plan. The significance of launch activities depends on the type of product. Typically, a launch focused on a release date is important in the consumer market. But in the enterprise market the focus on a hard release date is no longer the rule. Adoption of new products or versions takes a lot longer with enterprise customers than in the consumer market, therefore launch activities are spread over longer periods of time. There is a lot of literature about product launches like [Lawley07] or [Cooper00].

Integrated marketing in the software industry uses a combination of various marketing components. The MarCom Plan describes media planning as well as the campaign's creative strategy for advertising and public relations online and offline. Public relations have top priority in marketing communication for software companies. Leaders of successful software companies spend a lot of time discussing market trends, corporate visions, and strategies with the technical and business press as well as with analysts.

User conferences constitute another important forum for software companies. The company may organize such conferences for its products (e.g. SAP's SAPphire) or join industry conferences (e.g. the European Banking and Insurance Forum, EBIF, JAVAWorld, etc.). A software company needs its corporate management to be visible and approachable in such conferences and involve chief architects, community leaders, and product managers.

The chosen development methodology will impact the approach to orchestrating marketing. A typical marketing department will set plans, goals and budgets at the beginning of a new year or period and be unwilling to deviate from these plans in a significant manner. This lack of flexibility on the marketing side can create frustration in a high-pressure, quickly changing environment that is typical for a software development organization. Therefore, it is good practice to make agreements with the marketing department on the type of work and how much work they can do for a particular software product on an intermittent basis. For example, an SPM could negotiate that 10% of marketing resources be made available to product management to announce new product capabilities not yet committed at the time the annual marketing plan was finalized.

6.3.2 Typical Areas of Conflict

Marketing and product management frequently find themselves in conflict because of the strong interdependencies between the two roles. We highlight three common sources of conflicts and discuss ways to mitigate them.

- **Strategic Conflict: Brand Versus Product Investment**

A typical marketing department is inclined to invest in overall brand development because this will lead to a more beneficial impact for their KPIs. On the other hand, investment in product marketing better suits the product manager's KPIs. How to distribute marketing investments between brand development and specific product marketing is a strategic decision that should be made at the board level. A product manager needs to raise this issue when necessary.

- **Product Conflict: Roadmap and Requirements**

A roadmap is a heavily contested document that virtually all departments want to influence, including the marketing department. The interesting and potentially worthwhile marketing ideas are typically more than can be implemented, so a product manager needs to say no to most of them. At the same time, a product manager needs to be on the lookout for marketing which conveys the 'allure of innovation'. Although these specifics may not drive sales, they demonstrate to the target customers that the vendor is an 'innovative player' or 'thought leader' worthy of their business.

- **Communication Conflict: Product Launch**

The launch of a new product or product version requires careful orchestration of many different stakeholders within and outside of your organization. The marketing department is responsible for supplying all product promotion materials. However, asking them to drop everything and start working on a particular product when that product's next version is nearing technical completion will result in protest and conflict. It is best to make an organization-wide agreement on what is in a product promotion package and the lead time required for delivering a quality package. Product promotion materials can take many different forms aside from the classical brochures and slide deck, such as:

- Press conference accompanied by a press release
- Media buys, both online and offline (Google ads, bus stop posters)
- Product logo
- Copy (i.e. text) for the website
- Public relations deals with strategic partners
- Inclusion in the organizational newsletter
- Social media presence

- **Approaches to Addressing Conflicts with Marketing**

To avoid and mitigate conflicts with marketing, a software product manager can:

- Ask the Board to define trade-off criteria for brand versus product marketing
- Involve Marketing early and frequently in product strategy discussions
- Agree what a product promotion package entails and the time required for completion
- Have a regularly scheduled meeting with Marketing to exchange information and make decisions in a timely way.

6.3.3 SPM's Focus Areas for Orchestrating Marketing

There are some areas that an SPM needs to focus on when orchestrating marketing:

- Positioning of product in marketing plan
- Plan execution
- Product launch
- Value communication
- Channel and partner management
- Selective participation in marketing events
- Trading off brand marketing with product marketing

Measuring Marketing's work and success have historically been difficult. The more Marketing is focusing on the internet, the easier measurement becomes. Granular marketing-specific KPIs that reflect customer behavior may be collected to measure the success of communication efforts. Examples:

- Opens and clicks: the percentage of people that open communication messages and click on action links or buttons
- Email submissions: the number of emails submitted each day/week/month
- Requests for information: the number of requests for information (RFIs) or requests for proposals (RFPs) received
- Number of new customer contacts
- Number of new business opportunities
- Online conversions: conversion of all or specific online channels
- Number of trade show leads: the number of people contacted thanks to a trade show.

The marketing industry asserts that it is becoming data-driven, and software product management should embrace this trend.

6.4   Sales and Fulfillment

Companies establish a company-wide sales strategy within which individual product sales activities are planned and executed. The more a software company invests in sales, the higher the sales volume and profit margin usually are. The economic considerations described in Chap. 2 and the marketing leverage described in Sect. 6.3 explain this relationship. One important question is whether the main objective of the product strategy is growth or profitability. The former maximizes sales volume, the latter the number and price of licenses sold in the market. The answer depends on the position of the product in its life cycle (see Sect. 4.5).

Marketing measures create the necessary pull in the market and stimulate demand. Sales activities provide the supplemental push so that contracts are signed and products are purchased. Sales success determines the top line, i.e. the total corporate revenue and market growth. The actual split of responsibilities between Marketing and Sales may differ from company to company.

There are two approaches for a direct salesforce: inside and outside sales. Outside sales involve interacting with customers face-to-face. This is common in enterprise sales, where the sales process tends to be more complicated due to the complexity of the problem space and customer decision making. Inside sales operate remotely with sales representatives interacting with customers via the phone or internet. As the Internet grows in importance as a software channel and as more software is delivered as a service, the role of inside sales is growing.

Traditionally enterprise software vendors have targeted decision makers in IT departments and/or on the business side of customer organizations. More recently, there has been a trend to "product-led growth" [Bush19], also known as bottom-up sales. This means that potential users in enterprises become the primary target group. The product itself must be so convincing, intuitive and/or communicative that initial users are easily won over and become "sales agents" in their enterprises. This approach not only requires changes to Marketing and Sales, but to the product itself (see Sect. 3.7.3).

Fulfillment combines a number of back office processes and systems: ordering, billing, payment collection, and distribution. All of these are necessary to make the product available to customers for use. Fulfillment can be under Sales' responsibility, or with a central fulfillment unit. Manufacturing is usually not an issue for pure software products or services except for shrink-wrapped software. For licensed software, making the software available on a server for download is a common distribution method. In the case of Software-as-a-Service, the provisioning of software in clouds, i.e. hosting, is required; in this case, a server infrastructure must be established and maintained, usually by an operations organization. The product manager must define expected availability and any authorization required for the software to be downloaded or accessed.

The Sales and Fulfillment column in the SPM Framework lists the main tasks:

Sales planning addresses the development and negotiation of plans for all sales-related activities. Sales are projected and usually quotas assigned to sales forces, for a pre-defined timeframe, often a year. A sales plan will define target values and incentives. The plans can be product-specific, or for groups of products. They need to conform to corporate and product strategies and plans, and the Marketing plan.

Customer relationship management (CRM) means the systematic management of a company's interactions with customers, clients, and sales prospects. CRM includes customer communication, knowledge management, and customer requirements engineering. CRM must not only focus on short-term sales success, but also on long-term customer relationships. Maintaining contact with existing customers is extremely important, since satisfied customers are a reliable source of information and future revenue, especially in the software industry. In comparison, winning new customers is essential for further growth but requires far more time and effort than ensuring current customer satisfaction.

Operational sales mean the execution of the sales plan, tracking of the relevant measurements, and taking corrective actions when measurements deviate from the plan. Execution includes making offers, negotiation of contracts, and management of offers and contracts.

Operational fulfillment means ensuring smooth order and distribution processes, sufficient supply (in the case of physical distribution), meeting the terms of service level agreements (in the case of software-as-a-service), stable and easy online ordering and distribution, and smooth and correct billing and payment follow-up.

The product manager's orchestration responsibility includes the positioning of a product in the sales and incentives plan and tracking of plan execution. He has to be involved when any product-specific commitments are made to customers. This involvement is particularly important when customer requirements lead to trade-offs between the short-term sales and long-term product strategy, and when Sales has to deviate from the standard terms and conditions, price levels, or price structure. A product manager may also decide to be involved selectively in pre-sales meetings with key customers.

Understanding the Sales organization and related processes is important to software product managers because, as product advocates and as part of their orchestration responsibilities, their success will rely heavily on their ability to influence the motivation, willingness, and ability of the Sales organization to sell their product.

Representatives from a company's fulfillment function should provide fulfillment-related requirements to product management. These requirements may include pricing structures, licensing, and packaging models, required formats for digital assets, or physical properties of documentation and packaging. Professionals working with Fulfillment should also pass along input gathered from their interactions with channel partners.

6.4.1 Sales Motivation and Compensation

Compensation for sales professionals is different from that of other software organizational functions in that a significant proportion of their compensation is likely variable. Sales professionals are often compensated with commissions, which are related to the sales revenue or volumes of sales that they generate. As part of the sales planning process, sales professionals may be assigned a sales quota, expressed as a monetary figure representing the minimum amount of new revenue or license volume they are expected to create from particular products or services. Setting quotas can be a powerful way to incent sales professionals to focus on specific products or markets.

In one large organization, the sales plan cycle was about a month-long wrestling match of product managers each vying for special mention, special terms, special incentives for his product in the sales plan. Once the sales plan was delivered to the direct sales force, they would in turn spend several days analyzing the sales plan, comparing notes, looking for customer opportunities, prior to negotiating their own quotas and territories with their managers.

Customers are sometimes offered discounts from software list prices to encourage them to buy. Discounting is a powerful mechanism for sales professionals to convince customers to buy at all, or to accelerate buying decisions. Discounts, however, lower product-related revenue and over time may undermine the price structure and price levels which the product can command in the marketplace. We recommend strict governance rules for any pricing decisions (see Sect. 3.10). In any case, Product Management must monitor the discounting practices and balance the need to close sales with defined business objectives to manage this trade-off.

6.4.2   The Sales Organization

Sales organizations often report to a board level position responsible for sales or sales and marketing. Still, there is no single, widely accepted organizational structure for the Sales function within the company or for the Sales organization itself. Sales may be assigned based on a myriad of segmenting dimensions such as geography, industry, consumer segment, customer size, or a combination of them.

In B2B, the Sales responsibilities and activities of an account manager for existing customers are completely different from those required for new customer acquisition. The terms farmer and hunter may be used to describe these two different types of sales representatives. Depending on the size of the company and on the product, it can make sense to assign different people to each of these two tasks or even to establish special Sales units for new customers.

Vertical sales structures, organized by industry, have become increasingly popular and successful for both existing customer service and new customer acquisition. Today, practically every cross-industry software product vendor and most of the larger consulting and service companies have such a vertical sales structure, company size and critical mass of the Sales organization permitting. The attractiveness of the vertical structure lies in market expectations: many customers no longer seek information technology as such, but rather ICT (information and communications technology)-based solutions to improve their business processes. Therefore, vendors must be able to describe the advantages of ICT and its positive effects on the business processes of an industry or a single customer.

A customer does not expect the salesperson to be an expert in their industry. However, a customer expects that the salesperson knows the vendor's products and enough about the industry to explain how the offered products can result in financial benefit to him. The winning market player will be the one whose sales structures and processes can most convincingly communicate such benefits.

The disadvantage of a vertical structure is that it does not allow comprehensive, regional customer attention. In increasingly specialized ICT markets, the advantages of focusing on an industry clearly outweigh the disadvantages of not being able to provide regional attention. In some companies, the vertical sales organization even takes precedence over and has a more binding character than individual country or territorial organizations.

In a globalized world, giving regional attention to key customers is no longer possible. Sales organizations operating on a global scale to manage relationships with global customers are increasingly becoming a major competitive advantage. Many large ICT vendors have therefore implemented concepts such as global account management to provide one-stop service to global clients. This approach is also attractive in that it conceals any internal conflicts between individual Sales units from customers.

6.4.3 The Sales Cycle

The sales cycle is the name given to the series of steps required to identify potential customers and sell them a software product. The goal of Sales is to make the sales cycle as short as possible. Many definitions for the sales cycle are available from various sources, with many of them defining phases or stages (see Fig. 6.2).

The process of a customer buying a product is often referred to as the buying cycle. It is important that the stages of the vendor's sales cycle align with those of the customer's buying cycle, particularly for complex sales.

6.4.4 Typical Areas of Conflict: Sales

In most companies, the relationship between Software Product Management and Sales is conflict-laden. Typical areas of conflict include:

- **Getting Product-Related Commitments from Sales**

While a product manager wants reliable commitments regarding the sales volumes of his product, Sales is typically only willing to commit numbers for larger product groups, but not for individual products. Consequently, the product manager often complains that Sales is not sufficiently focused on his product. Sales will claim that the product does not fulfill the current market requirements. Those conflicts can only be overcome if both parties are forced to make commitments early in the

Phase	Description
Prospect	Prospecting involves identifying potential customers
Contact	The contact phase represents communicating directly with prospects identified in the previous phase.
Identify needs	The sales professional gathers information from the prospect to identify pains and needs and assess whether the vendor's offering can address these pains and needs.
Propose offer	The sales professional generates an offer. For complex solutions, e.g., enterprise B2B solutions, the sales professional relies on others, sometimes from the product team, to suggest the most attractive offer possible for the prospect.
Manage objectives	Once the prospect receives the offer, objections to the offer often arise. For example, the prospect may feel the offer is too expensive. This may result in sales persuasion or a revised offer.
Close	The sales professional generates a contract and gets a binding commitment from the prospect to pay for the software product.

Fig. 6.2 Stages of the sales cycle

development cycle of a product version. Such commitments can only be achieved if executive management enforces them.

- **Getting Product Feedback from Sales**

Sales professionals' contacts with prospects, clients, and competitors make them a valuable source of product-relevant information. The variable nature of their compensation and the inherent difficulty of their job prevent many sales teams from investing the time necessary to provide detailed feedback to product teams. Product managers and their leadership should underscore the unique value of information from the Sales organization and negotiate sufficient time and rewards for engagement with Sales leadership.

- **Sales Incentives**

Because of misaligned quotas and incentives, sales professionals may not be motivated to give some products the attention that the associated product managers expect. Product managers need to be aware of product-related incentives to understand whether their product is receiving the focus from Sales it needs to meet its business objectives.

- **Sales Price and Discounting**

To meet their sales targets for the current reporting period, sales people may be inclined to grant significant discounts to close deals in their pipeline. However, excessive discounts lower a product's overall revenue and profitability. Product managers must monitor discounting policy and practice to ensure that overall business objectives are not being unacceptably compromised to generate sales in the short term. Differing discounting policies between products can result in some products being heavily discounted to compensate for "discounting freezes" on others. Ideally, there are corporate pricing governance rules in place to prevent this (see Sect. 3.10).

- **Short-Term Customer Requirements vs. Longer-Term Market Requirements**

To secure sales, sales professionals may need to request features required by a small number of customers (or even a single customer). Product managers must take into account the opportunity costs of such investments, primarily related to diminished investment in features that are more broadly appealing. Features that are not widely used can generate significant development and maintenance costs over the life-cycle of the product, increasing complexity and eroding profitability. Product managers' discussion with sales may be more convincing if they help sales understand the business impact of investment alternatives and the cost impact of implementing features that aren't widely used. Having such explanations on the table will also be useful in case of internal escalation.

- **Impact of SPM Customer Engagement on Sales**

It is important or even critical for SPMs to have direct contact with customers for a variety of reasons. These include the gathering of feedback and validating product-related plans. Customer contact should be coordinated with sales to reduce the risk of endangering ongoing sales negotiations or the appearance that the different organizations within the software vendor are not aligned. It is also important that messaging be coordinated. Sometimes product managers are so eager to talk about upcoming features and enhancements that they can leave the customer with the impression he should wait to buy until those enhancements are delivered.

Approaches to Addressing Conflict: Sales
Product managers should agree on a formal engagement model with Sales. That model should include regular, timely face-to-face meetings to discuss strategic product-related topics:

- enlist the help of management to ensure the Sales organization has the appropriate incentives in place to ensure to position and sell the product manager's product (s),
- regularly review discounting policy and actual discounts given, to understand the impact of discounting on their product's revenue,
- ensure Sales understands the product strategy, in particular for which customer needs the product is optimized. In that way Sales can better qualify customers and

focus on those where the product is a good fit. This helps Sales to close deals faster, and reduces requests for "feature specials" that are needed only by one or very few customers,
- actively keep the sales organization apprised of customer engagement activities, including updating CRM or similar systems of record, and personally informing account representatives (where applicable).

6.4.5   Typical Areas of Conflict: Fulfillment

Working in Fulfillment is usually an unrewarding task. Everybody expects everything to work smoothly. Fulfillment staff only gets attention when something goes wrong. Special areas of conflict between product management and fulfillment can be:

- **Fulfillment Planning and Scheduling**

Fulfillment requires planning that may be heavily impacted by changes to release schedule. Frequent changes to release schedules or poor communication can be a source of conflict between software product management and fulfillment as these changes may result in wasted efforts and additional cost.

- **Non-standard Pricing of Packaging**

Fulfillment will have the ability to manage some product packaging and delivery schemes, to bill based on certain price structures. If SPM intends to deviate from those, negotiation needs to occur very early to allow Fulfillment to build the capability or to debate the necessity. Such deviation needs to be considered in terms of short and long term costs and in relation to corporate strategy.

- **Access Rights to Downloads**

SPM must work with Fulfillment to ensure that people downloading the software product have appropriate authorization, including meeting licensing terms.

6.4.6   SPM's Focus Areas for Orchestrating Sales and Fulfillment

There are some areas that an SPM needs to focus on when working with Sales and Fulfillment:

- Sales Plan product positioning
- Sales plan execution
- Product-specific commitments to customers (features and measurements)

- Handling of customer requirements (short-term sales vs. longer-term product goals)
- Monitoring for deviations from standard terms and conditions
- Monitoring for deviations from minimum price levels, price structure, or excessive discounting
- Selective participation in pre-sales meetings
- Smooth and correct order, billing, and payment processes
- Sales representatives' product skill levels
- In bigger companies: sales representatives dedicated to product family vs. cross-product
- Alignment of sales measurements with SPM's responsibilities (product vs. product group focus)

Measuring Sales' work and success is relatively straightforward. Measurements may be of revenue, number of licenses or contracts, and market share, either new or total. The selection of measurements depends on the stage of the product's life cycle (see Sect. 4.5) and the company's strategic focus.

6.5   Delivery Services and Support

The Service unit is responsible for product-related human services offered and provided to customers. Non-product-related services like custom software development or system integration are out of SPM scope.

The term "Delivery Services" means services that help customers to become productive with the software product. A typical scenario which might call for delivery services is that of a new customer who wants to start using the product. Another scenario is the existing customer who wants to migrate to a new version or new release of the product. These services include education, installation and tailoring. Such tailoring, even when based on a product's built-in tailorability options (see Sect. 3.6), is a customer-specific service that can entail a large project of configuration and customization.

The term "Support" stands for services that help existing customers to be continuously productive with the product. These services include operations, e.g. for SaaS products, maintenance, technical support, and a help desk to assist with technical and non-technical problems. In some companies, support may be organizationally separated from other services.

Product managers need to have a broad and deep understanding of customer pains to identify opportunities to address customer challenges with services. Services can be critical for customer adoption and retention, particularly for products that address complex problems.

Either the vendor or partners may provide services. Even companies that would prefer to relegate service delivery to partners may be compelled by customers to provide them as well: some customers expect a complete solution and don't want to establish an additional business relationship with a third party service provider. No matter how skilled the partner, some customers may also view the vendor as the ultimate source, expect most expertise from him, and want to hold him directly responsible for the success of the solution. Some customers may also believe that if their relationship is directly with the vendor he "will fix the code" if it does not do what the customer expects. Needless to say, such customer impressions are to be vigorously avoided.

The Delivery Services and Support column in the SPM Framework lists the main tasks:

- Service planning and preparation address the development and negotiation of plans for all product service-related activities during a given time period, often a year, including targets and incentives. The service plans need to be synchronized with product strategies, product plans, and marketing plans. Preparation includes development of a technical base (if required), forecast of demand (with SPM), resource management, skills development, and the development of marketing material (together with Marketing).
- Service Execution means execution of the service plan, tracking of the relevant measurements, and taking corrective actions when measurements show deviation from plan.
- Technical support refers to the fulfillment of contractual obligations, i.e. maintenance contracts with license products or of service-related elements of SaaS contracts. The typical support structure is:
  - Level 1: Help Desk
  - Level 2: Technical Maintenance
  - Level 3: Change Team (typically in or with Development)
- Customer requests need to be triaged into defects, requirements, and non-technical problems, and documented in a customer issue database.

Operations is a key element in all products offered with the SaaS (Software as a Service) delivery model or as a customer-specific managed service. In such cases, the vendor assumes the responsibility of operating the software at an internal or external data center, also known as a hosting service, and giving access to the customer. The quality requirements of this hosting service will be defined in a service level agreement that is part of the contract with the customer (see Sect. 2.4). The vendor's approach may include DevOps (see Sect. 5.1). In Technical Support, a call center on level 1 answers user telephone calls or other inputs. The call center staff need not have profound technical product knowledge but should be able to answer basic questions and differentiate between product failures and user errors. On level 2 dedicated product specialists deal with failure analysis and debugging. Level 3 usually involves a subset of actual product developers, known as the change team, and handles particularly difficult problems and fixes.

As a rule of thumb, levels 1 and 2 should be capable of handling 80–90% of the problems rising to their levels. Only 1–4% of all problems reported on level 1 should normally reach level 3. Significant deviations from this general rule, i.e. higher percentages reaching level 3, require prompt and thorough analysis. Deviations may signal a product quality problem or that level 1 and 2 staff members are poorly qualified, a problem that can be addressed by training. Such escalations to level 3 are a cost and resource issue as the change team at level 3 constitutes a scarce resource which could be coding new functions. However, forcing problems down to level 1 and 2 to make the measurements look good will result in horrible customer satisfaction and morale problems if the real source is poor quality.

Inputs from customer calls need to be categorized as bug reports, defects, feature requests, or non-technical problems and documented in a customer issue database.

A product manager's orchestration responsibility includes: management of product-related services as part of the product offering; tracking service execution; resource management; and skills development. Requirements management of delivery services and support includes service-level agreements (SLA) for service provisioning, e.g. response times on customer requests, and for operations, e.g. infrastructure availability. It also includes a compliance level of regulations and industry standards.

Product management also needs to provide volume forecasting for service planning, and information to support delivery services, support and operations for new product releases.

Product-related documentation is required both internally and externally. Internal documentation includes documents such as specifications, technical manuals etc. This documentation is usually Development-created and not intended for customers. External documentation refers to documentation intended for use by people outside of the product-owning company such as end users, customer IT people, other ecosystem actors or service partners. For end users' guidance, printed and/or online manuals, help functions, or step-by-step instructions need to be specifically developed and require collaboration between UX design, software development, technical support, and marketing. Ideally there are specialized technical writers who know how to create this kind of external documentation. But the product manager still needs to orchestrate these activities.

Another important product-success element is product-specific training offered to the company's sales and marketing, technical support, maintenance staff and, if applicable, to customers. In larger companies, the provision of training requires a multiplier approach. Developers and product managers conduct initial training for the training staff (train the trainers) who subsequently conduct the training. Such elaborate training programs require far-in-advance planning as lead times may be long. The responsible product manager must ensure that the relevant organizational units allot time and resources to the training and provide required workforce and budget as it is needed.

Support services interact with customers after the sale, often at particularly critical times, for example, when an issue is preventing the software from performing important functions. Service organizations also get deep insight into how customers use the software and which parts of the product cause customer dissatisfaction. It is for these reasons that it is important that SPMs regularly engage with Support. Product managers should seek to understand support requirements and challenges and prioritize features that improve support based on sound business criteria.

Although support enhancements don't generate the same customer excitement as features aimed at end users, such investments can improve customer satisfaction and reduce outages. As software support costs decline, the business performance of the software organization improves.

Professionals in Delivery Services and Support also need to understand the product's value proposition and roadmap and should know to whom to refer a customer if they discover product-related opportunities.

Although services can play an important role in providing good customer value, the definition and management of services require knowledge and skills that differ from those required to manage the software component of software products. Product managers should play a key role in shaping the product-related service strategy (see Sect. 3.8), identifying service opportunities, and defining service-related requirements for their product. Nonetheless, they should engage other professionals with the appropriate level of experience to do the detailed services definition, planning, and delivery.

Service organizations may be set up as peer organizations to Sales and Marketing. It is common for Services organizations to have a planning cycle and business model that is independent of the product organization (see Sect. 2.4).

6.5.1 Typical Areas of Conflict: Delivery Services

Delivery Services and Support may at times be in conflict with product management. We highlight the following sources of conflicts and discuss ways to mitigate them.

- **Getting Feedback About the Product from Delivery Services and Support**

Because they often help customers deploy and use software products, Delivery Services personnel can be rich sources of feedback on the product. Unfortunately, their incentives often encourage them to spend as much time as possible working on customer projects, leaving them and their leadership with little inclination to invest time engaging with product managers or providing them with feedback. Product managers should seek to develop relationships with members of the Delivery Services organization and should lobby for commitments to provide feedback to the product team. These commitments should include the definition of processes and guidelines for interfacing between the teams, budgeting a reasonable amount of time per year for the Delivery services organization to engage with the product team, and suitable integration of the software tools used by the two teams.

- **Sharing the Product Roadmap/Positioning with Delivery Services and Support**

Services spend a considerable amount of time with customers before and after the sale. During that time, they may be able to position new features or offerings with the customers. For this reason, product managers should invest time in sharing the roadmap and associated positioning with the Services organization.

- **Prioritizing Features for Markets vs. Individual Customers**

The Delivery Services organization's involvement in customer projects may make them advocates for specific product features with low appeal to other customers. Product managers should be prepared to explain investment decisions to Services personnel and underscore the necessity of meeting the needs of multiple stakeholders.

- **Product Enablement for Services Personnel**

Product managers should ensure that Delivery Services personnel receive adequate information and training related to the product, especially in conjunction with new releases. Inadequate enablement may result in low-quality work from them on customer projects or market perception that others, e.g. third-party service providers, have superior product knowledge.

- **Provisioning and Hosting**

With Software-as-a-Service offerings, the software organization is responsible for hosting services. Many companies work with external hosting providers. An in-house hosting approach offers opportunities for improving time-to-market with a DevOps approach (see Sect. 6.2.1), however. The key success factor for implementing DevOps is the definition of fast and flexible collaboration between Development and Operations.

- **Product Team Support for the Delivery Services and Support Organization**

The Delivery Services and Support organization may need support from the product team for solution design and bug resolution. Product managers should attempt to provide the help needed while minimizing the impact on product development.

- **Ensuring Customer Satisfaction with Support Issue Resolution**

Support professionals and organizations often have KPIs which include how many incidents they close and how quickly. This may tempt them into marking support incidents closed before the customer is satisfied with the resolution. Product management can manage this risk with frequent engagement with the Support organization and development of guidelines defining when Support should alert SPM about important issues.

- **Balancing Investment in Supportability Features with Other Priorities**

A product should be easy to support. Support investments must be balanced with investments in market demand. All too often, investments in supportability receive lower priority than customer-requested features. Unbalanced decisions result in low business performance due to support costs. SPMs should assess investments in supportability based on business criteria.

- **Ensuring Support Professionals Have Adequate Knowledge of the Product**

In order to provide adequate support for a product, Support professionals must be trained on product functions, both from an end-user and a "back-end" perspective. From a customer satisfaction perspective, it is in SPM's best interest to ensure that the Support organization not only understands the technical aspects of the product—information they often get from engagement with Development—but also understands the business purpose of the product. This gives them context that can be important in understanding the nature and magnitude of customers' support issues. The product team may need to supply product documentation specifically aimed at Support professionals in addition to documentation intended for customers.

- **Timely Communication of Support Issues that Impact Customer Satisfaction**

SPMs should work with the Support organization to define guidelines for when SPM should be made aware of issues that might affect customer satisfaction or business performance. Support should have a standard and regular way of communicating such issues to SPMs to make appropriate business decisions. No less important is that SPMs often engage with customers and should never be caught unaware of critical issues.

6.5.2 Approaches to Address Conflict: Delivery Services and Support

To avoid and mitigate conflicts with Delivery Services and Support, a software product manager should:

- Create formal plans to ensure that Service personnel understand both the business/functional and technical aspects of the products, including positioning.
- Define appropriate "handoffs" for customer queries regarding product roadmap, product strategy, and the value of the overall portfolio.
- Define reasonable practices to ensure that direct queries from Delivery Services and Support to Development do not distract them from their primary development mission.

- Make himself available to help Service personnel navigate the development organization as appropriate to ensure timely resolution of product-related issues encountered by the Service organization.
- Make support professionals aware of the important role they play in customer satisfaction, so they can better assess tradeoffs between this goal and support KPIs, like closing open issues as quickly as possible. SPMs would also benefit from influencing Support KPIs to balance speed with customer satisfaction.
- Play an active role in training Support personnel with each new release, including the business motivation.
- Consider investing some time working with or "shadowing" Support better to understand the daily challenges of the Support organization and their support-ability requirements.
- Actively seek supportability requirements from the Support organization and budget appropriately for those, for example in release planning.
- Agree clear triggers for when the Support organization should alert SPM to support issues.

6.5.3 SPM's Focus Areas for Orchestrating Delivery Services and Support

There are some areas that a product manager needs to focus on when orchestrating Delivery Services and Support:

- Consider and manage product-related services and documentation as part of the offering
- Service execution
- Service specialist skills
- Frequent analysis of incoming service calls: these are often good indicators for problems with quality, usability, and functional coverage,
- Resource management: avoid bottlenecks that impact Product Development, Sales, and customer satisfaction.

Service units usually follow a services business model (see Sect. 2.4) and are typically measured on revenue and customer satisfaction.

6.6 Orchestration Skills

6.6.1 Mindset for Influencing Without Authority

Product managers have the challenge of achieving "influence without authority, accountability without control" [Hall13]. This challenge is the same one faced by managers in a matrix organization.

Matrix Victim	Successful Matrix Manager
My goals are not clear.	Here are the commitments I have chosen.
I do not have a job description, and I am not clear what I should be doing.	This is what needs to be done.
I do not have the authority to get things done.	Who do I need to influence to get this done?
I cannot be accountable for things I do not control.	Where can I get the resources to meet my commitments?
My manager doesn't empower me.	What have I done to earn the right to take on more responsibility?

Fig. 6.3 Beliefs about matrix organizations [Hall13]

A certain mindset and leadership skills are required to succeed in such a role. Hall compares two very different mindsets regarding matrix work: a successful matrix manager "relishes the flexibility, autonomy, and breadth that the matrix gives them." This statement describes the approach that helps software product managers succeed in orchestrating other functions. Someone believing that things can only be achieved in a traditional organizational structure, "where managers thought they had all the answers and cascaded clarity, authority, and responsibility" will find it difficult to succeed in a matrix organization. This mindset is the one of the matrix victim, which is not helpful for orchestration tasks.

Hall summarizes key beliefs that characterize these two different mindsets (Fig. 6.3):

Sandy [Sandy20] puts his focus directly on influential product management with his four mindsets that need to be applied in parallel depending on the situation (see Fig. 6.4):

- **Explorer**:
  expands the solution space based on creative thinking, e.g. design thinking
- **Analytical**:
  makes decisions based on data,
- **Challenger**:
  challenges assumptions and ideas to counter confirmation bias,
- **Evangelist**:
  get buy-in from stakeholders and team through effective communication.

6.6.2 Sources of Power

Because the various company functions necessary to product success rarely report to the SPM organization, software product managers must find creative ways to

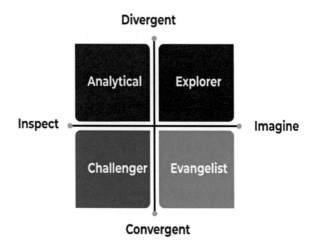

influence to achieve product vision, goals, and objectives. Understanding what power is, where it comes from, and how to increase it can help software product managers increase their influence.

Social communication studies have theorized that leadership and power are closely linked. They have further suggested that some forms of power affect one's leadership and success. That idea often is used in organizational communication and throughout the workforce.

The social psychologists French and Raven released a study in 1959 [FrenRav59], in which they defined the terms power, the ability to influence others, and identified the bases of power described in Fig. 6.5.

Product managers typically exert the most influence using referent and expert power. Depending on the organizational setup, their legitimate power is limited, and they have little or no reward or coercive power over other organizational functions.

6.6.3   Managing Conflict

Product managers must orchestrate across the organizational boundaries of an organization in order to be successful, without the power to direct other business functions. Consequently, conflict with other business functions will occur that prevents product managers from reaching their goals. Nevertheless, conflict is also beneficial for organizations. Disagreement necessitates two parties to negotiate to find a single, mutually satisfactory solution [ZarRub00], a solution that is often of superior value than if it had not have been negotiated [RaiRicMe07]. This chapter introduces selected approaches to conflict resolution, the human-process and techno-structural approaches [Rahim15], that include the possibility of intervention by a third party after escalation.

Basis	Characterization
Reward power	Reward power is based on a person being able to control the likelihood that another person will be rewarded. Close alignment of SPM with executive leadership may offer SPM some reward power.
Coercive power	Coercive power uses the threat of force to gain compliance from another with physical, social, emotional, political, or economic means. Typically, SPMs have very little coercive power over other functions as they have no direct management authority over them.
Legitimat e power	Legitimate power comes from an elected, selected, or appointed position of authority and may be underpinned by social norms. An employee's direct manager often can exert legitimate power because the organization has authorized that manager to influence the people that report to him or her. SPMs typically have some legitimate power granted to them by the organization. Some development life cycle models, like Scrum, empower the product owner, who may report to the product manager, by giving the product owner ownership of the product backlog.
Referent power	Referent power is based on one person's strong identification with another. A person identifying with another person is likely to adopt attitudes and beliefs similar to that other person. Referent power is often the primary source of power for software product managers. Product managers can increase their referent power by defining and executing a compelling product strategy and investing in trustful relationships with other organizational functions.
Expert power	Expert power is based on one person's perception of another's knowledge in a given area. For example, a person's thinking and behavior regarding a legal case might easily be influenced by advice from a lawyer. SPMs often have expert power based on their knowledge of stakeholders, the business aspects of the software product, and the domain addressed by the software product.

Fig. 6.5 Bases of power [FrenRav59]

The human-process approach "attempts to improve organizational effectiveness by changing members' attitudes and behavior regarding a conflict." The approach suggests achieving this goal by educating the concerned stakeholders on the five styles of handling interpersonal conflict. Figure 6.6 gives an overview, and Fig. 6.7 briefly summarizes each style, differentiated on two dimensions: concern for the self (how much a person attempts to satisfy his personal interests) and concern for the others (how much a person wants to satisfy other parties' interests).

The techno-structural approach attempts to "improve organizational effectiveness by changing the organization's structural design characteristics" or managing the amount of conflict by introducing organizational changes. A variety of

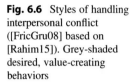

Fig. 6.6 Styles of handling interpersonal conflict ([FricGru08] based on [Rahim15]). Grey-shaded desired, value-creating behaviors

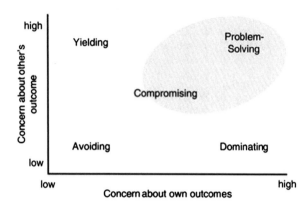

Yielding low concern for self, high concern for others	A party sacrifices his personal interests to satisfy the interests of the other party. The former reacts to a perceived hostile act of the latter with low hostility or even positive friendliness. During a negotiation, the former will attempt to play down the differences and emphasize commonalities between the two parties.
Dominating high concern for self, low concern for others	A competitive or dominating individual will do anything to achieve their personal objectives. Consequently, he or she ignores the needs and expectations of the other party. A dominating person tries to impose his will by sheer force, e.g. on subordinates, and commands their obedience.
Avoiding low concern for self, low concern for others	A party avoids negotiation by "I see no evil, hear no evil, and speak no evil." The party attempts to postpone an issue, withdraw from the situation, and refuse to acknowledge the conflict. When the conflict is avoided, the interests of neither party are satisfied.
Problem-Solving high concern for the self, high concern for others	Leads to full collaboration between parties. All try to be open, exchange information, and examine differences to reach a mutually acceptable solution. This style has two distinctive elements: confrontation and problem solving: "confrontation involves open and direct communication which should make way for problem-solving. As a result, it may lead to creative solutions to problems."
Compromising medium concern for self, medium concern for others	Compromising is characterized as give-and-take or sharing and often used to conclude negotiations rapidly. Both parties give up something to make a mutually acceptable decision. They might split the difference, exchange concessions, or search for middle ground. This style is in the middle of all other styles.

Fig. 6.7 Styles of handling interpersonal conflict, based on [Rahim15]

Devise and implement a common method for resolving conflict
A company-wide process for resolving disagreements prevents useless debate about who is right or wrong and haggling over small concessions. A well-designed conflict resolution process will reduce transaction costs and foster an environment in which innovative outcomes emerge from discussions. Unfortunately, no conflict resolution method is universally applicable. A conflict resolution method must offer a clear, step-by-step process and integrate the process in existing business activities to be effective. Processes used only in exceptions will be unsuccessful.
Provide people with criteria for making trade-offs
From time to time, two parties need to make zero-sum trade-offs between competing priorities – situations in which it is unclear which decision is best. Definition of criteria for making such choices must apply organization-wide. The criteria will foster productive discussion of common objectives.
Use the escalation of conflict as an opportunity for coaching
Senior management should view each escalation of conflict as an opportunity to teach employees about how to resolve conflicts effectively. Management should push their respective employees to consider "the needs of the other party, alternatives that might best address the collective needs of the other party, and the standards to be applied in assessing the trade-offs between alternatives." While this approach requires time from senior managers initially, it reduces the time senior managers need to spend on resolving escalated conflicts in the long term.

Fig. 6.8 Tactics for managing disagreement at the point of conflict

organizational change techniques exists. Weiss and Hughes introduce a comprehensive set of best practices for managing disagreements at the point of conflict [WeiHug05]. These practices enable employees to resolve conflicts themselves. Weiss and Hughes also suggest approaches for managing conflict when escalated up the management chain. When necessary, employees escalate a conflict to a superior, who decides on the employees' behalf. Weiss and Hughes recommend implementing three tactics for each type of conflict resolution. These tactics transform conflict from a major liability into a significant asset. We summarize the tactics in Figs. 6.8 and 6.9. Be aware that organizational corporate culture determines when escalations are acceptable.

6.6.4   Negotiation Skills

Negotiation is a discussion for reaching a shared agreement among multiple parties. As a leader in the product organization responsible for aligning the requirements and efforts of multiple stakeholders, negotiation is a critical skill for most software

Establish and enforce a requirement of joint escalation
In many conflicts, the parties try to get support from their direct leadership. Prevent a vicious circle by enforcing people to present disagreements to their management together. Now, the decision maker has a balanced view of the perspectives on the conflict, its causes, and possible solutions. Moreover, the number of problems that are escalated decreases.
Ensure that managers resolve escalated conflicts directly with their counterparts
An unresolved dispute tends to travel up the management chain until a senior manager with the appropriate organizational influence makes a unilateral decision. This dynamic breeds organization-wide resentment in the form of "we'll win next time, " making friendly conflict resolution increasingly difficult. Moreover, unilateral decisions lead to inefficiency, ill feelings, and bad decision-making. Instead of propagated escalation, managers should formally commit to dealing with escalated conflicts directly with their management counterparts in other departments.
Make the process for escalated conflict resolution transparent
Having resolved a conflict, managers at most companies announce the decision and move on. This behavior prevents employees from learning how to resolve similar issues in the future. Management should explain instead how the specific aspects were weighed and how the decision was reached. Not every single detail of the process needs sharing, but the relevant trade-offs should be honestly discussed and people enabled for resolving future conflicts.

Fig. 6.9 Tactics for managing conflict upon escalation

product managers. Product managers frequently negotiate regarding the following topics, among others:

- Release scope and timing with executive management, Development, and others.
- Budget for functions like Marketing and Sales.
- Contracts with third parties like software suppliers or service providers.
- Product pricing and discounting with individual customers.

The Harvard Negotiation Project developed the concept of principled negotiation as described in their seminal work on negotiation, "Getting to Yes" [FiUrPa12] that was originally published in 1981 and elaborated into a systematic approach to negotiation [RaiRicMe07]. The concept addressed what they considered non-productive negotiation approaches and tactics. Principled negotiation encourages negotiators to bargain over interests rather than positions. It defines four principles:

- Separate the people from the problem: by nature, people often conflate the relationship with the substance of the conflict. Fears and perceptions can be turned into better understanding by discussing each other's emotions.
- Focus on interests, not positions: a position is what a party in a negotiation is willing or unwilling to accept. Interests represent the party's wants or needs.

- Invent options for mutual gain: creatively think of options that address negotiation parties' interests.
- Insist on using objective criteria: these criteria provide a means of resolving differences in interests outside the context of the negotiating parties' wills.

Principled Negotiation also defines the concept of a Best Alternative to a Negotiated Agreement (BATNA, [FiUrPa12]), i.e., the most advantageous alternative course of action a party can take if negotiations fail and an agreement cannot be reached. A party in a negotiation should typically not accept an outcome that is less desirable than their BATNA. When negotiating or preparing for negotiation it is important to consider the other parties' BATNA as well as your own.

Former FBI negotiator Chris Voss [Voss16] suggests using negotiation tactics that take advantage of human psychology by exploiting well-known cognitive biases, for example the Framing Effect or Loss Aversion.

SPM Today and Tomorrow

7

Company founders usually intend their organizations to be viable long term economic institutions. In spite of all modernistic focus on short term results, executive management must have making the company's success sustainable as a key objective. Based on the concept of economic sustainability, this book emphasizes the importance of state-of-the-art software product management for the success of companies that have software (or software-intensive) products in their portfolios.

In this last chapter, we want to look into the future of SPM (Sect. 7.1), derive conclusions from analyzing the state of its practice (Sect. 7.2), and describe the ways in which SPM applies to different business scenarios (Sect. 7.3). Finally, we will present ISPMA, the International Software Product Management Association, and explain the ways you can get value from ISPMA (Sect. 7.4) as a software product manager or a company.

7.1 The Future of SPM

As experienced software product management practitioners and consultants, we have been convinced for a long time that the quality level of the work of SPM teams has a significant impact on the business success of companies across industries. Recently McKinsey [SrTrWaWa20, GnJiSrWa21] published evidence based on their research, not only for companies developing and providing software (-intensive) products, but also for corporate IT organizations across industries.

McKinsey uses a measure called "Developer Velocity Index" (DVI). It is not the velocity measure known in agile environments, but is a combination of 46 different drivers across 13 capability areas, with SPM being one of these areas. The McKinsey team demonstrated a strong correlation between DVI and the business performance of the whole company. Not surprisingly, software companies achieved the highest DVI scores, but McKinsey applied this approach across quite a number of industries. It turned out that 4 out of the 13 capability areas have the highest impact on business performance: tools, culture, product management, and talent management. In

© Springer-Verlag GmbH Germany, part of Springer Nature 2022
H.-B. Kittlaus, *Software Product Management*,
https://doi.org/10.1007/978-3-662-65116-2_7

product management "DVI scores are less sensitive to individual attributes and far more responsive to an integrated, balanced product-management function". McKinsey claims that this applies not just to product managers but that developers and other team members also need SPM knowledge and capabilities.

More recently, McKinsey focused their analysis on several companies in banking and retail industries. Previous findings were largely confirmed with SPM being a key factor affecting business success in the corporate IT organizations. "Successful companies also invest in the end-to-end operating model for the product management function. This model includes a holistic definition of products that covers any software that creates value for an internal or external user; long-term product road maps; specific product artifacts; review processes that emphasize product outcomes; and experimentation and usage data to refine offerings." [GnJiSrWa21]. McKinsey recommends education offerings for software product managers.

Since software is not only becoming increasingly pervasive in standard software products, but also as embedded software in other industries' products and services, there is increasing recognition of the value of software as a critical asset. This asset plays a major role in the sustainable economic success of the companies and therefore needs to be managed in a comprehensive business-driven way, which is exactly what Software Product Management (SPM) is about. With trends like Cloud, Internet of Things, Industry 4.0, fifth-generation telecommunication networks (5G), smart systems like self-driving cars etc., software is becoming the number one value driver in more and more industries. Harvard professor Michael Porter analyzed this development in two articles [PortHepp15, PortHepp14]. We are seeing increasing numbers of tightly integrated systems with software, hardware, telecommunications (ICT), etc. which redefine the relationship between human beings and technology.

With the growing importance of software, we are convinced that the establishment of and focus on software product management will enable the companies in all industries to cope more effectively with future business and technological challenges. And challenges will abound. Most companies in non-software industries are facing severe cultural and skills issues that make it difficult for them to embrace the opportunities that software can open up for their businesses. Serious change management is required top-down, i.e. from executive management, but also from the bottom up. Here software product managers can help as change managers who keep the organization on track towards "software thinking."

Corporate IT organizations have often operated as project-driven service organizations. There is increasing awareness that a corporate IT organization's portfolio of software applications constitutes sustainable assets not only for IT, but for the corporation as a whole. So a pure project view is not sufficient. Software assets require a life cycle view promulgated through the institution by the establishment of SPM. In total, these developments broaden the applicability of the concept of SPM across industries significantly.

In Asia and other regions in the world where the software industry has been primarily focused on providing offshore outsourcing services, there is increasing interest in establishing software product businesses. This is because offshore outsourcing is no longer growing as it was and in many of these regions there is growing demand for localized standard software products and internet services, e.g. in India. Companies who want to address this demand need to establish product organizations which include the role of software product manager and need to change their business model and culture (see Sect. 2.4).

Current new technologies produce unprecedented amounts of data about customers and things (as in "Internet of Things"). Access to this data, its aggregation and interpretation have become key assets within companies. This creates opportunities for "data products," i.e. offerings by vendors where the main deliverable is data. Such products already exist for certain markets like stock markets or pharmaceutical markets. The ways in which software product management can be adapted to the management of these data products continues to be a fertile area for research and consulting.

New technologies and data are now increasingly important to the work of product managers. We discussed data-analysis-driven and data-input-driven approaches to product planning in detail in Sect. 4.2. Software tools based on artificial intelligence are becoming relevant to software product managers, e.g. in eliciting new requirements [Rietz21].

Though ISPMA Fellow Members Andrey Maglyas and Samuel Fricker's software product management survey dates to 2014 [MaglFri14], we still consider their findings relevant today. Some results regarding the future of software product management (quotes from participants in quotation marks):

All respondents agreed that SPM would play an important role in the future. With advances in technologies and tough competition in the market, empowered, systematic, and consistent SPM is important for software organizations to excel. Overall, based on the answers from the respondents we can identify three directions on the future of SPM:

Increased Awareness and Importance

In many companies SPM is still immature today [MagNiSmo12]. Companies try various approaches to adopting software product management practices in order to deal with constantly changing markets and technology trends, but the definition of product manager roles and responsibilities are still far from mature, understood, and recognized [MagNiSmo13]. "There will be a better understanding of how important the product manager's contribution is to the success of software-based offerings (especially given that the technical feasibility is becoming less of an issue). Therefore, product managers will be increasingly recognized."

Certification, Standardization, and Education

As one of the respondents said: "It [software product management] will be more formalized, since the right product management is probably the most efficient investment you can make in a product, regardless of its place in the life cycle."

Product managers may be viewed as middle managers who act as a linchpin connecting different parts of the organization [FloyWool94]. In this role, product managers act as interpreters and implementers of decisions and also bridge strategic and operational levels [MagNiSmo13]. To perform the job well requires a deep understanding of the roles and responsibilities of SPM in general and the ability to map this to company-specific organizational structures and to work practices of functional units like marketing, sales, development, and support. When product managers learn everything through on the job training, that is to say, learning by doing, they frequently miss best practices already known and implemented in other companies. Therefore, education in product management will be the next milestone in accepting and spreading the discipline from self-learning to industry-wide best practices. A serious certification process will help encourage personal development of qualified software product managers and will make it easier for companies to identify them.

More Authority
"Authority" may take two different forms:

- Hierarchical authority in a management hierarchy enables SPMs to implement decisions they make within the team reporting to them.
- Personal authority based on personality, experience, recognition, and respect.

Product managers usually have no direct subordinates, and this differentiates them from other middle managers. It means that their hierarchical authority is limited and their role may be restricted solely to the role of advisor [MagNiSmo13] or "cross functional leadership with no authority." Many of the survey respondents expect to have more authority in the future. If they mean hierarchical authority we believe that is wishful thinking on their part and see no sign of companies giving more hierarchical authority to product managers, with rare exceptions. If they mean personal authority we agree with that assessment. The greater the value executive management sees in the product manager role, the more likely it is to promulgate that view, making it possible for a well-educated and experienced product manager to achieve higher levels of personal authority. This in turn makes it easier for a product manager to convince and influence customers, executives, and colleagues in the organization.

For the IT industry, hardware prices have been declining such that processor, storage capacity, and communication bandwidth are simple commodities. Cloud computing is firmly established and shows continuous significant growth rates. In many areas, capacity considerations are no longer the limiting factors that they used to be. This opens the door to a new phase of innovation with software as the key component. After a period of about 15 years in which innovation was very much driven by consumer business, innovation areas like Internet of Things, Industry 4.0, or Big Data are driven anew by enterprise business.

Corporate IT organizations find it increasingly difficult to stay on top of these many changes and innovations. Technology-driven start-ups come up with specialized new business processes and quickly take away market share, e.g. fin-techs in the financial services industry. "Digital Natives," the generation that has learned and became fluent with PC and online games, the internet and the smartphone before they could even talk, are now entering the workforce. They expect the same IT capabilities at their workplace that they are accustomed to at home, and they will not join a company that does not support their work and life styles adequately. Nor can a company benefit from their full abilities if it does not provide appropriate environments. The "Bring your own device" that many companies have implemented can be seen as a response to the challenge, but it will be insufficient.

Technological changes will continue to lead to innovative new business models, some of which will have significant disruptive power. The role of software product manager will become ever more important in finding ways to marry new technological solutions to business problems on a continuous basis, not just in software companies and corporate IT organizations, but across all industries.

These developments provide huge opportunities for research. We can only list some topics as examples:

- Analytics for software product management.
- Correlation between a product manager's use of data and product success.
- Correlation between a product manager's authority and product success.
- Correlation between software pricing approach and product success.
- Correlation between ecosystem strategy and product success.
- Software category building in different product scenarios and business scenarios.

7.2   The State of Practice

The role of software product manager is firmly established in North America. One can hardly find a software company which has not implemented such a role. In Europe, most software companies have established such a role as well. In Asia/Pacific and other parts of the world, where the role is not commonly established, we see examples of strong companies like Samsung, Infosys and specific Chinese companies that have adopted the role. We also see a growing trend towards adoption in corporate IT organizations and companies in non-software industries which produce software-intensive products and services.

While the term "software product manager" is the one most often used for the role, there are many other terms used as well (see Sect. 2.6). We have also observed differences in role definition and execution (see Sect. 2.6), often as a consequence of specific business environments (see Sect. 7.3).

Here are more quotes from the software product management survey that ISPMA Fellow Members Andrey Maglyas and Samuel Fricker conducted in 2014 [MaglFri14] (in quotation marks):

Skills and Education
Respondents frequently alluded to the need for SPM knowledge but decried a lack of specialized education, e.g. "Even small software companies can now build business applications just like Oracle, SAP, etc. but typically the smaller companies do not have trained SPM professionals. Therefore, the training becomes more important."

The respondents considered global competition, new markets, lowered entry barriers, and increased importance of sustainable strategies as the main drivers of the need for SPM education. They felt it was essential to acquire and train new skill sets to manage software products. Another lacking skill identified by the respondents is orchestration, or the coordination of all the multiple facets of software product organizations necessary to product success. Lacking skills and not finding the education they desire, product managers often learn by doing which can have a negative effect on the product.

To decrease the number of failures and bad decisions made by immature product management and to make the hiring process easier and more convenient, the respondents have proposed standardization and professionalization as a solution. The standardization should help to improve the "lack of consistency or consensus about product management roles and responsibilities across companies." Product managers have difficulty in finding comprehensive information work guidelines online. Standardization and professionalization would also address that need.

As SPM is a multi-disciplinary field, companies struggle with defining the skill requirements when appointing new product managers. "Companies don't know how to hire product managers. They tend to focus on just one facet of a multi-faceted job. For example, some will look for domain knowledge while others look for computer science training. I think an educational path would provide some degree of clarity."

Software Product Management Challenges
Lack of education and standardization in SPM are not the only challenges today. Although the respondents reported unclear definition of the role as one of the main challenges, we tend to consider this lack of clarity the result of other challenges like excess responsibility and insufficient authority. With too many responsibilities, a product manager may well be so busy with purely tactical activities like endless customer meetings that he has no time to focus on product strategy activities.

Another risk of being a "multi-purpose person" is being asked to perform many additional tasks ranging from development to user experience design to marketing, sales and support. However, while they may be in charge of many activities critical to product success, product managers rarely have authority in practice. They are "often not sufficiently empowered by management and cannot make market-facing decisions or resist development's technically motivated agenda." Such lack of authority is a characteristic that distinguishes technically oriented product managers from more business-oriented product managers or senior product managers [MagNiSmo13].

The other reported challenges related to general challenges of development and management of software products: customer understanding, rapidly changing environment, prioritization, coordination, and resource management. Product managers rarely have their own resources and must request them from higher management every time they require additional resources for the product [MagNiSmo13]. Thus product managers must identify resource gaps and predict resource shortages well ahead of time in order to obtain them from higher management on a timely basis.

Software Product Management Activities

To provide insight on the way SPM operates in practice, survey respondents were asked to name the most important SPM activities to manage a product properly. They mentioned: market analysis, requirements management, communication with stakeholders, customer analysis, roadmapping, orchestration, product life cycle management, product strategy, prioritization, vision, product planning, and product analysis. The ISPMA SPM Framework (see Sect. 2.5) covers each of these 12 activities either explicitly or implicitly.

Most companies embrace a subset of activities prescribed by the framework, primarily in the area of core SPM activities. However, many companies fail to assign important product strategy activities listed in the ISPMA SPM Framework to product managers, a serious omission which companies need to address to become more successful.

That the survey results show Customer Analysis as a key activity can be viewed in two ways. One interpretation is that knowing the market and what customers are doing with the product is highly important for product managers. The other interpretation is that in some companies SPM tasks are intermingled with marketing tasks.

"Having time to actually be a product manager—roles in every company are so different but overall, product managers seem to be the all-in-one job role, putting down fires, solving crises, running after budgets and resources, which leaves little to no room to actually know what your roadmap should look like." Therefore, prioritization is not only relevant to product requirements, but also to the actual self-organization of the product manager.

In general, there is no single magic recipe for the definitions of responsibilities and the organization of software product management. These questions need answers in the context of company objectives, products managed, existing company organizational structure, and company culture. We argue that Software Product Management has the responsibility for the sustainable success of a product in the market. Success depends on allowing the software product managers to focus on the important items and not be overwhelmed by urgent day-to-day tactical necessities.

7.3   SPM in Different Business Scenarios

The concept of software product management described in this book and in ISPMA's syllabi is business-context-agnostic and therefore applies to a wide range of industries. However, in some business environments there are specific considerations with respect to the advice given in the previous two sections of this chapter. The specific business scenarios are:

- Standard software products.
- Platforms.
- Software in software-intensive systems (embedded software).
- Software in professional (human) services (embedded software).

- Software managed by Corporate IT organizations (for one or multiple internal customers).

7.3.1   Standard Software Products

In this scenario the full contents of ISPMA's SPM Body of Knowledge is applicable—for both on-premise software and Software-as-a-Service (SaaS).

7.3.2   Platforms

We consider innovation platforms as software products (see Sect. 2.2.1). So the full contents of ISPMA's SPM Body of Knowledge is applicable with special emphasis on ecosystem management and tailorability strategy.

For transaction and coordination platforms (see Sect. 2.2.1) we assume two roles—the platform manager and the software product manager. The platform manager takes care of managing the domain-specific business aspects, in particular the balancing of the business model so that all stakeholders get sufficient benefits from using the platform. The role of platform manager is not fully covered by ISPMA's SPM Body of Knowledge nor by this book. The underlying software needs to be managed by one or more software product managers who act in a way very similar to product managers in corporate IT organizations (see Sect. 7.3.5).

7.3.3   Software in Software-Intensive Systems (Embedded Software)

The amount of software embedded in hardware components and systems is increasing at a quick rate (see Sect. 2.2). Software is turning into the number one value driver in more and more industries. Traditionally, hardware manufacturers had a life cycle view of their products that differed significantly from software vendors. With hardware, when the development of a version of a product is finished, the product goes into production. For an extended period, there is no further development, but only after-sales services to resolve defects in individual product instances, e.g. individual cars. Then after quite some time, a new development project starts for the next version of the hardware product, and the cycle begins anew. If the hardware product includes software components, hardware manufacturers have tended to treat embedded software in the same way as the hardware.

These days, this approach is no longer workable for more and more hardware products because there is increasing necessity for frequent software changes. So the life cycles of the software components become more similar to those of standard software products while the life cycles of the hardware components do not change substantially. Cost considerations motivate manufacturers to keep hardware components as stable as possible, with the result that hardware and software need to be managed at two very different speeds from a product management perspective (see also [LickKitt16]).

This difference presents significant challenges to a product manager responsible for a complete system of hardware and software components. The software components need to be managed from a software product management perspective, so if there is a product management team it makes sense to establish dedicated software product managers within it.

Most strategy considerations, in particular the business aspects, will be managed at the integrated product level. The software product manager will focus on positioning with regard to the other components of the product; on the scope of the software; on the business aspects directly related to the software portion, e.g. business cases and costing; and on make or buy decisions.

7.3.4 Software in Professional (Human) Services (Embedded Software)

As we pointed out in Sect. 2.4, business models for a software product business and a professional service business are fundamentally different. In particular, there are limits to the profitability of a professional service business that do not exist for a software product business. That is why professional service providers in all industries are trying to find ways to improve their profitability by replacing humans with standard software components in their professional service offerings. Sawhney has analyzed this approach in detail [Sawhney16]. He calls the software components products in order to point out that they need to be standardized and managed like software products, but they are not software products according to our definition since they are not sold as standalone products.

Nevertheless, the software components need to be managed from a software product management perspective. Depending on the type of service, the business manager responsible for the service may not—from a workload standpoint—be able to assume the software product management tasks as well. We recommend a dedicated software product manager who works in tight cooperation with the service business manager.

Most strategic elements, in particular business aspects, are managed on the service level. The software product manager will focus on positioning with regard to the other components of the service; on the scope of the software; on the business aspects directly related to the software part, e.g. business cases and costing, and on make or buy decisions.

7.3.5 Software Managed by Corporate IT Organizations

Numbers of corporate IT organizations in all industries are adopting the practice of software product management. Software components in an enterprise architecture, particularly applications, tend to have very long life cycles which require a strategic view and management continuity, difficult to achieve in a pure project organization. Some corporate IT organizations have also been transformed into profit centers which may have multiple customers inside and outside of the corporation for the same software components; that makes their business model appear very similar to one from a software vendor.

In corporate IT organizations, the role of software product manager sometimes has different names, e.g. application manager or (application) service manager (see Sect. 2.6). Strategy decisions need consideration in close cooperation with software product customers, be they companies, business units or corporate departments. A most important aspect is the positioning of the software product in the enterprise architecture of the corporation over time. The relevance of the business aspects depends on the design of the business relationship between the corporate IT organization and the companies, business units or departments in the corporation. If the corporate IT organization runs as a cost center, its focus will be on business cases, budgets and costing, while the overall business responsibility is on the business side. The more the corporate IT organization operates as a business unit of its own, the more relevant other business aspects become.

Relevant ecosystems are usually restricted to the technology side, i.e. software and other technology providers and software development partners. Since a corporate IT organization usually has the responsibility for Operations, i.e. the run-time production environment, risk management has the added burden of operational risk. While contractual issues at product level between corporate IT and software product customers, companies, business units or departments) are unlikely, contracts with software providers need special attention. Depending on industry and the manner in which corporation, company, or business unit is doing business, there may be specific legal or regulatory requirements.

Product planning also needs close management cooperation between the corporate IT organization and the companies, business units or departments who are software product customers. The business side of the enterprise architecture, in particular business process models and data models, play an important role with respect to requirements and integration. In product life cycle management, profit considerations and market share are typically not relevant unless the IT organization runs as a profit center and/or the corporation allows its business units to work with external competitors.

The relevance of strategic management considerations depends on the design of the business relationship between the corporate IT organization and its customers. If the corporate IT organization runs as a cost center its focus will be on innovation management and resource management. The more the corporate IT organization runs as a business unit of its own, the more relevant other strategic management aspects become.

On the orchestration side, marketing and sales are usually not relevant unless the corporation allows its business units to work with external competitors. An exception is customer relationship management with the company-internal departments and users as customers. Services usually include Operations, i.e. the run-time production environment governed by IT service management. The product manager monitors operations and may become directly involved in critical situations.

7.4   ISPMA

The International Software Product Management Association (ISPMA, www. ispma.org) is an open non-profit association of experts, companies, research institutes, and practitioners with the goal of fostering software product management excellence across industries. ISPMA was started in 2009 and legally established in 2011. As of January 2022, it has more than 2600 members worldwide. Hans-Bernd Kittlaus is ISPMA's current chairman and is a founding board member of ISPMA.

ISPMA aims at establishing software product management as a discipline of its own in both academia and industry, and disseminates and maintains a Curriculum and a Certifiable Body of Knowledge (SPMBoK). The SPMBoK is documented in syllabi that are the basis for training courses and certification exams:

- Foundation.
- Excellence in Product Strategy.
- Excellence in Product Planning.
- Excellence in Strategic Management.
- Excellence in Orchestration.
- SPM for Startups.

The Foundation and SPM for Startups modules are aimed at participants with up to 5 years of practical experience in the software area. They ought to have a fundamental understanding of the software business, but the training requires no specific technical or commercial competencies. The SPM for Startups module is intended for people involved in software product management in startups as well as those building new software products in mature businesses. That includes not only product managers themselves but also those with whom the product manager interfaces, i.e. founders, investors, incubators, accelerators, general management, marketing and sales, research and development, production, service and support, and controllers. The Excellence modules are targeted at product managers who already have the ISPMA Foundation Level Certificate or at least 3 years of comparable SPM experience.

ISPMA's results are applicable to the software industry, to vendors of software-intensive products and technical and human services in other industries (embedded software), and to corporate IT organizations in all industries.

The syllabi are available at no charge on the ISPMA web site. Commercial training providers and universities may offer training courses after approval by ISPMA. Independent certification agencies conduct certification exams and issue the certificates on behalf of ISPMA.

ISPMA also provides a platform for communication and exchange between its members, be it at conferences, in workshops and working groups, or on the internet.

There are different membership types:

- Fellow Member: Distinguished expert from industry or academia elected by the existing fellow members. Fellow members commit to contribute to ISPMA work results and represent ISPMA.
- Certified Member: Practitioner or academic member who has at least one of ISPMA's certificates.
- Subscribing Member: People from industry and academia who are interested in SPM.
- Company Member: Company or academic institution committed to excellence in SPM and which wants to support ISPMA. Company members nominate delegates who have the rights of fellow members.

ISPMA provides unique value to the SPM community, to professionals in training and certification, and to companies and academic institutions interested in SPM, value which is uniquely specialized compared to all other players in product management education:

- Focus on software only.
- More than 50 distinguished international experts from industry and academia as Fellow Members who cooperate tightly for continuous updates and improvements of the SPMBoK based on the latest developments in business, research, technology and methodology.
- Non-profit organization.
- Strict separation between
  - ISPMA as developer of curriculum, syllabi and exams (non-profit).
  - Training provider and trainers (commercial or academic).
  - Certification agencies.
- High quality of SPMBOK.
- High confidentiality of exam contents.
- High value of certificates (due to the separation described above).
- Free availability of syllabi.
- Frequent information on latest developments in SPM.
- Open platform for networking, exchange and cooperation.

With these elements, ISPMA helps individuals to learn about SPM and improve their SPM skills. ISPMA also helps companies which wish to establish or improve their SPM organizations. And ISPMA creates a basis for training providers and trainers who want to offer SPM training. All of these groups are welcome to become personal and company members of ISPMA.

Glossary

A glossary is a living document since language is continuously changing. New terms are introduced, existing terms may be changed slightly or completely redefined. This glossary is aligned with ISPMA's glossary (as of January 2022) the latest version of which can be found here: https://ispma.org/framework/glossary/.

Term	Definition
Brand Awareness	A measure of whether a brand is correctly identified by potential customers. Typically expressed as a percentage of a target market. There are many different approaches to measuring this statistic, but it typically means that a customer can respond to a brand after viewing its logo or packaging.
Business Case	A decision support and planning approach for comparing the costs and benefits associated with a proposed initiative.
Business architecture	Domain-specific architectural model that represents real world aspects of a business and how they interact.
Business Model	Description of the rationale of how an organization creates, delivers and captures value by interacting with suppliers, employees, customers and partners.
Business Model Archetype	A basic pattern of doing business. Available archetypes are creator, distributor, lessor and broker.
Category Maturity Life Cycle	A model that describes the rise, duration, and decline of a category of product or service in terms of total revenue or number of users.
Channel	A sequence of intermediaries through which goods and services as well as the compensation are transferred between a company and its customers.
Cloud Computing	Service and delivery model for the provisioning of IT components through the internet based on an architecture that enables a high level of scalability and reliability.
Company Board	The entity of a company which is responsible for the definition and communication of strategy, vision and mission to the rest of the company. Also, it has the managerial supervision of the different departments, including product management.

(continued)

© Springer-Verlag GmbH Germany, part of Springer Nature 2022
H.-B. Kittlaus, *Software Product Management*,
https://doi.org/10.1007/978-3-662-65116-2

Term	Definition
Competitor	A competitor of company A is another company that sells products and/or services to A's target market (or a subset thereof) which are similar to A's products and/or services.
Compliance Management	Management of the decision process, including which legal and regulatory requirements are relevant, and which non-legal standards and guidelines the organization wants to comply with. It also includes a governance approach that ensures that the defined compliance requirements are consistently implemented and audited in the organization. It may include participation in and/or influencing of defining external and internal rules, standards and guidelines.
Constraint	Business, project or design decisions taken in advance to ensure the solution fits business, managerial and contextual concerns. These decisions limit the solution space.
Continuous Delivery	Automated push of software into the production environment or delivery to customers.
Continuous Deployment	Combination of continuous integration and continuous delivery to automatically deliver code changes to customers.
Continuous Integration	Automated integration, build, and test of software in the development environment.
Conversion Rate	Metric for the number of customers who have completed a transaction on a web site divided by the total number of website visitors.
Copyright	A form of intellectual property right that gives the author of an original work exclusive rights for publishing, distributing and adapting the work.
Corporate Strategy	The basic long-term goals of an enterprise and the courses of action for carrying out these goals.
Cost Per Lead	Metric for the average amount of money invested to acquire a new lead.
Cost Structure	The types and relative proportions of fixed and variable costs connected to a business model.
Customer	A party that receives or consumes products and/or services from a second party.
Customer Insight	Knowing and understanding of the problems and the environment in which customers operate.
Customer Segment	A subset of existing and/or potential customers targeted by a common value proposition.
Delivery Model	A description of the mechanisms in which a product is made available to customers. Examples: Licensed product vs. Software-as-a-Service (SaaS).
Delivery Services	All customer-specific services provided to customers to help them become productive with the initial software product or when a new version is installed.
DevOps	Development methodology aiming for a tighter cooperation between Development and Operations to achieve better quality of software products, shorter time to market, and improvements in operational efficiency.

(continued)

Term	Definition
Embedded Software	Software parts of software-intensive systems that are not marketed and priced as separate entities.
Financial Management	Planning, tracking and influencing financial aspects (of a product).
Functional Requirement	A statement that identifies what a product or process must accomplish to produce required behavior and/or results.
Functional Support Plan	Describes the activities, deliverables, budgets, dependencies, and schedules for a business function to members of a cross-functional product team, on behalf of a product.
Innovation Management	The discipline of managing processes related to innovation. Innovation management allows the organization to respond to external or internal opportunities, and use its creative efforts to introduce new ideas, processes or products.
Innovation Platform	Technological foundation upon which the owner and other firms develop complementary innovations.
Intellectual Property	Exclusive rights that are granted by law to the owner(s) of intangible assets that result from creations of the mind, such as inventions, literary and artistic works, and symbols, names, and images used in commerce.
Key Performance Indicator (KPI)	A specific numerical measure that represents the progress towards a strategic goal, objective, output, activity, or further input.
Kano Analysis	A technique for understanding which product features will help drive customer satisfaction.
License	A set of rights concerning a licensor's intellectual property which a licensor grants to a licensee.
License Agreement	A legal document that describes a license and the related financial conditions.
Market	(a) The area of economic activity in which buyers and sellers of goods and services come together, and the forces of supply and demand affect prices. (b) A geographic area of demand for commodities or services. (c) A specified category of potential buyers.
Market Analysis	Analysis of all aspects relevant for a particular market in its current state and over the strategic time frame including market structure, competitors, market shares, customer preferences and behavior.
Market Segmentation	Division of a market into sub-sets called market segments that are distinct from each other, and homogeneous with regard to certain criteria.
Market Share	Percentage of revenue or volume that a particular player makes in a particular market or market segment in relation to the market's total revenue or volume.
Marketing	(a) The activities that are involved in making people aware of a company's products and making sure that the products are available to be bought. (b) The organizational and/or functional unit in an organization that is responsible for (a).

(continued)

Term	Definition
Marketing Communication (MarCom)	Set of marketing activities that concerns executing the marketing strategy to create communication deliverables including advertising, branding, graphic design, promotion, publicity, public relations and more.
Matrix Organization	Organizational structure in which individuals report to more than one person
Minimum Viable Product	The minimum feature set of a new product that is derived through a learning phase and that some customers are willing to pay for in the first release.
Mission Statement	Definition of the present activities or purpose of an organization by saying what it does for whom and how.
Net Promoter Score	Method to measure customer loyalty by asking a single 0-10 scale question: "How likely is it that you would recommend $BRAND$ to a friend or colleague?". Your promoter score is the percentage of customers who answer 9 or 10 subtracted by those who answer 0–6.
Non-Functional Requirement	A requirement that pertains to a quality concern that is not covered by functional requirements. Also referred to as → Quality requirement
Offering Architecture	Separately priced components of the product offering and their relationships to each other, and tailorability options in line with the tailorability strategy.
Open Source Software	Software that can be freely accessed, used, changed, and shared (in modified or unmodified form) by anyone. Open source software is made by one or more people, and distributed under licenses that comply with the Open Source Definition.
Partner	A party who joins one or more other parties based on an agreement that defines the terms and conditions of the relationship (partnership).
Patent	A patent is an exclusive intellectual property right for an invention granted to the inventor for a defined timeframe by an authorized body of a sovereign state. The right is granted for the territory of that sovereign state. It is the right to exclude others from making, using, offering for sale, or selling the invention. The types of inventions covered by patent law can be different from state to state.
Performance Management	Continuous tracking and analysis of selected KPIs relevant for business success, plus timely action taking if needed
Platform	A technical product that the platform owner as well as third parties use as a foundation for conducting their own respective businesses
Positioning	Definition of an approach to communicating a product to potential customers.
Pricing	All activities required to set, communicate, and negotiate prices in a convincing way.
Process Improvement	All activities to analyze, plan and execute changes in processes with the goal to optimize the defined process KPIs.

(continued)

Term	Definition
Process Model	An abstract description of one or more processes. A process model typically describes a process as a sequence of activities and the involved roles and responsibilities.
Product	A combination of goods and services, which a supplier/development organization combines in support of its commercial interests to transfer defined rights to a customer.
Product Analysis	Analysis of all business aspects relevant for a particular product in its current state and over the strategic time frame including KPIs like revenue, revenue distribution, footprints, and market shares.
Product Life Cycle	Describes the evolution of a product from its conception to its discontinuance and market withdrawal.
Product Life Cycle Management	The management of the business and technical aspects of a software product with regard to its position in its life cycle.
Product Line	A set of products based on a common platform with defined (static or dynamic) variability tailored to different markets and users.
Product Management	(a) The discipline which governs a product along the product life cycle with the objective to generate the biggest possible value to the business. (b) The organizational and/or functional unit in an organization that is responsible for (a).
Product Manager	A person responsible for → Product Management in an organization. An organization can have multiple product managers.
Product Marketing	Applying → Marketing to a → Product. Translates strategic marketing decisions to the product level.
Product Portfolio	Set of products or services offered by a company.
Product Portfolio Management	The activity of making decisions about investments in the products included in the product portfolio over the strategic timeframe.
Product Roadmap	A document that provides features or themes of the product releases to come over the strategic timeframe. The creation of a roadmap is influenced by the product strategy designed for this product.
Product Scope	Abstract description of the functional and quality characteristics of the product.
Product Strategy	(a) Combination of the strategic goals and measures for the product, i.e. aspects that need to be defined and managed for the strategic timeframe of the product. See corresponding column in ISPMA's SPM Framework. (b) Consistent documentation containing the following items and their evolution during the strategic timeframe: • Product vision • Product definition • Target market, potential segments • Delivery model • Product positioning • Sourcing

(continued)

Term	Definition
	• Business plan • Roadmap
Product Vision	Conceptual description of a future state of the product at the end of the strategic timeframe or even later, i.e. high-level descriptions of a product concept and a corresponding business model.
Product-Technology Roadmap	Overview of the relationship between product releases (product evolvement) and successive technology generations.
Quality Requirement	A requirement that pertains to a quality concern that is not covered by functional requirements. Also referred to as → Non-functional requirement.
Release	(a) Product release: an instance of the product that is delivered to customers, and maintained as part of product maintenance. (b) Pre-release: a result of development activity that is testable, e.g. the result of a sprint in Scrum.
Release Definition	The result of selecting the requirements to be implemented in the next release. Usually this result is documented including statements about the relationship between the selected requirements and strategic objectives.
Release Planning	The process of selecting the requirements for the next release.
Requirement	(a) A condition or capability needed to solve a problem or achieve an objective. (b) A condition or capability that must be met or possessed by a system or system component to satisfy a contract, standard, specification, or other formally imposed document. (c) A documented representation of a condition or capability as in definition (a) or (b). Three different types of requirements are distinguished: functional requirements, quality requirements and constraints.
Requirements Engineering	(a) The disciplined and systematic approach (i.e., "engineering") for elicitation, documentation, analysis, agreement, verification, and management of requirements while considering market, technical, and economic goals. (b) Activity within systems engineering and software engineering.
Requirements Management	Planning, executing, monitoring, and controlling any or all of the work associated with requirements elicitation and collaboration, requirements analysis and design, and requirements life cycle management.
Requirements Prioritization	The activity during which the most important requirements for the product are determined. As priorities change over time this activity is often targeted at the next release of the product.
Requirements Triage	An activity for early and fast acceptance/rejection of requirements.
Resource Management	The efficient and effective development of an organization's resources. In the software business resources are primarily people, existing software and systems that the software runs on or is developed on.

(continued)

Term	Definition
Return On Investment	Metric for the average amount of revenue divided by the related cost.
Revenue	Money collected by an organization in return for products and/or services.
Revenue Model	Set of all → revenue streams of a company.
Revenue Stream	Describes generation of compensation over time for a product, service or company as revenue or in non-monetary ways. Non-monetary aspects may be data or services in return.
Risk Management	The identification, assessment, and prioritization of risks followed by coordinated and economical application of resources to minimize, monitor, and control the probability and/or impact of unfortunate and/or undesired events.
Scenario	Description of a real or imagined situation under a defined set of assumptions.
Service	(a) Useful labor that does not produce a tangible commodity (as in "professional services"). (b) A provision for maintenance and repair (as in "software maintenance service"). (c) The technical provision of a function through a software component that can be accessed by another software component, often over a network and executed on a remote server (as in "web services" or "Software-as-a-Service").
Service Level Agreement (SLA)	Agreement between two or more parties about the target values a service-giving party has to achieve for the defined measures that are relevant for quality and cost of the service.
Software Ecosystem	A network of people and/or companies that forms around a software vendor or a product or product platform. The relationships in this network have the goal to achieve benefits for all participants and can be formalized or not. Formalized relationships are called partnerships.
Software Intensive System	A system where a significant part of the value originates from software.
Software Product	A product whose primary component is software.
Software Product Family	A group of software products which for marketing reasons are marketed as belonging together under a common family name.
Software Product Line	A set of software-intensive systems that share a common, managed set of features satisfying the specific needs of a particular market segment or mission, and that are developed from a common set of core assets in a prescribed way.
Software Product Management	The management of a software product or the software components of a software-intensive product over its life cycle with the objective of generating the biggest possible value to the business.
Software Product Management Competence model	Competence model that guides product management in process improvement.
Software Product Manager	Product manager of a software product or the software components of a software-intensive product.

(continued)

Term	Definition
Software Value Map	A decomposition of the "value" concept that details value of a software intensive product from the main areas of financial, customer, internal business process, and innovation and learning perspectives.
Software-As-A-Service (SaaS)	A delivery model for software that is used in cloud computing.
Sourcing	The process of ensuring that all required resources are available when they are needed.
Stakeholder	A person, group, or organization that has direct or indirect stake in an organization because it can affect or be affected by the organization's actions, objectives, and policies.
Strategic Marketing	The way a firm effectively differentiates itself from its competitors by effectively segmenting the market, selecting the appropriate targets and consistently developing a better value positioning to customers than its competitors.
Support	All product-related services provided to existing customers.
Tailorability	Enablement of the product for customer- or market-specific adaptations by providing properties that can be changed after system development.
Target Market	A set of market segments to which a particular product is marketed to.
Trade Secret	Something which has economic value to a business because it is not generally known or easily discoverable by observation such as an algorithm and for which efforts have been made to maintain secrecy.
Trademark	A distinctive identifier, such as a phrase, word or sign, for certain products or services as those produced or provided by a specific person or enterprise. Protection of trademarks depends on local law.
Transaction Platform	Intermediary or online marketplace that makes it possible for people and organizations to share information or to buy, sell, or access a variety of goods and services.
User	A person or thing that uses something i.e. products or services.
User Experience	Every aspect of the users' interactions with a software product or component with the purpose of shaping the user's behaviors, attitudes, and emotions about that product or component.
Value Communication	The process of connecting defined customer values with identified target markets for the product.
Value Proposition	Description of the benefits customers can expect from one product, or from the products and services of a company.
Virtual Team	A group of individuals who work together across time, space and organizational boundaries with links strengthened by webs of communication technology.

Terms of Use

References

[Aaker13] Aaker, D.A.: Strategic Market Management. Wiley (2013)

[Accion15] Accion: Pricing Your SaaS Product. https://content.accion.org/wp-content/uploads/2018/08/Pricing-Your-SaaS-Product.pdf

[AdnKap10] Adner, R., Kapoor, R.: Value creation in innovation ecosystems: how the structure of technological interdependence affects firm performance in new technology generations. Strateg. Manag. J. **31**(3), 306–333 (2010)

[AlNaPfRu17] Al-Alam, D., Nayebi, M., Pfahl, D., Ruhe, G.: A two-staged survey on release readiness. In: EASE'17 – Evaluation and Assessment in Software Engineering, pp. 374–383. ACM (2017)

[Allen06] Allen, P., Higgins, S.: Service Orientation: Winning Strategies and Best Practices. Cambridge University Press (2006)

[AlmSenBl16] Almquist, E., Senior, J., Bloch, N.: The elements of value. Harv. Bus. Rev. **September**, 46–53 (2016)

[Alvarez14] Alvarez, C.: Lean Customer Development – Build Products Your Customers Will Buy. O'Reilly. (2014)

[AndNar98] Anderson, J.C., Narus, J.A.: Business marketing: understand what customers value. Harv. Bus. Rev. **76**, 53–65 (1998)

[AndZei84] Anderson, C., Zeithaml, C.: Stage of the product life cycle, business strategy, and business performance. Acad. Manag. J. **27**(1), 5–24 (1984)

[Arthur96] Arthur, W.B.: Increasing returns and the new world of business. Harv. Bus. Rev. (1996)

[ArWeBriFi10] Artz, P., van de Weerd, I., Brinkkemper, S., Fieggen, J.: Productization: transforming from developing customer-specific software to product software. In: International conference on Software Business (ICSOB 2010), Jyväskylä, Finland, 2010

[AthLuc19] Athey, S., Luca, M.: Economists (and economics) in tech companies. J. Econ. Perspect. **33**, 209–230 (2019)

[AveBePe15] Avedillo, J.G., Begonha, D., Peyracchia, A.: Two Ways to Modernize IT Systems for the Digital Era. McKinsey Insights (August 2015)

[Axelos16] Axelos: ITIL practitioner guide. TSO, Norwich (2016)

[BaKaKuHi20] Balasubramaniam, N., Kauppinen, M., Kujala, S., Hiekkanen, K.: Ethical guidelines for solving ethical issues and developing AI systems. In: Morisio, M., et al. (eds.) Product-Focused Software Process Improvement, pp. 331–346. Springer International Publishing, Cham (2020)

[BasWebZh15] Bass, L., Weber, I., Zhu, L.: DevOps: A Software Architect's Perspective. Addison-Wesley, Upper Saddle River (2015)

[BaGeBuBi14] Baur, A.W., Genova, A.C., Bühler, J., Bick, M.: Customer is king? A framework to shift from cost- to value-based pricing in software as a service: the case of business intelligence software. In: Li, H., Mäntymäki, M., Zhang,

© Springer-Verlag GmbH Germany, part of Springer Nature 2022

H.-B. Kittlaus, *Software Product Management*,

https://doi.org/10.1007/978-3-662-65116-2

X. (eds.) Digital Services and Information Intelligence, pp. 1–13. Springer (2014)

[Bech15]   Bech, H.P.: Building Successful Partner Channels. TBK Publishing (2015)

[BekWeer10]   Bekkers, W., van de Weerd, I.: SPM Maturity Matrix. Technical Report UU-CS-2010-013, University of Utrecht (2010)

[BVSB10]   Bekkers, W., Weerd, I. van de, Spruit, M., Brinkkemper, S.: A framework for process improvement in software product management. European Conference on Software Process Improvement (EuroSPI 2010), Grenoble, France, 2010

[BenMcF13]   Benko, C.A., McFarlan, W.: Connecting the Dots. Aligning Your Project Portfolio with Corporate Objectives. McGraw-Hill, 2013

[BerAnd05]   Berander, P., Andrews, A.: Requirements prioritization. In: Aurum, A., Wohlin, C. (eds.) Engineering and Managing Software Requirements. Springer (2005)

[BGRTSF11]   Berntsson-Svensson, R., Gorschek, T., Regnell, B., Torkar, R., Shahrokni, A., Feldt, R.: Quality requirements in industrial practice – an extended interview study at eleven companies. IEEE Trans. Softw. Eng. **38**(4), 923–935 (2011)

[Besaha03]   Besaha, B.: Bounty hunting in the patent base. Commun. ACM. **46**(3), 27–29 (2003)

[Biering04]   Biering, S.: Preis- und Produktstrategien für digitale Produkte, untersucht am Beispiel des Software-Marktes (Dissertationsschrift). Haufe, Freiburg (2004)

[Blank13a]   Blank, S.: The Four Steps to the Epiphany, 2nd edn. K & S Ranch (2013)

[Blank13b]   Blank, S.: A New Way to Look at Competitors. https://steveblank.com/2013/11/08/a-new-way-to-look-at-competitors/ (2013) Accessed 25 Dec 2016

[Blank13c]   Blank, S.: Why the lean startup changes everything. Harv. Bus. Rev. **91**(5), 63–72 (2013)

[BlanDorf12]   Blank, S., Dorf, B.: The Startup Owner's Manual: The Step-By-Step Guide for Building a Great Company. K & S Ranch (2012)

[Blank10]   Blank, S.: Perfection by Subtraction – The Minimum Feature Set. http://steveblank.com/2010/03/04/perfection-by-subtraction-the-minimum-feature-set/ (2010) Accessed 25 Dec 2016

[BoGiRo06]   Bonaccorsi, A., Giannangeli, S., Rossi, C.: Entry strategies under competing standards: Hybrid business models in the open source software industry. Manag. Sci. **52**(7), 1085–1098 (2006)

[BonChu00]   Bontis, N., Chung, H.: The evolution of software pricing: from box licenses to application service provider models. Internet Res. **10**, 246–255 (2000)

[BCWAGPSA19]   Borg, M., Chatzipetrou, P., Wnuk, K., Alégroth, E., Gorschek, T., Papatheocharous, E., Shah, S.M.A., Axelsson, J.: Selecting component sourcing options: a survey of software engineering's broader make-or-buy decisions. Inf. Softw. Technol. **112** (2019)

[Bosch19]   Bosch, J.: How to Develop Software. https://www.linkedin.com/pulse/how-develop-software-jan-bosch/ (2019)

[Bosch12]   Bosch, J.: Building products as innovation experiment systems. In: International Conference on Software Business (ICSOB 2012), Cambridge, MA, 2012

[Bosch09]   Bosch, J.: From software product lines to software ecosystems. In: 13th International Software Product Line Conference (SPLC 2009), San Francisco, CA, 2009

[Boulding62]   Boulding, K.: Conflict and Defense: A General Theory. Harper & Brothers (1962)

[Bowles18]   Bowles, C.: Future Ethics. NowNext Press, Hove (2018)

[Brown08]   Brown, T.: Design thinking. Harv. Bus. Rev. **86**(6), 84–92 (2008)

[Brynjo03]   Brynjolfsson, E.: The IT Productivity Gap. Optimize Magazine, Issue 21, July 2003

[BrMaJaHe96] Bruckhaus, T., Madhavji, N., Janssen, I., Henshaw, J.: The impact of tools on software productivity. IEEE Softw. **13**(5), 29–38 (1996)

[BSA18] BSA: BSA Global Software Survey. https://gss.bsa.org/wp-content/uploads/2018/05/2018_BSA_GSS_Report_en.pdf (2018) Accessed 28 Sept 2021

[BuStTh10] Burke, A., van Stel, A., Thurik, R.: Blue ocean vs. five forces. Harv. Bus. Rev. **88**(5), 28–29 (2010)

[Burkov20] Burkov, A.: Machine Learning Engineering. True Positive (2020)

[BusZim12] Buse, R.P.L., Zimmermann, T.: Information needs for software development analytics. In: Proceedings of the 34th International Conference on Software Engineering (ICSE 2012 SEIP Track), Zurich, Switzerland, 2012

[Bush19] Bush, W.: Product-Led Growth: How to Build a Product That Sells Itself. Product-Led Institute (2019)

[Butje05] Butje, M.: Product Marketing for Technology Companies. Butterworth-Heinemann, Burlington (2005)

[BuDiHe12] Buxmann, P., Diefenbach, H., Hess, T.: The Software Industry. Springer, Heidelberg (2012)

[BuJaPo11] Buxmann, P., Jansen, S., Popp, K.M.: The sun also sets: ending the life of a software product. In: International Conference on Software Business (ICSOB 2011), Brussels, Belgium, 2011

[Buxm01] Buxmann, P.: Network effects on standard software markets: a simulation model to examine pricing strategies. In: Proceedings from the 2nd IEEE Conference on Standardization and Innovation in Information Technology, pp. 229–240. IEEE (2001)

[CagJon20] Cagan, M., Jones, C.: Empowered – Ordinary People, Extraordinary Products. Wiley (2020)

[Cagan08] Cagan, M.: Inspired – How to Create Products Customers Love. SVPG Press (2008)

[Carey09] Carey, P.: Data Protection: A Practical Guide to UK and EU Law. Oxford University Press (2009)

[Carlshamre02] Carlshamre, P.: Release planning in market-driven development: provoking an understanding. Requir. Eng. **7**(3), 139–151 (2002)

[CSLRH01] Carlshamre, P., Sandahl, K., Lindvall, M., Regnell, B., Natt och Dag, J.: An industrial survey of requirements interdependencies in software product release planning. In: 5th International Symposium on Requirements Engineering (RE'01), Toronto, Canada, 2001

[CheCheMe13] Chen, S., Cheng, A., Mehta, K.: A review of telemedicine business models. Telemed. e-Health. **19**(4), 287–297 (2013)

[Chesbrou05] Chesbrough, H.W.: Open Innovation: The New Imperative for Creating and Profiting from Technology. Harvard Business Review Press (2005)

[Choudary21] Choudary, S.P.: Platform Scale – For a Post-Pandemic World. Penguin Random House India (2021)

[Christen13] Christensen, C.A.: The Innovator's Solution. Harvard Business Review Press, Boston (2013)

[ClaHeyScho08] Classen, A., Heymans, P., Schobbens, P.: What's in a feature: a requirements engineering perspective. In: 11th International Conference on Fundamental Approaches to Software Engineering (FASE 2008), Budapest, Hungary, 2008

[ClSeRBC07] Cleland-Huang, J., Settimi, R., Romanova, E., Berenbach, B., Clark, S.: Best practices for automated traceability. IEEE Computer. **40**(6), 27–35 (2007)

[ClemNort15] Clements, P., Northrop, L.: Software Product Lines: Practices and Patterns. Addison Wesley (2015)

[CMMI18] CMMI Institute: CMMI V2.0 Development Model (2018)

[Cohn04] Cohn, M.: User Stories Applied: For Agile Software Development. Mountain Goat Software (2004)

[Cohn06]   Cohn, M.: Agile Estimating and Planning. Prentice Hall PTR (2006)

[CollThom02] Collberg, C.S., Thomborson, C.: Watermarking, tamper-proofing, and obfuscation – tools for software protection. IEEE Trans. Softw. Eng. **28**(8), 735–746 (2002)

[Condon02]   Condon, D.: Software Product Management: Managing Software Development from Idea to Product to Marketing to Sales. Aspatore Books (2002)

[CooEdg09]   Cooper, R.G., Edgett S.J.: Generating Breakthrough New Product Ideas: Feeding the Innovation Funnel. Product Development Institute (2009)

[CooEdg08]   Cooper, R.G., Edgett S.J.: Ideation for Product Innovation: What are the Best Methods?, pp. 12–17. PDMA Vision Magazine (March 2008)

[CoEdKl01]   Cooper, R.G., Edgett, S.J., Kleinschmidt, E.J.: Portfolio Management for New Products, 2nd edn. Perseus Books (2001)

[Cooper00]   Cooper, R.G.: Product Leadership – Creating and Launching Superior New Products. Perseus Books, Cambridge (2000)

[Coulter12]   Coulter, M.: Strategic Management in Action, 6th edn. Pearson Prentice Hall, Upper Saddle River (2012)

[CrolYosk13] Croll, A., Yoskovitz, B.: Lean Analytics – Use Data to Build a Better Startup Faster. O'Reilly (2013)

[CusGaYof19] Cusumano, M., Gawer, A., Yoffie, D.B.: The Business of Platforms. Harper Business (2019)

[Cusuma07]   Cusumano, M.: The changing labyrinth of software pricing. Commun. ACM. **50**(7), 19–22 (2007)

[Cusuma04]   Cusumano, M.: The Business of Software. Free Press (2004)

[Cusuma03]   Cusumano, M.: Finding your balance in the products and services debate. Commun. ACM. **46**(3), 15–17 (2003)

[DaFeFrPa18] Dalpiaz, F., Ferrari, A., Franch, X., Palomares, C.: Natural language processing for requirements engineering: the best is yet to come. IEEE Softw. **35**(5), 115–119 (2018)

[DavBrHo07]   Daviesa, A., Bradyb, T., Hobday, M.: Organizing for solutions: systems seller vs. systems integrator. Indus. Market. Manag. **36**(2), 183–184 (2007)

[Davis05]   Davis, A.: Just Enough Requirements Management. Dorset House (2005)

[DeLaat05]   De Laat, P.B.: Copyright or copyleft? An analysis of property regimes for software development. Res. Policy. **34**(10), 1511–1532 (2005)

[DemLec06]   Demil, B., Lecocq, X.: Neither market nor hierarchy nor network: the emergence of bazaar governance. Organ. Stud. **27**(10), 1447–1466 (2006)

[DenCle04]   Denne, M., Cleland-Huang, J.: Software by Numbers: Low-Risk, High-Return Development. Prentice Hall PTR (2004)

[DenLew17]   Denning, P.J., Lewis, T.G.: Exponential laws of computing growth. Commun. ACM. **60**(1), 54–65 (2017)

[DenDun03]   Denning, P.J., Dunham, R.: The missing customer. Commun. ACM. **46**(3), 19–23 (2003)

[Doerr18]   Doerr, J.: Measure What Matters: OKRs: The Simple Idea that Drives 10x Growth. Penguin (2018)

[DHKSU18]   Doorley, S., Holcomb, S., Klebahn, P., Segovia, K., Utley, J.: Design Thinking Bootleg. Stanford University (2018)

[Druck73]   Drucker, P.: Management: Tasks, Responsibilities, Practices, pp. 64–65. Harper and Row, New York (1973)

[Duboc19]   Duboc L., et al.: Do we really know what we are building? Raising awareness of potential Sustainability Effects of Software Systems in Requirements Engineering. In: IEEE 27th International Requirements Engineering Conference (RE), Korea, 2019

[Dunford19]   Dunford, A.: Obviously Awesome – How to Nail Product Positioning so Customers Get It, Buy It, Love It. Ambient Press (2019)

[DuJaKu18]   Dutt, A., Jain, H., Kumar, S.: Providing Software as a Service: a design decision(s) model. Inf. Syst. e-Bus. Manag. **16**, 327–356 (2018)

[Ebert07]   Ebert, C.: The impacts of software product management. J. Syst. Softw. **80**(6), 850–861 (2007)

[Ebert09]   Ebert, C.: Software product management. CrossTalk. **16**, 15–19 (2009)

[Ebert11]   Ebert, C.: Global Software and IT: A Guide to Distributed Development, Projects, and Outsourcing. Wiley, Hoboken (2011)

[EberBrin14]   Ebert, C., Brinkkemper, S.: Software product management – an industry evaluation. J. Syst. Softw. **95**, 10–18 (2014)

[EberDumk07]   Ebert, C., Dumke, R.: Software Measurement: Establish – Extract – Evaluate – Execute. Springer (2007)

[ElisBrow17]   Elis, S., Brown, B.: Hacking Growth: How Today's Fastest-Growing Companies Drive Breakout Success. Virgin Books (2017)

[EriAmrDa17]   Erich, F., Amrit, C., Daneva, M.: A qualitative study of DevOps usage in practice. J. Softw. Evol. Process. (2017)

[Fagerb05]   Fagerberg, J.: Innovation – a guide to the literature. In: Fagerberg, J., Mowery, D., Nelson, R. (eds.) The Oxford Handbook of Innovation. Oxford University Press (2005)

[Farmer06]   Farmer, E.: The gatekeeper's guide, or how to kill a tool. IEEE Softw. **23**(6), 12–13 (2006)

[FeFiHL05]   Feller, J., Fitzgerald, B., Hissam, S.A., Lakhani, K.R. (eds.): Perspectives on Free and Open Source Software. MIT Press (2005)

[FeRaBu17]   Fenn, J., Raskino, M., Burton, B.: Understanding Gartner's Hype Cycles, doc. no. G00251964. Gartner (2017)

[FiUrPa12]   Fisher, R., Ury, W.L., Patton, B.: Getting to Yes: Negotiating Agreement Without Giving In (upd. rev. ed.). Penguin (2012)

[FleBen15]   Fleisher, C., Bensoussan, B.: Business and Competitive Analysis: Effective Application of New and Classic Methods, 2nd edn. Pearson Education (2015)

[FleBen02]   Fleisher, C., Bensoussan, B.: Strategic and Competitive Analysis: Methods and Techniques for Analyzing Business Competition. Prentice Hall (2002)

[FloyWool94]   Floyd, S.W., Wooldridge, B.: Dinosaurs or dynamos? Recognizing middle management's strategic role. Acad. Manag. Exec. **8**(4), 47–57 (1994)

[FlyvBud11]   Flyvbjerg, B., Budzier, A.: Why your IT project may be riskier than you think. Harv. Bus. Rev. **89**(9), 23–25 (2011)

[ForJumKi18]   Forsgren, N., Jumble, J., Kim, J.: Accelerate – The Science of Lean Software and Devops: Building and Scaling High Performing Technology Organization. IT Revolution Press (2018)

[FotrFric16]   Fotrousi, F., Fricker, S.: Software analytics for planning product evolution. In: International Conference on Software Business (ICSOB 2016), Ljubljana, Slovenia, 2016

[FoFrFi14]   Fotrousi, F., Fricker, S., Fiedler, M.: Quality requirements elicitation based on inquiry of quality-impact relationships. In: IEEE 22nd International Requirements Engineering Conference (RE 14), Karlskrona, Sweden, 2014

[FoFrFiLG14]   Fotrousi, F., Fricker, S., Fiedler, M., Le Gall, F.: KPIs for software ecosystems: a systematic mapping study. In: International Conference on the Software Business (ICSOB 2014), Paphos, Cyprus, 2014

[FrenRav59]   French, J.R.P., Raven, B.: The bases of social power. In: Cartwright, D.P. (ed.) Studies in Social Power, pp. 150–167. University of Michigan Press (1959)

[Fricker12]   Fricker, S.A.: Software product management. In: Maedche, A., Botzenhardt, A., Neer, L. (eds.) Software for People – Fundamentals, Trends and Best Practices, pp. 53–81. Springer, Heidelberg (2012)

[Fricker14]   Fricker, S.A., Grau, R., Zwingli, A.: Requirements engineering: best practice. In: Fricker, S.A., Thümmler, C., Gavras, A. (eds.) Requirements Engineering for Digital Health. Springer, (2014)

[FricGru08]   Fricker, S.A., Grünbacher, P.: Negotiation constellations – method selection framework for requirements negotiation. In: International Working Conference on Requirements Engineering: Foundation for Software Quality (RefsQ 2008), Montpellier, France, 2008

[FricSFT16]   Fricker, S.A., Schneider, K., Fotrousi, F., Thümmler, C.: Workshop videos for requirements communication. Requir. Eng. 21(4), 521–552 (2016)

[FricSchu12] Fricker, S.A., Schumacher, S.: Release planning with feature trees: industrial case. In: 18th International Working Conference on Requirements Engineering: Foundation for Software Quality (RefsQ 2012), Essen, Germany, 2012

[FrGoBySc10] Fricker, S.A., Gorschek, T., Byman, C., Schmidle, A.: Handshaking with implementation proposals: negotiating requirements understanding. IEEE Softw. 27(2), 72–80 (2010)

[Gartner21a] Gartner Group: Gartner Market Databook, 1Q21 Update, March 2021

[Gartner21b] Gartner Group: Forecast Public Cloud Services, Worldwide, 2019–2025, 1Q21 Update, March 2021

[Gartner22]   Gartner Group: Gartner Magic Quadrant. https://www.gartner.com/en/research/methodologies/magic-quadrants-research (2022)

[Gartner13]   Gartner Group: Understanding Gartner's Hype Cycles. Gartner Group, Stamford, ID Number G00251964, July 2013

[GausWein89] Gause, D.C., Weinberg, G.M.: Exploring Requirements: Quality Before Design. Dorset House. (1989)

[Glinz08]   Glinz, M.: A risk-based, value-oriented approach to quality requirements. IEEE Softw. 25(2), 34–41 (2008)

[GnJiSrWa21] Gnanasambandam, C., Jindal, N., Srivastava, S., Wagle, D.: Developer Velocity at Work: Key Lessons from Industry Digital Leaders. https://www.mckinsey.com/industries/technology-media-and-telecommunications/our-insights/developer-velocity-at-work-key-lessons-from-industry-digital-leaders (2021)

[GopSand97]   Gopal, R.D., Sanders, G.L.: Preventive and deterrent controls for software piracy. J. Manag. Inf. Syst. 13(4), 29–47 (1997)

[GoFrPaKu10] Gorschek, T., Fricker, S.A., Palm, K., Kunsman, S.: A lightweight innovation process for software-intensive product development. IEEE Softw. 27(1), 37–45 (2010)

[GorsWohl06] Gorschek, T., Wohlin, C.: Requirements abstraction model. Requir. Eng. 11(1), 79–101 (2006)

[GoWoGL06]   Gorschek, T., Wohlin, C., Garre, P., Larsson, S.: A model for technology transfer in practice. IEEE Softw. 23(6), 88–95 (2006)

[Gorche11]   Gorchels, L.: The Product Manager's Handbook: The Complete Product Management Resource, 4th edn. McGraw Hill (2011)

[GotSei13]   Gothelf, J., Seiden, J.: Lean UX – Applying Lean Principles to Improve User Experience. O'Reilly (2013)

[GottGor12]   Gottesdiener, E., Gorman, M.: Discover to Deliver: Agile Product Planning and Analysis. EBG Consulting (2012)

[GreRuh04]   Greer, D., Ruhe, G.: Software release planning: an evolutionary and iterative approach. Inf. Softw. Technol. 46(4), 243–253 (2004)

[GriHau96]   Griffin, A., Hauser, J.R.: Integrating R&D and marketing: a review and analysis of the literature. J. Prod. Innov. Manag. 13(3), 191–215 (1996)

[Groenv97]   Groenveld, P.: Roadmapping integrates business and technology. Res. Technol. Manag. 40(5), 49–58 (1997)

[Haines21] Haines, S.: The Product Manager's Desk Reference, 3rd edn. McGraw Hill (2021)

[Hall13] Hall, K.: Making the Matrix Work – How Matrix Managers Engage People and Cut Through Complexity. Nicholas Brealey Publishing (2013)

[Harmon14] Harmon, P.: Business Process Change. Morgan Kaufmann (2014)

[HassTrac06] Hassenzahl, M., Tractinsky, N.: User experience – a research agenda. Behav. Inform. Technol. 25(2), 91–97 (2006)

[Hecker99] Hecker, F.: Setting up shop: the business of open-source software. IEEE Softw. 16(1), 45–51 (1999)

[Hender70] Henderson, B.: The Product Portfolio. The Boston Consulting Group, Boston (1970)

[HerrDan08] Herrmann, A., Daneva, M.: Requirements prioritization based on benefit and cost prediction: an agenda for future research. In: 16th IEEE International Conference on Requirements Engineering (RE'08), Barcelona, Spain, 2008

[Herzwurm10] Herzwurm, G.: Produktmanagement in der IT: Geschäftsmodelle und Produktpositionierung, 7. Fachtagung Software Management - Vom Projekt zum Produkt (FTSWM'2010), Aachen, Germany, 2010

[HerzPiet09] Herzwurm, G., Pietsch, W.: Management von IT-Produkten - Geschäftsmodelle, Leitlinien und Werkzeugkasten für softwareintensive Systeme und Dienstleistungen. Springer (2009)

[HerzPiet08a] Herzwurm, G., Pietsch, W.: Guidelines for the analysis of IT business models and strategic positioning of IT-products. In: 2nd International Workshop on Software Product Management (IWSPM'2008), Barcelona, Spain, 2008

[HerzPiet08b] Herzwurm, G., Pietsch, W.: Management von IT-Produkten. Geschäftsmodelle, Leitlinien und Werkzeugkasten für softwareintensive Systeme und Dienstleistungen. Springer (2008)

[HiAlCeBa13] Hillenbrand, P., Alcauter, S., Cervantes, J., Barrios, F.: Better branding: brand names can influence consumer choice. J. Prod. Brand. Manag. 2(4), 300–308 (2013)

[HoRoPL00] Hoch, D.J., Roeding, C.R., Purkert, G., Lindner, S.K.: Secrets of Software Success. Harvard Business School Press (2000)

[HooFar01] Hooks, I.F., Farry, K.A.: Customer-Centered Products – Creating Successful Products through Smart Requirements Management. Amacom (2001)

[HumMol11] Humble, J., Molesky, J.: Why enterprises must adopt Devops to enable continuous delivery. Cutter IT J. 24(8) (2011)

[HumFar10] Humble, J., Farley, D.: Continuous Delivery: Reliable Software Releases through Build, Test, and Deployment Automation. Addison-Wesley (2010)

[IanLev04a] Iansiti, M., Levien, R.: Strategy as ecology. Harv. Bus. Rev. 82(3), 68–81 (2004)

[IanLev04] Iansiti, M., Levien, R.: The Keystone Advantage – What the New Dynamics of Business Ecosystems Mean for Strategy, Innovation, and Sustainability. Harvard Business School Press (2004)

[ISO98] ISO/AWI TR 9241-1: Ergonomics of Human-System Interaction. Part 1: Introduction to the ISO 9241 Series (1998)

[ISPMA21] ISPMA.: www.ispma.org (2021). Accessed 20 July 2021

[ISTQB21] ISTQB: Certified Tester AI Testing (CT-AI) Syllabus, Version 1.0 (2021)

[JabiPeTa16] Jabbari, R., bin Ali, N., Petersen, K., Tanveer, B.: What is DevOps? A systematic mapping study on definitions and practices. Proceedings of the Scientific Workshop XP'2016

[JanBrCus13] Jansen, S., Brinkkemper, S., Cusumano, M.A. (eds.): Software Ecosystems: Analyzing and Managing Business Networks in the Software Industry. Edward Elgar Publishing (2013)

[JohGus00] Johnson, M.D., Gustafsson, A.: Improving Customer Satisfaction, Loyalty, and Profit: An Integrated Measurement and Management System. Jossey-Bass (2000)

[Jones08] Jones, C.: Applied Software Measurement: Global Analysis of Productivity and Quality. McGraw-Hill (2008)

[KaSeTT84] Kano, N., Seraku, N., Takahashi, F., Tsuji, S.: Attractive quality and must-be quality. J. Japanese Soc. Quality Control. **14**(2), 147–156 (1984)

[KapNor96a] Kaplan, R.S., Norton, D.P.: Linking the balanced scorecard to strategy. Calif. Manag. Rev. **39**(1), 53–79 (1996)

[KapNor96b] Kaplan, R.S., Norton, D.P.: Using the balanced scorecard as a strategic management system. Harv. Bus. Rev. **74**(1), 75–85 (1996)

[KarlRyan97] Karlsson, J., Ryan, K.: A cost-value approach for prioritizing requirements. IEEE Softw. **14**(5), 67–74 (1997)

[Karlsson06] Karlsson, L.: Requirements Prioritisation and Retrospective Analysis for Release Planning Process Improvement. Ph.D. Thesis at Lund University, 2006

[KaReTh06] Karlsson, L., Regnell, B., Thelin, T.: Case studies in process improvement through retrospective analysis of release planning decisions. Int. J. Softw. Eng. Knowl. Eng. **16**(06), 885–915 (2006)

[KarTRBW06] Karlsson, L., Thelin, T., Regnell, B., Berander, P., Wohline, C.: Pair-wise comparisons versus planning game partitioning – experiments on requirements prioritisation techniques. Empir. Softw. Eng. **12**(1), 3–33 (2007)

[KatSha94] Katz, M.L., Shapiro, C.: Systems competition and network effects. J. Econ. Perspect. **8**, 93–115 (1994)

[KatSha85] Katz, M.L., Shapiro, C.: Network externalities, competition, and compatibility. Am. Econ. Rev. **75**(3), 424–440 (1985)

[KhuFrGor15] Khurum, M., Fricker, S., Gorschek, T.: The contextual nature of innovation – an empirical investigation of three software intensive products. Inf. Softw. Technol. **57**(1), 595–613 (2015)

[KhuGorW13] Khurum, M., Gorschek, T., Wilson, M.: The software value map—an exhaustive collection of value aspects for the development of software intensive products. J. Softw. Evol. Process. **25**(7), 711–741 (2013)

[KhuKhuGo07] Khurum, M., Khurum, A., Gorschek, T.: A Model for Early Requirements Triage and Selection (MERTS) Utilizing Product Line Strategies. In: 11th International Software Product Line Conference (SPLC 2007), Kyoto, Japan, 2007

[KimBeSp14] Kim, G., Behr, K., Spafford, G.: The Phoenix Project. IT Revolution Press. (2014)

[KimMaub15] Kim, W.C., Mauborgne, R.: Blue Ocean Strategy: How to Create Uncontested Market Space and Make the Competition Irrelevant – Extended Ed. Harvard Business School Press, Boston (2015)

[KiPhSu12] Kimes, S.E., Phillips, R., Summa, L.: Pricing in Restaurants. Oxford University Press (2012)

[KittMang22] Kittlaus, H.-B., Mangipudi, H.: Software Product Management for Startups – The ISPMA-Compliant Study Guide and Handbook (2022)

[KittSalt22] Kittlaus, H.-B., Saltan, A.: Cloud product vision, market positioning, strategy, and pricing. In: Hajizadeh, Y. (ed.) Building Cloud Software Products – Innovation, Technology, and Product Management. Springer (2022)

[Kittlaus20b] Kittlaus, H.-B.: Platform – What Do We Mean? https://www.linkedin.com/pulse/platform-what-do-we-mean-hans-bernd-kittlaus/ (2020)

[Kittlaus20a] Kittlaus, H.-B.: Increasing Diversity in Software Product Planning and Development Approaches. https://www.linkedin.com/pulse/increasing-diversity-software-product-planning-hans-bernd-kittlaus/ (2020)

[Kittlaus19]   Kittlaus, H.-B.: Customer-Specific Tailorability of Your B2B Software Product – The Good, the Bad and the Ugly. https://www.linkedin.com/pulse/customer-specific-taylorability-your-b2b-software-product-kittlaus/ (2019)

[KittFric17]   Kittlaus, H.-B., Fricker, S.A.: Software Product Management – The ISPMA-Compliant Study Guide and Handbook. Springer (2017)

[Kittlaus15]   Kittlaus, H.-B.: One size does not fit all: software product management for speedboats vs. cruiseships. In: International Conference on Software Business (ICSOB 2015), Braga, Portugal, 2015

[Kittlaus14]   Kittlaus, H.-B.: Geschäftsmodelle. In: Hilber, M. (Hrsg.) Handbuch Cloud Computing, pp. 29–53. Dr. Otto Schmidt Verlag (2014)

[Kittlaus12]   Kittlaus, H.-B.: Software product management and agile software development: conflicts and solutions. In: Maedche, A., Botzenhardt, A., Neer, L. (eds.) Software for People – Fundamentals, Trends and Best Practices, pp. 83–96. Springer (2012)

[KittClou09]   Kittlaus, H.-B., Clough, P.: Software Product Management and Pricing – Key Success Factors for Software Organizations. Springer (2009)

[KiRaSch04]   Kittlaus, H.-B., Rau, C., Schulz, J.: Software-Produkt-Management – Nachhaltiger Erfolgsfaktor bei Herstellern und Anwendern. Springer (2004)

[Klemens06]   Klemens, B.: Math You Can't Use – Patents, Copyright, and Software. Brookings (2006)

[KnZeKo16]   Knapp, J., Zeratsky, J., Kowitz, B.: Sprint: How To Solve Big Problems and Test New Ideas in Just Five Day. Transworld Digital (2016)

[KnasLeff20]   Knaster, R., Leffingwell, D.: SAFe® 5.0 Distilled: Achieving Business Agility With the Scaled Agile Framework. Addison-Wesley (2020)

[Kolb14]   Kolb, D.: Experiential Learning: Experience as the Source of Learning and Development. Pearson Education (2014)

[Kollm16]   Kollmann, T.: E-Business, 6th edn. Springer (2016)

[KKTLD15]   Komssi, M., Kauppinen, M., Töhönen, H., Lehtola, L., Davis, A.: Roadmapping problems in practice: value creation from the perspective of the customers. Requir. Eng. 20(1), 45–69 (2015)

[KostScha01]   Kostoff, R., Schaller, R.: Science and technology roadmaps. IEEE Trans. Eng. Manag. 48(2), 132–143 (2001)

[KotArm15]   Kotler, P., Armstrong, G.: Principles of marketing, 16th edn. Prentice Hall (2015)

[KowUla17]   Kowalkowski, C., Ulaga, W.: Service Strategy in Action. Service Strategy Press. (2017)

[Kruchten96]   Kruchten, P.: A rational development process. CrossTalk. 9(7), 11–16 (1996)

[KruCas14]   Krüger, R., Casey, M.: Focus Groups: A Practical Guide for Applied Research, 5th edn. SAGE Publications (2014)

[Kude12]   Kude, T.: The Coordination of Inter-Organizational Networks in the Enterprise Software Industry: The Perspective of Complementors. Peter Lang Verlag (2012)

[KuSiKa12]   Kumar, L., Singh, H., Kaur, R.: Web analytics and metrics: a survey. In: International Conference on Advances in Computing. Communications and Informatics (ICACCI'12) (2012)

[LarVod10]   Larman, C., Vodde, B.: Practices for Scaling Lean & Agile Development. Addison Wesley (2010)

[Lawley07]   Lawley, B.: Expert Product Management: Advanced Techniques, Tips and Strategies for Product Management & Product Marketing. Happy About (2007)

[Lazzar04]   Lazzaro, N.: Why We Play Games: Four Keys to More Emotion Without Story. Report, XEO Design (2004)

[LeCBölPe13] Le Callet, P., Böller, S., Perkis, A., et al.: Qualinet White Paper on Definitions of Quality of Experience. European Network on Quality of Experience in Multimedia Systems and Services, 2013

[Leffing11] Leffingwell, D.: Agile Software Requirements. Addison-Wesley (2011)

[LeKaVä07] Lehtola, L., Kauppinen, M., Vähäniitty, J.: Strengthening the link from business decisions to requirements engineering: long-term product planning in software product companies. In: 15th IEEE International Requirements Engineering Conference (RE'07), New Delhi, 2007

[LRKMM19] Leite, L., Rocha, C., Kon, F., Milojiicic, D., Meirelles, P.: A survey of DevOps concepts and challenges. ACM Comput. Surv. **52**(6), Article 127 (2019)

[Lemay17] Lemay, M.: Product Management in Practice. O'Reilly UK Ltd (2017)

[LeLiLe20] Lewrick, M., Link, P., Leifer, L.: The Design Thinking Toolbox: A Guide to Mastering the Most Popular and Valuable Innovation Methods. Wiley (2020)

[LickKitt16] Lick, P., Kittlaus, H.-B.: Software product categories in the automotive industry and how to manage them. In: International Conference on Software Business (ICSOB 2016), Ljubljana, Slovenia, 2016

[LinWuWen12] Lin, C., Wen, Z., Tong, H., Griffiths-Fisher, V., Shi, L., Lubensky, D.: Social network analysis in enterprise. Proc. IEEE. **100**(9), 2759–2776 (2012)

[LinFen03] Linden, A., Fenn, J.: Understanding Gartner's Hype Cycles. Gartner Group, Mai (2003)

[LoKaVäKo09] Loehtola, L., Kauppinen, M., Vähäniitty, J., Komssi, M.: Linking business and requirements engineering: is solution planning a missing activity in software product companies? Requir. Eng. **14**(2), 113–128 (2009)

[LoMcRyCo17] Lombardo, C.T., McCarthy, B., Ryan, E., Connors, M.: Product Roadmaps Relaunched: How to Set Direction while Embracing Uncertainty. O'Reilly Media (2017)

[Lucassen17] Lucassen, G.: Understanding user stories: computational linguistics in agile requirements engineering. Ph.D. dissertation, Utrecht University (2017)

[LuDaWeBr16] Lucassen, G., Dalpiaz, F., van der Werf, J., Brinkkemper, S.: Improving agile requirements: the quality user story framework and tool. Requir. Eng. **21**(3), 383–403 (2016)

[LuPiBo18] Luz, W.P., Pinto, G., Bonifácio, R.: Building a collaborative culture: a grounded theory of well succeeded DevOps adoption in practice. In: ACM/IEEE International Symposium on Empirical Software Engineering and Measurement, 2018

[LynnAkg01] Lynn, G.S., Akgün, A.E.: Project visioning: its components and impact on new product success. J. Prod. Innov. Manag. **18**(6), 374–388 (2001)

[LyAbVaWr99] Lynn, G.S., Abel, K.D., Valentine, W.S., Wright, R.C.: Key factors in increasing speed to market and improving new product success rates. Ind. Mark. Manag. **28**(4), 319–326 (1999)

[MNJR15] Maalej, W., Nayebi, M., Johann, T., Ruhe, G.: Toward data-driven requirements engineering. IEEE Softw. (2015)

[MaglFri14] Maglyas, A., Fricker, S.: Preliminary results from the software product management state-of-practice survey. In: International Conference on Software Business (ICSOB 2014), Paphos, Cyprus, 2014

[MagNiSmo13] Maglyas, A., Nikula, U., Smolander, K.: What are the roles of software product managers? An empirical investigation. J. Syst. Softw. **86**(12), 3071–3090 (2013)

[MagNiSmo12] Maglyas, A., Nikula, U., Smolander, K.: What do practitioners mean when they talk about product management? In: 20th IEEE International Requirements Engineering Conference (RE), Chicago, IL, 2012

[MaiGiRob04] Maiden, N., Gizikis, A., Robertson, S.: Provoking creativity: imagine what your requirements could be like. IEEE Softw. **21**(5), 68–75 (2004)

[MaNiSmFr17] Maglyas, A., Nikula, U., Smolander, K., Fricker, S.A.: Core software product management activities. J. Adv. Manag. Res. **14**(1), 23–45 (2017)

[MatMat98] Matheson, D., Matheson, J.: The smart organization: creating value through Smart R&D. Harvard Business School Press, Cambridge (1998)

[MathKou10] Mathioudakis, M., Koudas, N.: Twittermonitor: trend detection over the Twitter stream. In: 2010 ACM SIGMOD International Conference on Management of Data, 2010

[Maurya12] Maurya, A.: Running Lean: Iterate from Plan A to a Plan that Works. O'Reilly and Associates (2012)

[McFarland12] McFarland, C.: Experiment!: Website Conversion Rate Optimization with A/B and Multivariate Testing. New Riders Publishing (2012)

[McGee04] McGee, K.: Heads Up – How to Anticipate Business Surprises and Seize Opportunities First. Harvard Business School Press, Boston (2004)

[McGiTuLa78] McGill, R., Tukey, J., Larsen, W.: Variations of box plots. Am. Stat. **32**(1), 12–16 (1978)

[McGrat01] McGrath, M.E.: Product Strategy for High Technology Companies, 2nd edn. McGrawHill, New York (2001)

[MessSzy03] Messerschmitt, D.G., Szyperski, C.: Software Ecosystem – Understanding an Indispensable Technology and Industry. MIT Press, Cambridge (2003)

[Meyer08] Meyer, R.: Partnering with SAP. Books on Demand, Norderstedt (2008)

[MileHub94] Miles, M., Huberman, A.: Qualitative Data Analysis. Sage Publications (1994)

[MilWed13] Miller, P., Wedell-Wedellsborg, T.: Innovation as Usual. How to Help Your People Bring Great Ideas to Life. Harvard Business Review Press, Boston (2013)

[MilMor99] Miller, W.L., Morris, L.: 4th Generation R&D: Managing Knowledge, Technology, and Innovation. Wiley, New York (1999)

[Mintzb13] Mintzberg, H.: The Rise and Fall of Strategic Planning: Reconceiving Roles for Planning, Plans, Planners. Free Press (2013)

[MinAhlLa08] Mintzberg, H., Ahlstrand, B., Lampel, J.: Strategy Safari: The Complete Guide Through the Wilds of Strategic Management, 2nd edn. Financial Times Prentice Hall (2008)

[MivBen14] Mival, I., Benyon, D.: User Experience (UX) design for medical personnel and patients. In: Fricker, S., Thümmler, C., Gavras, A. (eds.) Requirements Engineering for Digital Health. Springer (2014)

[Moore93] Moore, J.F.: Predators and prey: a new ecology of competition. Harv. Bus. Rev. **71**(3), 75–83 (1993)

[Moore04] Moore, G.A.: Inside the Tornado: Strategies for Developing, Leveraging, and Surviving Hypergrowth Markets, Harper (2004)

[Moore04a] Moore, G.A.: Darwin and the demon: innovating with established enterprises. Harv. Bus. Rev. **82**(7-8), 86–92 (2004)

[Moore08] Moore, G.A.: Dealing with Darwin: How Great Companies Innovate at Every Phase of Their Evolution. Portfolio/Penguin. (2008)

[Moore14] Moore, G.A.: Crossing the Chasm. Harper, New York (2014)

[MorWin90] Morrison, S.A., Winston, C.: The dynamics of airline pricing and competition. Am. Econ. Rev. **80**, 389–393 (1990)

[Myers00] Myers, J.H.: Measuring Customer Satisfaction: Hot Buttons and Other Measurement Issues. American Marketing Association (2000)

[NagHogZ14] Nagle, T.T., Hogan, J.E., Zale, J.: The Strategy and Tactics of Pricing – A Guide to Growing More Profitably, 5th edn. Pearson (2014)

[NagHog05] Nagle, T.T., Hogan, J.E.: What Is Strategic Pricing?. Strategic Pricing Group Insights (Monitor Group) (2005)

[NaChRu18] Nayebi, M., Cho, H., Ruhe, G.: App store mining is not enough for app improvement. Empir. Softw. Eng. **23**(5), 2764–2794 (2018)

[NayRuh15] Nayebi, M., Ruhe, G.: Analytical product release planning. In: Bird, C., Menzies, T., Zimmermann, T. (eds.) The Art and Science of Analyzing Software Data, pp. 550–580. Morgan Kaufman (2015)

[NeeSiCe98] Neef, D., Siesfeld, G.A., Cefola, J. (eds.): The Economic Impact of Knowledge. Elsevier (1998)

[ÖzePhi12] Özer, Ö., Phillips, R.: Oxford Handbook of Pricing Management – Introduction. Oxford University Press (2012)

[OshKoWil11] Oshri, I., Kotlarsky, J., Willcocks, L.P.: The Handbook of Global Outsourcing and Offshoring, Revised, 2nd edn. Palgrave Macmillan (2011)

[OstPign14] Osterwalder, A., Pigneur, Y.: Value Proposition Design. Wiley (2014)

[OstPign10] Osterwalder, A., Pigneur, Y.: Business Model Generation. Wiley (2010)

[ParAlsCho16] Parker, G.G., Van Alstyne, M.W., Choudary, S.P.: Platform Revolution. W.W. Norton (2016)

[PearEnsl04] Pearce, C.L., Ensley, M.D.: A reciprocal and longitudinal investigation of the innovation process: the central role of shared vision in product and process innovation teams (PPITs). J. Organ. Behav. **25**(2), 259–278 (2004)

[Peine14] Peine, K.: Situative Gestaltung des IT-Produktmanagements, unv. Diss., Universität Stuttgart (2014)

[PepRyl06] Peppard, J., Rylander, A.: From value chain to value network: insights for mobile operators. Eur. Manag. J. **24**(2–3), 128–141 (2006)

[PetWoh10] Petersen, K., Wohlin, C.: Measuring the flow in lean software development. Softw. Pract. Exp. **41**(9), 975–996 (2010)

[PhaFarPr07] Phaal, R., Farrukh, C., Probert, D.: Strategic roadmapping: a workshop-based approach for identifying and exploring strategic issues and opportunities. Eng. Manag. J. **19**(1), 3–12 (2007)

[PhaFarPr04] Phaal, R., Farrukh, C., Probert, D.: Technology roadmapping – a planning framework for evolution and revolution. Technol. Forecast. Soc. Chang. **71**(1), 5–26 (2004)

[Pichler20] Pichler, R.: How to Lead in Product Management – Practices to Align Stakeholders, Guide Development Teams, and Create Value Together. Pichler Consulting (2020)

[Pichler16] Pichler, R.: Strategize: Product Strategy and Product Roadmap Practices for the Digital Age. Pichler Consulting (2016)

[Pichler10] Pichler, R.: Agile Product Management with Scrum. Addison-Wesley (2010)

[PohlBoLi05] Pohl, K., Böckle, G., van der Linden, F.: Software Product Line Engineering: Foundations, Principles, and Techniques. Springer (2005)

[PohlRupp11] Pohl, K., Rupp, K.: Requirements Engineering Fundamentals. Rocky Nook Computing (2011)

[Popp19] Popp, K.M.: Best Practices for Commercial Use of Open Source Software, 2nd edn. Books on Demand (2019)

[Popp13] Popp, K.M.: Mergers and Acquisitions in the Software Industry - Foundations of Due Diligence. Books on Demand. (2013)

[Popp12] Popp, K.M.: Leveraging open source licenses and open source communities in hybrid commercial open source business models. In: International Workshop on Software Ecosystems (IWSECO 2012), Cambridge, MA, 2012

[Popp11a] Popp, K.M.: Software industry business models. IEEE Softw. **28**(4), 26–30 (2011)

[Popp11b] Popp, K.M.: Hybrid revenue models of software companies and their relationship to hybrid business models. In: International Workshop on Software Ecosystems (IWSECO 2011), Brussels, Belgium, 2011

[PoppMey10] Popp, K.M., Meyer, R.: Profit from Software Ecosystems. Books on Demand (2010)

[Popp10] Popp, K.M.: Goals of software vendors for partner ecosystems – a practitioner's view. In: International Conference on Software Business (ICSOB 2010), Jyväskylä, Finland, 2010

[PortHepp15] Porter, M.E., Heppelman, J.: How smart, connected products are transforming companies. Harv. Bus. Rev. **93**(10), 96–114 (2015)

[PortHepp14] Porter, M.E., Heppelman, J.: How smart, connected products are transforming competition. Harv. Bus. Rev. **92**(11), 64–88 (2014)

[Porter08] Porter, M.E.: The five competitive forces that shape strategy. Harv. Bus. Rev. **86**(1), 78–93 (2008)

[Porter98] Porter, M.E.: Competitive Strategy. Free Press (1998)

[Porter85] Porter, M.E.: Competitive Advantage. Free Press (1985)

[Porter79] Porter, M.E.: How competitive forces shape strategy. Harv. Bus. Rev. **March–April**, 137–145 (1979)

[PragInst19] Pragmatic Institute, Inc.: Pragmatic Framework (2019)

[Pritch15] Pritchard, C.L.: Risk Management: Concepts and Guidance, 5th edn. CRC Press (2015)

[PruAdl06] Pruitt, J., Adlin, T.: The Persona Lifecycle: Keeping People in Mind Throughout Product Design. Elsevier (2006)

[PruGru03] Pruitt, J., Grudin, J.: Personas: practice and theory. In: ACM Conference on Designing for User Experiences, San Francisco, CA, 2003

[Rahim15] Rahim, M.A.: Managing Conflict in Organizations, 4th edn. Transaction Publishers (2015)

[RaiRicMe07] Raiffa, H., Richardson, J., Metcalfe, D.: Negotiation Analysis – The Science and Art of Collaborative Decision Making. The Belknap Press of Harvard University Press (2007)

[RajlBenn00] Rajlich, V., Bennett, K.: A Staged Model for the Software Life Cycle. IEEE Computer. **33**(7), 66–71 (2000)

[RaaMoBia13] Raatikainen, M., Komssi, M., Dal Bianco, V.: Industrial experiences of organizing a hackathon to assess a device-centric cloud ecosystem. In: IEEE 37th Annual Computer Software and Applications Conference (COMPSAC 2013), Kyoto, Japan, 2013

[Reichh96] Reichheld, F.F.: The Loyalty Effect: The Hidden Force Behind Growth, Profits, and Lasting Value. Harvard Business School Press, Cambridge (1996)

[RegnBSO08] Regnell, B., Berntsson Svensson, R., Olsson, T.: Supporting roadmapping of quality requirements. IEEE Softw. **25**(2), 42–47 (2008)

[RegnBrin05] Regnell, B., Brinkkemper, S.: Market-driven requirements engineering for software products. In: Aurum, A., Wohlin, C. (eds.) Engineering and Managing Software Requirements. Springer (2005)

[RegHNBH01] Regnell, B., Höst, M., Nattoch Dag, J., Beremark, P., Hjelm, T.: An industrial case study on distributed prioritization in market-driven requirements engineering for packaged software. Requir. Eng. **6**(1), 51–62 (2001)

[Ries11] Ries, E.: The Lean Startup. Crown Business (2011)

[Ries09] Ries, E.: Minimum Viable Product: A Guide. http://www. startuplessonslearned.com/ 2009/08/minimum-viable-product-guide.html (2009)

[Rietz21] Rietz, T.: Designing AI-based systems for qualitative data collection and analysis. Ph.D. dissertation, Karlsruhe Institute of Technology (2021)

[RobRob06]   Robertson, S., Robertson, J.: Mastering the Requirements Process, 2nd edn. Addison-Wesley (2006)

[Royce70]   Royce, W.: Managing the Development of Large Software Systems. IEEE WESCON (1970)

[Rubin12]   Rubin, K.S.: Essential Scrum: A Practical Guide to the Most Popular Agile Process. Addison-Wesley (2012)

[RufEbe04]   Ruffin, M., Ebert, C.: Using open source software in product development: a primer. IEEE Softw. 21(1), 82–86 (2004)

[Ruhe10]   Ruhe, G.: Product Release Planning: Methods, Tools and Applications. CRC Press (2010)

[RuheSal05]   Ruhe, G., Saliu, M.: The Art and Science of Software Release Planning. IEEE Softw. 22(6), 47–53 (2005)

[RusKan03]   Rust, R.T., Kannon, P.K.: E-Service: A New Paradigm for Business in the Electronic Environment. Commun. ACM. 46(6), 37–42 (2003)

[Samuel03]   Samuelson, P.: Trade secrets vs. Free speech. Commun. ACM. 46(6), 19–23 (2003)

[Sandy20]   Sandy, K.: The Influential Product Manager – How to Lead and Launch Successful Technology Products. Berrett-Koehler Publishers (2020)

[Sawhney16]   Sawhney, M.: Putting products into services. Harv. Bus. Rev. 94, 82–89 (2016)

[Schmid03]   Schmid, K.: Lösungen für Probleme des Requirements Engineering für Produktlinien. Softwaretechnik –Trends. 23(1), 20–21 (2003)

[Schmidt02]   Schmidt, M.: The Business Case Guide. Solution Matrix (2002)

[SchoHeTB07] Schobbens, P., Heymans, P., Trigaux, J., Bontemps, Y.: Generic semantics of feature diagrams. Comput. Netw. 51(2), 456–479 (2007)

[SchoHerz17] Schockert, S., Herzwurm, G.: Agile software quality function deployment. In: 23rd International QFD Symposium, Tokyo, ISQFD 2017

[SchKuPop13] Schütz, S., Kude, T., Popp, K.M.: The impact of software-as-a-service on partner management. In: International Conference (ICSOB 2013), Potsdam, Germany, 2013

[SchwSuth20] Schwaber, J., Sutherland, J.: The Scrum Guide – The Definitive Guide to Scrum: The Rules of the Game. https://www.scrumguides.org (2020)

[Schwaber02] Schwaber, K.: Agile Software Development with Scrum. Pearson International (2002)

[Schwind07]   Schwind, M.: Dynamic Pricing and Automated Resource Allocation for Complex Information Services. Springer (2007)

[SegMeDu11]   Segetlija, Z., Mesarić, J., Dujak, D.: Importance of distribution channels – marketing channels – for national economy. In: 22nd CROMAR Congress: Marketing Challenges in New Economy, Pula, Croatia, 2011

[SheeGall15] Sheen, R., Gallo, A.: HBR Guide to Building Your Business Case. Harvard Business Review Press, Boston (2015)

[ShPlCoJa13] Shneiderman, B., Plaisant, C., Cohen, M., Jacobs, S.: Designing the User Interface: Strategies for Effective Human-Computer Interaction, 5th revised edn. Addison-Wesley (2013)

[ShoWar07]   Shore, J., Warden, S.: The Art of Agile Development, O'Reilly Media (2007)

[SiMoMeKa12] Simonetto, M., Montan, L., Meehan, J., Kaji, J.: Structuring and Managing an Effective Pricing Organization. Oxford University Press (2012)

[SkelPais19] Skelton, M., Pais, M.: Team Topologies: Organizing Business and Technology Teams for Fast Flow. It Revolution Press (2019)

[SodhSodh07] Sodhi, M.N., Sodhi, N.N.: Six Sigma Pricing: Improving Pricing Operations to Increase Profit. Pearson FT Press (2007)

[SolisWang11] Solis, C., Wang, X.: A Study of the Characteristics of Behaviour Driven Development. In: IEEE 37th EUROMICRO Conference on Software Engineering and Advanced Applications, Oulu, Finland, 2011

[SongMon98] Song, M., Montoya-Weiss, M.: Critical development activities for really new versus incremental products. J. Prod. Innov. Manag. **15**(2), 124–135 (1998)

[SrTrWaWa20] Srivastava, S., Trehan, K., Wagle, D., Wang, J.: Developer Velocity: how software excellence fuels business performance. https://www.mckinsey.com/industries/technology-media-and-telecommunications/our-insights/developer-velocity-how-software-excellence-fuels-business-performance (2020)

[Standish16] Standish Group: Chaos Report 2016

[StoSmu15] Stompff, G., Smulders, F.: The right fidelity: representations that speed up innovation processes. In: 19th DMI: Academic Design Management Conference, 2015

[StuSte12] Stuckenberg, S., Stefan, B.: Software-as-a-service development: Driving forces of process change. In: AIS PACIS Proceedings, Paper 122, 2012

[SvGoFTSM10] Svahnberg, M., Gorschek, T., Feldt, R., Torkar, R., Saleem, S., Mu, S.: A systematic review on strategic release planning models. Inf. Softw. Technol. **52**(3), 237–248 (2010)

[TapWil06] Tapscott, D., Williams, A.D.: Wikinomics – How Mass Collaboration Changes Everything. Portfolio/Penguin (2006)

[Teece10] Teece, D.J.: Business models, business strategy and innovation. Long Range Plan. **43**(2), 172–194 (2010)

[Tessarol07] Tessarolo, P.: Is integration enough for fast product development? An empirical investigation of the contextual effects of product vision. J. Prod. Innov. Manag. **24**(1), 69–82 (2007)

[TetGar15] Tetlock, P.E., Gardner, D.: Superforecasting – The Art and Science of Prediction. Crown (2015)

[Thomk20] Thomke, S.H.: Experimentation Works: The Surprising Power of Business Experiments. Harvard Business Review Press (2020)

[Thomp14] Thompson, L.: The Mind and Heart of the Negotiator, 6th edn. Pearson Prentice Hall (2014)

[Torres21] Torres, T.: Continuous Discovery Habits. Product Talk LLC, Amazon (2021)

[Trendow13] Trendowicz, A.: Software Cost Estimation, Benchmarking, and Risk Assessment: The Software Decision-Makers' Guide to Predictable Software Development. Springer (2013)

[Tukey58] Tukey, J.W.: The teaching of concrete mathematics. Am. Math. Mon. **65**(1), 1–9 (1958)

[UlrEpp11] Ulrich, K., Eppinger, S.: Product Design and Development. McGrawHill (2011)

[UN15] United Nations: The 17 Goals. https://sdgs.un.org/goals (2015)

[VähRau05] Vähäniitty, J., Rautiainen, K.: Towards an approach for managing the development portfolio in small product-oriented software companies. In: 38th Annual Hawaii International Conference on System Sciences (HICSS'05), Hawaii, USA, 2005

[VAKaPoJa13] van Angeren, J., Kabbedijk, J., Popp, K.M., Jansen, S.: Managing software ecosystems through partnering. In: Jansen, S., Brinkkemper, S., Cusumano, M.A. (eds.) Software Ecosystems: Analyzing and Managing Business Networks in the Software Industry, pp. 85–102. Edward Elgar (2013)

[Vasudeva14] Vasudeva, V.N.: Open Source Software and Intellectual Property Rights. Klüwer Information Law Series (2014)

[Vogels14] Vogels, W.: The Story of Apollo - Amazon's Deployment Engine. www.allthingsdistributed.com/2014/11/apollo-amazon-deployment-engine.html (2014). Accessed 25 Dec 2016

[Voss16]   Voss, C.: Never Split The Difference. Penguin Random House (2016)

[Waldo08]   Waldo, J.: Scaling in games and virtual worlds. Commun. ACM, vol. 51, no. 8, August 2008, pp. 38-44

[Waltl13]   Waltl, J.: Intellectual Property Modularity in Software Products and Software Platform Ecosystems. Books on Demand (2013)

[Weber20]   Weber, L.: Software Product Management – Tips and Templates. Amazon (2020)

[Weber17]   Weber, L.: The Product Marketing Manager. Amazon (2017)

[WBNVB06]   Weerd, I. van de, Brinkkemper, S., Nieuwenhuis, R., Versendaal, J.M., Bijlsma, A.: On the creation of a reference framework for software product management: validation and tool support. In: International Workshop on Software Product Management (IWSPM'06), Minneapolis, MN, 2006

[WMDUHW05]   Weill, P., Malone, T.W., D'Urso, V.T., Herman, G., Woerner, S.: Do Some Business Models Perform Better than Others? A Study of the 1000 Largest US Firms. MIT Center for Coordination Science, Boston, Working Paper No. 226 (2005)

[Weinst04]   Weinstein, A.: Handbook of Market Segmentation: Strategic Targeting for Business and Technology Firms, 3rd edn. Haworth Press (2004)

[WeiHug05]   Weiss, J., Hughes, J.: Want collaboration? Accept – and actively manage – conflict. Harv. Bus. Rev. **83**(3), 93–101 (2005)

[WenSny00]   Wenger, E., Snyder, W.: Communities of practice: the organizational frontier. Harv. Bus. Rev. **78**(1), 139–146 (2000)

[Wiegers03]   Wiegers, K.: Software Requirements. Microsoft Press (2003)

[Winer99]   Winer, R.S.: Marketing Management. Prentice Hall (1999)

[WohAur05]   Wohlin, C., Aurum, A.: What is important when deciding to include a software requirement in a project or release? In: International Symposium on Empirical Software Engineering (ISESE 2005), Noosa Heads, Queensland, Australia, 2005

[WuBuRa20]   Wu, C., Buyya, R., Ramamohanarao, K.: Cloud pricing models: taxonomy, survey, and interdisciplinary challenges. ACM Comput. Surv. **52**(6), 1–36 (2020)

[XuJYHKO09]   Xu, Q., Jiao, R., Yang, X., Helander, M., Khalid, H., Opperud, A.: An analytical Kano model for customer need analysis. Des. Stud. **30**(1), 87–110 (2009)

[Zaca19]   Zacarias, D.: 20 Product Prioritization Techniques. Folding Burritos (2019)

[ZarRub00]   Zartman, I.W., Rubin, J.Z.: The study of power and the practice of negotiation. In: Zartman, I.W., Rubin, J.Z. (eds.) Power and Negotiation, pp. 3–28. University of Michigan Press (2000)

[ZowCou05]   Zowghi, D., Coulin, C.: Requirements elicitation: a survey of techniques, approaches, and tools. In: Aurum, A., Wohlin, C. (eds.) Engineering and Managing Software Requirements. Springer (2005)

Index

Printed in the United States
by Baker & Taylor Publisher Services